CW01239010

CAPE TOWN

THE MAKING OF A CITY

An Illustrated Social History

1662   1795

1840

1870

CAPE TOWN

THE MAKING OF A CITY

An Illustrated Social History

NIGEL WORDEN

ELIZABETH VAN HEYNINGEN

VIVIAN BICKFORD-SMITH

DAVID PHILIP PUBLISHERS
1998

First published 1998 by David Philip Publishers (Pty) Ltd,
208 Werdmuller Centre, Newry Street, Claremont 7708, South Africa,
and in Europe by Verloren Publishers, P.O. Box 1741, 1200 BS Hilversum,
The Netherlands

© 1998 Nigel Worden, Elizabeth van Heyningen & Vivian Bickford-Smith

ISBN 0-86486-435-3 (David Philip)
ISBN 90-6550-161-4 (Verloren Publishers)

All rights reserved

Design and lay-out	Sarah-Anne Raynham
Cover design	Abdul Amien
Cartography	James Mills-Hicks
Reproduction	Hirt and Carter, Cape Town
Printing and binding	Tien Wah Press, Singapore

Contents

7 PREFACE

8 ACKNOWLEDGEMENTS

9 LIST OF ABBREVIATIONS

11 CHAPTER ONE
'More the Name than the Reality'
Cape Town 1620–1662

35 CHAPTER TWO
From Cabo to Kaapstad
Cape Town 1662–1795

85 CHAPTER THREE
'A Singular Mix'
Cape Town 1795–1840

151 CHAPTER FOUR
The British Town
Cape Town 1840–1870

219 CHAPTER FIVE
The Search for Order
Cape Town 1870–1899

265 REFERENCES

275 INDEX

Preface

THIS HISTORY of Cape Town is first and foremost about its people. Chronologically, they range from seventeenth-century Khoi herders, trying to maintain their societies in the face of European encroachment, to incipient 'South Africans' on the eve of war almost 250 years later. Cape Town was never homogeneous in its social composition, and the varied human experiences of the place that we have endeavoured to capture in this book have reflected numerous social divisions, including those of class, ethnicity, gender and religion.

This history is also about the changing and enduring relationships between people and the physical places in which they lived. We examine Cape Town's development from its early years as a settlement hemmed in by mountains and by an apparently hostile and alien hinterland, looking out to sea, its umbilical cord still tied to the European and Asian societies which had given it birth. By the end of the nineteenth century Cape Town had become a city which stood confidently poised as the capital of a key colony in the British Empire.

Fresh perspectives on Cape Town life have been provided by paintings, maps and, from the 1850s, photography as well as more conventional documentary sources. The changing ways in which both visitors and residents depicted the town say much about how its outward appearance altered over three centuries. But they also reveal a great deal about how the *mentalité* of Capetonians – their understanding of the world they inhabited – also changed.

This illustrated social history of Cape Town has been a long time in the making. Robin Hallett played a crucial role in instigating the study of Cape Town's past in the 1970s. He organised the first of six Cape Town history workshops at the University of Cape Town in 1978. From 1990 the Centre for Scientific Development began to fund research through the Cape Town History Project, located in the History Department at the University of Cape Town. Although considerable original material has been included here, this book would not have been possible without the plethora of mostly unpublished academic work on the city's past that has been generated over these years. There are, of course, still gaps, and topics that are treated unevenly; and this history, like all histories, is necessarily the interpretation of its authors. Nonetheless we hope that readers will recognise something of the origins of 'their' Cape Town in these pages.

A companion volume, *Cape Town in the Twentieth Century*, will also be published shortly.

Acknowledgements

THIS BOOK would not have been possible without the assistance of many people.

We should like to thank Sarah-Anne Raynham whose design and lay-out have transformed our script into this handsome book; James Mills-Hicks for the maps and figures; and our photographer, Jean Brundrit. Russell Martin has been a skilful editor and patient publisher, encouraging us throughout.

Our thanks go to the Cape Tercentenary Foundation who helped sponsor the cartography, and the Centre for Scientific Development of the Human Sciences Research Council for their support of research into Cape Town history over six years. They are in no way responsible for our opinions.

Students who participated in the research of the Cape Town History Project made an invaluable contribution. They include Teun Baartman, Andrew Bank, Naomi Barnett, Harriet Deacon, Marijke du Toit, Kevin Greenbank, Craig Iannini, Mark Irvine, Kirsten McKenzie, Rosemary Ridd, Terri Strauss, Andrew Walker, Kerry Ward and Joanne Winter. In addition, a number of students conducted interviews for us under the aegis of the Tutu Fund Vacation Students, including Paula da Gama, Thavie Mchunu, Victor Modise and N. Radebe.

Cape Town is remarkably fortunate in its librarians and archivists, who have dealt with us patiently for many years. It would be invidious to mention individuals – there have been so many – but this book would not have been possible without the assistance of the staffs of Jagger Library at the University of Cape Town, the South African Library and the Cape Archives. We thank them most sincerely. A number of other libraries, museums, art galleries and institutions have generously made their resources available to us, including the Algemeen Rijksarchief in The Hague, Atlas van Stolk in Rotterdam, the Brenthurst Library (especially Marcelle Weiner and Diana van Nierop), the Charles Bell Heritage Trust (Dr Frank Bradlow), the Genadendal Museum (Dr I.H.T. Balie), MuseumAfrica (Kathy Brookes), the South African National Cultural History Museum, the South African National Gallery, the William Fehr Collection (Lalou Meltzer), and the National Council of Women. We thank Ian Black of the Land Survey Department, as well as Mrs Williams, both of the Cape Town City Council.

Many people have given us advice and assistance. Our thanks go to Jim Armstrong, Margaret Cairns, Achmat Davids, Jill Fletcher, Kirsten McKenzie, Vincent Kolbe, Nigel Penn, Howard Phillips, John Rennie, Helen Robinson, Robert Ross, Christopher Saunders, Phillida Simons, Terri Strauss, Kerry Ward, Brian Warner and our colleagues in the History Department at the University of Cape Town.

Finally, we should also like to thank in particular Arthur Davey, Claudia Pienaar and James Patrick for their personal, and practical, support.

Abbreviations

CA   Cape Archives

CTCC   Cape Town City Council

DRC   Dutch Reformed Church

DSAB   *Dictionary of South African Biography*

QBSAL   *Quarterly Bulletin of the South African Library*

SACA   *South African Commercial Advertiser*

SAL   South African Library

SANAC   South African Native Affairs Commission

UCT   University of Cape Town

VOC   Vereenigde Oost-Indische Compagnie

VRJ   *Journal of Van Riebeeck*

VRS   Van Riebeeck Society

YMCA   Young Men's Christian Association

YWCA   Young Women's Christian Association

meest Z.O. en aldwer half jaer
meest N.W. en beyde zo fel dat men
beswaarlyke gaan kan. Heir is nu
een Storm uijtgebeelt.

Cros ost 88
een alder

CHAPTER ONE

'More the Name Than the Reality'

Cape Town
1620–1662

ON 3 July 1620, Andrew Shillinge and Humphrey Fitzherbert, commanders of two English East India Company fleets bound for Surat and Bantam, took 'quiet and peaceful possession' of Table Bay and 'of the whole continent near adjoining', in the name of 'the High and Mighty Prince James, by the Grace of God King of Great Britain'. Naming Lion's Head 'Ye Sugar Loaf', Signal Hill 'King James Mount' and Devil's Peak 'King Charles Mount', they planned the establishment of a 'plantation' (in imitation of that set up by the Virginia Company at Jamestown several years earlier) to ensure the refreshment of the English Company's ships on their way to India, adding that they hoped much from 'the Blacks, when there is a government to keep them in awe … time no doubt will make them [our] servants'.[1]

This is not, of course, the usual account of the origins of Cape Town. Shillinge and Fitzherbert's claims were not followed up, and nothing came of the episode. But it serves to set Jan van Riebeeck's occupation of the shore of Table Bay in a rather different context. For the Dutch occupation in 1652 was only one of a series of contacts and claims by European travellers passing the Cape on the way to the Indian Ocean. Indeed the claims on behalf of the English East India Company in 1620 were provoked by the prospect of a similar move by its rival, the Dutch East India Company (VOC), with whom it was in bitter conflict in Bantam and Java.

Table Bay and its striking domination by Table Mountain had exercised an ambivalent fascination among Europeans since they first learnt of its existence when in 1503 the Portuguese explorer Antonio de Saldanha sailed into the bay by mistake, thinking he had already rounded the Peninsula. On the one hand it was a place of mystery and allure. From at least the time of Dante, Europeans thought that an earthly paradise existed somewhere on a mountain beyond the deserts of Africa and in the sixteenth and early seventeenth centuries they readily associated Table Mountain with such a place. Physical descriptions of the area of modern Cape Town evoked exotic and luxuriant images. Thus in the year of the English occupation, a Frenchman, Augustin de Beaulieu, described

> forests of tall trees, as thick as apple-trees with no fruit on them and of a very hard wood … all along the mountains there is an infinity of game, such as roebucks, deer as large as harts, partridges and all sorts of game, and on the mountains are great numbers of monkeys, marmots, lions, lynxes, foxes, porcupines, ostriches, elephants and other beasts unknown to me.[2]

But there was another side to this image. The Cape was wild and stormy, most strikingly embodied in Camoens's *Lusiads* by the 'fearsome monster' Adamastor, who

Previous pages: Khoikhoi in a south-easter gale, by an unknown early eighteenth century artist. (SAL INIL 6253)

'Forests of tall trees, as thick as apple-trees with no fruit on them and of a very hard wood … all along the mountains there is an infinity of game, such as roebucks, deer as large as harts, partridges and all sorts of game, and on the mountains are great numbers of monkeys, marmots, lions, lynxes, foxes, porcupines, ostriches, elephants and other beasts unknown to me.'

Augustin de Beaulieu

The names given by the English in 1620 to the mountains around Table Bay were still marked on John Sellar's map of 1675. (SAL PHA: Table Bay)

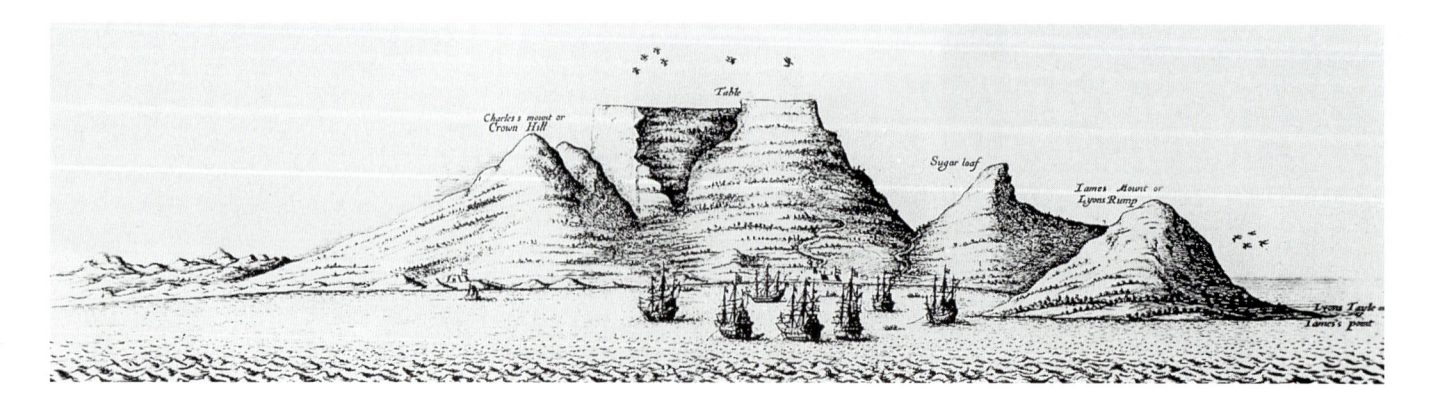

Seventeenth-century maps confidently positioned the fabulously wealthy kingdom of Monomotapa in the African interior. (SAL KCA. AS. 1683. Mallet)

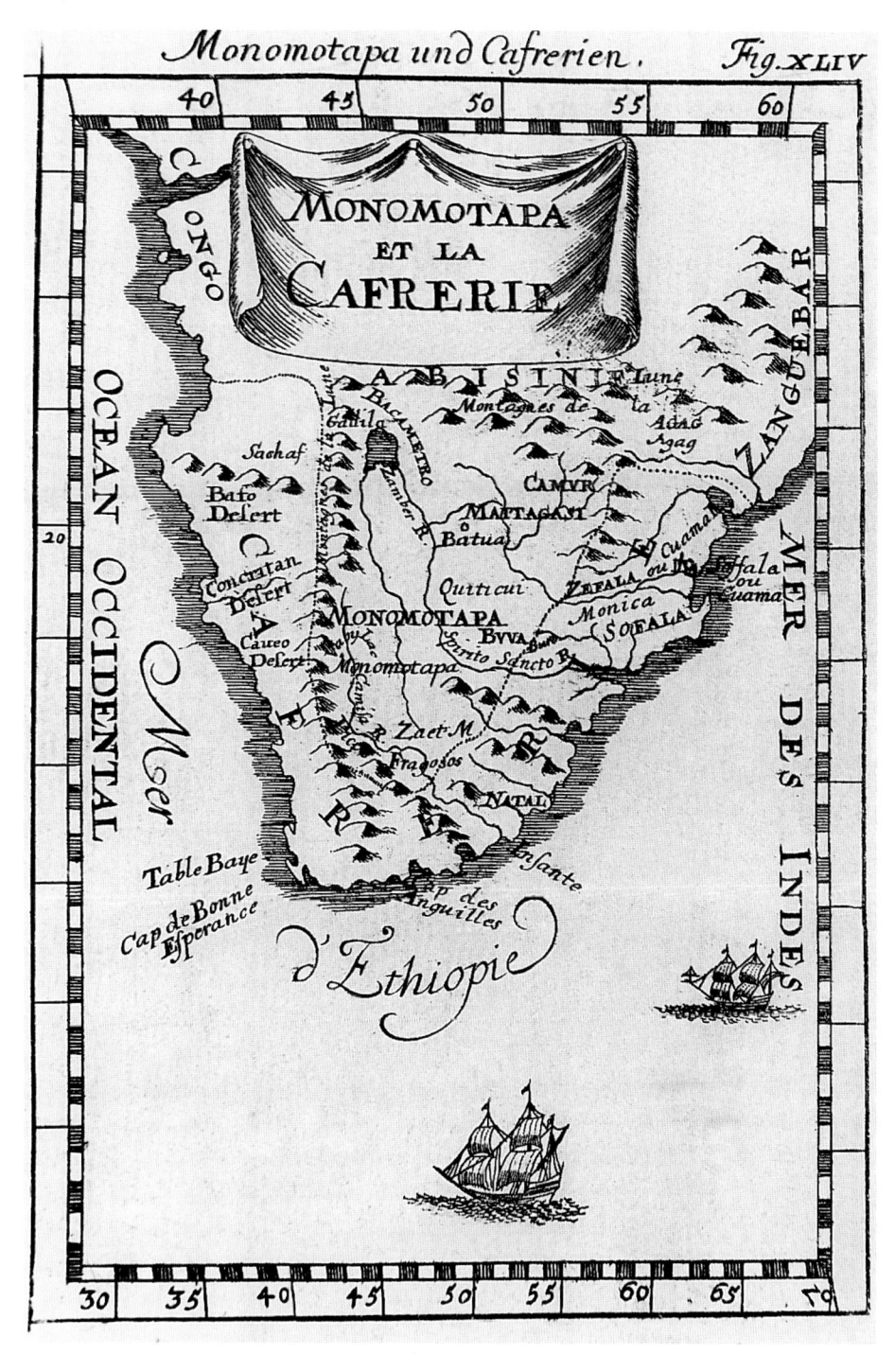

'I am that mighty hidden Cape, called by you Portuguese the Cape of Storms ... until now it has remained unknown: your daring offends it deeply'.

Camoens, *The Lusiads*

declared, 'I am that mighty hidden Cape, called by you Portuguese the Cape of Storms ... until now it has remained unknown: your daring offends it deeply.'[3]

And paradise contained its serpents, marking it as a place of danger as well as exoticism. In 1510, Francisco de Almeida, the first viceroy of the Portuguese Indies, brought his fleet into Table Bay in search of fresh water. Some of his crew went to a nearby settlement of Khoi pastoralists, on the site of modern Salt River, to barter for sheep and cattle. Their attempts to kidnap two of the Khoi led to a punch-up and the return of a soldier with 'face bloodied and some teeth broken'. In revenge Almeida together with 'the flower of the Portuguese nobility' marched to the village to teach the Khoi a lesson in European superiority. They captured not only cattle but also 'children they had found

'MORE THE NAME THAN THE REALITY' 13

in the houses'. The Khoi retaliated, forced them back to the shoreline and there killed Almeida and fifty others.[4] Before long, Europeans were depicting the inhabitants of this paradise as ferocious cannibals, an image which was to survive well into the seventeenth century.

This dramatic episode also explains subsequent Portuguese caution about involvement at Table Bay. But in the early seventeenth century, the site again attracted interest, this time from the English and Dutch, both of whom had formed trading companies to challenge Portuguese domination of the lucrative trade with Asia. Dutch failure in 1607–8 to oust the Portuguese from Mozambique led to a search for other mid-way ports of call for water and fresh meat supplies. Both St Helena and Mauritius were occupied but Table Bay, as the only known and sheltered source of fresh water along the southern African coast, was more regularly visited.

English as well as Dutch ships obtained fresh water and attempted to barter copper and iron for meat with the Khoi, often setting up tents along the shoreline while negotiating the process. Such trade was not easy: as early as 1610 the Khoi refused to accept iron in return for their cattle and sheep, doubtless because the local market was saturated. Autshumato (called 'Harry' by the Europeans), chief of the Strandloper or 'Watermen' Khoi, was taken by the English to Bantam in 1631–2, and then used as a trading agent after his return to Table Bay, although his role as custodian of dispatches and letters left by passing fleets was more significant than that of cattle trader.

This highly inaccurate depiction of the death of Almeida at Table Bay, published in Holland in 1707, shows a fanciful Khoi settlement with pyramid and palm trees. (CA M7)

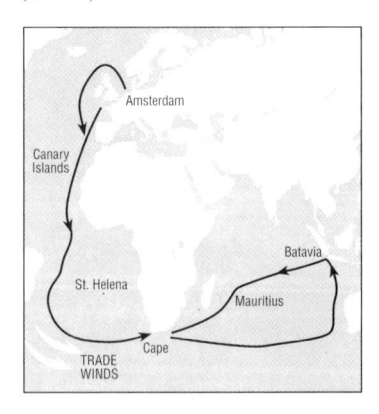

Vessels from Europe could pick up on the South Atlantic trade winds, avoid the West African coast and make straight out from the Canary Islands to the mid-Atlantic, sighting land only at the Cape before catching the monsoon trades into the Indian Ocean.

English or Dutch ships in Table Bay and their tents along the shore were thus regular sights in the seventeenth century, and the image of a luxuriant and plentiful land seemed confirmed, even if the Khoi cattle trade was not as abundant as the callers hoped. But the ambivalence of paradise's darker shadows continued. The English used Robben Island as a penal colony in 1615 in a foretaste of its later notoriety; stories of cannibalistic local inhabitants who ate their visitors continued to titillate European readers into the 1620s; and the Dutch used Table Bay in 1636 as a depository for mutineers, who were thrown overboard with leaded weights attached.[5] The bay's reputation as the 'Cape of Storms' was furthered by the numerous shipwrecks that took place in and around it and the castaways who ended up on its shores.

A drawing made in 1634 by the English traveller Peter Mundy shows a tent for sick passengers and sailors along the shore next to the fresh-water stream. A clearly defined track runs along the shoreline.

A. The Topp of the great hill called the Table. B. The goeing upp thereto betwene a monstrous Clefte or opening. C. A prettie brooke which cometh from the said openinge and runneth by the Tent. D. The Tent where the sicke men ly ashoare. E. James his Mounte. F. The Sugar Loafe. G. The Valley or plaine under the Hill. H. Charles his Mounte, being certain Rocks on the Topp of a Hill resemblinge a Castle afarr off. I. The place where our shipp rode called Table bay and by some Saldania Bay. K. The Buttresses or supporters under the Table being of the Nature of Charles his Mounte, seemeing artificiall.

(SAL, *Travels of Peter Mundy in Europe and Asia*)

The experience of one such group, the castaways from the *Haerlem* in 1648, is often cited as the cause of the VOC occupation of the Cape four years later. Certainly the report written by the survivors of this VOC shipwreck recommending permanent Dutch settlement did much to influence the directors of the Company. Van Riebeeck responded to it and was subsequently appointed commander of the expedition that established a settlement in 1652. But this was by no means the first shipwreck in the bay and the Dutch were well aware of its facilities long before this date. The 1652 occupation was a pre-emptive move to exclude the English with whom the Dutch were at open war, just as the 1620 claims by the English had aimed at excluding the Dutch. Van Riebeeck carefully checked that there were no English vessels in Table Bay before laying claim to its shore.[6]

His expedition also needs to be seen in the broader context of the activities of the trading companies in the Indian and South Atlantic oceans. By the mid-seventeenth century, the VOC had expanded its operations from trading carrier to occupier and colonist in Java, Bantam and the Celebes. The volume of its shipping between Europe and the East had sharply increased since the 1620s and the need for a permanent refreshment stop on the way grew more acute.

The report of the *Haerlem* survivors highlighted the inadequacies of St Helena and Mauritius, both of which lacked sufficient resources. It also addressed the lurking fears that Europeans still had of the local inhabitants of Table Bay. Testifying to the friendliness of the Khoi during their period of enforced stay, the writers denied that they were 'brutal and cannibals' and claimed rather that previous hostilities were as much the fault of the Europeans as of the locals.[7] Moreover, they argued that a permanent settlement would bring about closer contacts with the Khoi, enabling them to learn Dutch so that 'living on good terms with them, some of their children may afterwards be employed as servants and educated in the Christian religion, by which means ... many souls will be brought to the Christian Reformed religion and to God', a useful combination of conversion and labour supply familiar in the theory of European colonisation since the Spanish conquest of the Americas.[8] Van Riebeeck, drawing rather on the darker image of the Cape, failed to agree that the Khoi were so amenable: 'they are not to be trusted, being a brutal gang, living without any conscience ... I have heard from many who have been there and who are trustworthy, that our people have been killed without any cause whatever.'[9]

This statement drew attention to the most significant difference between Table Bay and St Helena or Mauritius: it was not an uninhabited island but the tip of a continent populated for millennia. Skeletons and the tools of hunters and gatherers from the Middle and Late Stone Age, some dating from about 30,000 years ago, have been discovered at sites on the modern Foreshore, Maitland, Peers Cave at Fish Hoek and across the southern part of the Peninsula and Cape Flats. Faunal remains of sheep from 1600 years ago, and cattle bones dating from at least AD 700, have been found at sites across the south-western Cape, revealing the later presence of pastoralist communities. There has been much controversy amongst archaeologists as to whether hunter-gatherers and pastoralists represented two distinct waves of human occupation or whether the hunter-gatherers slowly adopted domestic livestock and evolved into pastoralists. But the weight of evidence at present suggests the former scenario, with the earlier San hunter-gatherers retreating to remoter mountainous sites, such as the Piketberg, away from the encroachment of Khoi pastoralists onto grazing lands.[10] There seem to have been no San communities left in the Cape Peninsula by the seventeenth century, the cattleless 'Watermen' encountered by Europeans along the shore of Table Bay being rather Khoi pastoralists who had lost their stock.

The soils of the south-western Cape, and therefore the vegetation which grows on them, lacked sufficient nutrients to permit the Khoi cattle herds to stay for long periods in one place. They therefore had to move seasonally around the region. For instance, the Cochoqua moved annually between Saldanha Bay and the Swartland. As the Cape Peninsula provided good summer pasturage, at least two groups of Khoi, the Gorachoqua and the Goringhaiqua, used the shores of Table Bay as part of an annual transhumance pattern. They usually arrived in the Peninsula in November, grazing their cattle at Table Bay and often also in the region of modern Sea Point and Hout Bay, moving on across the Cape Flats in January. The 'Peninsular' Goringhaiqua also migrated to the southern Peninsula during the summer.

Although the Cape Khoi had trading contacts with the agricultural communities of the eastern Cape and the interior, arable farming had not emerged in the south-western Cape by the seventeenth century. There were good reasons for this – the region is a

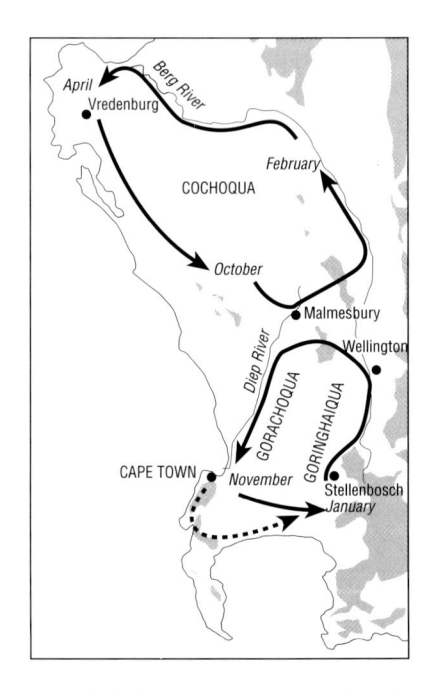

Annual Khoi transhumance patterns in and around the Cape Peninsula. (After Andrew Smith in M. Hall (ed.), *Frontiers*, p. 136)

winter rainfall zone and the indigenous millet and sorghum are summer rainfall crops. The Khoi were thus dependent upon cattle and sheep for subsistence, trade and the accumulation of wealth, and they were therefore reluctant to barter limitless numbers of cattle and sheep with European visitors. The economic imperatives of this pastoralist society were to conflict sharply with those of the Dutch settlement.

The 'Instructions for the officers of an expedition fitted out for the Cape of Good Hope to found a fort and garden there', given in 1651 to Van Riebeeck by the VOC directors in Amsterdam, were unambiguous about the kind of settlement they planned for Table Bay. They envisaged a dual role for the station: as a defensive post against both 'the natives, who are a very rough lot' and potential European rivals as well as a source of fresh food for passing vessels. This was to determine the physical layout of the post. The expedition's first duty was to build 'a defensive fort', then 'as soon as you are in a proper state of defence you shall search for the best places for gardens, the best and fattest ground in which every thing planted or sown will thrive well, which garden shall be properly enclosed … '[11] By the end of the first month work on both projects was under way.

The focus on fort and garden was to provide both the basis for Cape Town's later physical layout and the key symbols of its early function. The defensive fort was a visible assertion of power, a statement of presence which announced a permanence lacking in the tents of earlier European shelter at Table Bay. It housed not only garrisons but also official residences, sleeping quarters for Company employees, storehouses and administration offices.[12] But it was also an indicator of weakness, of alien presence in a landscape which the Dutch did *not* dominate, reflecting the need to huddle in a single defensive building. This tension between permanent assertiveness and vulnerability was to remain a feature of the VOC settlement at Table Bay throughout its first decades.

'As soon as you are in a proper state of defence you shall search for the best places for gardens, the best and fattest ground in which every thing planted or sown will thrive well, which garden shall be properly enclosed … '
Instructions to Van Riebeeck, 1651

John Sellar's 1675 illustration of the first fort at Table Bay was made several years after its collapse. It shows a much sturdier structure than had in fact existed. (SAL PHA: Table Bay)

Van Riebeeck followed his instructions and set about constructing a fort, employing both the local garrison and sailors and soldiers from passing ships.[13] But it was a temporary and precarious structure of earthen ramparts and wooden walls, which Van Riebeeck and the VOC directors feared could be easily overwhelmed by 'nimble Hottentots', as well as the English or French with whom the Dutch were in a state of rivalry and sometimes open warfare.[14] In fact its worst enemies were rain and mudslides, and it almost completely collapsed in 1663. Only after this was the stone structure erected which survives today.

The setting out of a market garden of fruit and vegetables – ornamental flowers were

'MORE THE NAME THAN THE REALITY' 17

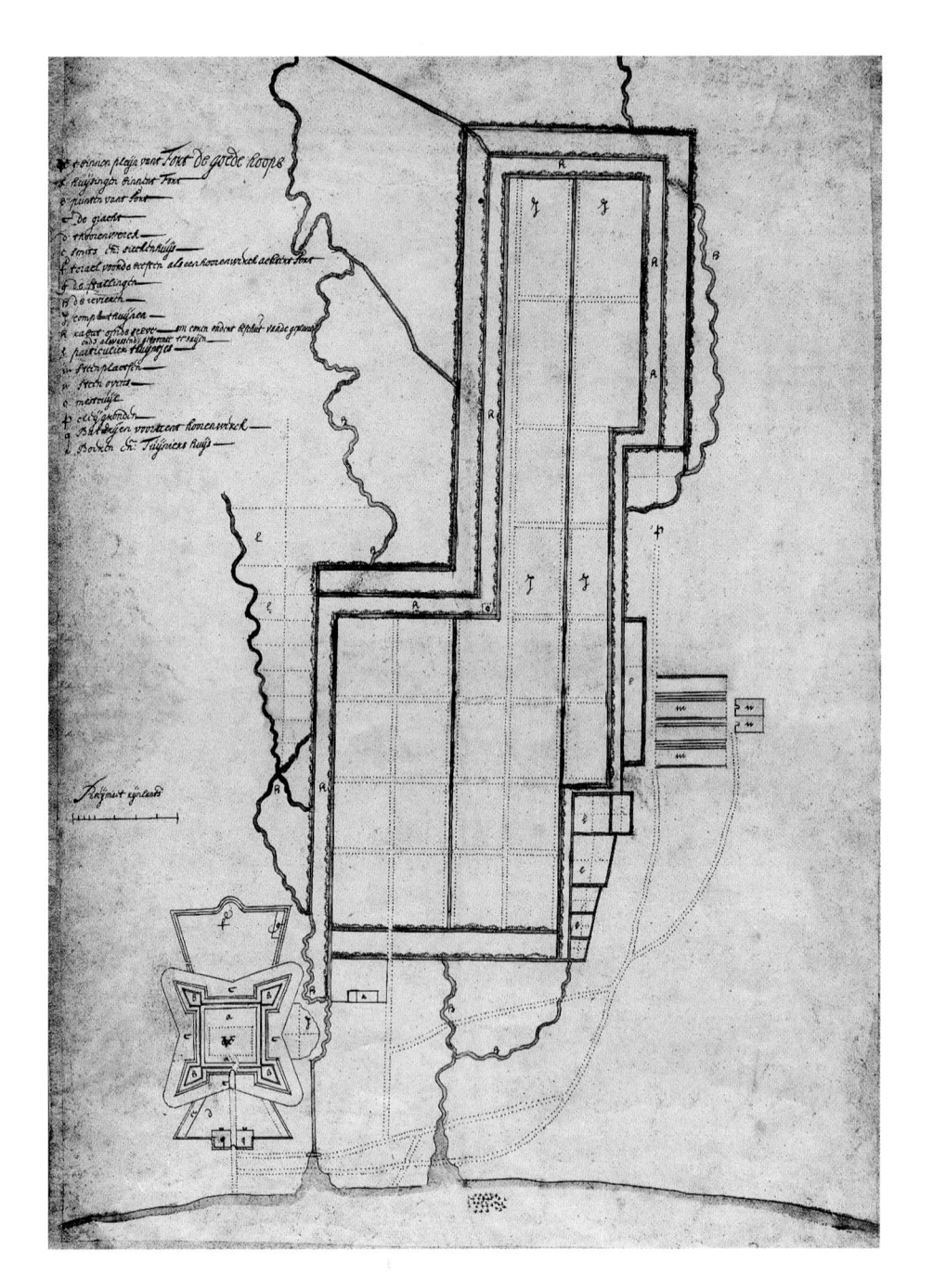

This 1656 map of the settlement at Table Bay shows the early layout, giving the appearance of control over a tamed and transformed environment. The fort (*a*) and garden (*j*) were sited on either side of the fresh-water stream descending from the mountain, channelled into irrigation ditches (*h*) around the garden and flowing into the bay alongside the fort walls. Neat lines demarcate the garden boundaries and its internal divisions into cultivated strips and vegetable beds, while the four-cornered mound of the fort asserts a dominating presence. The map even shows the footpaths between garden, fort and coastline, in a confident assertion of boundaries. Hendrik Boom's house (*r*) is clearly marked to the right of the fort, as are some of the farms established around the garden (*l*). (Algemeen Rijksarchief VEL 820)

not to be introduced until the 1770s – was a more direct claiming of the landscape and a less common feature of Dutch colonial settlements. In Batavia garden plots were situated outside the Dutch town and were tended by local inhabitants or Chinese cultivators. At the Cape, there was no such indigenous cultivation and the Company gardens were situated alongside the fort. They were tended by Company employees under the direction of Hendrik Boom, an Amsterdam gardener who was the only Dutchman to reside outside the fort, in a small house built next to the garden. The garden was a constant source of concern to the VOC, with frequent requests for seeds being made to Amsterdam and Batavia, progress on their growth reported in dispatches, and alarm at the devastations of winds, rain and the encroachments of wild animals, Khoi and visiting sailors on the scrounge or the spree. Thorn trees were planted as protection against all of these threats, thus enclosing and marking out a special space.[15]

'... the clothing, skull and bones of the soldier given up for lost on the 30th of last month were found at the extremity of the Lion Mountain, about 30 roods from the beach. The cranium was half bitten off, so it is presumed that he was devoured by a lion.'

Van Riebeeck's Journal,
12 September 1659

But the world over which the Dutch had no control came right up to the walls of the fort. From the start the men at the fort were forbidden to roam far from it because of the dangers such wanderings entailed. On 12 September 1659, 'the clothing, skull and bones of the soldier given up for lost on the 30th of last month were found at the extremity of the Lion Mountain, about 30 roods from the beach. The cranium was half bitten off, so it is presumed that he was devoured by a lion.'[16]

To the ravages of animals were added those of the elements. The first winter of 1652 was exceptionally cold, with snow on Table Mountain. In subsequent years winter rains and flood streams from the mountain inundated the fort and garden, while ferocious south-easterly winds in summer flattened crops.[17] There were constant emergency repairs to be made. To add to these difficulties the health of the garrison and of crew from passing ships left much to be desired. Indeed one of the functions of the settlement was to provide recuperation for those weakened by long sea voyages. In February 1653 the surgeon reported so many cases of 'dropsy, dysentery, fevers and pains in the joints' that 'we are being rendered almost impotent and the fortification works etc. are greatly retarded'.[18]

Such descriptions give the lie to the confident assertions of maps. Indeed, rather than providing the intended support for the VOC's trading vessels, the early Cape settlement was in its initial stages completely dependent on food supplies shipped from Amsterdam and Batavia for its survival. In June 1654 complete starvation was only averted by the timely arrival of the *Tulp*, which had been sent to Madagascar in search of rice.[19] The situation improved somewhat during the spring months when the garden crops grew, but the state of the settlement throughout Van Riebeeck's ten-year period of command (1652–62) was always precarious. As late as 1662, it was still dependent on the arrival of rice supplies from Madagascar.[20] And for much of the first decade of the settlement, emergency provisions of penguins, seal meat, cormorants and eggs came from Robben Island. As early as 1654, a vegetable garden was dug on the island and flocks of sheep were placed there, safely out of the way of natural (and human) predators. The 'pantry' of Robben Island thus saved the early Cape Town garrison from starvation.

But beyond the fort and garden lay another landscape. On 28 April 1652 a posse of soldiers ventured around the southern side of Table Mountain. In an evocation of the early image of the Cape as paradise, Van Riebeeck reported finding there 'the most beautiful, wide and level ground consisting of exceeding fine garden soil and clay lands ... traversed by the loveliest fresh rivers'.[21] Cultivation of these lands was at this stage outside Van Riebeeck's remit. But he harped on the theme, particularly when the Table Bay settlement proved to be so fragile.

Shortage of manpower was a problem. Visiting crews protested at being made to work while stopping over at the Cape and would certainly not have taken kindly to cultivating their own food supplies. And resident Company employees were reluctant to start new cultivation without any incentive. By 1655 some had been permitted to grow vegetables on small plots of their own near the fort, and to sell them to passing crews; further incentives were also given to some Company employees who were leased herds of cattle in return for provision of milk to the fort. But in all these cases they continued working for the Company and received their monthly wages. Company wage-earners could not be spared from their labours at the fort and elsewhere for full-time farming outside the Table Valley. Yet such cultivation seemed essential if the settlement was to survive.

The solution finally approved by the VOC directors in October 1657 was to release some employees from their contracts, thus saving on their wages and replacing them with others, and to grant them freehold lands along the Liesbeek Valley to enable them to set up as agriculturists since 'agricultural work will be done much better by private individuals than by the Company'.[22] Seed, tools and an initial loan were provided on credit, although the 'free burghers', as they were known, were kept under strict check. Although their produce was destined for the ships in Table Bay, while that produced from the Company garden provided the needs of the garrison, the burghers were obliged to sell their produce to the Company at fixed prices, were restricted in their direct access to ships, forbidden to trade with the Khoi and were not even permitted to cross Company lands without permission.[23]

The establishment of free burgher farming was of immense significance. It extended the frontier of the VOC settlement into the Liesbeek Valley and in so doing marked out neatly rectangular blocks, in a further mapping and naming of the landscape which would become the basis of suburban expansion in the nineteenth century. Moreover, in reaction to the unsuccessful system used by the Dutch West India Company in New Netherland (New York), where areas of land were leased to 'patrons' who then brought out settlers from Europe, the Cape freeholders marked the beginnings of individual and private colonisation at the Cape. But it was hardly a triumphant act: 'this was a gesture of despair rather than a signal of great expectations'.[24] And the free burghers did not find their position much easier than they had as Company employees. Crop failures and inadequate cultivation techniques gave them little profit, and most remained heavily indebted to the Company. Like the garrison, they were dependent on rice provisions from outside the Cape.[25] By the end of 1658 they were in virtual open revolt against the Company. Contrary to the myth that the first free burghers were the enthusiastic founding fathers of white South Africa, by 1707 some 40 per cent of the 570 burghers whose fate is known had either applied to return to Company service, been given permission to leave the colony or stowed away in departing ships.[26]

The extension of cultivation around the side of Table Mountain also worsened relations between the Dutch and the Khoi. The land on which Cape Town was later developed had long been an integral part of the transhumant pasturage routes of the Goringhaiqua ('Peninsular' or 'Kaapmans' as the Dutch called them) and the

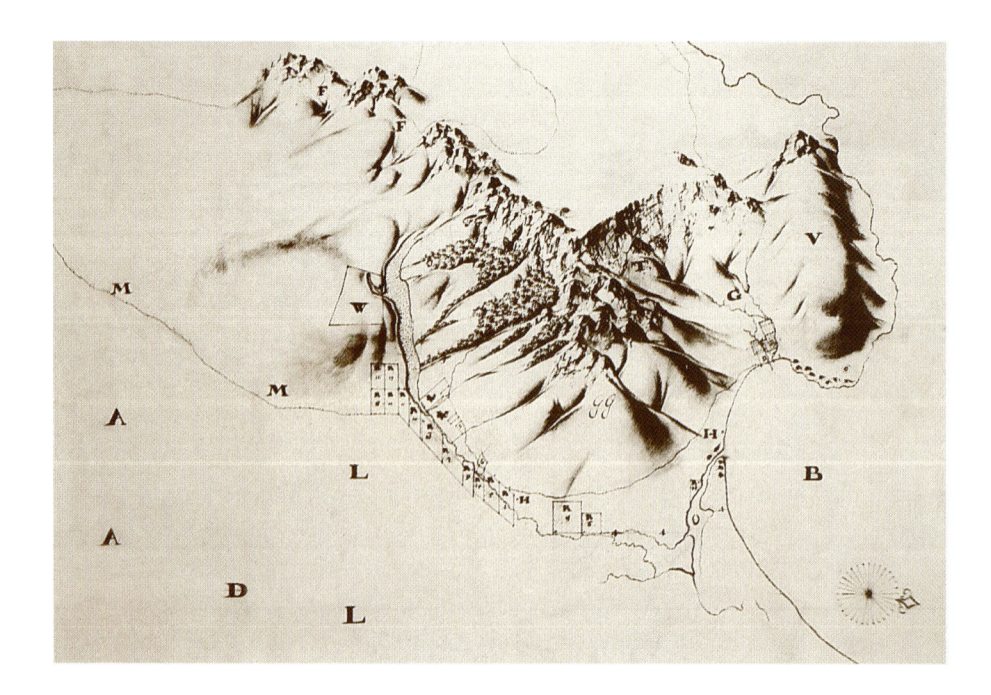

Map showing the first land grants in the Liesbeek Valley to free burghers. The line *M* marked the limit of the area 'most suitable for Cape burghers to build and farm', forming the first boundary of the colony. (CA Map 3/9)

Gorachoqua and also provided marine shoreline subsistence for the Goringhaicona ('Watermen' or 'Strandlopers'). In addition, during the course of the early seventeenth century the Cochoqua ('Saldanhars') extended their grazing routes down from Saldanha Bay and the Swartland to Table Bay, attracted by both the good summer grazing pastures and trade with European visitors. To the Khoi, as in all pastoralist societies, stock, rather than land, acted as the marker of wealth. Groups of pastoralists grazed land for specific periods, and were accustomed to following set routes throughout the year, but did not 'occupy' specific sites permanently. From the late sixteenth century local Khoi opposed Europeans if they appeared to be staying too long at Table Bay and refused to barter with them.

The VOC settlement lay directly in the path of Khoi grazing routes. When the Dutch arrived in April, they encountered only the stockless Goringhaicona. But in December the Cochoqua appeared, showing little respect for the neatly ordered boundaries of Dutch maps: 'the Saldanhars again came with thousands of cattle grazing in the vicinity of the fort, indeed almost entering through the gate and being kept out of the gardens with difficulty.'[27]

The Dutch were pining for beef and mutton and hoping to obtain stock to supply the Batavian returning fleet. The Cochoqua were not, however, interested in bartering any of their herds for copper trinkets. The Company journal records the frustrations felt by Van Riebeeck, whose dislike and mistrust of the Khoi had been evident in his comments on the *Haerlem* report:

> would it matter so much if one deprived them of some 6 or 8 thousand cattle? For this there would be ample opportunity, as we have observed that they are not very strong   indeed they are extremely timorous. Often only 2 or 3 of them drive a thousand cattle within range of our cannon, and it would therefore be quite easy to cut them off.[28]

He was restrained by the knowledge that the Company directors had ordered him to barter and not to make war, as well as by the hope that through the intermediary of Autshumato regular trading would eventually be obtained. Moreover, the settlement was by no means as powerful as its journal suggested. As we have seen, it was extremely fragile and vulnerable in its first years. Without knowledge of the power of the Cochoqua or the numbers of their allies who could come to their defence, direct attack would have been risky.

Some cattle were obtained from the Goringhaiqua who migrated each summer across the Cape Peninsula. But by mid-1653 they too were alarmed that the Dutch were showing no signs of leaving. They attempted to persuade them to do so by making off with some of their cattle and killing the herder. To pastoralists, for whom cattle represented the basis of subsistence and investment, this would have been sufficient to ensure the collapse of the Dutch interlopers. But the Dutch, basing their presence on occupancy of land and the physical boundaries of fort and garden, did not respond accordingly. Instead they strengthened guards on the herds and demanded compensation, but they were still dependent on Autshumato and other intermediaries to obtain the stock they required to provision both themselves and the passing fleets.

In 1654–6 tensions rose further. The Cochoqua refused to accept Dutch pretensions of controlling the land permanently, and showed their contempt by grazing their cattle across the garden and shoreline, mixing them with the Company's own herds. The

'The Saldanhars again came with thousands of cattle grazing in the vicinity of the fort, indeed almost entering through the gate and being kept out of the gardens with difficulty.'

Van Riebeeck's Journal,
18 December 1652

Goringhaiqua told the Dutch firmly during their summer migrations of 1655 that 'we were living upon their land and they perceived that we were rapidly building more and more as if we intended never to leave, and for that reason they would not trade with us for any more cattle'.[29] That same night

> it happened that about 50 of these natives wanted to put up their huts close to the banks of the moat of our fortress, and when told in a friendly manner by our men to go a little further away, they declared boldly that this was not our land but theirs and that they would place their huts wherever they chose. If we were not disposed to permit them to do so they would attack us with the aid of a large number of people from the interior and kill us, pointing out that the ramparts were only constructed of earth and scum and could easily be surmounted by them and that they also knew how to break down the palisades.[30]

The Dutch were forced to back down, but the episode demonstrated their vulnerability even more directly than disputes over cattle grazing. The Khoi were contesting the central symbols of their presence and power in the same way that Dutch occupation of pasturage threatened the symbols of Khoi existence.

When the English traveller Thomas Herbert visited Table Bay in 1627, he depicted Khoi bartering sheep in exchange for copper. By the time this was published in the Netherlands in 1658, the Khoi were less willing to trade with the Dutch, who had occupied their grazing lands. Open conflict broke out the following year. (SAL PHA: Khoisan)

22 CAPE TOWN 1620–1662

'[Autshumato] visited the fort ... and asked where he and the Kaapmans were to live and graze their cattle now that we were ploughing the land everywhere. They were told to remain where they were now living, that is in the country towards the mountain range in the interior.'

Van Riebeeck's Journal,
27 July 1657

Arguments about pasturage near the fort and garden continued. In 1656 the Dutch were more assertive, telling the Goringhaiqua to move their cattle 'further behind the Lion Mountain ... out of sight of the Company's settlement'.[31] When Autshumato asked in July 1657 'where he and the Kaapmans were to live and graze their cattle now that we were ploughing the land everywhere, they were told to remain where they were now living, that is in the country towards the mountain range in the interior'. This attempt to break down the transhumance cycle would, as Autshumato pointed out, lead to disaster.[32]

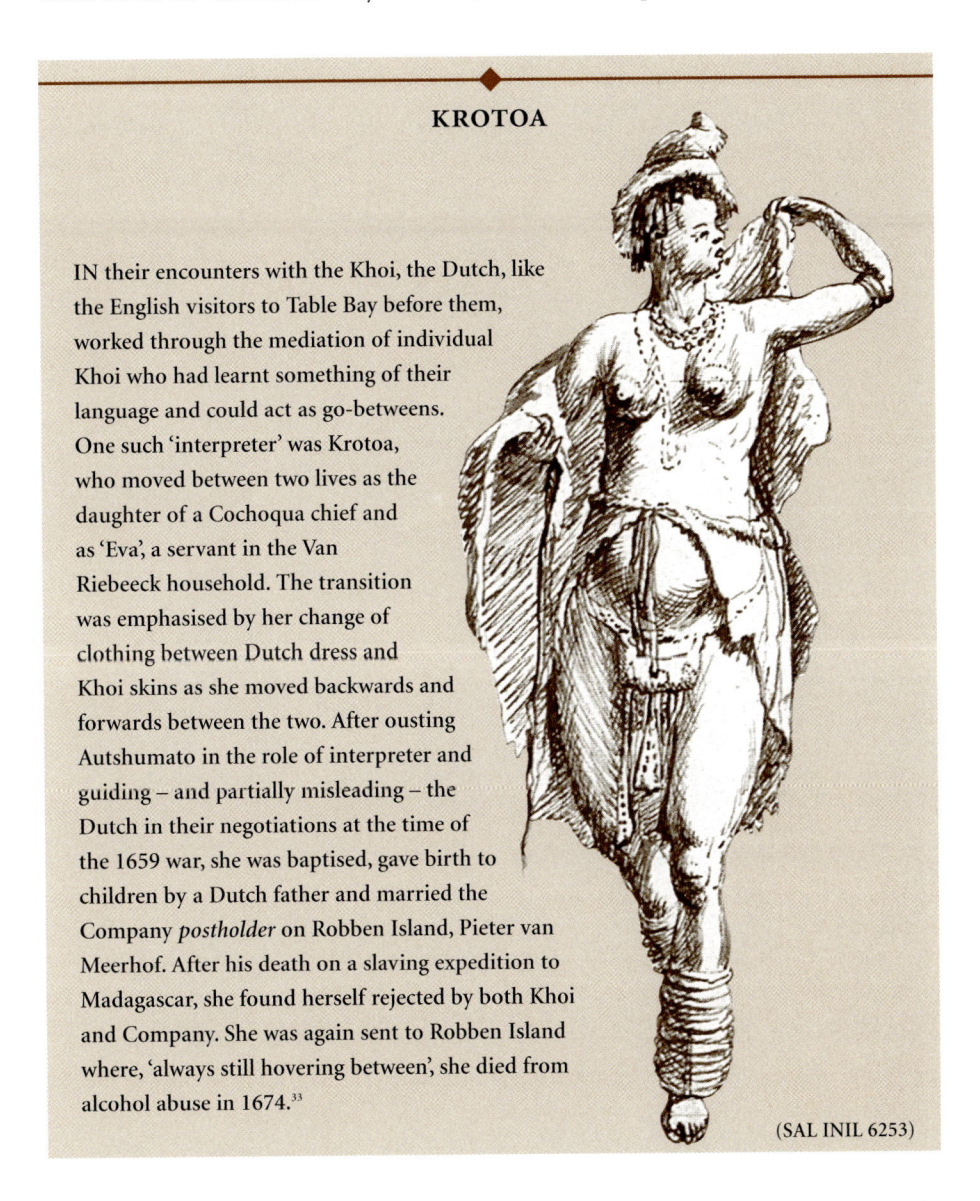

KROTOA

IN their encounters with the Khoi, the Dutch, like the English visitors to Table Bay before them, worked through the mediation of individual Khoi who had learnt something of their language and could act as go-betweens. One such 'interpreter' was Krotoa, who moved between two lives as the daughter of a Cochoqua chief and as 'Eva', a servant in the Van Riebeeck household. The transition was emphasised by her change of clothing between Dutch dress and Khoi skins as she moved backwards and forwards between the two. After ousting Autshumato in the role of interpreter and guiding – and partially misleading – the Dutch in their negotiations at the time of the 1659 war, she was baptised, gave birth to children by a Dutch father and married the Company *posholder* on Robben Island, Pieter van Meerhof. After his death on a slaving expedition to Madagascar, she found herself rejected by both Khoi and Company. She was again sent to Robben Island where, 'always still hovering between', she died from alcohol abuse in 1674.[33]

(SAL INIL 6253)

The establishment of free burgher farms along the Liesbeek in 1658 thus came in the context of growing tensions and disputes over access to land in the Peninsula. The Khoi refused to accept these new encroachments on their pasture lands and insisted on continuing to graze their cattle as before, breaking down the hedges built to exclude them. During 1659–60 open conflict broke out, the free burghers formed a militia company and sent their families to the greater security of the fort. On 6 April, the eighth anniversary of Van Riebeeck's landing, 'peace was concluded' but not without a further exchange of grievances. The Khoi

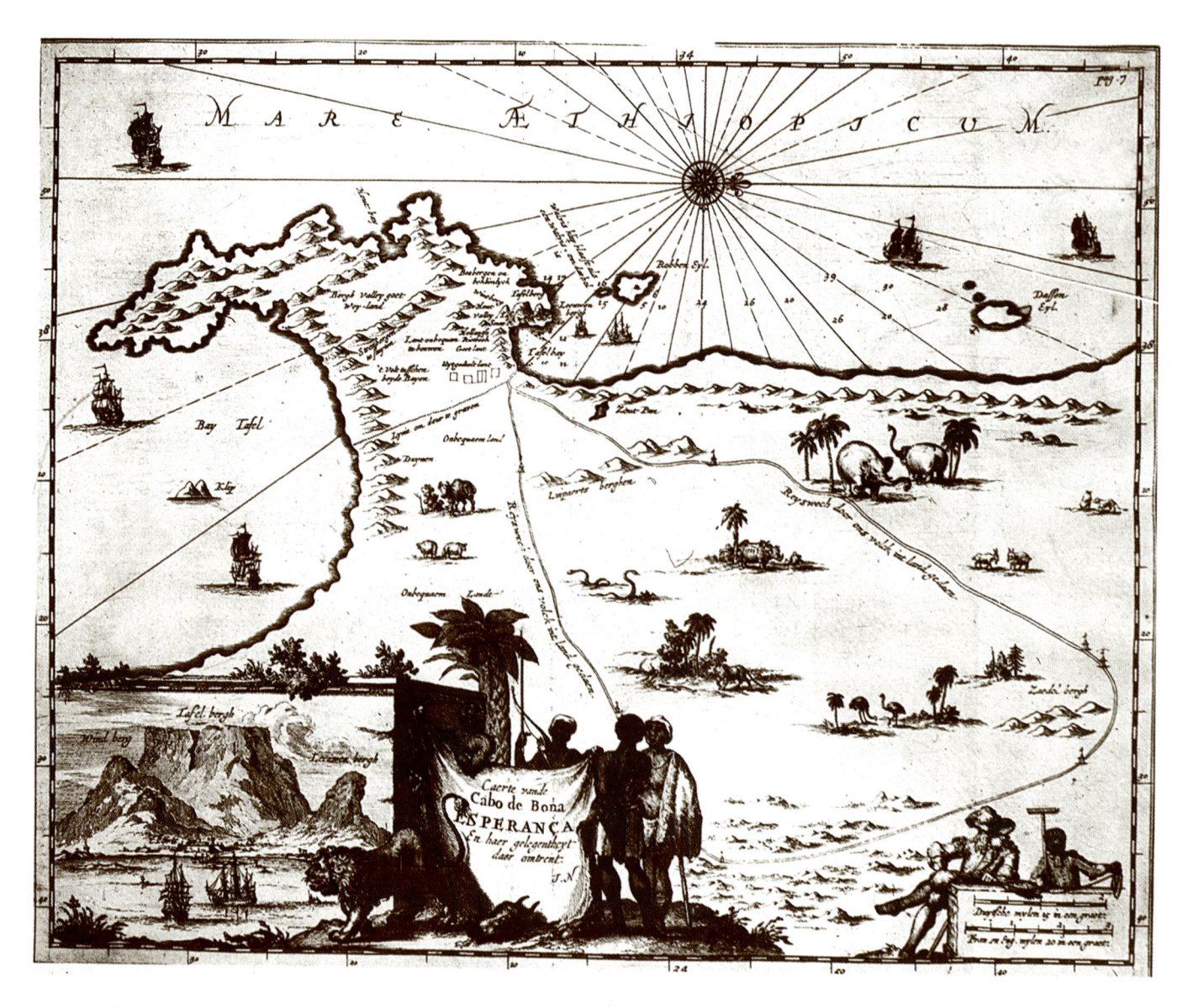

A map prepared in 1659, showing the extent of free burgher farms, proposals for a canal to cut across the Peninsula, and the terrain beyond inhabited by wild beasts and monsters. (CA M70)

strongly insisted that we had been appropriating more and more of their land, which had been theirs all these centuries, and on which they had been accustomed to let their cattle graze. They asked if they would be allowed to do such a thing supposing they went to Holland ... 'As for your claim that the land is not big enough for us both, who should in justice rather give way, the rightful owner or the foreign intruder?' ... Eventually they had to be told that ... their land had fallen to us in a defensive war, won by the sword, as it were, and we intended to keep it.[34]

The Dutch thus decided to claim the site of modern Cape Town by right of conquest, and not by the occupation of an 'empty land'. The Khoi were firmly told that they could only pass through the Table Bay settlement on laid-out footpaths.[35] By December 1660 Van Riebeeck was complaining that the Liesbeek and Table Valley areas were insufficient for the needs of the Company herds and farms and the following year proposed confining the Goringhaiqua to the southern part of the Peninsula 'in the Hout and Bergh Valleys'.[36]

By 1660 the presence of the VOC post was thus transforming not only the shoreline of Table Bay but the whole of the Cape Peninsula. Various proposals were made to stake

24   CAPE TOWN 1620–1662

'This belt will then be so densely overgrown that it will be impossible for cattle or sheep to be driven through and it will take the form of a protective fence, like those which some lords and squires mark off the boundaries of their territories in certain parts of Germany and in the district of Cologne ... '

Van Riebeeck's Journal, 23–25 February 1660

out physically the mapped space of fort, gardens and farms as protection against Khoi 'intrusions'. In a striking reflection of the Company's predilection for islands, far removed from threatening and untamed hinterlands, the VOC directors recommended the digging of a channel between the Salt and Liesbeek rivers, cutting right down to False Bay – a scheme which Van Riebeeck soon declared to be impracticable. Instead palisades were constructed along the Salt River bank and watchtowers set up along the Liesbeek Valley with an elaborate system of flag signalling back to the fort.[37] Following Van Riebeeck's observations of the effectiveness of thick hawthorn hedges in Barbados, he ordered the planting of 'bitter almond trees and all sorts of fast-growing brambles and thornbushes' along the boundaries of the farms, including the outlying land he had appropriated for his own use on the site of modern Wynberg.[38]

The limits of what would later become Cape Town's southern suburbs were being laid out. In these ways physical symbols of the VOC's self-defined settlement were imposed on the landscape, both excluding the alien world of the rest of Africa and giving a sense of security by reconstructing a more familiar European landscape:

> This belt will then be so densely overgrown that it will be impossible for cattle or sheep to be driven through and it will take the form of a protective fence, like those which some lords and squires mark off the boundaries of their territories in certain parts of Germany and in the district of Cologne. They also have circular watch- or guard-towers here and there with heavily barred entrances to protect the farmers from attacks from outside. Our already completed watchtowers and their adjacent barriers will serve a similar purpose in our case ... Within the compass of this hedge, the whole settlement and all the grain farms, forests etc. will be beautifully enclosed as in a half-moon, and everything will be well protected against raids by the Hottentots.[39]

The impact of the Dutch presence on the natural environment of the Peninsula was not confined to pasture lands and hedges. The natural wildlife was being steadily hunted out – encouraged by the premium that the Company paid for the shooting of lions and leopards. Robben Island was populated by sheep which the Company hoped would breed in isolation from Khoi rivals, while the seals of the coastline were hunted for their oil and flesh. Timbers of the Table Bay area were swiftly falling to the axe. By 1658 Van Riebeeck was lamenting the 'reckless destruction' of the forests and restricting felling to a post on the southern side of the mountain named 'Paradise', although he also paid Khoi to bring timber in to the fort from further afield.[40]

The 'Paradise' post was ironically part of the process that was rapidly destroying the landscape of the paradise of earlier European descriptions and imagination. Paradise was now being pushed back across the Cape Flats, where expeditions reported seeing 'in the direction of the Mountains of Africa [the Hottentots Holland range] thousands of antelope, steenbok and eland, but it was as impossible to overtake them on horseback as it is to catch a bird in flight'.[41] Africa now lay outside the physical and mental boundaries of the tamed landscape of the southern Peninsula, yet it continued to exercise a particular fascination. Expeditions were mounted in search of the mythical and fabulously wealthy 'Emperor of Monomotapa', whose 'residence' and 'most of his gold' were believed to be within striking distance of the hills visible from the slopes of Table Mountain.[42]

Who resided within the boundaries of this world so carefully set apart from Africa?

The unknown African continent beyond the Cape Peninsula is named Monomotapa in John Sellar's 1675 map. (SAL PHA: Table Bay)

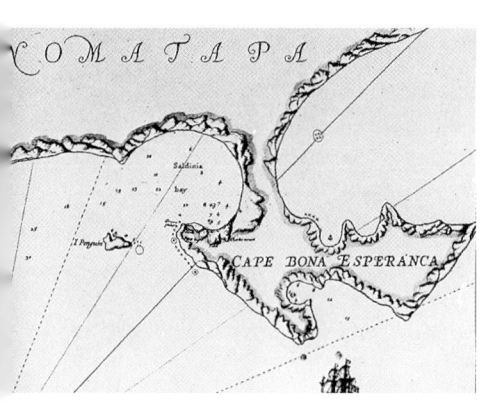

The population of the early settlement was overwhelmingly male. The laying out of fort and garden had been accomplished by the 181 men who arrived in 1652, assisted when possible by passing crews. They had been recruited in the Netherlands, although many of them came from other parts of northern Europe, and some had already seen service in the East Indies. Death reduced their number to 133 by 1656, a figure which fell further to under 100 when some were released as free burghers in 1658. The Company considered reducing the number of its men at the Cape after the completion of the fort in 1655, but conflict with the Khoi persuaded them to supplement the garrison with new recruits who arrived in the course of 1660–1. However, the Company was unwilling, or unable, to spare sufficient numbers to carry out the varieties of work of construction, land clearance and cultivation, defence and ship provision required of the settlement. The total number of VOC employees had only marginally risen to 120 by 1662, a figure which the directors in Amsterdam ordered should not be exceeded, 'yea, if possible even less, since we are now about to be at peace with all European nations'.[43]

The establishment of free burghers eased the situation somewhat, although they were from the Company ranks and were only gradually replaced. In 1658 there were 51 free burghers, all of them male; a few were joined by their wives from Holland, one of whom disguised herself as a man in order to obtain pay on the Company rolls and a free passage.[44] But the mainstay of the workforce of the early settlement came neither from VOC employees nor from the free burghers. Over half of the population of the settlement recorded in the journal of 1658 were slaves.

Chattel slavery formed the backbone of the labour force of the Dutch Cape. Initially the use of slaves followed the pattern of Dutch Batavia, where slaves from elsewhere in the East Indies and India were used as domestic servants in the households of both Chinese and Company residents. In the first few years eight female and three male slaves were servants in the household of Van Riebeeck and other Company officials, and one worked in the gardens. But, lacking adequate supplies of Company employees and aware of their expense and 'unruliness', Van Riebeeck soon appealed for further supplies of

Population of the VOC settlement, 30 May 1658[45]

Garrison	80
Sick	15
Dutch women and children	20
Healthy and sick slaves of the Company	98
Freemen	51
Male and female slaves of freemen	89
Exiles	7
TOTAL	**360**

An early eighteenth-century illustration of an over-dressed Cape farmer supervising a slave with a hoe. (CA L1379)

slaves to do the dirtiest and heaviest work.⁴⁶ The Batavian authorities replied that none were immediately available, but a new impetus was given to the search for slave supplies after the introduction of free burgher agriculture. The first shipload of 228 slaves arrived from the Guinea coast in 1658, and shortly afterwards the chance capture of a Portuguese slaver bound for Brazil brought 174 Angolans, mainly children, to the Cape. These were highly unusual sources: the Guinea trip was made in secret and it was the only time that the VOC undertook an expedition to the West African coast, monopolised by the Dutch West India Company. About half of the slaves were sent on to Batavia, a quarter distributed to the free burghers, and the rest kept by the Company and housed in the fort.

The precedent for slave labour was thus established although neither free burghers nor Company was enchanted with the first supplies. Many ran away and some free burghers returned their slaves to the Company in case they found themselves indebted for slaves who had deserted. By September the number of Company slaves had fallen to 83, 'including those returned by the freemen for fear of desertion ... made up of 34 men and 49 women. They are mostly old and useless, and about 30 are mad, ill or crippled, and can be of no particular service. We shall be relieved of this burden, however, as they will soon die off.'⁴⁷ This experience did not in the long term put either Company or free settlers off, and Dutch Cape Town remained heavily dependent on slave labour.

As yet, nothing has been said about Cape Town itself. There is a good reason for this. The development of a town was not the intention of the VOC either in 1652 or in the subsequent decade. The settlement was to be an outpost, a garrison, garden and some arable farmlands. Its inhabitants were to ensure the provision of meat, vegetables and grains, not to form an urban community. In this the Dutch Cape was expected to follow the example of the VOC stations in Mauritius and St Helena, rather than urban Batavia. Moreover, before the establishment of farming along the Liesbeek in 1658, the very permanence of the station was in some doubt. A particular problem was the violence of winds and storms that sometimes made Table Bay unsafe for shipping. The VOC directors were thus continually searching for better sites, up the Cape coast (where they initially favoured the more sheltered harbour of Saldanha Bay until it was shown to have no fresh-water supplies) and in the Southern Atlantic (Tristan da Cunha was considered at one point as an island to replace St Helena). They retained ambitions as late as 1662 to conquer the Portuguese stations along the Mozambique coast.⁴⁹

There was thus no commitment to an urban settlement on the shores of Table Bay. In 1661 the Company directors wrote with some displeasure to Van Riebeeck that 'From your letters we have remarked that you are gradually tending towards the building of a town there and the enlarging of the colony; but as we look upon it here this idea should be abandoned.'⁵⁰ Van Riebeeck hastened to deny any suggestions that he had acted against the Company's wishes.

> Our idea of laying out a town here has always been very little ... we no longer allow any freemen to reside near the fort except those who had previously accepted a good sized piece of ground for raising wheat, as we can very well feel the burden of freemen, exclusive of agriculturists, and therefore will allow no more than there are already, for whom, should they build any houses here, we have, that they might be erected in proper order as an incipient town, marked off 50 roods, outside the fort's walls, so that at present it seems to have more the name than the reality; if we had not opposed it all the freemen would have left the country and come to live near the Fort.⁵¹

SLAVE WIVES

Although most slaves remained in bondage throughout their lives, some were freed and a few married Company burghers at a time when other women were in short supply. The first recorded example of such a marriage came on 6 July 1658:

'*Jan Sacharias of Amsterdam is a local bachelor and freeman, 27 years of age, who had given promise of marriage to the young woman Maria, born in Bengal, 20 years of age, former slave of the sick comforter Pieter van der Stael. She had been bought into freedom by the same Jan Sacharias for this purpose, as is shown by the transfer to that effect produced today, and he has requested that they might be legally joined in holy matrimony. The Council of this Fortress having established that they are both free persons, who according to their own statements are not in any way bound to any other person in this regard and having been assured that Maria not only understands Dutch perfectly but speaks it clearly and has a fair knowledge of Christ according to the Reformed religion, has decided to grant the young people their fair request.*'⁴⁸

But this reply reveals that more had in fact taken place on the shores of Table Bay than the building of a fort and the laying out of a garden.

The origins of an urban community can be traced to experiments which Van Riebeeck carried out before the creation of free burghers. Cattle and pigs were leased to married Company employees, to be herded in the vicinity of the fort. Their wives were primarily responsible for this duty. The belief that the women of the garrison should be made economically active was further demonstrated when in 1656 the wives of the fort were given permission to make shirts 'in order to make a stuiver without loss to the Company, since they were complaining that there was so little to earn.'[52]

More significant was the arrangement that Annetje Boom, wife of the Company's gardener, who had accompanied her husband on the initial journey in 1652, should lease the Company's milk cows. In return for 'being willing to take the risk' and to enable her to maintain her eight children since 'she cannot make ends meet on her husband's board money alone', she was given permission to keep a tavern 'for the purpose of providing men from passing ships with lodging and refreshment'.[53] Annetje Boom's tavern may not have been in the purview of the Heren XVII, but it suited Van Riebeeck, who by this stage was tired of having to provide board and lodging at the fort for every visitor to Table Bay.[54] All the same, it was still to be kept in the Company's financial interests: Annetje had to agree to obtain all her provisions from the Company and the prices she could charge were also subject to its approval.

Female employment in this overwhelmingly male world thus set the precedent for non-agricultural activities in the vicinity of the fort. Some of the new free burghers found the attractions of such work preferable to the uncertainties of agriculture. Several free-burgher grants in 1658–9 specified other employment, such as tailor, carpenter, surgeon and baker.[55] And the profitability as well as popularity of the first tavern with both visitors and the garrison led to requests for others. The free-burgher surgeon was permitted to keep an inn for an initial three-year probationary period, where his surgical skills were sometimes useful in patching up the wounds produced by brawls in his tavern. By the end of 1657 there were four taverns alongside the fort and garden, and by 1659 the 'town burghers who live near the fort' were 'granted the privilege' of being permitted to sell a wide variety of goods to passing seamen although they were not permitted to board ships in the harbour until the Company had the chance first of disposing of goods at its own – and usually higher – prices.[56]

The rhythm of life in the settlement was closely linked to the arrival of ships. The main period of activity was between December and May, especially when the Batavia return fleets arrived. In the second half of the year far fewer ships made their way to Europe, although some arrived en route to Asia. 'As soon as a ship has anchored at the Cape', reported one visitor in 1660, 'those in charge give a part of the soldiers and crew leave to go ashore to refresh themselves there. Those who have been the most sick during the voyage are sent ashore first each in turn, and go into the town, where they get board for seven or eight stuivers a day, and for this sum are well entertained.'[57] The earnings to be made alongside the fort and harbour were certainly more attractive than those of the farmers of the Liesbeek, most of whom were heavily in debt. This accounts for the Heren XVII's demand that even the burghers residing near the fort should also cultivate plots of land.

The growth in the number of buildings by 1661 was sufficient to 'amaze' the Cochoqua chief Gonnema, who had not seen the site since 1653, and for one French visitor to be impressed by the 'fine town inhabited by all sorts of folk who live near [the

'Our idea of laying out a town here has always been very little ... at present it seems to have more the name than the reality ...'
Van Riebeeck, 9 April 1662

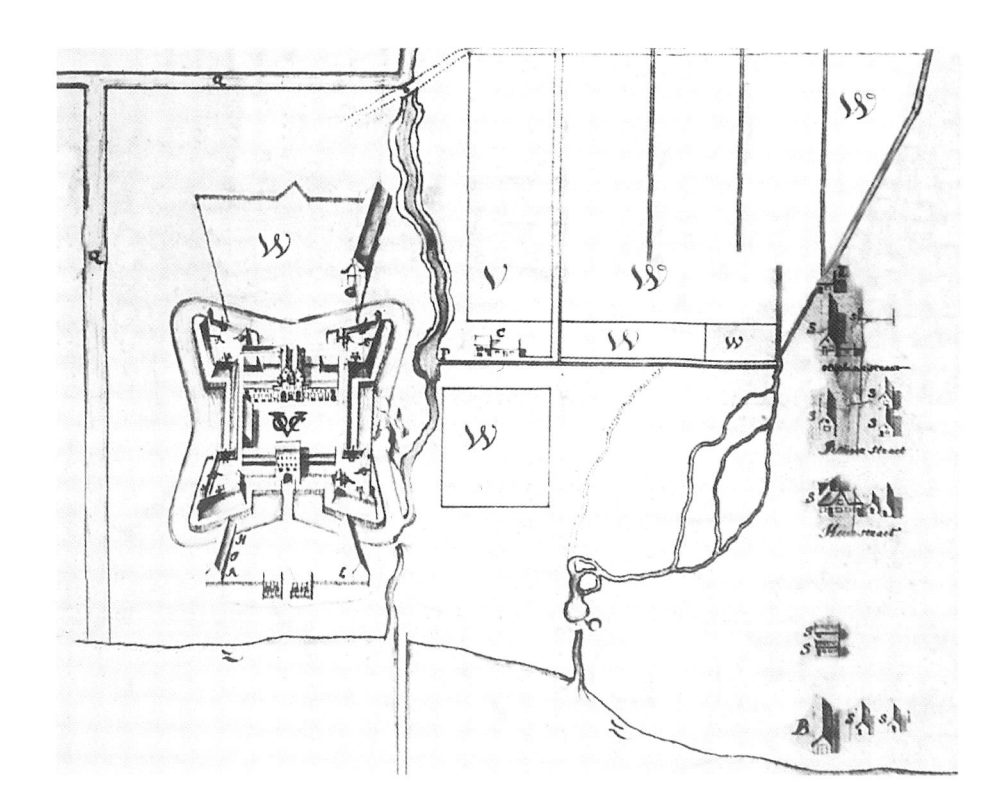

Map dated 1660, showing the changes since 1656 (see p. 18). Several new Company structures are marked: the jetty (built in 1658, though constantly in need of repair) and a small hospital along the shoreline (*B*). In addition 'Freemen's houses' (*S*) are now shown to the right of the fort and garden, with the names of three streets: 'Oliphants' (later Hout Street), 'Reijger' and 'Heerestraat' (later Castle Street). (CA Map 2/19)

fort]'.[58] References were now being made to a 'town', as distinct from the Company fort and the free burgher farms. In the period of heightened tension between the Dutch and the Khoi in May 1659, a 'town burgher militia' was drawn up, modelled on the burgher corps of Portuguese communities in India, and consisting of 'the burghers who live close to the fort (who are called the town burghers)'.[59]

An incipient sense of community amongst the 'town burghers' was shown in their request in the following year for the appointment of one of their number as superintendent of the pigs that they owned.[60] But each of these 'town burghers' had close links to a rural base. They also farmed plots of land on the boundaries of the Company's own gardens, and the first holders of deeds to land in this area also owned agricultural land, two of them along the Liesbeek and two in Table Valley.[61] There were no clear boundaries demarcating the divide of town and countryside. Farms on the slopes of mountains surrounded the earliest buildings. Indeed, as Van Riebeeck emphasised in 1662, this was a town with 'more the name than the reality', being minute in size, firmly in the shadow of the fort and lacking an economic, political or social structure distinct from the rest of the settlement.

Its residents were also firmly under the control of the Company. The VOC was a highly hierarchical organisation, in which rank was minutely detailed and authority exercised through an elaborate network of rank and order. Van Riebeeck, as commander, headed the Council of Policy (Politieke Raad), which met weekly in the fort and carried out 'all functions of government, legislature, executive powers and jurisdiction', at least until the appointment of a Council of Justice in 1685. This in turn was subordinate to the governor-general in Batavia, and under the ultimate authority of the Heren XVII in the Netherlands.

Employees of the Company held rank in a military hierarchy, which took effect from the moment men signed their contracts, operated aboard the ships and was transferred on to land at the Cape. The authority of the Company was invasive in every aspect of

The governor-general's residence, Batavia. (CA M71)

life in the settlement. Not only did it distribute pay, organise the work and determine promotions of its employees, but it also approved land grants, solemnised marriages and allocated slaves to the free burghers, who were no less obliged to show loyalty and devotion to the Company after their release from contract than were the employees. They were granted some say in the administration of the settlement, being permitted to nominate annually four of their number to sit on the Council of Policy when it determined matters pertaining to them; from the four, the commander selected two. These were usually chosen on the grounds of their 'experience'. In 1661 the 'free sawyer' Leendert Cornelissen was dismissed from this position since,

> instead of setting the freemen an honourable and dignified example [he] has been behaving in a more and more debauched manner by drinking, celebrating, fighting, brawling, and swearing, and thus not only bringing into disrepute his own character and the important office which he holds, but also tarnishing the lustre of the Council on which he has a seat and which considers abuses committed by free burghers, and has the right to cast a vote of censure.[62]

For the Council acted as both judge and punisher of miscreants. The Cape inhabitants had to follow the Batavian codes, with which Van Riebeeck had considerable familiarity after his period of work in the Batavian Castle. These were supplemented by special *plakkaten* (statutes) issued from the Cape fort. In order to ensure that they were carried out, a provost-marshal and executioner was appointed as early as December 1652 'to instil fear into the common people'.[63] Characteristically of the seventeenth century, punishments were brutal and public spectacles, the sentence often symbolically emphasising the offence committed. Thus four sheep thieves were condemned in 1658 to hard labour for periods of between five and sixteen years, but 'in addition all four are to stand exposed with sheepskins on their heads and shoulders'.[64]

Although the Dutch identified themselves as 'Christians' in opposition to the 'heathen' slaves and Khoi, their understanding of Christianity was not always that of the established Reformed Church. Indeed, the mental world inhabited by many VOC recruits who came from a rural Europe was marked by elements of popular culture and religion far removed from that of urban Amsterdam. In one intriguing glimpse into such a world, we hear of a Company soldier in the fort who lost a ring and believed that it had been stolen. In order to find the culprit he placed a key into a Bible at the beginning of St John's gospel, said 'Has — taken my ring?' several times with different names, and, when the Bible 'turned round of itself,' stated that 'You see who has been pointed out'. This mixture of magic and the pages of the Bible of Reformed Christianity clearly shows the incomplete conquest of formal religion over its more popular manifestations.[65]

Just as the VOC's attempts to formulate an ordered landscape were foiled by both natural and local enemies, so its hierarchical and legalistic social order was frequently challenged. For to many the Cape 'paradise' seemed more like purgatory. From the early days of the VOC settlement, there was opposition to the hard work required of the men. In the first few years the only break came on Sundays and on 6 April, anniversary of the 1652 landing, which was to be observed 'for all time' as a 'day of thanksgiving and of prayer' – although by 1656 it had been replaced by a more practical holiday granted after the departure of the return fleet in June, a period which caused heavy work at the harbour.[66] This was little compensation for many who resented the life of drudgery working at the Cape in place of the riches and adventures they had anticipated in the service

'Instead of setting the freemen an honourable and dignified example [Leendert Cornelissen] has been behaving in a more and more debauched manner by drinking, celebrating, fighting, brawling, and swearing ...'

Resolution of Council of Policy,
5 October 1661

Opposite: Wouter Schouten's drawing of Table Bay in 1658 showing the first fort and houses and small vessels conveying passengers and goods from the shore to ships in the harbour, with a group of Khoi in the foreground. The exaggerated shapes of Table Mountain and Lion's Head conveyed an image to European readers of an exotic and extraordinary landscape. (William Fehr A19)

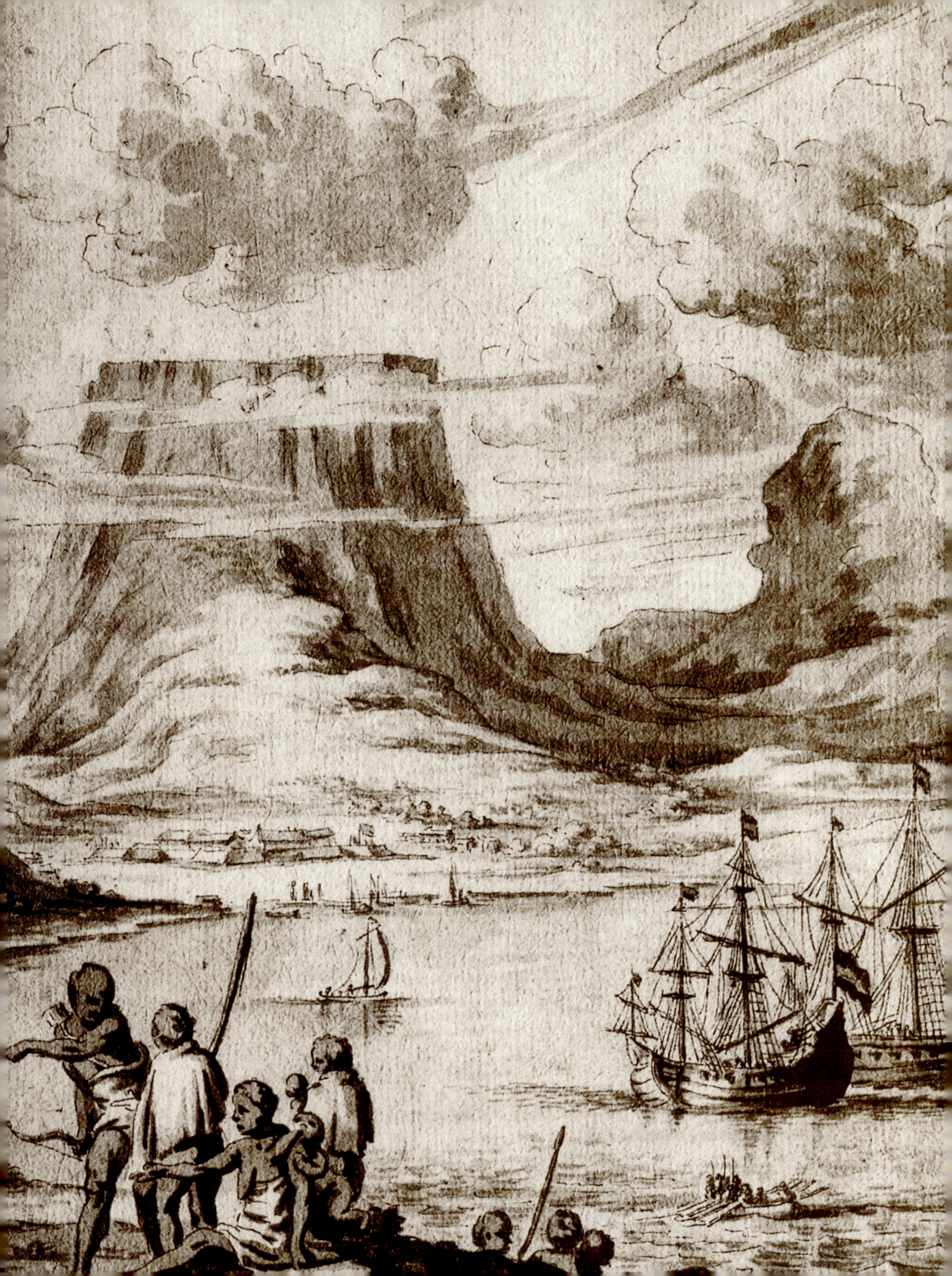

of the VOC in the East Indies. Complaints about poor food and cramped living conditions in the early fort were frequent, sometimes leading to near mutiny. In May 1654 Jan Danielssen, arquebusier who had arrived with Van Riebeeck's fleet, was reported wandering around the settlement with two knives saying, 'If it happens again like last year that we get so little to eat, yet have to work all the same, I shall finish the Commander with the knives.' After a spell in the fort's prison, he confessed that he had indeed uttered such words but only 'in a state of dejection' without ever intending to carry out his threat. He was sentenced to be keelhauled and put in chains for six months with pay docked for three of them.[67]

One common response to the 'purgatory' of the Cape was desertion. As early as September 1652 several employees escaped aboard passing ships, and in 1655 a group attempted to commandeer the yacht *Roode Vos* from Saldanha Bay and sail it to Brazil.[68] The return fleets regularly carried stowaways; in 1658, after 21 had so absconded, it was recognised that 'this desertion takes place every year and is difficult to prevent',[69] although troops were stationed on the shore when the fleet was due to sail, and free burghers, their servants and slaves were forbidden to go on board any vessel in the harbour.

Slaves also ran away, although most often by disappearing overland rather than aboard ships, where they would be readily detected. Most hoped to reach eventually their homes in Angola, in as great an ignorance of the geography of the Cape hinterland as their owners. The Khoi were offered rewards to return them, though usually without success, even after they were told that the runaways planned to attack and possibly also eat them.[70] By August 1658, the Company was growing afraid of the implications of continued slave desertions, particularly since in the same year it had abandoned its settlement at Mauritius, at least partly because of attacks from runaway slaves in the forests. It was reported that

> the number of male and female slaves who are now fugitives amounts to 28 and they are becoming a formidable group. Moreover, it is feared that they will gather at a certain place known to all the slaves, to which they will all flee and there attempt to form a strong group, and because they are much bolder and braver than the Hottentots and will multiply in the course of time, the Hon. Company will have good cause to fear them more than the natives unless steps are taken in time.[71]

As a result the Council of Policy agreed to put all the male Company slaves in chains and to provide fetters for free burghers 'to put their slaves in irons'.

In this context of fear of slave runaways and of open conflict with Khoi, the settlement was rocked by the discovery of a plot from within, which in the words of an early eighteenth-century visitor 'might readily have been the ruin of the whole Colony'.[72] In December 1659 a group of '4 English, 4 Scotch and 2 Dutch servants of the Company as well as a black convict, 2 servants of the free burghers and 15 slaves' plotted to capture the fort and murder its inhabitants and then sail away in the *Erasmus*, an empty vessel in the harbour.[73]

According to Johan Saar, a Company employee who arrived at the Cape while this episode was being investigated, this plot was caused by the desperation of Company employees who, although they had signed on in Holland as soldiers, were being treated by the commander 'as harshly and as miserably as if they had been less than serfs and

Departure of VOC fleet from Amsterdam. (CA M65)

> 'The number of male and female slaves who are now fugitives amounts to 28 and they are becoming a formidable group ... because they are much bolder and braver than the Hottentots and will multiply in the course of time, the Hon. Company will have good cause to fear them more than the natives unless steps are taken in time.'
>
> Resolution of Council of Policy, 28 August 1658

> 'Why do you stay in this damned Cape?' 'What are you doing staying in this cursed country?', 'Come jump in the boats we shall hide you', 'Whoever likes to go, let him get into the boat. Amsterdam, Zeeland, Rotterdam, Hoorn, Enckhuysen &c; get in, the ships are ready to leave'. 'All this was screamed out about all the freemen's dwellings, and more shameful and disdainful language about this place was made use of.'
>
> Sailors from the return fleet, 22 March 1660

slaves'.[74] The combination of slaves and over-worked Company servants, including British soldiers who had been recruited and brought to the Cape during the Khoi conflicts of the previous months, was potentially lethal.

The plot was discovered before damage could be done, but an episode occurred several months later which further revealed the discontent seething in the early Cape Town settlement. In March 1660, 20 Company servants, 18 free burghers and 3 convicts managed to get away on the return fleet.[75] Other stowaways, 26 in number, were captured, but on the promise that they would not be punished, they agreed to explain to a by now thoroughly alarmed Council why they had tried to leave. They had been encouraged by the sailors from the fleet, who after running riot in the town – invading the garden, pulling up the cabbages and attacking the gardener when he tried to prevent them – ran through the streets crying, 'Why do you stay in this damned Cape?' 'What are you doing staying in this cursed country?', 'Come jump in the boats we shall hide you', 'Whoever likes to go, let him get into the boat. Amsterdam, Zeeland, Rotterdam, Hoorn, Enckhuysen &c; get in, the ships are ready to leave' and other such inducements. 'All this was screamed out about all the freemen's dwellings, and more shameful and disdainful language about this place was made use of.'[76]

At least forty people took the opportunity and their reasons clearly indicate the misery that life in the settlement could entail. Joost Pietersoon of Leiden complained that he was working in the smithy though he had enlisted as a soldier and 'was therefore not bound to make locks or work in the shop'. Lucas Jansz, a soldier from Groningen, stated that his pay was inadequate and that he 'could not bear the want of shoes and stockings'. The freeman Hans Ras of Angel stated that he did not know how he was to pay the servants he kept on his land and that although he wished to buy slaves 'he could not get any'.[77]

This episode, taking place within a few months of the *Erasmus* plot and in the wake of the threat of destruction by the Khoi, underlines the insecurity and misery felt by many of the first inhabitants of Cape Town. Together with the unsatisfactory costs that the settlement was still incurring for the Company, it led to considerable scepticism on the part of its directors. After Van Riebeeck's departure to become governor of Malacca in May 1662, the Batavian authorities lamented that the reports received from the Cape had been wildly over-optimistic: 'To make the Cape appear more than what it in reality is, experience has taught us to be mere bragging.'[78]

Indeed the background to the establishment of the VOC settlement had not been straightforward. And ten years after its foundation, the future of Cape Town was still very uncertain.

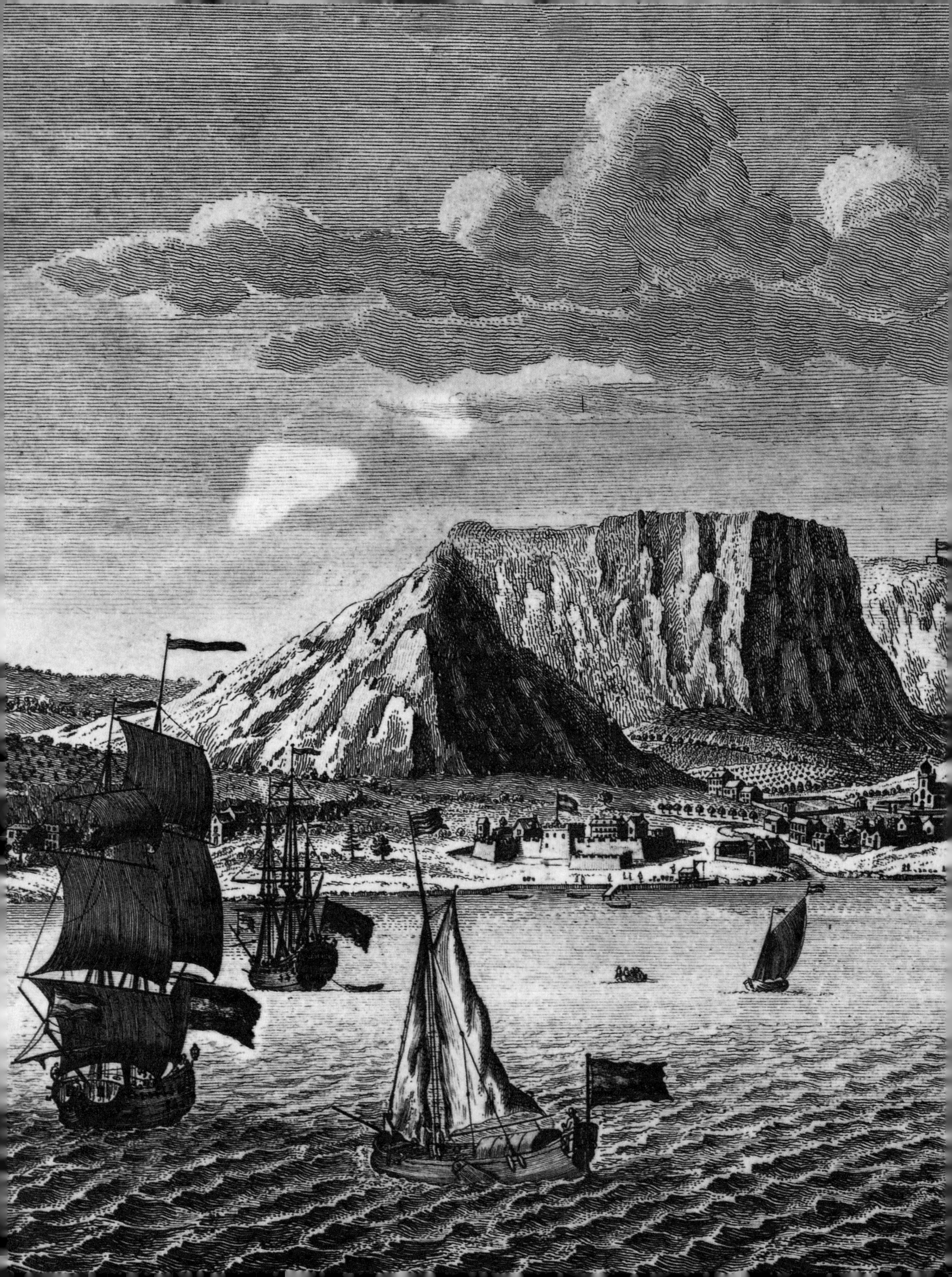

CHAPTER TWO

FROM CABO TO KAAPSTAD

CAPE TOWN
1662–1795

THE MORNING of Saturday 8 April 1752 began wet and windy, but as the day went on the clouds cleared. This was a fortunate sign. For Rijk Tulbagh, the new governor of the Cape, had decided to make his mark by commemorating 'a hundred years of peaceful occupation of this land'. At midday cannons were fired from the Castle and the batteries along the shore of Table Bay, answered by the VOC, English, French and Danish ships in the harbour. A volley was sounded from the top of Signal Hill, and Tulbagh invited the leading Company officials and officers of the garrison, the most prominent of the citizenry and the captains of visiting ships to a banquet at the Castle. Outside in the town celebrations took place in a rather less formalised manner. The chief mate of the British ship *Drake* and a fellow crew member ended the evening in a drunken brawl and were robbed by several Dutch sailors in the back streets along the shoreline.[1]

The day had not all been drunken revelry. In the morning the colony's elite had gathered in the Groote Kerk for a service of thanksgiving and commemoration. In a sermon which must have lasted well over an hour, *predikant* Petrus van der Spuy extolled the virtues of the Cape as it had grown 'ever larger and stronger' since Jan van Riebeeck formally declared the Company's possession of the site on 8 April 1652. Giving thanks to the God who 'is our God, we are his people', he exhorted his listeners to 'Give praise in the town! Give praise in the countryside!'[2]

These were the rhetorical words of a formal commemoration, but they are suggestive. The Cape colonial settlement had certainly grown and prospered since the early years of its uncertain existence. At its economic and political centre was Cape Town, which by the middle of the eighteenth century was beginning to emerge as a distinctive urban community with physical, social and cultural features that clearly demarcated it from the rest of the colony. The shift was marked by nomenclature. Whereas the settlement at Table Bay was initially referred to merely as de Kaapsche Vlek (the 'Cape settlement') or simply Cabo ('the Cape'), by the mid-eighteenth century both visitors and locals were beginning to call it Kaapstad, the 'Cape Town'. Its role was still that of an outpost in the larger and much more profitable Dutch trading empire whose centres were in Amsterdam and Batavia, and it was fundamentally shaped by the migration of people and goods between Northern Europe, the Indian Ocean and the Far East. But in the process it was beginning to acquire a distinct character of its own.

It was only in the 1670s, a decade after Jan van Riebeeck had left for the greater luxuries of Malacca, that the VOC finally committed itself to a permanent settlement at its Table Bay outpost. For the VOC was in the process of making a fundamental shift in its trading policy. The profits of the spice trade were falling, and there were limits to the extent to which the Company could penetrate further into the established intra-Asiatic routes of the East Indies. Instead the VOC turned more towards the cotton and silk trade of India and China, with shipping direct from Bengal or Ceylon back to the Netherlands via the Cape. This also brought the VOC into more immediate competition with British and French interests in the Indian Ocean and highlighted the importance of the Cape. The danger of rivals was underlined when the French attacked the outpost at Saldanha Bay in 1670. And so in 1672, when the United Provinces of the Netherlands were at war with both Britain and France, the Company declared itself to be 'the true and lawful possessors of this Cape district', a region including Table, Hout and Saldanha bays, and marked the fact by the 'payment' of tobacco, beads, brandy and bread valued at 115 rix-dollars to Schagger (or Osingkhimma), the 'captain' of the Goringhaiqua Khoi. This action was clearly intended as a statement of exclusion to European rivals rather than as

Previous pages: Johannes van Ryne's fanciful view of Cape Town published in 1754. Apart from the distorted mountains, it incorrectly portrays the Castle as a European-style fortress with high walls and turrets, and it shows the Reformed church (in the wrong location) with a Germanic onion dome. (William Fehr GHML81/11)

This anonymous watercolour of *c.* 1700 makes no attempt to depict the Cape Town settlement accurately. Its value lies rather in its symbolism – a townscape with straight road, fences, church, houses and planted trees, peopled with Dutch figures and a horse, signifying the permanence of a new colonial settlement and the domestication of an alien landscape. (William Fehr A3)

Plan of the new Castle with seals of the VOC. (William Fehr GH81/6)

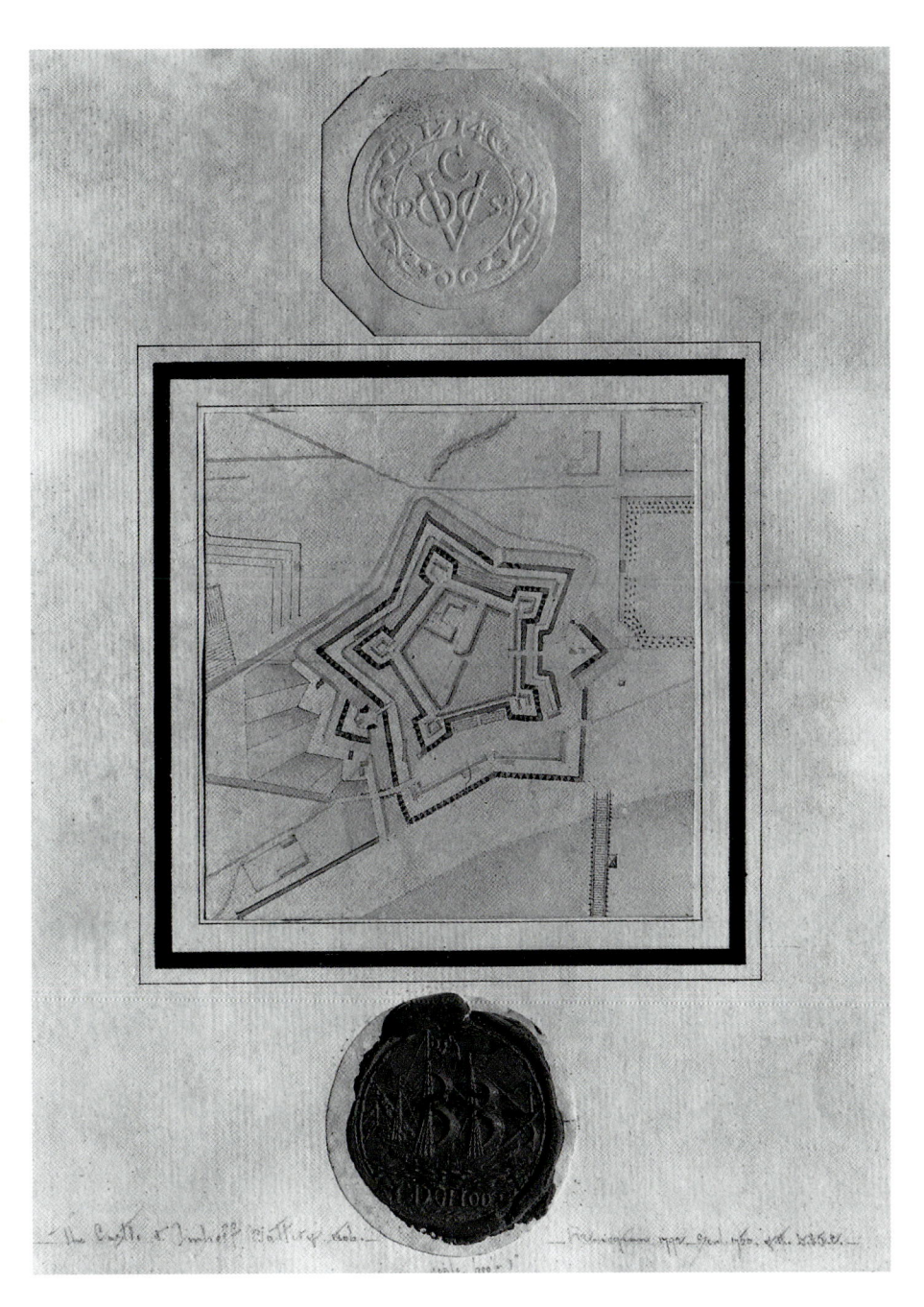

a legitimising purchase from the Khoikhoi. Indeed the 'purchase' was less significant than the attacks made on the Cochoqua Khoi by a Dutch raiding party in the following year, an episode which led to several years of continuing conflict and the ultimate extinction of independent Khoikhoi societies in the south-western Cape.

The claims to permanence took other forms. In 1666 work had begun on building a new stone fort to replace Van Riebeeck's mud and wooden stockade. The new Castle, completed in 1674, was an altogether grander affair, sited on the eastern side of the settlement to defend it from attack both by sea and from the interior (across Salt River), and at the point where the mountain stream met the shoreline and was conveniently channelled into its moat. Not that attack was likely to be averted by such a shallow (and ill-constructed) moat, but all self-respecting European castles had to have one, and the symbolism of a more permanent colonial presence was clear. At the laying of the foun-

FROM CABO TO KAAPSTAD 37

dation stone, Commander Zacharias Wagenaer delivered an oration which was even more explicit:

> Our conquests are extending further and further and all the black and yellow people are being suppressed. We are building a stone wall out of the earth that thundering cannon cannot destroy. Before, against our Hottentots, our walls were built of earth. Now we can boast of stone against other enemies. In this way we frighten off the Europeans, as well as the Asians, the Americans and the wild Africans. In this way holy Christendom is made known and finds a place in wild, heathen lands. We praise the almighty reign of God and say in unison: Augustus' empire, victorious Alexander and Caesar's great kingdom – none of these had the honour of laying a stone at the end of the earth.[3]

Despite the setbacks of the early years, the VOC had now committed itself to defending a permanent settlement from its heart on the shores of Table Bay. Although there were scares of French attacks during the European hostilities of the 1740s, the Dutch Cape was not to be threatened again until its conquest in 1795 by the British. Its primary function remained as a port of call for the replenishment of ships on their way to and from Asia. Once burgher farming was established beyond the Liesbeek and into the Hottentots Holland and Boland hinterland after the defeat of the Khoi in 1679, Cape Town's role also developed as the only port and hence the only point of contact between the colony and the outside world. By the time of Tulbagh's centenary celebrations, almost a quarter of the Cape's free population lived in Cape Town and were beginning to shape a distinctive kind of society.

Spatial Organisation

Cape Town's slow physical emergence into a town is reflected in the comments and perceptions of travellers and visitors. By 1714 the minister François Valentyn was impressed by the changes that had taken place over the past thirty years:

> When one lands at the Cape one sees an open plain with a good number of houses, nearly all whitewashed and looking attractive and ornamental from the roads ... when I came here in 1685 the houses stood pretty far apart, and were very few in comparison with today. In 1714 I myself counted about 254, large and small, at the Table Bay, not counting some public buildings such as the Rope Store and other buildings of the Hon. Company.[4]

'We praise the almighty reign of God and say in unison: Augustus' empire, victorious Alexander and Caesar's great kingdom – none of these had the honour of laying a stone at the end of the earth.'

Zacharias Wagenaer, 1674

E.V. Stade's view of Cape Town in 1710 shows the Castle and jetty and several streets of houses on the right. Between the Castle and houses, a bridge crosses the stream from the mountain. (Algemeen Rijksarchief Topo 15-86)

Steady physical growth continued. In 1759 Jacob Francken commented that 'during the last 25 years it has been increased by the addition of various streets, so that now it is rather a city than a village'.[5]

Not everyone was so impressed. In 1710 Johanna van Riebeeck, who had lived all her life in the East Indies, and been married in turn to the governor of Colombo and the governor-general of Batavia, made a journey to Europe and recorded her impressions of the settlement which her grandfather had founded some sixty years earlier and about which she must have heard a great deal:

> This place looks prettier and more pleasant from the sea than it does when you are on land. It is a miserable place. There is no grass and the roads near the castle and in the town are covered with holes and ruts, as if wild pigs had been rooting in them ... There is nothing pretty to be seen along the shoreline ... the castle is very peculiar ... the other houses here resemble prisons ... One sees here all sorts of peculiar people who live in very strange ways.[6]

Clearly, Cape Town of the early eighteenth century was far removed from the more sophisticated establishments of the VOC in Batavia and Ceylon. It was still a relatively primitive place, whose outward image of neat and whitewashed houses concealed a less organised and pleasant reality.

Unlike most European cities, or the fortified citadel of Batavia, Cape Town lacked town walls, and so the distinction between urban, peri-urban and rural was never absolute. Cape Town was still a very rural settlement in appearance and nature. But the surrounding countryside was also transforming so as to respond to the needs of the growing town. Many town dwellers had small vegetable plots on the slopes of Table Mountain and Devil's Peak. A widow living on Signal Hill in the 1730s made a living selling milk in the town.[7] Farms at Salt River and along the Liesbeek provided vegetables, corn, milk and butter for the town.[8] By 1774 a new road between Rondebosch and Cape Town was considered necessary to accommodate the daily traffic of carts and wagons. Salt pans were developed in the Tijger Valley 'three miles from the Castle', and the lower reaches of the Salt and Liesbeek rivers were extensively fished by townspeople.

The growing town denuded the region not only of its indigenous human inhabitants but also of its flora and fauna. By the 1740s, 'with the exception of a so-called stag or doe, there is hardly any game within a radius of 20 or 24 miles from the Castle'.[9] Even the ubiquitous baboons were not seen as regularly in the gardens above the town by the middle of the eighteenth century.[10] Natural timber also swiftly succumbed to the axe. Restrictions on wood cutting in Table Valley were introduced in 1687 but the scarcity of wood was a serious problem throughout the VOC period, driving up the cost of planks, boards and beams, and encouraging the shift from wooden to brick and plaster buildings.[11] The destruction of the natural vegetation cover on the mountain slopes led to sheet-wash removal of layers of topsoil, which were carried along the channels through the town into the bay. Shallowing resulted, 'so that the house ... built by the sea-shore is now further from it, and time after time they have been obliged to lengthen the quay that has been made in the harbour'.[12]

The physical shape of the growing town represented the statement of an imposed colonial order on an alien environment: it had little in common with the more haphazard growth of European and South-East Asian ports. Although lacking city walls, its outer limits were marked by the naming of streets at its edges as 'Buiten': Buitengracht,

'This place looks prettier and more pleasant from the sea than it does when you are on land. It is a miserable place. There is no grass and the roads near the castle and in the town are covered with holes and ruts, as if wild pigs had been rooting in them ... There is nothing pretty to be seen along the shoreline ... the castle is very peculiar ... the other houses here resemble prisons ... One sees here all sorts of peculiar people who live in very strange ways.'

Johanna van Riebeeck, 1710

Buitenkant, Buitensingel. The new Castle dominated the point at which the mountain stream entered the sea, but was also sited to the east of the old stockade in order to enable the ordered growth of burgher houses around the Company gardens. Some of the burgher houses which had been built near to it were demolished.[13] The planned physical separation of Castle and town was emphasised by an intervening stretch of open ground (the parade ground, or *plein*), which was levelled and improved by commandeered burgher slaves in the 1730s after potholes caused several accidents to people and wagons.[14] The *plein* was something of a no-man's-land between town and Company headquarters.

The town itself was established according to a strict grid pattern of streets (which today still forms the shape of central Cape Town) with regular square 'blocks' occupied by dwelling houses. This was even replicated in the layout of the Company gardens where pathways continued the street patterns and vegetable beds mirrored housing blocks. Mountain streams were channelled into watercourses alongside the Company gardens, down the main 'Heerengracht' and round the parade ground into the sea, in an imitation of Dutch urban canals. Land grants were under the control of the Company, which thus attempted to ensure the ordered development of building. Initially grants were made to approved burghers without payment. Although they were usually in freehold rather than leasehold tenure, once sold the Company charged a municipal rate 'of the 10th or 20th penny of the rent it is judged it would let for annually'.[15]

The key landmarks of Dutch Cape Town were its public buildings, all of them owned

This picture of the houses above Stal Plein at the end of the eighteenth century shows the rural character of upper Cape Town. Large residences for the wealthier town burghers were built at the upper end of the setttlement in the 1780s. (William Fehr C42)

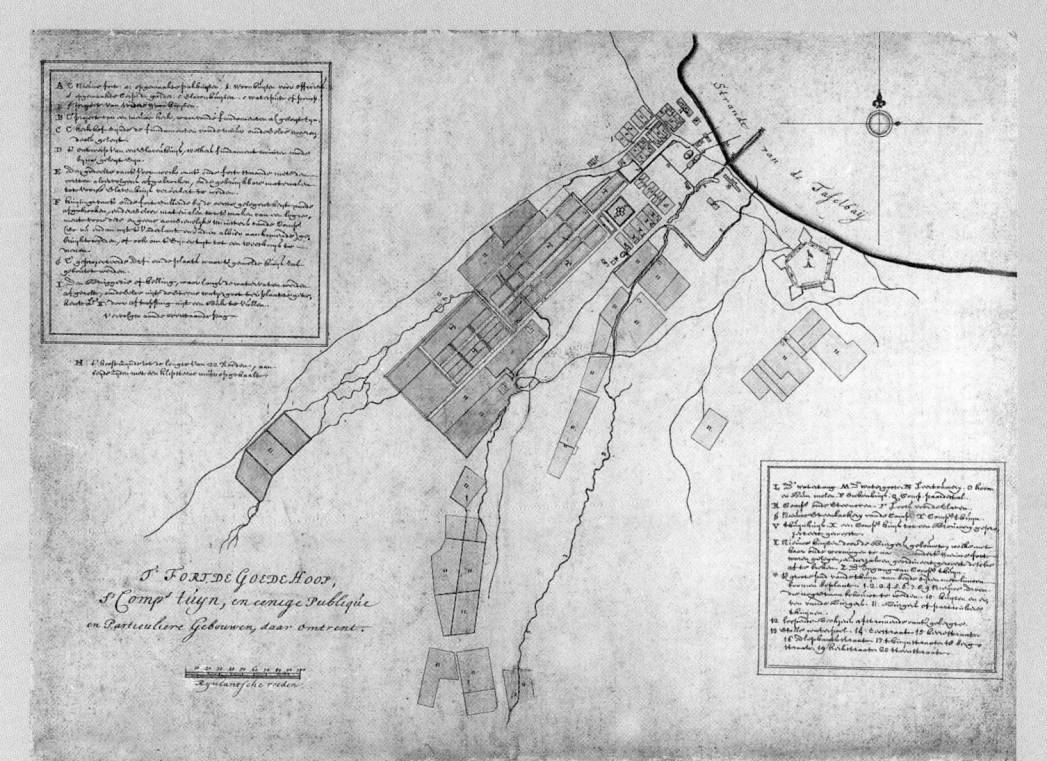

A plan drawn up *c.* 1700 entitled 'The fort of Good Hope, the Company gardens and several public and private buildings around them'. Burgher houses (*Y*) have now appeared around the church and additional *erven* (1–9) are marked out for further building along the newly named Kerk and Steen streets. The settlement is still surrounded by extensive 'burgher or private gardens' (11), which were mainly used for market gardening. (Algemeen Rijksarchief VEL 828).

By 1767 building had expanded to the west of the town, with square blocks, each containing between 10 and 12 houses, surrounding the market square (*B*). Privately owned 'gardens' (39) continued to exist around the Company gardens in the upper part of town. The extension of fortifications from the Castle (*A*) in a series of batteries along the coast (1–5) is clearly visible, as are the sandbanks along the shoreline and the two graveyards on the slopes of Signal Hill, one for free burghers and one for slaves (37). (Algemeen Rijksarchief VEL 838)

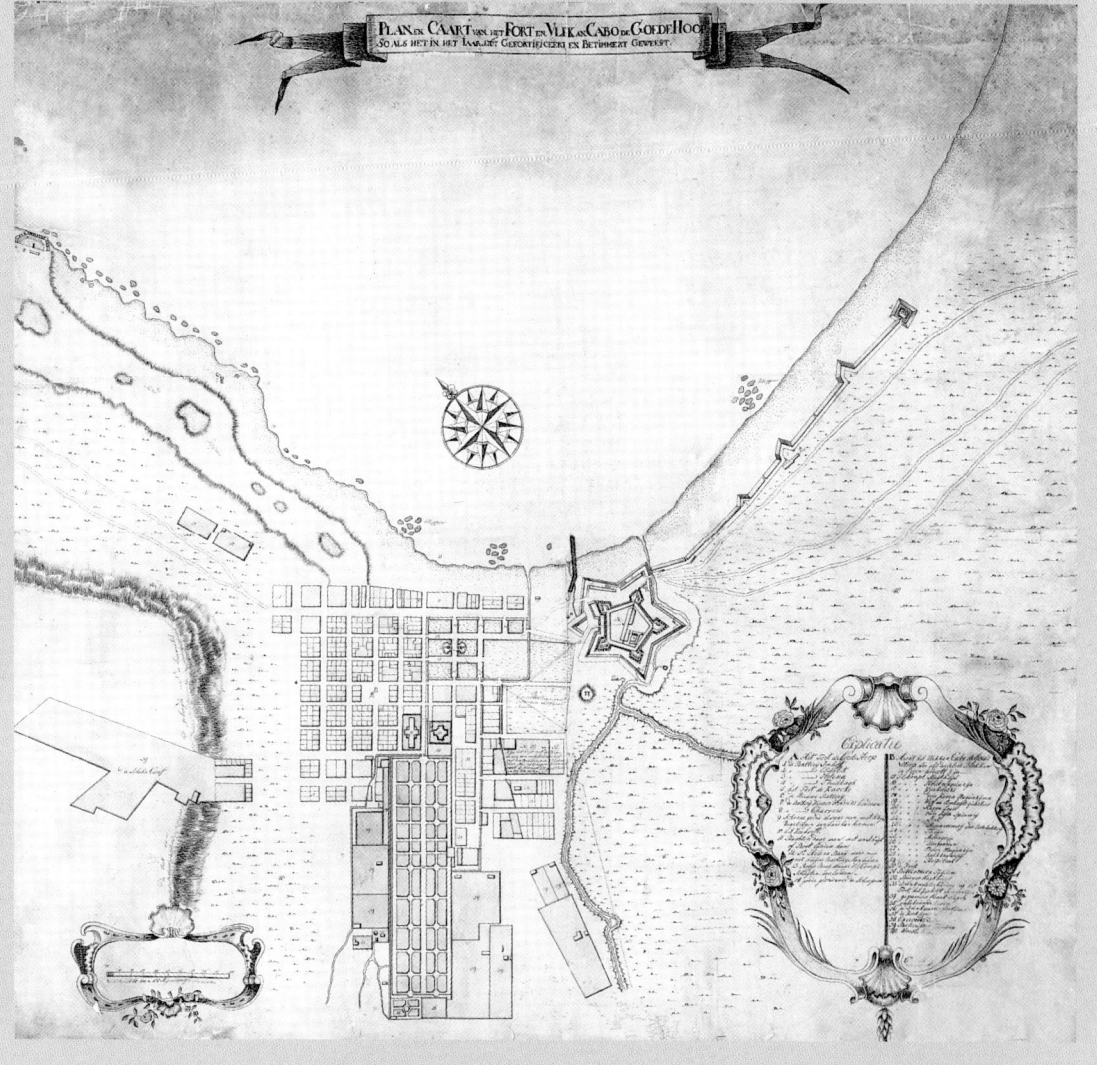

FROM CABO TO KAAPSTAD 41

Johannes Rach's panorama of Cape Town from Table Bay, 1762. Rach joined the VOC as a gunner in 1762 and spent two years at the Cape before continuing to Batavia. The paintings he made during this time provide a detailed visual record of Cape Town in the mid-eighteenth century. (Atlas van Stolk, Rotterdam)

by the Company, and strategically located in prominent sites. From the sea the Castle dominated the landscape. This key building impressed most visitors. It was situated above the wooden jetty by which disembarking crew and passengers came ashore, as well as at the entry point to the town on the road from Salt River and Rondebosch. A patrol guardhouse was built on the road between the outer bastion of the Castle and the shore. 'All waggons, pedestrians and horsemen that come to town from the interior must pass by this patrol so that the corporal on guard may note the products such as grain, wine or wood with which the waggons are laden', thus enabling the authorities to check produce coming into the town and to levy taxes.[16] Further batteries were built along the shore and at Salt River mouth to pre-empt enemy landings; the Chavonnes Battery was built in 1715 'at a creek between the rock-strewn shore beyond the Lion Mountain'. In the 1780s, at a time of heightened military activity, a further series of batteries was added around the town.

The Castle was a community in itself. It housed the garrison, key administrative offices, living quarters for the governor and senior officials, and the Company bakery,

View inland from the Amsterdam Battery, built on the shoreline in 1781–6. It was a large structure, with living quarters for the gunners, and facilities for the making of red balls, or heated shot. (UCT Archives)

Johannes Rach's view of the town from the east in 1762, showing the domination of the Castle and the wastelands outside its walls. The figures include Khoi shepherds, a Khoi mother and child, and two Europeans fighting with knives. The land just outside Cape Town still retained some of the characteristics of a frontier of interaction between the colonial newcomers and the indigenous inhabitants of the Cape. (Atlas van Stolk, Rotterdam)

together with 'workshops for blacksmiths, wheelwrights, locksmiths, coppersmiths, tinkers, carpenters, joiners, turners, glaziers, gunstock-makers, etc.'[17] Indeed each bastion of the Castle had its own internal organisation and structure of control. But the Castle could not contain all the activities of the Company employees and as early as 1688 some soldiers were lodged in barracks outside the Castle walls. Along from the jetty was the slaughterhouse, situated on the shore to enable offal to be washed away, as well as a 'very long and large warehouse'.[18] In the course of the eighteenth century warehouses and workshops were constructed in blocks along this line (modern Strand Street) and extending up to the crossing with the Heerengracht.

Viewed from the harbour, the town was thus fronted with Company warehouses and workshops, many of them by the middle of the eighteenth century being doublestoreyed. The line of vision then extended up the Heerengracht, on which key public buildings were situated. The most prominent was the Reformed Church whose spire appeared above the other buildings. This 'very fine edifice' was the only church permitted in town until the building of the Lutheran Church on Strand Street in 1780.[19] Inside the Groote Kerk, pews were allocated to Company officials and town burghers in strict order of rank. A few 'free seats' were also available but it was the duty of the church warden to ensure that orderliness was strictly maintained and that 'the ladies are not insulted in their positioning which brings about great commotion and disorder'.[20] Above the church portal was inscribed in Latin:

> I am the comfort of all the sick and suffering
> The fountain of salvation if ye but go to this Heavenly Bath
> If ashamed of your deeds ye hasten hither
> Ye shall be saved by the possession of this treasure[21]

FROM CABO TO KAAPSTAD

Double-storeyed workshops and warehouses along the shore, *c.* 1790. Painting by Samuel Davis. (William Fehr A28)

Directly opposite it, across the Heerengracht, was a portal with another Latin inscription offering a different kind of healing:

> This house receives with its hospitality those broken by disease and the weariness of travel, and generously administers healing aid. May Africa dread thy Laws, O Netherlands, and thy name, ordained by fate to tame the nations.[22]

This mixture of hospitable caring and threatening assertion of colonialism was a fitting combination. For the weary and sick in this building were the soldiers and sailors of the Company's fleets and armies. It became the site of the Company hospital in 1697, when it was realised that previous accommodation in a corner of the fort (described as a 'death house') was inadequate for the number of sick crew brought ashore.[23] The hospital could house 225 patients and, except in times of smallpox epidemic, proved sufficient until the 1770s, when foundations were laid for a new building behind the Company gardens. Its rooms were damp in winter and stuffy in summer. Dysentery was rampant. Patients suffering from infectious diseases were not always isolated, and poor food did not aid recovery, neither did 'the air fouled by various odours due to perspiration and the presence of many patients suffering from dysentery or diarrhoea'. Mentzel commented that 'the conditions at the hospital more often send a person to his grave than the disease itself'.[24]

Across from the hospital lay another fortress, the Slave Lodge, a large and windowless brick building which housed the Company's slaves. Behind this were the stables, for a brief time housing not only horses but also the governor's pet zebras. Dominating the upper reaches of the town were the Company gardens, designed in the seventeenth century for profit rather than pleasure. Because of increasing Dutch interest in botanical specimens the gardens acquired a key role from the late seventeenth century as a point of collection of local plants for scientific purposes; this gradually came to replace its original purpose of growing basic foodstuffs as the colony became more self-sufficient. Company slaves employed there would apparently report anyone observed picking the fruit, although by the mid-to-later eighteenth century, as Company dependence on its own produce decreased, it did become more of a pleasure garden.[25]

But between these landmarks lay a less ordered townscape. The spaces between blocks were unpaved, turning to mud in winter and dust bowls in summer. Regular complaints were made about offal and refuse in the streets. The water supply channelled from the mountain streams was erratic, for these overflowed during heavy rains and ran

> **STREET SIGNS**
>
> *I*n 1790, for the first time street signs were posted on boards. Berg (modern St George's) Street was renamed Venus Street. The board of this name was positioned on the house of the *predikant* Serrurier, much to his embarrassment since it attracted ribald comments from passing sailors who assumed that 'Venus' advertised rather more carnal pursuits. The sign was removed at his request, and the street reverted to its original name.[26]

44 CAPE TOWN 1662–1795

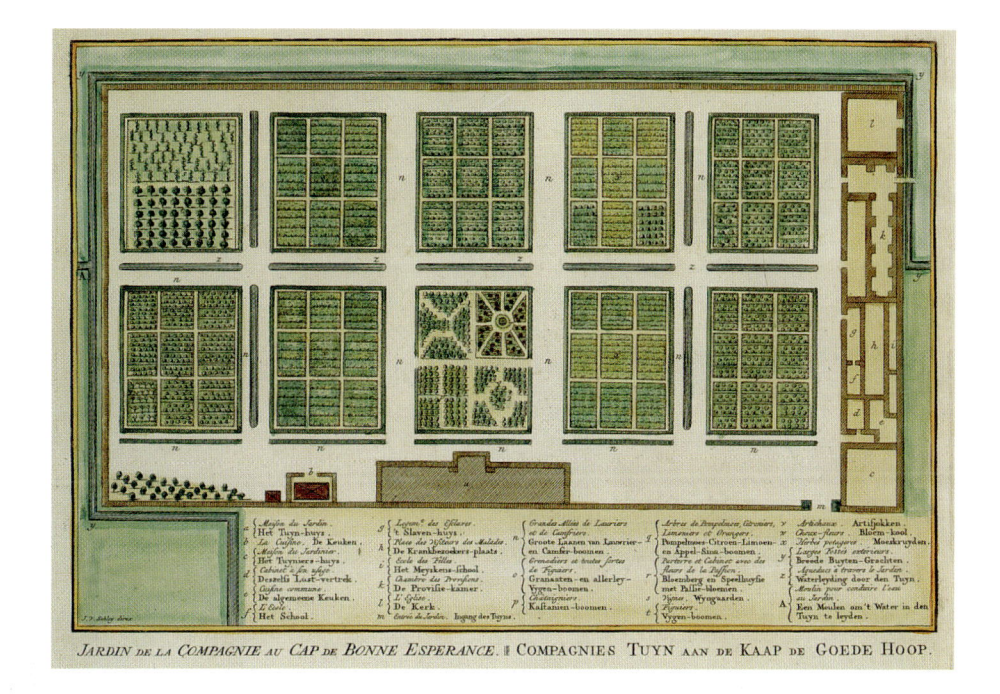

A plan of the Company gardens from P. Kolb's *Naaukeurige en uitvoerige Beschryving van die Kaap de Goede Hoop* (1727). Kolb was greatly impressed by its formalised design, with rows of trees (*o, p, q, t*), a small vineyard (*s*) and vegetable beds (*v, w, x*), surrounded by a broad outer canal (*y*) and irrigated by aqueducts (*z*). (William Fehr GH84/8)

Two blocks west of the Heerengracht was the square on which the Burgher House was built. According to Mentzel, 'in appearance [this] differs little from an ordinary burgher dwelling' (vol. 1, p. 132). It overlooked the town's market-place, thus offering little competition to the ordered status of the Company's public buildings and spaces. In 1755, however, it was rebuilt in the grander style shown in this picture by Johannes Rach of 1762. (CA M166)

An ox wagon driving across the Parade Ground at the bottom of the Heerengracht, 1762. Drawn by Johannes Rach. (CA M163)

dry in summer.[27] Only a few of the larger houses had connecting teak-and-copper water pipes. The main source of water was the well in the centre of the square opposite the Burgher House. This caused most interest when it was rumoured in 1732 that a treasure of gold coins was hidden at its bottom, although enterprising attempts to retrieve them came to nothing.[28]

Cape Town was a market centre, into which cattle and sheep were regularly herded. Attempts to prevent them from wandering through the streets were often made, but the frequency of regulations issued in the seventeenth century against this indicates just how unsuccessful they were.[29] Valentyn commented in 1726 that 'an enclosure or corral should be made to house the animals of the people coming from without, so that they are not compelled to let them roam everywhere contrary to the *plakkaten*', but it seems that nothing was done.[30]

Plots of cultivated land were marked on early maps and continued to exist on the western side of the town throughout the eighteenth century. Although some early commentators drew attention to the 'pretty gardens', it appears that these were less ornamental than practical vegetable plots.[31] Only those houses on the outer streets had

FROM CABO TO KAAPSTAD 45

Cape Town in 1777–8

The panorama above was painted by Robert Jacob Gordon. Of Scottish descent, he became commander of the VOC garrison at the Cape from 1780 to 1795. The complete panorama, drawn on 22–3 June 1778, shows a 360° view from the ship *Neptune* anchored in Table Bay.

The detailed section depicts the view from Devil's Peak around to Signal Hill. Among the places annotated by Gordon are the site of the proposed Lutheran Church in Strand Street, the Chinese graveyard on Signal Hill, the Fort Knokke Battery on the 'road to False Bay', and Platteklip Gorge, the 'way up to Table Mountain'. (Algemeen Rijksarchief Topo 15-120)

The panorama (to the right) of Cape Town at the same period is by Johannes Schumacher, a German soldier and artist who accompanied Gordon on a number of expeditions to the Orange and Fish rivers and assisted him in his drawings of the landscapes and people encountered.

It shows the town from the top of Signal Hill ten years after the 1767 map on page 41. From this angle the jetty and the rectangular blocks of burgher houses are clearly visible. At this stage they were confined to the town side of the Buitengracht, although building started on the slopes of Signal Hill in the subsequent two decades. Farms and gardens surround the town and dominate the lower slopes of Table Mountain. (CA M165)

46 CAPE TOWN 1620–1662

FROM CABO TO KAAPSTAD 47

garden plots, demarcated by sheep shinbones; those in the city blocks, however, had no such yards.[32]

Before the 1750s there appears to have been little residential specialisation in the town. Poorer and wealthier residences adjoined each other, often in the same block. The large houses were not all in the same streets. Rented and owner-occupied properties stood cheek by jowl, and in one block several shops, a tavern and a prestigious town house were all to be found.[33] Cape Town at this stage was not large enough to make such spatial distinctions and, unlike Batavia in the mid-eighteenth century, there were no demarcated 'quarters' for different categories of residents. While the Company garrison lived at the Castle and its adjoining barracks, other Company employees lived out in rented rooms around the town. For their part servants and slaves lodged with their owners, while free blacks lived alongside other burghers. Nonetheless, many of the town's taverns and cheaper rented rooms were closer to the shoreline, which was described in 1752 as 'a dismal spot';[34] on the other hand blocks on the Heerengracht were of higher value and prestige. Towards the end of the century poorer and wealthier parts of the town were becoming more distinct.

The first burgher houses in Cape Town were built of wood and were rudimentary. Timber shortage, and the danger of fires, led to regulations requiring the use of clay and brick by the 1680s, and in 1691 for the same reasons a *plakkaat* forbade lean-tos and interior fireplaces in rooms other than the kitchen. Walls were whitewashed and sometimes shutters were painted, usually green, giving an appearance which struck some visitors particularly favourably. The poet de Marre, for instance, recalled Cape Town for its '*witte muren*'.[35] The earliest houses had only one or two rooms, but by the 1680s a few larger dwellings were built, often with workshops attached, such as shoemaker Barent Bakker's residence in Zeestraat. By the turn of the century a few double-storeyed buildings were appearing, although these were very much the exception. Before the 1720s there appears to have been little specialisation of room function; thereafter the division of bedrooms and living parlours became more apparent in the middle-range and

House building with clay and water. Drawn by Lady Anne Barnard. (CA AG15,689)

One of the most elaborate private houses in late-eighteenth-century Cape Town at the corner of Burg and Strand streets. It is thought to have been at one time the residence of the fiscal. The pinnacles collapsed in the earthquake of 1809. Painted by Samuel Davis, 1790. (William Fehr A30)

48 CAPE TOWN 1662–1795

Het Gezigt van het Staadhuys van Cabo de Goede Hoop. Met de selfs Grunmart en Gebergtens.

Fear of fire led to regulations forbidding thatch, and requiring flat roofs and internal shutters on town houses. This was especially the case after the slave arson fires of 1736. Rach's drawing of Greenmarket Square in 1762 gives an intriguing indication of both styles: on the left are older houses with sloping thatched roofs and external shutters while on the right are 'new style' dwellings with flat roofs and interior shutters. The well was the main source of water for the town during the summer months when there was little rain water in the streams channelled from the mountain. (W. Fehr, *The Old Town House*, Cape Town, 1955)

wealthier households. Yet specialised room function was not as developed as in the Netherlands, and the 'drawing-room' did not emerge until the nineteenth century.

A distinctively Capetonian town house began to develop in the eighteenth century, as urban burghers became increasingly marked out from rural farmers in their occupations and material culture. This diverged considerably from Dutch patterns. The *galderij* emerged as a public display room in a style which was unique to the Cape; at the same time some of the earliest houses inhabited by free-black or 'mixed couple' households developed features more reminiscent of Euro-Asian structures in Batavia.[36]

Peopling the Town

Although considerably smaller than the VOC headquarters in Batavia, the population of Cape Town grew steadily. By the 1750s it exceeded that of the VOC's second Asian port in Ceylon.

The largest number of Cape Town inhabitants were Company employees. Until the 1730s there were less than 1000 of them but numbers increased steadily after then, reaching over 3000 by the end of VOC rule.[37]

The elite of the employees were the officials, primarily of Dutch birth, who were carving out a career in the Company's administration and who held high-ranking offices. Following the mercantile orientation of the VOC, many were given commercial titles:

FROM CABO TO KAAPSTAD 49

The 1731 Census

The most complete record we have of the population of Dutch Cape Town comes from a survey taken in 1731 when Governor Jan de la Fontaine ordered an assessment of the financial status of the free-burgher population of the colony.[38] By adding in information about the Company's own employees and slaves as well as the *bandieten* (people sentenced to forced labour, including many from the VOC's Asian centres), we can obtain a relatively full breakdown of the town's population. Both the Khoi and the wives of senior Company officials are missing from these records, although their numbers were small. A more serious omission from the surviving records is the slaves who were privately owned by VOC officials (since such slaveholding was frowned upon by the VOC directors). Their numbers may well have been greater than those owned by private burghers and the VOC combined.

	Total	Adults Male	Female	Children
VOC employees	959	959	–	–
Free burghers	585	151	127	307
Free blacks	200	51	60	89
VOC slaves	566	±250	±250	66
Private slaves	767	424	187	156
Bandieten	80	78	2	0
Khoi	?	?	?	?
TOTAL	3157	1913	626	618

There are several striking features evident in these figures. Cape Town's population was small, only just over 3000, of whom the largest category (a third) was Company employees. Some 45 per cent of the population were in Cape Town against their will, either as slaves or as prisoners. Cape Town was also an overwhelmingly male city. Despite the absence from the figures of the few wives of Company officials, it appears that 75 per cent of the adult inhabitants were men, the large majority of whom were either slaves or single Company employees. Only the free burghers and some Company officials were able to form nuclear families. As far as can be judged from the sources, this general pattern varied little between the 1660s and the 1760s, and it had a profound effect on the economic, social and cultural characteristics of VOC Cape Town.

opperkoopman (senior merchant) being one of the most senior officials, under whom were the *onderkoopmannen* (junior merchants) and *boekhouders* (bookkeepers), who earned between 30 and 100 guilders a month. A small number of employees held specific professional posts as *predikanten*, school teachers, surgeons and apothecaries. Others were skilled in particular crafts, such as wagon drivers, carpenters, bakers, smiths and builders, and were employed in the Company's timber yards, workshops and storehouses, where they earned between 14 and 20 guilders a month.

But the majority were unqualified soldiers, earning 9 guilders or less, who lived in the Company barracks. They rarely, if ever, saw military action, although they lived a regimented life, organised into battalions and required to parade daily for roll-call – and 'woe betide any man who is absent overnight without leave'.[39] The main task was sentry duty but they also carried out a variety of other duties including construction work and woodcutting at Paradijs in Newlands Forest. A small group were posted to Robben Island where they guarded prisoners held there as well as tending sheep and vegetables, which were provided to ships unable to land on the main shore in stormy weather. And there was always a sizeable proportion of employees who were in the Company hospital – some 31 per cent by 1773 – most of whom had been landed in Cape Town because they were too sick to continue to Asia.[40]

The large majority of VOC employees were recruited in Europe and entered a five-year renewable contract. Many of the unskilled soldiers and general employees were

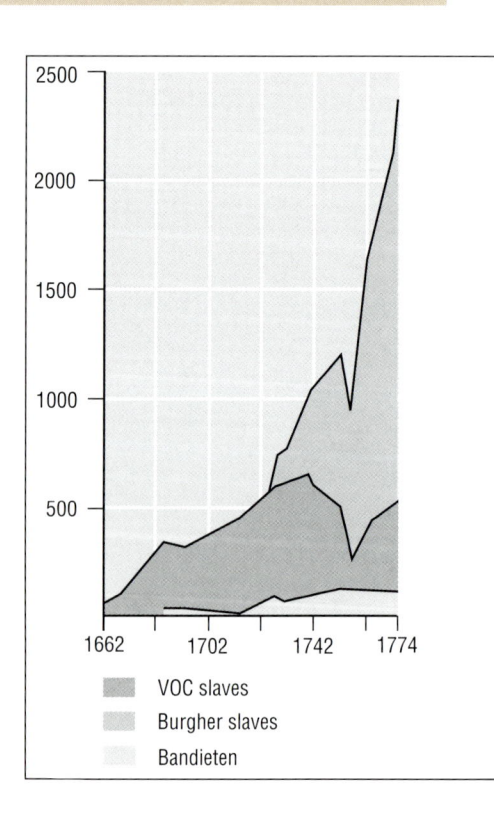

50   CAPE TOWN 1662–1795

drawn from the lowest ranks of European society, some after journeying large distances to the Netherlands. Thus, for instance, men from places as diverse as Norway, Amsterdam, Antwerp, Hamburg, Stockholm and Göttingen were working alongside each other in the Cape timber yards in 1731, and others in the town included recruits from Scotland, England, France, Denmark, Switzerland and Russia. The majority of soldiers were German, since in the words of one (admittedly German) observer, 'Hollanders make good sailors but poor soldiers.'[41] Most arrived at the Dutch ports penniless, and were advanced food, lodging and clothing against future wages until their ships sailed. Few qualifications were required beyond the ability to carry a musket. At least some were hoodwinked into a contract they did not fully understand. One German soldier in Cape Town in the 1770s had been shipwrecked off the coast of Holland. After using the 'trifle' he obtained from the sale of his shoe buckles he was grateful to meet an 'acquaintance' in Amsterdam who took him to an inn, but after eating and drinking he was prevented from leaving by the landlord who

> then began to make some enquiries about his residence, means of support &c. and, as he could not pay his reckoning, absolutely refused to let him go. When mustered on board of ship, whither he had been carried, without having previously been to the East-India House and received there, he complained to the director; but, as the poor fellow could not possibly pay for what the kidnappers had received of the Company to fit him out, he was obliged, willy-nilly, to sail for the Cape, where he arrived sick and was taken to the hospital. This poor man ... soon regained his liberty by running away, and getting on board of one of the English ships that lay in the road.[42]

Most VOC employees in Cape Town were of comparatively recent arrival, for there was little incentive for a soldier to remain in service long after his five-year contract had expired since his pay was only minimally increased. A distinction soon developed between the few *oorlamme*, or seasoned employees who had served for a period of time and knew the ropes, and the majority of *baaren*, or newcomers.

Most had not aimed at a career in Table Bay, for they were enticed into VOC service by the lure of wealth in the more exotic East Indies. But the majority were so sick that they had little choice. Between 40 and 60 per cent of new arrivals had been landed in Cape Town because they were too ill to continue after the lengthy and unhealthy journey cooped up in the holds of an unhygienic ship. They spent their first few weeks or months in the Company hospital and thereafter most stayed on. Of the 130 who landed in 1731/2, only 37 continued to other parts of the VOC empire although a few returned after careers in the East. Of the remainder 37 stayed in Company service at the Cape until they died, 44 returned to Europe without ever seeing the Indian Ocean, 5 became free burghers and 7 ran away and were never heard of again.[43]

As economic conditions in central Europe improved in the course of the eighteenth century, fewer recruits volunteered for VOC service. Instead many sailors and soldiers were taken from the unemployed proletariat of Dutch towns, numbers of whom already suffered from disease or malnutrition before embarking. By the early 1770s, some 23 per cent of new recruits died on the outward voyage. Homeward-bound vessels from Batavia and Ceylon were thus increasingly manned by Asian crews: out of the 1417 sailors who came to Cape Town from Asia in 1792, 233 were Indians, 101 Javanese, 504 Chinese and only 579 (40 per cent) were Europeans.[44] Cape Town's transient population

Cape Town population figures, 1662–1774 (Data from UCT Cape Town History Project compiled from a variety of sources in the Algemeen Rijksarchief and the Cape Archives)

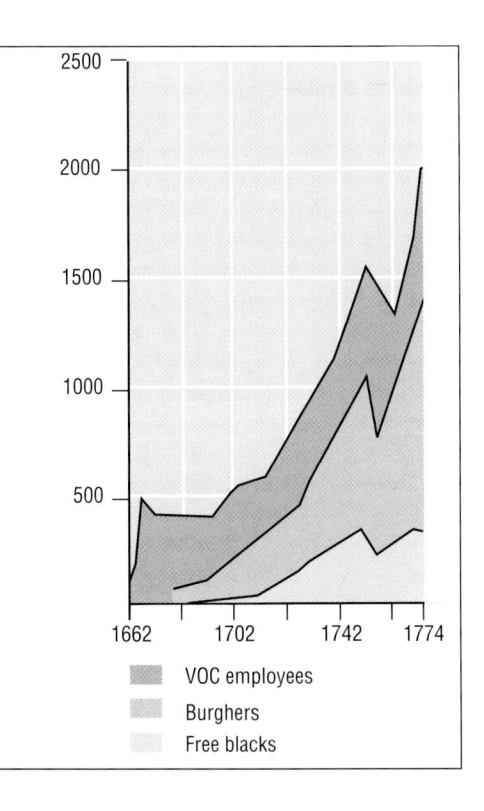

of VOC employees was thus being drawn from all parts of the Indian Ocean world.

As part of this trend, the Company began from the 1730s to recruit some of the sons of Cape burghers into its service. In 1731, 18 of the 51 administrators were Cape-born, and by 1773 the number had increased to 38 out of 66.[45] Most eighteenth-century governors had previous experience of service at the Cape: Hendrik Swellengrebel was appointed in 1739 as the first Cape-born governor. The distinction between the higher ranks of the administration and the brief sojourners who came as ordinary employees and soldiers was thus further accentuated.

But for most low-ranking employees, life at the Cape offered little prospect of promotion or financial gain. Following the practice of the Prussian army, some soldiers who possessed particular skills became *pasgangers*, making extra money for themselves by paying fellow soldiers to undertake their sentry duty while they carried out activities as diverse as carpentry and wig-making, though they still remained bound to the garrison militia.[46] A few employees applied for permission to contract out of the Company service and work as *knegts*, or overseers, on settler farms. This was one of the major ways in which Company employees obtained farming experience; the most successful of them could later apply for burgher status. Soldiers were forbidden to marry, and could only do so if they became free burghers. One observer commented that 'in many respects they are treated worse than slaves'.[47] It is thus scarcely surprising that they had a low reputation in the town, forming part of a restless and temporary underclass that featured regularly in the criminal cases brought to the Court of Justice. Cases of neglect of duty, falling asleep, drunkenness or absenteeism litter the court records.

Desertion was a serious problem. Each year there were cases of soldiers fleeing from the Castle. The most successful were those who already had contacts among the settler farmers of the hinterland with whom they could seek refuge. Others were less fortunate. Jacob Boerij of Zurich and two of his fellow drinking mates planned to jump over the Castle wall at night and run away in 1748. After hurting themselves in the process, they were arrested. The authorities, determined to make an example, ordered them to draw lots to decide who should be executed by firing squad. Boerij lost.[48] In 1722, in an attempt to stem the problem, an amnesty for deserters was issued although it had relatively little impact.

Others escaped as stowaways or were secretly recruited onto passing foreign ships. Christian Clos of Hanover was arrested on 25 September 1745 as he tried to leave the Cape on an English vessel. Despite his claims that he was drunk and did not know what he was doing, the fact that he was dressed in English uniform and had packed up his few belongings disproved his argument and he was sentenced to flogging and three years' hard labour without pay.[49]

The fluid and temporary character of a large part of the population was further emphasised by the presence of shipping crew in the port. Dutch Cape Town's prime function was to provide supplies, repairs and a period of recuperation to passing ships. At least fifty Company ships a year were obliged by order to call at the Cape on their way to the East Indies or Ceylon. To these were added vessels of other European powers, notably the British and French, but also some Swedish, Danish and Flemish vessels. Foreign ships had to pay anchorage fees and were occasionally denied provisions, particularly in the earlier years of the settlement when they were in short supply. Their numbers fluctuated: in the period 1700–14 there were 1070 ships in total anchoring in the harbour, of which 683 (64 per cent) belonged to the Company and 387 (36 per cent) were foreign.[50] In the mid-eighteenth century the numbers fell, especially when France

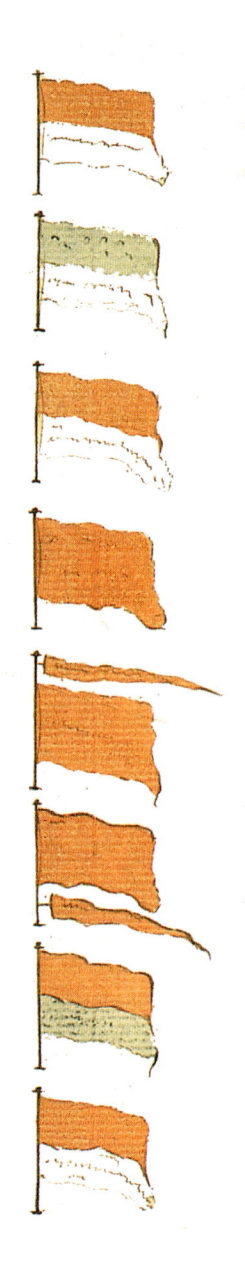

Varieties of flag signals flown from Lion's Rump in 1797. (CA BO180,19)

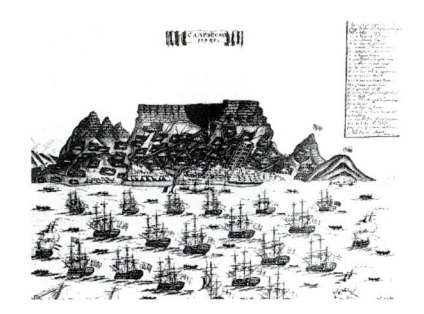

A formalised view of the British fleet in Table Bay on its way to India in 1748. (CA E8376)

was at war with the English and their Dutch allies, but in 1748 the harbour was packed with ships of the joint Anglo-Dutch fleet making their way to attack the French possessions in the Mascarenes and India. The numbers of foreign ships greatly increased in the 1780s and 1790s.

The rhythms of Cape Town's life were fundamentally shaped by the number of ships at anchorage in Table Bay. The average length of stay of VOC vessels in harbour was between 20 and 30 days, determined not only by the loading of provisions but also by the need to wait for linking vessels for the transmission of mail and other official instructions.[51] There was a strong seasonal character to shipping patterns, with summer and autumn being the busiest periods. Much activity in the town was focused in this period; the winter months, by contrast, were relatively quiet. During bad weather it was often difficult for ships to enter harbour. Attempts were made between 1743 and 1748 to build a breakwater at Mouille Point, but work was made difficult by the strong currents and the project was abandoned as too expensive. Windy conditions meant that ships had sometimes to anchor near Robben Island, from which emergency provisions were rowed out to them in small boats. From 1742 vessels arriving in autumn or winter had to enter False Bay, where winds were less severe, and a small provision store and harbour was developed at Simon's Town. The site was not ideal. There was no fresh water and provisions had to be carried either overland from the town or around the coast of the Peninsula in smaller ships.

The arrival of a ship in harbour was cause for much activity. An elaborate signalling system was established whereby flags were flown from the top of Signal Hill to indicate to VOC vessels that the post was still safely in Company hands. The flag codes of alternating blue, white and red stripes were changed at the start of each year.[52] After sighting a vessel, the commanding soldier posted at the flagstaff fired a cannon and signalled the direction from which the ship was coming. A corporal then ran down the hill to inform the authorities, 'and it often happens that the poor fellow has to ascend and descend 4 or 5 times in a day which is inconceivably fatiguing'.[53]

De Vis Shipwreck

*I*n 1740 the Captain of *De Vis* mistook the light from the Chavonnes Battery on the shore for that on Robben Island and ran aground. An ingenious method of hauling the crew ashore in the galley cauldron was devised and the operation, which proceeded throughout the following day, provided an entertaining spectacle for the town's inhabitants. It was painted on the spot by Jürgen Leeuwenberg, who chose to portray the moment when the ring on the cauldron snapped and three sailors were plunged into the sea – according to Mentzel, because one had filled his pockets with looted ducats; he drowned as a result.[54]

(SAL INIL 6598)

One visitor wrote in 1772, 'we were hardly come to anchor before a crowd of black slaves and Chinese came in their small boats to sell and barter for clothes and other goods, fresh meat, vegetables and fruit, all of which our crew were eager to procure'.[55] However, most of the necessary supplies for the onward journey were provided from the Company's warehouses. Fresh water supplies were as important as food, and the mountain streams were channelled into pipes which ran to the end of the jetty. Minor repairs could be carried out in the Company shipyards along the shoreline, although the Cape lacked the facilities for major work and shortage of good-quality timber was a problem.

Shipping in the harbour meant crews in the town. Shore leave was regarded as a privilege rather than a right, although in practice almost all crewmen obtained it. While sailors from some vessels remained on board overnight, many others found accommodation in town for the month or more that passed before they set sail. *Shageerijen*, or 'pot houses', and tents were specially erected along the shore to accommodate sailors in conditions that were little better than those on board ship. During the summer and autumn months the streets of the town were crowded with strangers; so much so that it was possible for one deserter in 1732 to hide without being spotted for two weeks.[56] In the early days of the settlement visiting crewmen could well have outnumbered the local population.

With some money in their pockets, and eager to spend it on drink, prostitutes and illicit trading goods, many sailors remembered their stay in Cape Town primarily for the fights they were involved in and the money they had spent. This was often cause for conflict. In 1731 a pub brawl broke out when a group of sailors called Cape soldiers *schelmen* and *Caabse gauwdieven* (rascals and Cape pickpockets) – possibly a reference to the high costs of drink and other Cape provisions.[58] And in 1752 the corporal in charge of the night patrol arrested two sailors as they left a bar at 11 p.m., on the grounds that they had stayed out after the 10 p.m. curfew. Taking them back to the Castle, he proceeded to beat them up, shouting, 'We've caught a couple of wolves here, let's give it to them!' and

A wide variety of boats gather around VOC vessels anchored at the site of the modern Cape Town Waterfront. This 1762 drawing by Rach shows fishing boats with nets and small shelters on board, reminiscent of South-East Asian *prahus* and likely to have been built and owned by free-black fishermen. The building on the shore is the Chavonnes Battery (called the 'Water Kasteel'). (Atlas van Stolk, Rotterdam)

Sailor Songs

Seventeenth- and eighteenth-century Dutch sailor songs depict Cape Town as an oasis of women and wine.[57]

Aan de Caap hoord en wilt verstaan,
Daar de meisjes dagelyks verkeeren
Al in het huys De Blaauwe Haan,*
Daar wyze dagelyks converzeeren.

Een frissche roemer Kaapsche wyn
Zal hem, die geld heeft, smaaklyk zijn.
Zo proeft men reeds op d'eersten stond
De vruchten van de Kaapschen grond.

[*Name of a Cape tavern]

'We were hardly come to anchor before a crowd of black slaves and Chinese came in their small boats to sell and barter for clothes and other goods, fresh meat, vegetables and fruit, all of which our crew were eager to procure.'

Carl Thunberg, 1772

'Take that, wolf.'[59] Since 'wolf' is not a usual Dutch term of abuse, this image of the predator sailor roving through the town is indicative of the tensions that could exist between passing sailors and the resident garrison.

In contrast to this constantly shifting, male-dominated group of VOC employees and sailors, Cape Town's free burghers formed a more stable sector of the population. It was not, however, the Company's intention that there should be a large population of free settlers in the town: the idea of releasing VOC employees from their contracts was that they should become farmers, providing the Company with grain and meat for its garrison and the ships. For this reason the number of free-burgher households in the town remained small. And by no means all of those who obtained burghership remained at the Cape: the 1731 survey included the names of 57 who had returned permanently to Europe in the preceding twenty years, although it is not known how many of them had lived in the town.

Of the 185 identifiable free-burgher households in Cape Town in 1731, 50 per cent consisted of married couples, while a further 22 per cent were headed by widowed men or women with children. The free-burgher population was thus becoming more balanced in gender terms than any other sector of the town's population. Some men had brought out their wives and children from Europe after attaining free-burgher status, and in the late 1670s women of marriageable age were imported from orphanages in Amsterdam and Rotterdam; these 'had no difficulty in finding husbands'.[60] In time, how-

WOMEN IN DISGUISE

*T*here are several examples of women disguising themselves as men and joining the Company as soldiers or sailors in order to reach the East, as a VOC sailor's song recalls:

Wat hoort men niet al vreemde dingen,
Een meisje hier uit Rotterdam;
Die toen 't fortuin haar tegen gingen,
Soo straks een resolutie nam.

Tot een zieleverkoper gestreden,
Alhier juist in de Brede Straat,
Nam zij dienst voor een matroos op heden
En weer op 't schip voor soldaat.[63]

Some such women were landed at Cape Town if discovered, although in a few cases they were sent home, despite being 'instantly asked in marriage by several of the inhabitants'.[64] Not all were free to accept. Lumke Thoole of Emden married one Thys Gerrits in Emden in 1716, but after eight days he joined the VOC, leaving her with her mother-in-law. Unhappy with this arrangement, she dressed up as a man, travelled across the Netherlands and also joined the VOC. On board her sex was discovered and she was put off the ship in Cape Town. There she quickly married Abraham Hartog, one of the richer burghers in the town. However, she was subsequently recognised by a fellow Emdenaar who sent word to her first husband, then in the VOC service in Thailand. He got leave to come to Cape Town, where Lumke was tried for bigamy, divorced from both husbands and shipped back to Europe, where she disappears from the historical record.[65]

Opposite: A VOC sailor. (F. Gaastra, *Geschiedenis van de VOC,* Leiden, 1991, p. 80)

ever, free burghers married the daughters of their fellow colonists, most of whom, in contrast to European patterns, wed at a young age.[61] Not all married free burghers, however: marriage to a high-ranking Company official provided an increase in social status. By the middle of the eighteenth century, all of the senior officials on the Council of Policy were married to free-burgher wives. Some Cape Town daughters also married visiting officials. Mentzel commented that 'many soldiers marry the daughters of respectable and wealthy burghers, and the highest members of government, the clergy, and the officers of various grades will take to wife simple burghers' daughters'.[62] Marriage to Cape widows by Company employees seeking their burgher rights was a ready means to wealth and rank. In Cape Town, in contrast to the country districts, some free-burgher men also followed the example of Batavia and married manumitted slaves and other 'free black' women.

In general terms the demographic increase of the burgher population was rapid; the free-burgher women at the Cape married at a younger age than their counterparts in Northern Europe.[66] In 1731 the average number of children in Cape Town free-burgher households was 3.5, a figure which compares with 2.9 in free-black households.[67] But at the same time, as in most pre-industrial societies, the mortality rate was relatively high. One English visitor to Cape Town in 1764 commented of its Dutch inhabitants that 'their lives in general do not exceed fifty years, and vast numbers die between forty and fifty, so that an old man or woman is really a wonder'. She blamed a variety of factors for this, including the 'state of the body ... being mostly gross fat people, occasioned partly by their diet (for they dress their victuals with a vast quantity of grease and butter and the children live in the same manner) and partly by their want of exercise, which they make very little of'.[68] But also significant in her list was the impact of smallpox and the inability of Capetonians to deal with it. Medical attention, and knowledge of the cause of disease, were indeed rudimentary, the 'doctors' in the town being little more than 'quick fix' surgeons.[69]

Mentzel, who lived at the Cape in the mid-eighteenth century, stressed that Cape Town 'free burghers' were distinguished from 'the country folk' and commented that the town was developing as a centre for specialised craft activities in the expanding colony:

> The number of people a colony can maintain depends entirely upon its development and the variety of occupations that exist ... No one can do without shoemakers and tailors, and I doubt whether there is another town in the whole world which has so many tailors in proportion to its population as the town at the Cape. All human needs are inter-dependent, and there is probably no trade that is not, in one way or another, assisted by some other craft. Nothing is more essential for each artisan in this country than the possession of his own home and hearth. Hence the number of house-builders is ever on the increase. First a village arose in Table Valley, and this gradually grew into a town, which now contains 1,200 houses.[70]

It was the growing community in Cape Town of free inhabitants that provided the crafts required both for the surrounding farmers and for the transient population and ship crews. In this, Cape Town differed strikingly from other VOC ports such as Batavia or Colombo, where crafts were mainly carried out by Chinese or other Asian inhabitants.

The VOC intended that Cape Town free burghers should only engage in occupations which would be to its benefit. There was no manufacturing in the town, apart from sev-

'Their lives in general do not exceed fifty years, and vast numbers die between forty and fifty, so that an old man or woman is really a wonder.'

Mrs Kindersley, 1764

eral short-lived attempts (in the late 1720s and again in the 1780s) to set up a silk-spinning factory.[71] In the 1670s, blacksmiths, tanners, shoemakers, tailors, butchers and bakers were all granted permission to practise their skills in the town and its vicinity, since the Company realised that this would be cheaper than carrying out such activities itself. But they were still restricted. Bakers were obliged to pay an annual licence fee of 26 rix-dollars and no one was permitted to sell meat for Company use or to ships in harbour. Permission to brew beer was only granted on a monopoly basis for an annual fee, and the brewery was situated at Papenboom along the Liesbeek. The Company long refused to allow burghers free access to the several mills which it had built around the town; it was only after the 1730s that a burgher water mill was erected above the Company gardens. Retailing was also restricted. In 1670 the widow Barbetjie Geens was granted permission 'to open a little shop for the sale by retail of drapery' but she had to purchase her supplies from Company stores. In 1676 she was also given special permission to brew 'sugar beer', a poor person's drink that was widely consumed in some of the households around the town.[72]

By 1731 the burgeoning town had specialists in a variety of crafts and trades. Few were professionals, apart from a surgeon and two teachers; the Company held the function of occupations such as lawyers and clerks. Most free burghers provided services and small-scale artisan manufacture for the community of residents and transient visitors. Shoemaking and bricklaying appear to have been occupations primarily undertaken by unmarried men, while widows mainly kept shops or lodging-houses, one was a washerwoman and three women (two of them widows) were recorded as *slegte vrouwen*, or prostitutes.

The most popular source of income was the keeping of lodging-houses, a profitable activity in a town with such a transient population. Passing visitors, crew and farmers who were in town for market, as well as unmarried senior Company officials, needed lodgings.[74] Several travellers commented on the difficulties of obtaining accommodation in Cape Town when the harbour was full, and everyone complained at the high prices they were forced to pay in season.[75] Lodgings ranged greatly in quality. Officers, visitors and Company administrators occupied private lodgings in the better-quality residences, which in the 1760s charged on average a rix-dollar a day including three meals. These satisfied at least one visitor: 'it must be admitted that for the money they entertain the folk unusually well, serving up continuously fresh food very well prepared and in abundance at each meal.'[76] However, 'extras make the bills mount up' and some of the more lavish landlords arranged dances and parties for visiting officers, 'where good wine and dainties are consumed in abundance, all of which is ultimately put on the bill.'[77] Some regular visitors and ship captains always stayed at the same lodging-houses when in Cape Town. Competition for such profitable guests could be fierce. In 1720 the English captain John Gordon decided to move out of Bastiaan Colijn's lodging house to stay with Amos Lambregts, a friend employed by the Company. The Colijn daughters proceeded to abuse Lambregts roundly for luring away their guest, spicing their attack with accusations of his sexual incompetence and his wife's infidelity.[78]

Ordinary crewmen were accommodated in cheap and crowded rooms in houses along the shoreline. Here they were usually provided with a midday meal of bread and wine or beer. Many of the poorer householders in the town let out sleeping space in the summer season. The renting of rooms on a longer term was also frequent in eighteenth-century Cape Town. Many of the estate inventories reveal that houses had tenants, ranging from poorer soldiers living in small rooms in the houses of free blacks, to Company

~
OCCUPATIONS
OF CAPE TOWN FREE BURGHERS,
1731[73]
~

	Married men	Single men	Single women/ widows
Surgeon	1		
Teacher		2	
Thatcher	2	2	
Bricklayer	2	5	
Woodcutter	1		
Silversmith	1		
Coppersmith		1	
Turner	6	1	
Tailor	6	1	
Butcher	1		
Baker	6	3	2
Wagonmaker	2		
Carpenter	4	2	
Shoemaker	2	8	
Cooper	3	3	
Plumber	1		
Blacksmith	3		
Saddlemaker	3	1	
Barber	1		
Miller	1		
Painter		1	
Brewer	1		
Fisherman	4		
Bellringer	1		
Lodging-house keeper	21	2	3
Shopkeeper	4		5
Wineseller	2		
Innkeeper	4		
Pagter [contractor]	2		
Craft *knegt*	9		
Washerwoman			1
Prostitute			3

FROM CABO TO KAAPSTAD

officials and long-term visitors in larger residences. Almost all of the houses in Ward 13, which was located on and around Strand Street, took in lodgers or had tenants by the end of the century.[79]

Some of the wealthier wine farmers who had urban properties ran wine shops from their homes, stocked with their own produce.[80] At the lower end of the scale, there was a thin line between lodging-house, wine shop and *taphuis* (bar). As could be expected in a port, there was a large number of such establishments, and according to a rather concerned Council of Policy in 1665 they were the most prosperous enterprises in town.[81] The wine store near the Company stables was kept by the enterprising widow van der Berg, who in addition to drink provided refreshment hampers to visitors making the obligatory climb up Table Mountain, complete with slaves to carry the provisions.[82] There were occasional attempts by the authorities to limit the number of *taphuisen*, but this was a somewhat futile move in a town full of thirsty single men. Tavern names which regularly appeared in the records include the familiar De Goude Leeuw (The Golden Lion), Het Blaauwe Anker (The Blue Anchor) and Het Witte Hart (The White Heart) as well as the wryly appropriate 't Laatste Stuivertje (The Last Farthing) situated on the shore, and the rather curiously named Schotse Tempel (Scottish Temple), an institution which trod the narrow line between wine store, tavern and brothel from at least the 1720s to the 1770s.

Despite frequent and repeated appeals, the free burghers were not permitted until the 1790s to organise trading vessels of their own which could compete with the Company's own interests. But this did not prevent informal activity on a smaller scale, both by Company officials and by free burghers. Mentzel began the chapter on 'the daily life of the burghers' in his detailed account of the Cape in the 1730s by pointing out that it was a considerable advantage for a Cape Town resident to own a house

> because it may be most conveniently used for trading purposes … it is soon known if certain articles of merchandise are available at [the] house. The trade thus conducted is casual, depending upon what purchases this official may make or what bargains he may drive with passing ships. It stands to reason that stock articles cannot be expected, but a varied and miscellaneous assortment of goods is found. These private stores are replenished in many ways; by the purchase of goods from ships' officers, by ordering directly from merchants in Holland upon a commission basis, or buying locally at public auction. No matter how acquired, the fact remains that every man in the town, be he free burgher, or official, *pasganger* or free worker, yea even a common soldier, is at the same time a huckster and a trader.[83]

Such retail trading was haphazard and although 'it is possible to buy every conceivable article of merchandise, never at the same place, or at the same time, or at the same price'.[84] Considerable profits could be made by buying from ship captains, particularly in the summer, and selling, often by auction, in the winter and spring months when supplies were low. Officers from outward-bound ships sold wines, beer, cured hams, cheese, clay pipes, tobacco and haberdashery; those returning from Asia sold printed cottons, chintzes and other cloths, rice and tea in this way. Goods from other parts of Europe and India were brought by foreign vessels, ranging from Swedish timber and copper to Chinese silks and Bengal chintzes.[85] Cape Town house inventories sometimes recorded large amounts of goods which were clearly not for domestic consumption, such as the 9000 fish hooks, 24,000 almonds and 2580 slop bowls found in

---

OTTO MENTZEL'S ACCOUNT OF THE CAPE

The most detailed contemporary account of life in eighteenth-century Cape Town comes from a Prussian, Otto Mentzel, who arrived in 1733 as a VOC soldier. A man of education, he was hired as a teacher of the children of high-ranking officials and also worked as a clerk at the Castle.

His departure was unexpected. In 1741 he was delivering letters to a ship in harbour, which set sail with him on board. He arrived in Zeeland with only the clothes he was wearing and the five guilders he had in his pocket. He entered the Prussian civil service and never returned to Cape Town, but he was sufficiently incensed by the inaccuracies of several published accounts of the colony to write in 1785 his *Geographical and Topographical Description of the African Cape of Good Hope, wherein is described the boundaries, internal and external conditions, constitution, form of government, judicial and police systems, military and provisions for defence, revenue, trade, local privileges, urban and rural industries, occupations, customs, habits and mode of life of the Christian as well as the heathen inhabitants.*

Although written largely from memory some fifty years after his stay in Cape Town, it is a remarkably vivid and accurate work and one of the few accounts by a resident who knew the town as well as the countryside.

the house of Anna Smuts and senior surgeon van Sittert in 1755.[86]

Although strictly illegal, there were no cases of prosecution in the courts for trading in such goods since 'the Company is well aware of this state of affairs and suffers it to continue because it has long since been unable to supply the increasing needs of a growing population from its own official stores. It is well satisfied in the knowledge that this illicit trading provides a livelihood for a large sector of the population.'[87] And one sector of the population in particular – there is considerable evidence that it was the wives of burghers and officials who provided the mainstay of the informal house-trading system:

> in view of it being unofficial, and often secretive, it seldom absorbs the entire attention of the individual ... the actual disposal of the purchases rests largely with the wives; the burghers usually practise a definite and regular craft such as that of blacksmith, joiner, shoemaker, tailor and so forth, while their wives often earn more than they by means of trading.[88]

When the house of the Company's lieutenant Rudolf Allemann burnt to the ground in 1732, not only was his furniture destroyed but, significantly, '*Madame* Allemann had a considerable stock of imported goods laid in, notably tobacco, soap from Marseilles, tea, coffee-beans, preserves and fine salt. All this was destroyed.'[89] This operation of the extensive black market by the wives of Cape Town was a powerful inversion of the usual domination by males of trade and business in eighteenth-century Northern Europe. Indeed women played a much more active part in the economic life of the town in the VOC period than was the case later, not least because Dutch inheritance laws permitted daughters to acquire property and capital from parents on an equal basis to sons.

The burgher population of Cape Town was thus primarily dependent on the goods and markets provided by outsiders – either farmers coming to town or, more profitably, ship crews with money to spend. Many visitors found the price of goods and services in Cape Town excessively high. The account of Elias Hesse, who stopped over on his way home from the East Indies in 1683, showed the kind of reputation that Capetonians had already acquired by that date: 'such passing of time ... for a whole month pretty well emptied my purse of the money brought from the Indies ... here money only is regarded, and nothing else, as in other places in the Indies, and without it one can do little.'[90] Prices were certainly inflated during the season when the ships were in, and sailors complained that they were 'milked' ashore, but 'the ships being gone off, the town was left quiet and empty, and everything was cheap again'.[91] To locals the predominant image was of the returning sailor or soldier with nothing better to do with his full purse than spend it. One such anecdote, doubtless apocryphal, is nonetheless suggestive of local perceptions:

> According to local informants there was never a more godless or drunken crew than that which arrived with the first return fleet from Batavia in 1741, throwing their ducats around as if they were stones ... Amongst them was a sailor who met a man wearing a pair of canvas shoes to whom he said: 'What will you take for those shoes?' 'Well now', answered the man, 'what will I take? Give me a handful of ducats for them, I bet you won't dare do that!' 'Of course,' replied the sailor, and he took a large handful out of his bag and threw them on the ground saying, 'It's nothing to me; give me the shoes.' And the man didn't think twice about it but snatched up the money and asked the sailor if he might like to buy his stockings as well.[92]

'In view of [private trading] being unofficial, and often secretive, it seldom absorbs the entire attention of the individual ... the actual disposal of the purchases rests largely with the wives; the burghers usually practise a definite and regular craft such as that of blacksmith, joiner, shoemaker, tailor and so forth, while their wives often earn more than they by means of trading.'

Otto Mentzel

One of the few pictures that we possess of an eighteenth-century Cape Town burgher family inside their own home, this shows a large stock of wine casks in the adjoining room, although it is not clear whether this was a wine cellar or a trading store. Officially its owner, Joachim Wernich, was a gardener and painter. Painting by Pieter Regnault. (Koopmans-De Wet)

Even when measured against the officials or burghers, the largest single category of Cape Town's population was slaves. Although the majority of Cape slaves worked on the wine and wheat farms, a significant number spent their lives in the town. In 1731, slaves formed 42 per cent of the recorded urban population.

The experiences of Cape Town slaves were by no means uniform. The largest group was owned by the Company itself and housed in the Slave Lodge, near the entrance to the gardens. Almost half of the Company slaves were women; the children they bore inherited their mothers' status. But mortality outstripped fertility and the majority of Company slaves were imported, many of them directly from Madagascar and Mozambique on Company vessels. Others were brought from the East Indies.

Company slaves were the general labourers in all the Company's facilities, performing both domestic and clerical work in the offices and hospitals and manual labour at the workshops, building sites and outposts. Mentzel recorded that 'six to ten slaves attend the patients by day and night' and prepared the food in the Company hospital whilst others dug the graves of those who had died.[93] Some slaves, usually those who had been born in the Lodge, worked with the Company's carpenters, coopers, smiths and potters and learnt skills of their own. Work was usually supervised by overseers or *mandoors*, themselves slaves who had risen to positions of trust.

At night all Company slaves in the town were locked up again in the Lodge, which was under the control of a Company *opzichter*, who lived in a separate but adjoining building. Living conditions in the Lodge were appalling. Most slaves slept in cramped rooms, many without hammocks. It appears that there was something of a hierarchy within the Lodge. At the top were the *mandoors*, many of whom had been born in the Lodge and were responsible for the distribution of food and clothing rations; in the middle could be found skilled artisans with some privileges, many (but not all) of whom were half-castes or from the East Indies; and at the bottom were the great majority of ordinary labourers, most of whom were imported from Madagascar and Mozambique.[94] Lunatics were also consigned to special rooms in the Lodge, and it

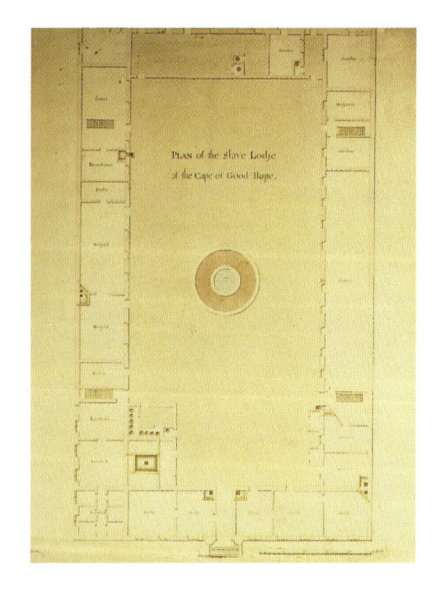

Floor plan of the Company Slave Lodge in 1798. On the left was the slave hospital, with two separate rooms for 'lunatics'; on the right a long room for the Company slaves and smaller rooms for the overseers. There was a large well in the centre. (William Fehr E41)

occasionally acted as an overflow from the neighbouring hospital.[95]

Also housed in the Slave Lodge were some of the *bandieten,* although most were imprisoned on Robben Island or at one of the batteries. The *bandieten* were criminals sentenced to hard labour for periods ranging from six months to life.[96] The large majority (73 per cent of the 435 *bandieten* listed between 1728 and 1748) were local Company employees on short sentences who had fallen foul of VOC regulations. Others were European employees from different parts of the VOC empire, particularly Batavia and Colombo. That the Cape was seen as an undesirable alternative to the East is evident from the fact that second-time offenders were often sent to Cape Town. For instance the soldier Lodewijk Rets of The Hague was banished to Robben Island for 25 years in 1744, after reprieve from a death sentence, for breaking out of Batavia prison and causing mayhem for seven weeks around the town. A number of *bandieten* in Cape Town were Asians. Occasionally these were East Indian rulers that the VOC wished to rid itself of, such as the 'Prince of Ternate', who spent 26 years in exile (1722–48) and died in Cape Town. Most, however, were criminal offenders.

Some *bandieten* were pardoned before the expiry of their sentences; others died in hospital. A few succeeded in escaping – as with slave and soldier runaways, most were never recaptured. While most of the white *bandieten* who did live out their term were subsequently returned to Europe, a few of the Asians were employed as policemen and executioner's assistants (called *caffers*). They were permitted to carry arms and were housed in the Slave Lodge. Others merged into the 'free black' population of the town.

The majority of urban slaves, at least by the end of the seventeenth century, were privately owned. Of the free-burgher households enumerated in 1731, 66 per cent included slaves, and only some of the younger single men, the three prostitutes and the poorest burghers were without them. In contrast to the larger slaveholdings on hinterland farms most urban households had less than five slaves, though some of the lodging-house keepers had over ten. The free burghers obtained slaves directly from the Company, which auctioned those it did not want to keep for itself, or from ships returning from the East Indies and Ceylon which usually carried a few slaves on board. Some burghers speculated in slaves, as in so many other goods, buying them from passing ships and selling them to farmers upcountry.

The wide variety of places of origin meant that Cape Town's slave population brought with them an eclectic mix of the cultures and languages of the Indian Ocean world. Certainly, colonists developed ethnic stereotypes of their slaves, distinguishing between those of Indonesian, Indian, Malagasy and African origin. The last mentioned were considered the most suited to farm labour but a number also lived and worked in the town. The single most common place of origin for Cape Town slaves throughout most of the eighteenth century, as in Dutch Batavia, was the island of Sulawesi (Celebes), especially those of Bugis origin.[97]

Slavery in Cape Town followed the pattern of Batavia, where the VOC had encountered an urban slave system already in existence when they established control in the East Indies. In precolonial Java slaves were kept within households, both for domestic labour and for social prestige, but were also permitted to seek their own subsistence as skilled labourers or even retailers. In Dutch Batavia and at the Cape something of this practice was retained, although in a very different context. Thunberg describes how, 'in the houses of the wealthy, every one of the company has a slave behind his chair to wait upon him. The slave has frequently a large palm leaf in his hand by way of a fan to drive away the flies.'[98]

An offender is led away by one of the *caffers*, the Asian *bandieten* employed as policemen in the town. Detail from drawing by Johannes Rach. (CA M166)

The personal slave of Hendrik Cloete, owner of Groot Constantia wine estate, holds his master's pipe. The sketch was sent by Cloete to a friend and the caption reads, 'Here I am at my table smoking your excellent tobacco.' (Swellengrebel Collection, Hilversum)

In addition to domestic work, slave women who had given birth were frequently required to suckle their owners' children as well as their own. Domestic chores which took place outside the house included fetching water from the communal pumps and carrying it home in buckets yoked over the shoulders, collecting firewood from the ever-diminishing supply of natural timber on the mountain slopes, and washing clothes in the streams flowing from Devil's Peak and Platteklip Gorge, where 'you will see almost daily, especially in fine weather, more than a hundred slaves busy with the family washing'.[99]

Occasionally burgher slaves were commandeered by the Company for special public works, such the aborted breakwater mole in the 1740s, the levelling of the parade ground in 1762, the building of a new road to Rondebosch in 1774, and fortification construction in the 1780s. A more regular task of domestic slaves was the hawking of their owners' produce. This included the produce of bakeries and the vegetables grown in the gardens in and around the town. A dispute arose in 1706, when some Cape Town bakers who did not have slaves complained of unfair competition from those who did. In 1754 it was forbidden for slaves to hawk goods apart from edibles, in an attempt to curb the thriving market in stolen goods.

Some slaves were skilled artisans such as tailors and carpenters and were hired out by their owners to the inhabitants of the town. Others made an income for their owners by fishing, in boats owned by free blacks or poorer burghers. This could be a considerable source of profit. 'The usual terms', wrote Mentzel, 'are that the hirer should pay to the owner of the slave 4 rxds. per month and provide the slave with food and tobacco but not with clothes.'[100]

Slaves who hawked goods or earned their own livelihood were required to return to their owners with a pre-arranged amount of *coelie geld*, a sum increased during the time when the fleets were in harbour. Thunberg observed in 1773 that every slave selling wood in the town was 'obliged to earn for his master two skellings daily, which makes about 80 rixdollars in a year; so that in a few years the master gets his purchase-money back again.'[101] There are several cases of punishment for those who returned with less. For instance January van Tutocorijn, slave of the widow Melt van der Spuy, returned home one day in September 1737 without *coelie geld*, was given a hiding by his mistress and sent out again without food. Hungry and cold, he sneaked into a neighbouring

Slave woman suckling a child, by Lady Anne Barnard. (SAL INIL 7055)

Slave washerwomen working at a stream on the slopes of Table Mountain in the 1830s. Platteklip Gorge was a favourite place for washing laundry throughout the eighteenth and nineteenth centuries. Drawn by J.C. Poortermans. (Library of Parliament)

Fish hawkers, drawn by H.C. De Meillon. (© The Brenthurst Press ART. 82/34)

Ceremonial *kris* from the Dutch East Indies, dating from 1757. In Java and Sulawesi the *kris* had a mystical and ritual significance. (William Fehr GH85/4)

house, took some bread and fell asleep in the attic, where he was discovered, arrested and flogged again, this time by the authorities.[102]

Such maltreatment may have been unusual, and it is likely that there was less overt brutality by domestic owners than on the farms of the country districts. Paternalism and deference dominated master–slave relationships in the household, although this did not of course preclude physical chastisement. And house slaves were always subject to the supervision of their owners, since there were few Cape Town houses with separate slave quarters. Some owners, such as Joachim von Dessin, resolved the tensions inherent in this relationship by sending their slaves to the *caffers* for punishment rather than performing the act themselves.[103] But there are also cases of owners who beat and flogged their slaves at whim. For instance, when Abraham Cloppenburg returned home at the curfew (10 p.m.) one Saturday night and found the table set for supper but the food not yet ready, he grabbed his slave Barkat van Timor by the scruff of the neck and ordered another of his slaves, Timor van Bali, to sjambok him in the kitchen. In desperation Barkat picked up a knife and stabbed Cloppenburg, then ran up to the attic of the house, where he barred himself in overnight and passed the time throwing bottles, pots and stones out of the window on to the heads of people passing below. *Caffers* broke into the attic from the flat roof the following morning and Barkat was arrested and subsequently sentenced to death for assaulting his owner. But the court also formally reprimanded Cloppenburg for maltreating his slaves and warned him of the dangers this caused for the whole community.[104]

Cape Town slaves resisted their owners in a variety of ways, ranging from running away, to poisoning, physical attack, arson and, less dramatically, working slowly and inefficiently or staying out for lengthy periods after acquiring sufficient *coelie geld*. Three separate fires broke out in the town in 1735–6 caused by slave arsonists, some of whom had secretly made their way to the Dutch settlement from the runaway slave community at Cape Hanglip on False Bay.[105] In the subsequent year there was a plot to poison the town's water supply. Runaways came from both the ranks of the Company and the private slaves. Between 1720 and 1753, 44 male Company slaves deserted and were never recaptured.[106] Others hid for shorter periods in the hills and mountains around the town. Acts of more desperate resistance included 'running amok', when slaves lashed out at everyone around them, including fellow slaves, in a suicidal frenzy. Jacob Haafner, who was in search of work in Cape Town in 1767, left his job of looking after the large number of slaves owned by one of the inhabitants because 'so many of them were Malays or Bougies, who are a vengeful and treacherous nation who will not think twice about murdering their opponents with poison or with a *kris*, a sort of snake-shaped dagger'.[107]

The authorities were acutely aware of the dangers that a large population of slaves posed to the security of the town and passed a barrage of regulations in an attempt to control them: these were brought together in a major 'slave code' in 1754. Slaves found in the town or on the mountain were required to show 'passes' signed by their owners. Slaves of more than three masters were not permitted to gather together in groups, an evident attempt to curb plots. No slave was allowed to carry arms. They were not permitted in the streets of the town after 9 p.m., an hour earlier than other inhabitants. They could also be arrested if they did not carry lanterns in the evening – an attempt to prevent plotting in dark corners. In 1760, after the murder of Michiel Smuts and his family by a group of slaves who then fled into the hills, Table Mountain was temporarily put out of bounds.

Not all slaves remained in bondage for life. Although the level of slave manumission at the Cape was considerably lower than in Asian slave societies or even in other Atlantic colonies, a small number of slaves were freed by their owners. Between 1715 and 1791, just over 1000 manumissions were made in the colony. The majority were female, Cape-born and lived in Cape Town. Many were freed on the death of their owners by will, an act which bestowed charity at no cost to the owner. Some were the mothers of their owners' children, and some were freed to become their wives. Almost a quarter were manumitted by free blacks, many of whom had purchased their own kin in order to set them free.[108]

The most distinctive feature of Cape Town's population which set it apart from the rest of the colony was the presence of people defined as *vrijzwarten* ('free blacks'). The number of first-generation free blacks in Cape Town was not large. At the end of the seventeenth century there were only 40 in the town and the highest number in the course of the eighteenth century was still less than 400. However, the offspring of free blacks and other parents were not always identified as such in the records, and many of their descendants merged imperceptibly into the free population.

Although the term 'free black' was used from the seventeenth century, they were separately listed in the population records only from the 1720s, when they were removed from the general burgher militia lists, and the category was only applied to people living in Cape Town. The majority were ex-slaves and their descendants, though the category also included the occasional free immigrant, such as Abdul Wasie, who came to the Cape as 'a free servant of his Batavian master' but chose to stay on when his employer returned to Asia.[109] Others were ex-*bandieten* who did not return home after the expiration of their sentences. Analysis of the names in the census returns suggests that the geographical origins of the free blacks varied little over time, with approximately similar proportions being born in South Asia, Indonesia and at the Cape, and a smaller number of Malagasy names.

Free blacks carried out a variety of other activities identical to those of the poorer free burghers. Some rented out rooms, and ran lodging-houses or eating places. Others practised crafts, sometimes in the workshops of free burghers, and several, especially in the late seventeenth and early eighteenth centuries, were market gardeners. Of the 96 free-black householders listed in the 1731 census, 36 owned slaves, although usually only one or two at most.

The majority of free blacks lived by fishing, an occupation central to the port town and one which gave it a distinctive character. According to Mentzel, 'No single person or boat owner is in a position to engage in fishing on a large scale because the co-operative labour of several persons, boats and a net is essential for success.'[110] Pooling of resources was essential to free-black fishermen, who lacked large amounts of capital but had close kinship networks in the town. While men carried out the fishing, women and children scaled, gutted and dried fish along the shoreline and sold the product in the town. Free-black fishing families formed the first identifiable occupational labouring community in Cape Town, which dominated the foreshore area up to the early twentieth century.

Some free blacks owned properties in the town, particularly in the earlier years of the settlement. In the seventeenth century these were mainly centred around Zee Street at the lower end of the town; by 1710 free-black *erven* had extended up to Heere (present-day Castle) and Oliphant (Hout) streets. Angela of Bengal, who had served in Van Riebeeck's household, acquired her freedom in 1666 and was granted a plot of land in Heere Street, on which she built a small house and ran a profitable business supplying

'No single person or boat owner is in a position to engage in fishing on a large scale because the co-operative labour of several persons, boats and a net is essential for success.'
Otto Mentzel

Properties and land owned by free blacks in Cape Town in 1659–1710. (After J.L. Hattingh, 'Grondbesit in die Tafelvallei', *Kronos,* vol. 10)

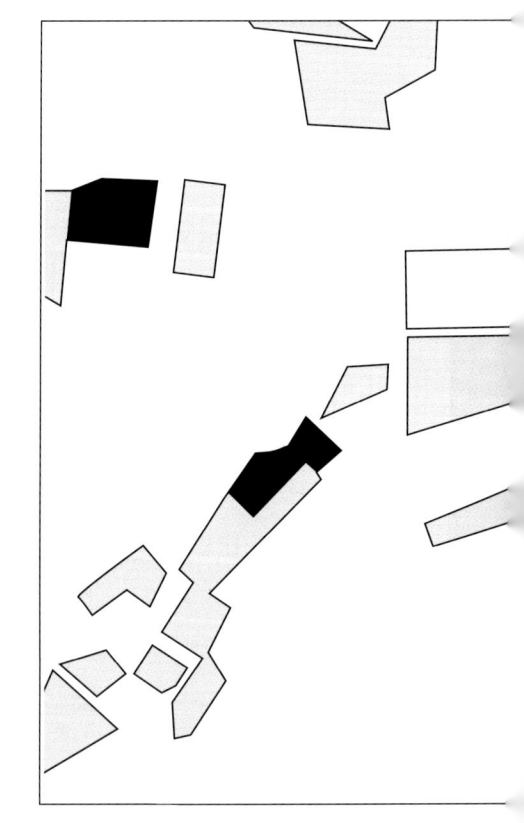

Free blacks fishing in Table Bay, as depicted by Charles Bell in 1833. (© The Brenthurst Library ART. 179/6)

Free-black erven

vegetables to passing ships until her death in 1712. She met Johanna van Riebeeck, the granddaughter of her former owner, when she visited the Cape in 1710 and gave her a 'little packet of seeds' as a present.[111]

But most free blacks were too poor to buy property and lived in hired rooms. Appolonia van der Caab, who died in 1762, lived with her husband and three (or possibly five) children in a single hired room, which was furnished with a four-poster bed, a clothes chest, cooking implements, four chairs, candlesticks and a 'tin chamberpot'.[112] A fair proportion of the smaller two- or three-roomed houses hired in Cape Town from the 1750s onwards were occupied by free-black or mixed free-black and free-burgher couples.[113]

The Chinese community in Cape Town formed a tiny but fascinating group. They were sent initially as *bandieten* convicts and exiles to the Cape by the VOC authorities in Batavia. Although hundreds were dispatched, only a few dozen survived their sentences and became free at the Cape. Some repatriated to Batavia with the Indonesian slave women they consorted with, who became the mothers of their children. Only one was baptised.[114] Juko, a Chinese *bandiet* from Batavia, obtained freedom and was baptised as Abraham de Vyf. He subsequently married the freed slave Maria Jacobs van Batavia, obtained a building plot in the town in 1702, and in 1710 won permission to return to Batavia with his wife and two children, although he died before this could take place.[115]

Many Chinese kept links with the strong Batavian Chinese community. Die-si-en, who had been banished to the Cape in 1738 'after unfortunately and innocently becoming implicated in a fraud shortly after his arrival in the city of Batavia, knowing no other language but the Chinese', appealed in 1751 to be allowed to return home to join 'his family and friends'.[116] It appears that those Chinese who remained in Cape Town became relatively prosperous, by running chophouses, fishing, selling vegetables and making candles, an occupation which they monopolised in the town.[117] Certainly they were a source of envy to many of the poorer citizens, including the rebel Estienne Barbier who, always short of money, complained that the government was favouring them above

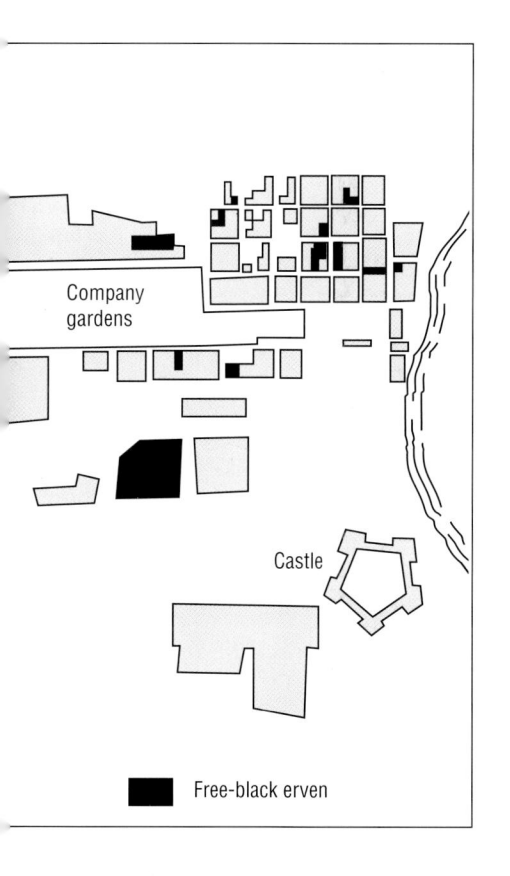

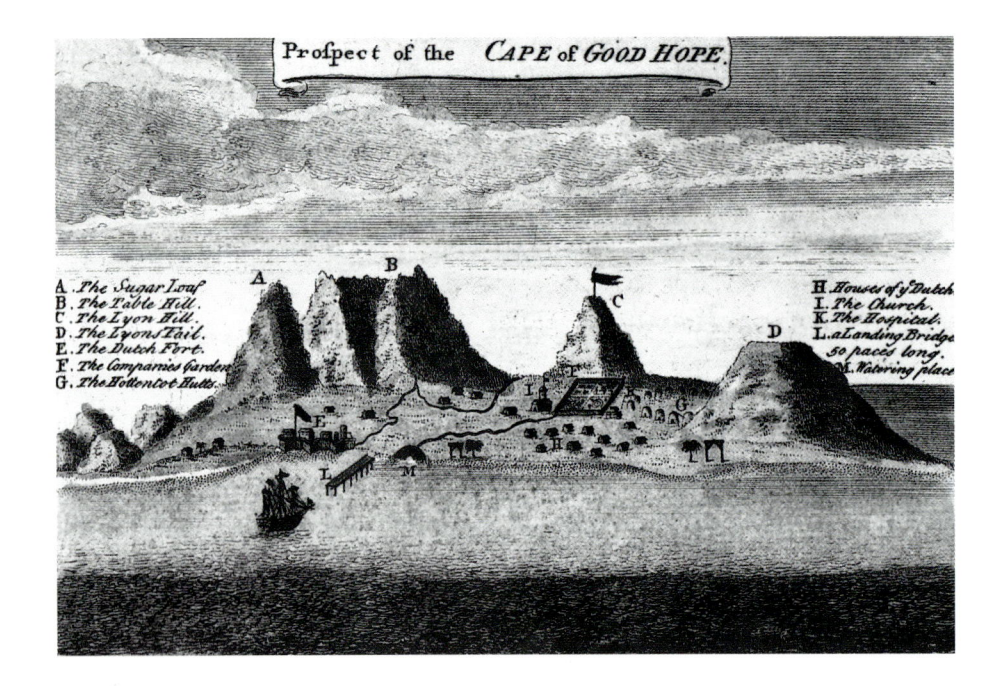

An early view of Cape Town (c. 1690) showing 'Hottentot hutts' near 'Lion's Hill'. (William Fehr GH87/1)

'white men' in the colony.[118]

The official records do not include Khoi in their tallies of the town's population. After being used as labourers to help build the new Castle, they were officially excluded from inhabiting the area by the 1676 'land sale'. A map from *c.* 1690 shows 'Hottentot hutts' on the slopes of Signal Hill.[119] These were likely to have been temporary structures, characteristic of the precolonial pastoralists and symptomatic of the exclusion and segregation of the indigenous inhabitants from the town itself. Khoi men sometimes worked on a casual basis as porters at the harbour or ran errands, but as an English visitor commented in 1711, they 'have a great love of liberty, and an utter aversion to slavery. Neither will they hire themselves in your service for longer than from morning to night, for they will be paid and sleep freemen and no hirelings.'[120] Rach's drawing of 1762 shows Khoi dressed in karosses, though they may not have been considered inhabitants of the town. Mrs Kindersley wrote in 1765 from Cape Town that Khoi servants 'alter

---

SMALLPOX

Smallpox was the most devastating of diseases to affect the town, and there were three major outbreaks of it, in 1714, 1755 and 1767.[123] On each occasion it appears that the slaves and free blacks were particularly badly affected, perhaps because they lived in more crowded living conditions, but in 1755 the burghers and Company employees made up nearly half of the fatalities. Despite careful regulations to prevent infected people or linen coming ashore from ships, it appears that this was in fact the origin of infection on each occasion. The 1755 epidemic hit Cape Town particularly hard. Overall, 2072 people died between May and October of that year. Bodies were found lying in the streets and mass graves had to be dug. All social activities were suspended, and taverns and eating houses were shut. Emergency hospitals were set up on an uninhabited farm and in barns on the outskirts of the town. Those who could fled into the country districts, some taking infection with them. It was not until March of the following year that the epidemic came to an end. In striking contrast to the centenary celebration four years previously, 7 April 1756 was declared a day of 'prayer, fasting and thanksgiving'. Although smallpox returned eleven years later and emergency hospitals were again set up in available private houses, the mortality levels were lower, doubtless as a result of immunity developed from the previous epidemic.

'Khoi servants ... alter their appearance and dress like slaves, but sometimes return to their own people and to their own manners.'

Mrs Kindersley, 1765

These two images show Khoi in eighteenth-century Cape Town. The upper picture, drawn by an unknown artist *c.* 1700, shows a Khoi man in traditional dress while the figures in the lower image (a detail from Johannes Rach's picture on p. 43) are Khoi in more Westernised clothing. (SAL INIL 6264; Atlas van Stolk, Rotterdam)

their appearance and dress like slaves, but sometimes return to their own people and to their own manners'.[121] Such a move between two worlds had been going on since the time of Krotoa (Eva). By the late eighteenth century Khoi society in the western Cape had been devastated both by smallpox and the loss of grazing land to colonial farmers. In 1770 some of the survivors were living in Cape Town more permanently: 'having come to live in the town, [they] support themselves by honest gain, by selling meat and cattle to the townsmen, and partly by hiring out their labour for money', but it has been estimated that there were only 56 of them altogether in the Table Valley area by 1787.[122]

WEALTH, POVERTY AND RACE

Some visitors commented on the apparent homogeneity of income of the town's free inhabitants. Mrs Kindersley, the intrepid Englishwoman who stayed in Cape Town in 1764–5, wrote:

> Most of the inhabitants were born here and here most of them will be buried; not having, in general, either inclination or abilities to go to Europe; they are mostly connected and doubly connected here by marriages and intermarriages; they have houses and land, their gains are not sufficient to enable them to return to the mother country with fortunes; but certain, and sufficient to enable them to live with comfort here ...
>
> I was never in a place where people seem to enjoy so much comfort; few are very rich, none miserably poor; great riches would be useless, as they have no means of spending; those who have just the necessaries of life are therewith content, because they never expected more; their ideas and their wants are few, and there is that happy constitutional dulness in the Dutch, which keeps them perfectly satisfied without either business or pleasures to occupy their minds.

Mrs Kindersley's stereotyping of 'Dutch dulness' and uniformity may well have been typical of English prejudices and of someone who came from a society of greater social and economic complexity. Although it was not until the nineteenth century that the divide between a very wealthy elite and a permanently impoverished sector of the urban population became fully apparent, there were certainly growing disparities of wealth and capital amongst the free burghers as Cape Town became a more complex society in the later eighteenth century. Analysis of probate and deeds records has revealed that from the 1750s to 1770s some polarisation of property sizes was occurring. An elite group of wealthier and larger householders was emerging, often connected to each other through matrilineal networks.[124] Most had links with the Company, as office-holders or as long-standing beneficiaries of the monopoly licence system.

Most of the wealthier Cape Town burghers had rural connections, with properties in both town and countryside. Indeed many had obtained their capital in agriculture and had then invested in urban properties. As early as 1708 the burgher councillors in the town complained that there were a number of farmers from Stellenbosch and Drakenstein 'who own houses in the Table Valley where they carry on business affairs' but who were able to evade burgher militia duty.[125] Notable among them was Martin Melck, who arrived at the Cape in 1746; by a series of judicious marriages to wealthy, but short-lived, widows he had by 1776 obtained ten grain and wine farms (of which the largest was Elsenburg) as well as five warehouses, a private residence and two plots of land in the town. (He bequeathed his storehouse at the top of Strand Street to the

Lutheran Church.)¹²⁶ Mentzel described such people as the 'capitalists' of Cape Town,

> who live in town but own estates in the country, which are worked by slaves and managed by an overseer or steward ... these landed gentlemen visit their farms from time to time, especially in the spring, see that everything is in order, give the necessary instructions to their managers and then return to their comfortable town houses to live in peace and plenty.¹²⁷

All the same the urban farm-owning 'capitalists' were but a small elite of the town's free burghers. Few of the others had many capital resources when they left Company service. If they failed to obtain access to lucrative Company leases or contracts they were dependent on their skills as artisans to build up some capital. Credit could be obtained by loans, normally at 5–6 per cent interest from wealthier residents, although sureties in the form of property were usually required and this excluded the many free burghers who rented rooms or houses. Some burghers did succeed in acquiring workshops or retail outlets in this way, but many were less successful and had to survive by working for others. Nine free burghers, some of them with families, were listed in 1731 as *knegts* (servants), working for *taphuisen* owners, shoemakers, a baker and a blacksmith. Others were listed with no occupation at all, although, as we have seen, they may well have had some income from illicit trading or small-scale hawking.

According to the 1731 enumeration, many of the citizens lived in debt, and some, such as the school teacher Jeremiah Roux, were described as *armer als arm*. A number of new burghers who had struggled in the town gave up and returned to Europe. Cape-born burghers who had no 'home' to return to in Europe were dependent on the charity of their kin or, failing that, the authorities. Begging without licence was forbidden, as it was in the Netherlands,¹²⁸ although Mentzel describes how one Dutch sailor, 'who had apparently some home experience in begging, tried the same game here. He was unlucky enough to call on this errand at the door of Mijnheer van der Henghel, the Fiscal, who rewarded him so richly with the cat that all further desire for begging left him for the rest of his life.'¹²⁹

In the 1670s and 1680s the Company had provided free rice rations for poor burghers and free blacks who were without food.¹³⁰ But the usual means of poor relief came from a special fund set up by the church diaconate.¹³¹ Regular grants were made to cripples, widows without income, the blind and the sick who had no family to support them, while indigent citizens could make appeal for special grants. Funding was only granted to those who proved that they could not find work or means of maintenance; by the 1770s doctors' reports were required to prove incapacity. Occasional help was given to impoverished visitors to the town, but only in exceptional circumstances, such as shipwreck survivors.

The usual form of relief was small cash, food or clothing handouts. However, for the long-term poor some accommodation was provided. There was no poor house in Dutch Cape Town, but in 1732 two small houses were built 'behind the Schotse Tempel' tavern on the foreshore and rooms were made available on a temporary basis. These were in such poor repair that they were pulled down in 1765; the diaconate then hired five other houses to use for the same purpose.

The poor fund also supported free blacks, although in 1705 the deacons agreed that the maximum payment for them should be 2 rix-dollars a month, a figure far short of the 5 rix-dollars usually paid to burghers. Certainly, poverty levels among the free blacks

A white *knegt*. *Knegts* were Company employees who contracted out of Company service and worked as overseers on farms or as servants in the town. Some returned to Europe after a period of time, while a few earned enough to pay off their contracts and became free burghers. (SAL INIL 6261)

were as high as for the rest of the population, if not more so. Those who entered freedom from slavery or convict imprisonment were unlikely to have many resources, although as time went on some were freed into a kin network that provided general support. The 1731 listing does not give details of occupation for free blacks, but many of them are described as being without possessions. That some lived a desperate existence on the margins of Cape Town is revealed in an entry in the Company journal for 4 February 1708: 'The body of an old black, known as Paay Moor, found dead in the gardens in a small hut. He was accustomed to beg his food in the town ... It is believed that he died of natural disease and great poverty.'[132]

'The body of an old black, known as Paay Moor, found dead in the gardens in a small hut. He was accustomed to beg his food in the town ... It is believed that he died of natural disease and great poverty.'
Company journal,
4 February 1708

The discriminatory levels of poor relief thus raise important questions about the extent to which race was a determining factor in the social structure of early Cape Town. It is clear that race was not identical to class in VOC Cape Town. Some free blacks were property owners and some free whites were paupers. There was no absolute racial division of labour. The small professional and administrative sector, being Company employees, tended to be of European origin or the sons of Cape burghers who had European ancestry whereas the slaves, coming from Africa and Asia, were not white. But although slaves held a very different legal status, some of them performed work that differed little from the Company soldier or free-burgher labourers. Africans, Europeans and Asians could all be found amongst Cape Town's artisans and labourers. In general, free blacks tended to be poorer than free whites if only because, as John Barrow observed in 1798, 'the body of the poor ... consists chiefly of that class of people who in their early days were denied the means of making any provision against old age: emancipated slaves and a few people of colour'.[133]

The main categories used by contemporaries to describe people were not 'black' and 'white', but 'Christian' and 'heathen'. Although the two systems of terminology were similar, the emphasis lay on cultural assimilation rather than fixed racial status. The concept of rigidly divided races defined somatically did not emerge until the mid-nineteenth century. The term 'free black' had 'less to do with colour than with a former servile (or criminal) status' and was not a heritable status.[134]

Racial origin was much less of a barrier to social mobility in early Cape Town than was the case in the rural districts. This was especially true for women. From early on, both Company officials and free burghers married free-black women, some of whom they had themselves manumitted from slavery. In this they followed the pattern of early Dutch Batavia, where Company officials were encouraged by the VOC to marry local women and where a distinctive mestizo culture emerged in the late seventeenth century as a result.[135] At the Cape the wives of VOC officials were not recorded, but there is much evidence of 'mixed couples' in the inventories and population registers. The first marriage recorded at the settlement took place between Jan Woutersz of Middelburg and Catharina of Bengal.[136] In 1692, 4 of the 34 Cape Town free burghers had ex-slave wives; in 1752 there were 7 evident free-black names amongst the wives of free burghers. But it appears that in the course of the eighteenth century the practice of male burghers marrying free-black wives declined. This reflected a similar trend in Batavia where official policy began to disapprove of mestizo households; it also reflects the greater availability of wives from the 'pool' of burgher daughters.[137]

The offspring of such unions were not described as 'free blacks' or by any other racial category of the kind used in the Atlantic colonies. Key Cape Town families, such as the Bassons and Vermeulens, were descended from both European and Asian ancestors.[138] The terms *halfslag* and *heelslag* were used in the slave baptism records, but only to indicate whether the father of the child was 'Christian' or 'heathen', and the nomenclature was not used more widely.[139]

Casual sexual contact between male burghers and female slaves was not unusual. The brewer Willem Menssink even attempted to persuade his wife that sex with slaves was the 'Cape custom' (although his habit of actually bedding them next to her went beyond the usual norms).[141] But racial origins were less significant than legal status. Children born out of wedlock to slave or free-black women did not escape being labelled after the status of their mothers even if their fathers were white. The main source of Company slaves lay in the children born to women in the Slave Lodge of sailor and soldier fathers, who were permitted entry between 8 p.m., when slaves were locked in, and 9 p.m. The offspring were classified as 'slaves'. Maternal legal status was thus all-important. As one historian has argued, 'people who were genetically of dominant "black" or slave origin could be free burghers and others who were of dominant "white" genetic origin could remain in slavery'.[142]

Yet it is not true to say that race played no part in the social structure of Cape Town. Awareness of race was certainly evident at all levels of society. In 1698 a Company official in the Castle broke up a fight between a free black and a free burgher on the Kat balcony, shouting, 'You black dog, how dare you lay hands on a Christian.'[143] Significantly, both assailants were described as 'school teachers'; the difference here was one of race, not class. Awareness of race and racial exclusivity came to play a more significant role over the course of the VOC period, especially at higher social levels. It appears that in the eighteenth century the higher-ranking citizens and Company officials chose wives of European ancestry, while 'mixed couples' tended to be at the lower end of the social scale.

In 1722 the free blacks of Cape Town were formed into a separate militia. Although it could be argued that this was at least recognition of their obligation to undertake military functions of a kind demanded of other male free burghers, their duties differed. They did not carry arms, and their purpose was to put out fires and prevent the looting of shipwrecks. Since both arson and looting were offences commonly associated with slaves, 'it was a thoroughly explicable form of symbolic inversion ... that it was the manumitted slaves who had to justify their freedom, as it were, by combating the efforts of their former fellows in bondage'.[144]

By the middle of the century, as in Batavia, clearly discriminatory laws were being passed against free blacks. In 1765, free-black women were forbidden to wear clothing in public which 'placed them on a par with respectable burghers' wives' and several *plakkaten* in the 1770s imposed more severe punishments for free-black offenders than for free burghers. By the 1790s, free blacks had to carry passes, in the same way as slaves. It seems that the higher-ranking echelons of Cape Town society were seeking to exclude the pretensions of those beneath them – and many of those beneath them happened not to be of pure European ancestry. The emerging division within the town was between a racially more (but by no means completely) exclusive wealthy elite and a poorer and racially more complex population.

Administering the Town

There could be no mistaking the fact that the VOC ruled Cape Town. As the chief settlement in the colony it was the central locus of VOC power. Here were based the Company rulers, their authority embodied in the institutions of the Castle, courts and church. Although three free burghers, chosen by the governor from a list of nominations, formed a Burgher Council and held advisory positions on the Council of Justice,

---

Armosyn Claasz

*A*rmosyn (a name meaning 'fine silk') was born as a Company slave and lived until the age of 38 in the Slave Lodge, where she was matron to the children. She had four children of her own, all by different fathers, some of whom may well have been white. By 1704 she had obtained her freedom as a 'free black' and owned a plot of land near Church Square in 1711. But her children were still slaves. All eventually were manumitted, but some of Armosyn's grandchildren were born before this happened and remained slaves all their lives. Others, born later, married free burghers and some obtained considerable wealth and were progenitors of major burgher families, such as the Slabberts and Britses.[140]

they lacked the power to exercise decisive judgments over their peers; all the same they benefited considerably from the patronage that ensued.[145]

The burgher councillors formed their own local body which, although relatively impotent in major issues, did play a role in the day-to-day administration of Cape Town. They collected a regular tax from householders, from which was built the Burgher House. From 1714 each burgher was also required by the Burgher Council to perform night-watch duty about once a month and to patrol the streets of the town, investigating any cases of fire, housebreaking or undue disturbance. They had the right to arrest curfew offenders and place them overnight in the Burgher House jail. They were also called upon to inspect the canal and water channels and to ensure that they were not 'fouled' by the slaves.[146] *Burgherwagt* duty was not popular: there are several cases of burghers failing to report or slinking home early. Their effectiveness was also minimal. One surviving record book faithfully records the nightly watch checking in and out every day from 1762 to 1769, though it only mentions nine incidents over the seven-year period, seven arrests of slaves going about without lanterns, and two false alarms in response to what were thought to be cries for help.[147] But since the *burgherwagt* had strict instructions not to interfere with the Company militia patrols and their sphere of responsibility, and had no right to enter private houses, they had little effective power over most incidents of crime in the town.[148]

By the 1780s the burghers were demanding greater control over their own administration. In response the Committee of the High Court was established in 1786 to act as a municipal commission for the town, consisting of three VOC officials and three of the burgher representatives on the Council of Policy. Its powers were broadened in 1793 with the appointment of two *wykmeesters* (wardmasters), for each of the 23 districts into which the town was divided. These were 'respectable householders' whose function it was 'to ensure that no irregularities took place' and that the streets were kept clean.[149] Cape Town was acquiring a local administration more appropriate to its increasing size, although it was not to obtain its own municipality until 1840.

'It has been deemed necessary to divide the town into wyken [wards] and to appoint wykmeesters to ensure that no irregularities take place.'

Resolution of Council of Justice, 1793

Urban Culture and Leisure

During the eighteenth century men and women in Cape Town begin to define themselves as distinct both from Europe and from the surrounding rural districts. Mentzel reported that Cape Town inhabitants were better informed than their rural counterparts, but had little interest in, or concern about, the affairs of Europe, resenting those who told them that life there was better than at the Cape.[158] Such pride in the Cape was also reflected in the comments of one free-burgher woman to the traveller Sparrman that people must have left Europe for reasons of poverty and she had no desire to go there and experience the same.[159] Instead, a new and distinctively urban pattern of culture and leisure was emerging which emphasised the mixture of North European and Indian Ocean influences prevalent in the port.

This was immediately apparent to visitors to Cape Town. In the coins of their change they could receive Dutch guilders, German schellings, Spanish reals, the Negapatnam pagoda or Colombo fanum, East Indian rupees, Javanese bronze, or Arab piastres. In the streets they would hear comparatively little 'High Dutch', but rather a mixture of a number of Northern European languages and dialects, the distinctive Portuguese- and Malay-based creoles of the kind found in the East Indies, together with smatterings of Chinese, Malagasy and occasional words from Khoi languages.

Traces of a Dutch culture were limited mainly to material and oral forms, rather than

From Cabo to Kaapstad 71

Rituals of Power and Status

The power and authority of the VOC and its representatives were publicly and ritualistically emphasised at every possible opportunity. Cape Town thus witnessed many rituals of state. The admiral of the annual returning fleet from Batavia to the Netherlands was greeted with gun salutes on entry into Table Bay and a formal reception committee on the jetty consisting of the governor, Council of Policy members and other officials in uniform. Great concern was caused in 1786 when the commissioner-general of the East Indies was expected and it was discovered that 'the Company's carriages, the State Coach excepted, are so old and worn that they can no longer be used'.[150] The installation of a new Cape governor was an occasion of great pomp and spectacle which involved a march of all Company officials and the leading free burghers in rank from jetty to Castle, where they swore formal allegiance. Whenever the governor left or returned to the Castle his progress was announced by the blowing of trumpets, the firing of salutes and the mustering of the guard. At church Company officials occupied the pews in absolute order of rank and precedence.

But perhaps the greatest public display of pomp was demonstrated at state funerals. That of Governor Baron Pieter van Reede van Oudtshoorn took place on Saturday 17 April 1773. Flags at the Castle and on ships in Table Bay flew at half-mast and the church bell tolled every half-hour from 7 a.m. until the burial at 2 p.m. At that hour, 'amid the continuing tolling of bells and the firing of minute guns from the Imhoff Battery and from the ships of the Honourable Company and foreign nations', a lengthy procession wound its way from the Castle up the Heerengracht to the church. The order of the procession, as recorded in the minutes of the Council of Policy, provided a visual spectacle of the ranked orders of the leading figures in the colony, the burghers falling in line behind the hierarchy of officials.[151] Indeed, so important was it at all times to reflect the proper hierarchy that if any key official was absent from the town, a substitute took his place.[152]

Rituals of authority were also clearly demonstrated in the proceedings of the Court of Justice. The reading of sentence, and its carrying out, provided, as in most eighteenth-century European and colonial societies, a public spectacle. Public floggings, hangings and, to modern sensibilities, excruciatingly gruesome executions were, above all, displays of authority. The execution ground lay outside the Castle walls, next to the road inland,

The state funeral of Baron van Oudtshoorn in Cape Town in 1773. (CA M172)

The gibbet and wheel for limb-breaking, c.1700. (William Fehr A66)

A wealthy burgher couple, a poorer inhabitant and a slave holding an umbrella in the market square, 1762. In the background a slave carries water. Differing social ranks were indicated by contrasting styles of dress. (Detail of drawing by Johannes Rach on p. 49).

where the largest number of people would pass the bodies of those victims who were left 'exposed to the air and the ravages of the birds', in the formulaic words of their sentences. Some offences had other specific places of punishment. Deserting soldiers ran the gauntlet of their regiments on the parade ground, while homosexual couples were tied together with leads on their feet and ceremoniously drowned in the harbour.

The shame of association with places of punishment was in itself a sentence. Lesser offenders were often sentenced to stand on the scaffold, sometimes with a rope around their necks: the shame of being thus exposed was regarded as suitable punishment. Johanna Wilkers, whose husband had left the Cape and who was accused of 'leading a lewd life' since, was sentenced to stand in church on three successive Sundays with a placard around her neck reading, 'I am an adulteress'. Another couple were tied onto the backs of donkeys to roam the town. The humiliation of such exposure was acute in a society in which public status mattered so much.[153]

The need to assert status through visible symbols was also apparent in clothing regulations. Batavian sumptuary laws, which were adapted to the Cape in 1755, restricted the wearing of particular kinds of clothes to persons of certain ranks. Only *opperkoopmannen* (senior officials) could wear velvet, only *onderkoopmannen* (junior officials) could have gold or silver shoe buckles, while emancipated slave women were forbidden to wear silk, lace or hooped skirts and were confined to chintz or striped linen. Slaves were obliged to dress in 'totally plain' clothes, unless they belonged to high-ranking officials, in which case they could wear livery. But none were supposed to wear shoes. Only the wives and widows of high-ranking officials were permitted to walk the streets followed by more than two slave women. Such rules to maintain visible social hierarchy were also applied to the Cape, where the privileges were extended to the burgher councillors.

The maintenance of the symbols of rank was a matter of vital importance. Violent disputes broke out when the order of precedence in pew seating at church was broken.[154] When carriages met in the streets, those occupied by people of lower rank were expected to give way; in one case failure to do so almost caused a serious accident and was a point of honour.[155] The need to defend 'honour' and reputation was not confined to the town's elite. A dispute between two rival female *taphuis* owners in 1665 arose after one had said to the other, 'I heard ... you were such a lady in the Fatherland ... in fact [you were] a workhouse prostitute and your father was in the rasphouse.'[156] The entire workforce of 20 men in the Company smithy downed tools in 1752 when the head blacksmith, Jan Krieger, found two spades missing and accused the workers of being responsible. As they later explained, it was not Krieger's usual harshness that upset them (he regularly hit them) but the insult to their 'honour' which was at stake, and they demanded the right to appeal to the governor to have their reputations restored, refusing to return to work until this was done.[157] It is indicative of the social order in VOC Cape Town that this unique incident of a collective dispute between workers and their employer was caused by threats to status and reputation rather than working conditions or wages.

Letter in Bugis written by the Stellenbosch slave Upas. (CA CJ373)

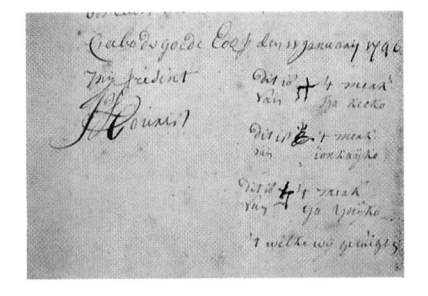

Slave manumission record with the Chinese signatures of the owner, Tja Kekko, and two witnesses, Ion Kaijko and Tja Tjoenke, dated 11 January 1746. (CA C1240)

literary ones. Between 1657 and 1707 only just over half of the free burghers in the colony as a whole could sign their names, with a slightly higher number of men than women.[160] The proportion appears to have been greater in town than in the countryside. In the eighteenth century almost all the town's free burghers could sign, but this was by no means always the case for the lower ranks of the VOC employees, and it is rare to find slave signatures. Of course ability to sign one's name was only the minimum level of literacy. We have very few private papers or letters showing a wider degree of education among burghers. Some Asian cultures were more literate than others, and there is an example of a letter written by a Cape slave in the Bugis language.[161] Most Chinese inhabitants signed their names in characters.

Although many Cape Town households in the seventeenth century had at least a few books, mainly theology, law and travel accounts, book ownership declined as the eighteenth century progressed.[162] There was no printing press or newspapers, and the only library, bequeathed by Joachim von Dessin in 1761 and under the charge of the church sacristan, was described by the traveller Stavorinus, who visited it ten years later, as 'a long room with a few bad books which are similar to those found in Batavia and which have the same pompous titles'.[163] A catalogue drawn up some years later shows a preponderance of theological and jurisprudence books of the kind found in the Netherlands, together with Diderot's influential *Encylopédie*. But it also contained items more reflective of the Asian world: two 'Malay bibles', three books printed in Colombo in Sinhalese and a collection of travel accounts emphasising the East Indies and Siam.[164]

This decline in book reading was doubtless the result of the increasingly Cape-born character of the burgher population and the rudimentary nature of educational provision in Cape Town. By the 1770s there were seven schools listed, with a total of 696 children, including a number of slaves. The main school was run by the church deacons. Requirements for its teachers, apart from membership of the Reformed Church, included the ability to speak and write good Dutch, to 'write a good letter', to sing 'David's psalms decently' and to have 'a reasonably good grasp of arithmetic'.[165] They thus appear to have provided little more than a basic elementary education. Wealthier burghers employed private teachers but they seem to have offered little more. In the Slave Lodge literate slaves acted as teachers to the children; these classes specifically excluded privately owned slaves.

The old Reformed Church building, drawn from Church Square by John Comfield in 1824. To the left is the Company Slave Lodge, which was converted into government offices in the early nineteenth century. (William Fehr C76)

The control of the Reformed Church over education was matched by its monopoly over public worship in the town, at least until the building of a Lutheran church in 1780. Catholics were forbidden to worship openly and their children were usually baptised in the Reformed Church.[166] As in Batavia, the Cape church was more subservient to the interests of the authorities than was the case in the Netherlands. The Company employed the *predikanten* (ministers) and the *ziekentroosters*, or unordained men who carried out predominantly pastoral work.

Yet although the free burghers placed great store by the baptism of their children, actual attendance at the Cape Town church, except on festival days or other special occasions, was slender. In the eighteenth century the governors and Council of Policy members were not regular members of the congregation and the church was rarely full.[167] In this the Cape Town population revealed greater similarity to Reformed Church members in the Netherlands than to their fellow colonists in the rural districts. But there is little evidence of the precise nature of religious belief. The uncertainties of storms, plague and fires were misfortunes which could be attributed to sinfulness, and public days of prayer were held on such occasions. As in Europe, a lingering belief in magical potions and witchcraft still existed at the beginning of the eighteenth century.[168] It was only in the 1780s that something of a revivalist movement developed in Cape Town which led to a more direct and personal pietism.

Although in theory baptism and membership of the Reformed Church were open to all, in practice they were restricted overwhelmingly to free people (including free blacks). The majority of the Company slave children were baptised, but rates for privately owned slaves were extremely low and declined through the eighteenth century. Although baptism did not in theory lead to manumission, Cape Town owners believed that their slaves would remain more marketable and hence 'safer investments' if they

FROM CABO TO KAAPSTAD 75

Germans in Cape Town

The number of Germans in VOC service meant that by the end of the eighteenth century an estimated 28 per cent of Cape Town's free burghers were of German origin, and although most intermarried with Dutch speakers, a German-speaking community retained its own identity and exists to this day.

Some Germans arrived with the Württemberg regiment in 1787–8 and stayed. One was the surgeon-major, Friedrich Liesching, one of Cape Town's first professionally trained physicians who established the well-known Liesching & Co. apothecary.

In 1779, after much petitioning, permission was finally granted for the building of a Lutheran church on land provided by Martin Melck, the poor German VOC servant who had made good through advantageous marriages and sharp business practice. It was opened in 1780. The church was not permitted to rival the Dutch Reformed Church and in 1786 a dispute arose when a child of Dutch parents was baptised by the Lutherans.[169] The majority of its congregation were German speakers: seven out of the eight church council members were German, the eighth being Swedish. A German hymnbook was used although it was not until 1819 that the number of German-speaking children necessitated the appointment of a German, rather than Dutch-speaking, teacher and catechist.[170]

---

were not baptised. There was no missionary proselytisation before the end of the eighteenth century.

Instead of Christianity, then, many of Cape Town's labouring classes adhered to other beliefs. Tamtanko and Theepesio, two Chinese inhabitants, bought a pig with some of the money they had stolen after a succession of six burglaries in and around the town in 1705, 'to offer as a thanksgiving to their so-named idol Joosje since their mission had turned out so successfully'.[171] The similarity of the phonetic transcription of 'Joosje' to the joss sticks offered to ancestors in Chinese religion may indicate the presence of such characteristic practices in Cape Town. There was a separate Chinese burial ground, alongside the slave cemetery on the slopes of Signal Hill, which had Chinese oval tombstones; here 'small rattans are stuck up, fastened with cotton-threads so as to form an arch or a vaulted roof over the tomb'.[172] Other slaves, especially from India and parts of South-East Asia, may have come from Hindu societies, although hitherto no records have been found to suggest direct Hindu practices at the VOC Cape.

A distinctive feature of the emerging urban culture of the eighteenth century was the growth of Islam. Many Cape Town slaves came from Islamic societies, particularly in the northern parts of Madagascar and the East Indies. To these Muslims were added some of the political exiles and convicts based at the Cape. The most famous, Sheikh Yusuf, was a member of the Makassar nobility who had journeyed to Mecca and was an important Sufi scholar who rose to prominence in the Sultanate of Banten. After backing the wrong side in a war of succession – wrong because the VOC supported the rival – he was captured and exiled first to Batavia, then to Ceylon and finally to the Cape. He arrived in Cape Town in 1694 with a retinue of 49 followers, including his wife, 2 slave women,

The Lutheran Church and, to the right, Martin Melck's house, drawn by Lady Anne Barnard in 1797. The swags on the church collapsed in the earthquake of 1809 and the existing tower was added only later. (SAL INIL 7058)

The site at Faure venerated by Cape Muslims as the tomb of Sheikh Yusuf, although there is a rival burial place in Indonesia. The tomb was built by Hadji Sulaiman Shah Mohammed in 1927.

Drawing by George French Angas of the Chinese burial ground on Signal Hill, 1 July 1843. (© The Brenthurst Press ART. 18/5)

12 children and 12 imams. Although he was exiled to a farm outside the town at Zandvliet (modern Faure), according to popular tradition he conducted prayer meetings in private homes and slave quarters and has thus been seen as the 'founding father of the South African Muslim community'.[173] But the origins of Cape Town's Islamic community were not the work of a single man: as important was the shared Islamic heritage of many of the South-East Asians, slave and free, in the town.

It was not until the end of the eighteenth century that public practice of Islam was permitted. However, oral traditions, backed by strong circumstantial evidence, suggest that Islam was also spread by other *shaykhs* and their followers among the *bandieten* and exiles who were placed on Robben Island, at Constantia and in other parts of the Peninsula, even before Sheikh Yusuf's arrival. In 1744 two *bandieten* who were sentenced to work in chains on Robben Island, Tuan Said and Hadji Mattarm, were listed as 'Mahommedan priests'. Tuan Said, who is thought to have originated from Yemen, was released after eleven years and worked in Cape Town as a *caffer*, a job which gave him access to the slave quarters and accounts for the magical reputation he acquired for entering through locked doors at night.[174]

Throughout the eighteenth century some of the mystical traditions of the *tasawwuf* Sufi order were maintained, and *tariqa* brotherhoods were possibly established at meetings of slaves, free blacks and *bandieten* in the forests and hills around Cape Town, thus providing the origins for the number of holy *kramat* shrines that exist on Robben Island, at Constantia and on the hills around the modern city.[175] In 1785 two slaves ran away from Cape Town with an Islamic talisman which they said they had obtained from a 'Mohamedan priest' to protect them from capture.[176]

The maintenance and growth of Islam and other religions provide one indication of a culture within the town which was distinct from the dominant ethos of the Company and free burghers. Further signs of the social divisions of the town are revealed in the leisure patterns of its population.

The high-ranking Company officials and the leading burghers formed an exclusive social elite; marriages between officials and burgher daughters cemented such ties. They attended celebrations at the Castle on special occasions, such as the birthday of the Prince of Orange or of the governor. The departure of the return fleet was usually cause for festivity, and on New Year's Day the burgher councillors and their wives were formally received at the Castle. New Year revelries in the town were rather more boisterous affairs: the burgher Willem Boomsaijer was fined in 1753 for firing off random shots from his house window.[177]

This association of Company and ships' officers and the more respectable free burghers was also encouraged by 'dances and receptions' arranged in the larger homes. Musicians were often slaves: Joachim von Dessin owned a slave cook 'who was a fine musician', and his estate included two trumpets, two violins, a 'cello, bass recorder and two hunting horns'.[178] Music was also performed at special occasions such as burgher weddings when feasts were held at the house of the bride's parents, 'who spare no pains to deck their tables with everything that money can buy'.[179]

On such occasions, men and women ate in separate rooms. Further gendered division is apparent in other leisure activities amongst the burghers. The institution of the social visit was a female activity, whereas 'men do not pay each other compliments or make ceremonial calls.'[180] Men did meet for coffee, tobacco or card playing in each other's homes rather than in public.[181] There were no coffee houses or news clubs of the kind found in eighteenth-century Northern Europe, but a men's club was established in

FROM CABO TO KAAPSTAD 77

View of the Society House beneath Lion's Head in 1767 with figures on the stoep and a slave with a wheelbarrow. (Jacob Haafner, *Lotgevallen en vroegere Zeereizen*)

1766; it owned a small *sociëteitshuis*, or Society House, on the Sea Point slopes of Signal Hill.[182] The frequent auctions held in the town were predominantly male social gatherings, as much occasions for entertainment as for business, although there were usually also a few women purchasers.[183]

Common recreations revealed in the estate inventories of wealthier burgher households in the early to mid-eighteenth century included backgammon and card playing, as well as sewing, embroidery and knitting.[184] The material culture of Cape households as revealed in these inventories, which included Bengal cottons and Indonesian cloths, also displayed considerable Eastern influences.[185] The presence of such items as *rijsblokken* and *stampers* speaks of the influence of Asian wives in the free-black and mixed households.[186]

The leisure and culture of the majority of Capetonians took place, however, in public places. Festivities of a more popular nature than the dinner parties and balls of the governor were held at the annual burgher militia review, where prizes were awarded for shooting competitions held on the parade ground. The Castle garrison occasionally arranged dog fights, and according to Mentzel,

> On the first day of each month there is a fête day, when the whole guard relaxes and indulges in feasting, drinking and merry making. A generous supply of meat, wine and vegetables is distributed; after dinner the band plays; dancing follows, and is continued until the wine is exhausted ... Sometimes some mummery is staged by those of the garrison who are gifted with histrionic powers. The players garb themselves in ludicrous manner but the entertainment is often good; gifts of wine are pressed upon them, often more than they can drink.[187]

Drink played a central part in the popular culture and leisure of Cape Town's working population. Dutch sailors had a particular reputation in Europe for being heavy drinkers. Both cheap wine and beer were widely consumed; beer was a favoured drink for the ordinary soldiers and sailors, and to be seen drinking it was a marker of low social status. Le Vaillant describes how

The occasional knife fight or duel was pre-arranged. A hint of this is perhaps given in Rach's picture of the Castle, in front of which two people are fighting with knives, one apparently dressed as a sailor. (Atlas van Stolk, Rotterdam)

> 'One day as I was walking with Mr Boers, he made me observe a man seated at the door of his house, who seeing we were near him, began calling to his slave with a loud voice, to bring him forth some red wine, though the Fiscal assured me, he had not a single bottle at his command, and that he had most likely not drunk of it ten times in his life; when I had passed him some little way, I turned and saw that it was beer his slave had brought him.'
>
> François le Vaillant, early 1780s

one day as I was walking with Mr Boers [the fiscal], he made me observe a man seated at the door of his house, who seeing we were near him, began calling to his slave with a loud voice, to bring him forth some red wine, though the Fiscal assured me, he had not a single bottle at his command, and that he had most likely not drunk of it ten times in his life; when I had passed him some little way, I turned and saw that it was beer his slave had brought him.[188]

The *taphuis* was the centre of social life for Cape Town's labouring classes. Here Company soldiers, sailors, free blacks, poorer burghers and slaves met and drank together, and the common leisure space of the tavern overrode the formal legal distinctions of slave and free.[189] Taverns were not only drinking houses but also places of 'diversion and recreation' that included dancing, facilities for tobacco smoking and sometimes billiard tables.[190] Some taverns also acted as brothels and at least one was a source of opium.[191]

The Company attempted to control this public leisure space, but without great success. Card playing and dice were supposedly forbidden in *taphuisen*, and all taverns had to close by the curfew hour of 10 p.m.[192] Such laws were not universally applied: in 1744 a corporal from the Castle was prevented by the lieutenant from arresting 'an English doctor' for breaking the curfew because 'he was a civilised man and would do no harm'.[193] Some attempts were made to prevent slaves from going to *taphuisen*, but little came of this and the only regulation was that they were not to be served drink after 9 p.m.[194] Regulations to prevent Company militia entering *taphuisen* proved fruitless, though entry was forbidden to soldiers on active duty.[195]

The *taphuisen* were sources of anxiety to the more 'respectable' inhabitants. In 1752 the burgher councillors complained that 'by these canteens that are situated in the heart or the middle of the town, all honest citizens are not only very much disquieted but exposed to great dangers by ... all sorts of excesses being committed by the baser Europeans and slaves under the influence of drink'. They proposed that licences should only be granted 'along the sea shore', adding that there would be no loss of revenue since 'the small change of the common people and the slaves must be drunk out no matter where they are'.[196] This attempt to segregate the centres of popular culture met with very little approval from the tavern keepers and the proposal came to nothing, but it is indicative of the growing separation of elite and popular social sectors of the town's population by the mid-eighteenth century.

Outside the *taphuisen*, the lower orders of Cape Town entertained themselves in the barracks of the garrison or in the open. Baboon-baiting was a peculiarly Cape adaptation of the popular European bear-baiting:

> 'In the town, tame baboons are sometimes kept, made fast to a pole. Their agility in climbing, leaping and dodging anyone that offers to strike them, is almost incredible.'
>
> Carl Thunberg, 1773

In the town, tame baboons are sometimes kept, made fast to a pole. Their agility in climbing, leaping and dodging anyone that offers to strike them, is almost incredible. Though one of these baboons was tied up, still it was impossible at the distance of a few yards to hit him with a stone. He would either catch the stone, like a ball, in his hand, or else avoid it in the most surprising and nimble manner.[197]

Gambling and cockfighting were favourite pastimes, particularly of slaves. Cockfighting was an important part of Javanese and Balinese popular culture and its presence amongst Cape Town slaves may well have reflected this. Rangton van Bali, a free black, had no less than eight packs of cards amongst his possessions, and there are a number of cases in the criminal records of slaves who stole money for gambling.[198]

FROM CABO TO KAAPSTAD

(J.W. Heydt, 1742; Koninklijk Instituut voor Taal-, Land- en Volkenkunde, Leiden)

Table Mountain

A CLIMB to the top of Table Mountain was, as now, obligatory for most visitors. Mentzel made an excursion with a party including slaves to carry the food, and 'did full justice to a boiled ham, a roast leg of mutton, and cold corned beef'.[199] But the appeal of romantic landscape had not yet reached eighteenth-century sensibilities. Abraham Bogaert, who made the climb up Platteklip Gorge in 1702, found it 'much toil and no little danger' and was repelled by its 'unpleasant precipice', 'valleys beset with thick jungles and horrible caves'.[200] Others described it as an 'unpleasant landscape', and the view from its top as one of 'horror'.[201]

Dominating the town, the mountain was also a region outside the control of its inhabitants. Fantasies about 'fearsome lights', remarkably shaped stones and baboons who raped people on the mountain were all recorded by (perhaps over-gullible) visitors.[202] A real danger was the presence of *drosters* (runaway slaves), whose fires could be seen from the streets of the town, a constant reminder to Capetonians of their vulnerability. 'The presence of escaped slaves was well known, but pursuit was dangerous, since the hunted men could hide themselves among the rocks and stone their pursuers to death.'[203] In 1760, after a group of slaves had murdered a Cape Town family and fled into the hills, orders were made preventing slaves from climbing the mountain, ostensibly because those collecting firewood 'make a fire near where they are working, which serves them to light their pipes, and dress their victuals ... when they leave work at night [they] often neglect to extinguish the fires which spreading ... the night following the town and road are presented with a most magnificent spectacle ... for the elevation and extent of the fire, renders the mountain a much more tremendous spectacle than Mount Vesuvius at the height of its eruption'.[204] But prevention of contact between the town slaves and the *drosters* was as important a consideration. In return for 'bread, meat and fish' provided by the slaves, the *drosters* would help with the cutting of timber.[205]

80 CAPE TOWN 1620–1662

BOOM AND BUST

By the late eighteenth century, the VOC was losing its trading position in the Indian Ocean. In 1780 a British fleet set sail to capture the Cape and only the swift arrival of troops sent by French allies, anxious to protect their supply route to Mauritius and Réunion, saved Cape Town from English invasion. In addition to the French regiment (which was withdrawn to Pondicherry in 1784), mercenaries were hired from the Luxembourg (which in spite of the name was French), Swiss and Württemberg regiments, all paid from Cape government funds.[206] A military defence expert, C.J. van de Graaff, was appointed as governor in 1785 and immediately set about strengthening the defences of the town. The fortifications that were subsequently erected (on the slopes of Table Mountain, Lion's Rump, Hout Bay and False Bay) were mainly built by new VOC recruits. At the same time work was slowly proceeding on a new hospital, an enormous two-storey building (on the present site of Caledon Square police station), designed to house 1500 patients; this was begun in 1772 but remained unfinished eighteen years later. The completed sections were used as barracks for the French troops in 1781, and in 1789 housed the mercenary battalions on one floor and invalids on the other. As a result of all this construction work and the increasing size of the militia, the Company establishment rose from less than 2000 in the 1770s to well over 3000 by 1789.

The presence of this sudden influx of newcomers had a considerable impact on Cape Town. Commissioner de Mist commented sternly in 1802 that 'the protracted stay of the French fleet during the war of 1781–4, and the foreign regiments in occupation have entirely corrupted the standard of living at the Cape, and extravagance and indulgence in an unbroken round of amusements and diversions have come to be regarded as necessities'.[207] A German visitor reported in 1784:

> I am having an excellent time as there is no end of amusement and congenial society ... It is not surprising to find French styles in great vogue, for is not the Cape almost a French dependency? Whatever styles may have been favoured formerly, I can vouch from personal observation that the coiffure of today is Parisian in every detail; not in vain were so many hairdressers included in the Pondicherry garrison.[208]

French dictionaries found their way into some (meagre) household libraries and French was spoken at social gatherings, where army officers and the town's leading burghers socialised.[209] French soldiers fitted out a room in the barracks as a theatre and invited the public to performances of Beaumarchais's new comedy *The Barber of Seville*.[210]

The impact of foreign troops was not confined to the social elite. The rank and file spilled out of the barracks into the taverns of the town, bringing with them their money, and also their grievances. Disputes arose over pay and poor conditions in the barracks. A mutiny broke out in the Württemberg regiment in 1789 in protest against bad food and to demand the same pay as the regular VOC garrison, with no deductions for equipment. Fights took place in the town; at one point these came close to armed conflict. Troops were subsequently confined to barracks after the evening roll-call in an attempt to reduce the brawling, much to the displeasure of the tavern keepers and prostitutes of the town who had been doing a roaring trade.[211]

The troops had to be provisioned and supplies from rural areas poured into the town. An increasing number of ships called at Table Bay. Although the VOC no longer

The new barracks, started in 1772 but only completed after the end of VOC rule. Drawn by Lady Anne Barnard. (CA AG15693/5)

'It is not surprising to find French styles in great vogue, for is not the Cape almost a French dependency? Whatever styles may have been favoured formerly, I can vouch from personal observation that the coiffure of today is Parisian in every detail.'
Anonymous visitor, reported in 1784

dominated the trading routes around the Cape, foreign vessels were taking their place. One striking indication of this was the replacement in the 1780s and 1790s of slave supplies from VOC posts in India and the East Indies by imports from East Africa, the Mascarenes and Mozambique brought by French and, later, Portuguese traders.[214] François Duminy, captain of such a French vessel, later entered the VOC's service,

Captain de Meuron arriving in Cape Town with the Swiss regiment in 1783. He is being rowed ashore by slaves. (William Fehr A87)

The Patriots

Not all Cape Town burghers secured advantage from the economic boom of the 1780s. A clique who had connections with VOC officials benefited to the disadvantage of the rest.[212] As a result a group of disaffected burghers petitioned the VOC and in 1784 visited the Netherlands, appealing directly to the States-General and in particular to its Patriot faction, which opposed the Orangist establishment. As a result some concessions were made. Trade with foreign ships was permitted after the needs of the Company had been satisfied.

The petitioners used some of the rhetoric of the Enlightenment, and there are signs that the Cape Town burghers closely followed the events of the American Revolution as well as the Patriot challenges to the Dutch establishment. Although there was hardly a large reading public in VOC Cape Town, some Enlightenment literature, such as Rousseau's *Emile* and works by Voltaire and Descartes, reached the town and was listed in auction catalogues in subsequent decades.[213] Yet ideals of 'freedom' and 'equality' were strictly limited in a colonial context.

As in the Americas, there was no support for notions of social equality with slaves or free blacks. But there was also little development at the Cape of a unifying settler self-identity of the kind then emerging in the American colonies. The concerns of the Cape Town 'Patriots' were rather with the impact of Company economic policies that were dividing the town into distinct factions. In this a specifically urban identity was revealed, and when Patriot delegates went to the Netherlands a split between urban and rural representatives took place.

resided in Cape Town and made large profits from slave trading. His house in upper Cape Town was surrounded by high walls and designed with narrow slit windows to ensure that slaves held there ready for sale could not escape.[215] Cape Town was also becoming a valuable supplier of goods for the wider south-west Indian Ocean region. The French alliance brought merchants from the sugar plantation colonies of Île de France (Mauritius) and Bourbon (Réunion), who turned to the Cape for supplies for the French naval garrison based at Port Louis.

The result was an economic boom for Cape Town. The Council of Policy commented in 1786 on its general prosperity, marked by outward signs of finery in dress and furnishings, the increase in housing construction and the investment by a number of burghers in landed property and heightened borrowing.[216] Lodging-houses made large profits and charged high prices, and the number of bakers, butchers and liquor licences increased markedly. Inventories of Cape Town houses in this decade also show a general increase in material prosperity, listing more valuable items such as fine porcelains and matching glassware.[217]

It was during this period that several Company officials organised import companies, such as La Febre & Co. and Cruywagen & Co., with the participation of some of the wealthier and favoured town burghers. Although such private profiteering by VOC employees was officially banned, it had been common practice for them to engage in small-scale commercial activity when possible. In contrast to the lucrative possibilities in the Indies, Cape Town had not hitherto offered much prospect of profit. But by the late 1770s and 1780s this situation was changing and a local mercantile community was beginning to emerge for the first time.

The boom soon came to an end, however. Payment of mercenaries and the flurry of building activity had been financed by the issue of paper money. By the late 1780s, inflation soared as a result. The VOC itself was in dire financial straits. In 1790–1 building work was abandoned and most of the mercenaries were dispatched to the East Indies.[218] Cape Town's 'golden age' of prosperity was over. As the Dutch naval officer de Jong stated in 1792, it might have appeared a 'fairy land' but 'the appearance of well-being and prosperity was largely made of tinsel' and indebtedness and inflation now meant that 'money has turned to chalk and stone, loses its value from day to day and is hardly worth anything any longer'.[219] Prices soared, but profits slumped.

Attempts to redeem the situation by the visiting commissioners Nederburgh and Frijkenius in 1793 led to the founding of a Loan Bank, the shoring up of the value of paper currency by silver imports, as well as the opening up of whaling and trade to St Helena and Madagascar to free burghers. But such concessions came too late, for shipping figures fell after 1790 to levels before the 1780 boom. Moreover, the terminal decline of the VOC made recovery difficult. Expenditure remained well ahead of revenue. Sympathy for the Patriot cause was growing not only among the burghers but also among some of the Company officials, and resonated with the conflict of Patriot and Orangist forces in the Netherlands, backed respectively by French and British support. When war in Europe broke out in 1792, Cape Town was once again vulnerable to foreign attack.

'Money has turned to chalk and stone, loses its value from day to day and is hardly worth anything any longer.'
Cornelis de Jong,
1792

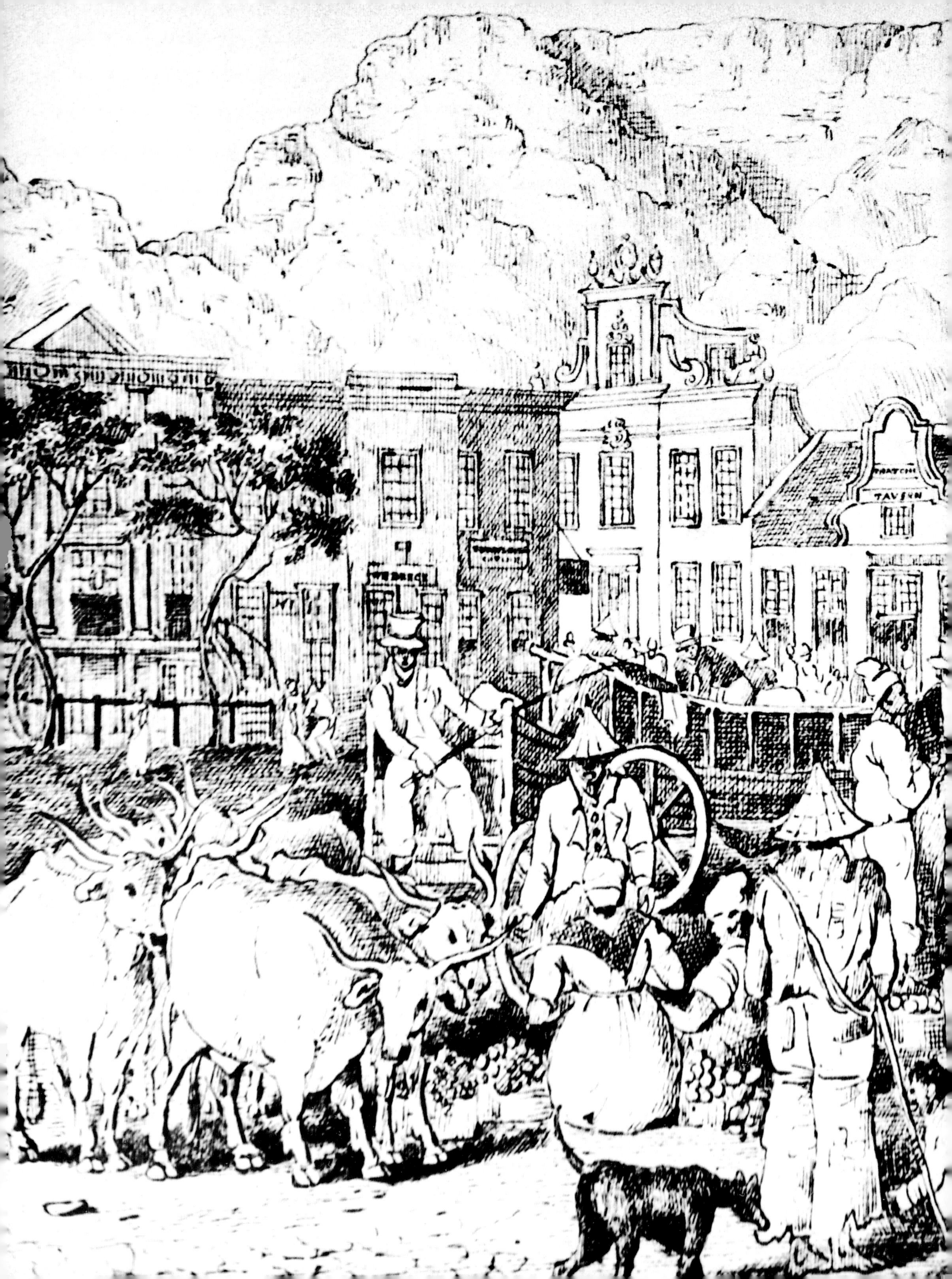

CHAPTER THREE

'A Singular Mix'

Cape Town
1795–1840

A contemporary illustration by J.C. Frederici of the Battle of Muizenberg of 1795, depicting British ships (*E*) firing on the Dutch encampment at Muizenberg (*B*), the landing of British troops (*D*) and the retreat of the Dutch towards Cape Town (*C*). (Library of Parliament)

O N 11 June 1795 a British fleet under Admiral Keith Elphinstone and Major-General James Craig sailed into False Bay. Amongst their papers was evidence of the English settlement at Table Bay in 1620, to be used to justify Britain's prior claims to the Cape. For the British were determined to prevent this strategic colony, the 'Gibraltar of the Indian Ocean', from falling into the hands of revolutionary France, whose armies had occupied the Netherlands.

The subsequent British invasion of the Peninsula from False Bay was a swift affair. The red flag of war (the 'blood flag') was hoisted on the Castle for the first time since Cape Town's foundation. Burghers from the town and country districts were mustered and set up camp at Wynberg to defend the city. Panic set in and many Cape Town families fled to Stellenbosch 'dreading the calamities of war'.[1] Fortification ditches were hastily erected around Cape Town and a Khoi regiment fought a delaying action near Muizenberg. But the poor state of the Cape militia and defences and a swift British advance as far as Driekoppen (modern Mowbray) meant that little could be done. The Dutch surrendered 'seeing the impossibility of defending Cape Town, and anxious to spare it from assault and plunder', and the 1200 British infantry and 200 artillery marched into the town.[2]

The terms of the surrender were conciliatory. Officials and burghers had to swear an oath to King George, but rights of property were guaranteed, no reparations were demanded and the value of the local paper currency was upheld. The British saw their occupation as temporary, extending only for the duration of the French threat. They stayed until 1803, when by the Treaty of Amiens they ceded the colony to the new Dutch

Previous pages: Charles D'Oyly's drawing of Greenmarket Square in 1832 shows Cape Town's wide diversity of occupation and population. Vegetable hawkers mix with country traders, top-hats with the conical *toedangs*, and behind them the Town House stands next to the Thatched Tavern. (CA A2999)

Lady Anne Barnard's panorama of the town, drawn from the Castle in the late 1790s, shows the British flag flying over the ramparts. (CA AG15693/6)

Anton Anreith's wry pediment on the back of the Supreme Court building (formerly the Company Slave Lodge), added in 1814, depicts a lethargic lion and accusing unicorn on the British coat of arms. (UCT MACM: Old Supreme Court)

Batavian government (the VOC having by this time been liquidated), choosing rather to keep Ceylon.

Although the subsequent Batavian period saw little challenge to British interests in the region, strategic issues came again to the fore when Anglo-French hostilities resumed in 1806. The British attacked Cape Town once more, this time from Bloubergstrand, and after a short engagement, in which the German mercenary regiment fled, resumed control over the town and the colony in January 1806. Their occupation was finally confirmed only at the end of the Napoleonic Wars in 1814, but it was clear that this time Cape Town was to remain in British hands. In common with other British colonial acquisitions at the time, the Cape was established as a Crown Colony administered by a civilian governor based in Cape Town.

The antipathy of some Dutch Capetonians towards their new rulers was palpable. Army officers complained in 1797 that Cape Town was 'dull in the extreme, and that the natives did not wish to make it pleasant to the English as they disliked them and showed them no civilities of any kind'.[3] The tensions inherent in this situation were revealed by an episode in 1798 when the Burgher Senate (a body of six leading Dutch citizens) refused to permit Governor Macartney to use the Town House in Greenmarket Square for a dinner to celebrate the king's birthday:

> 'His Lordship, not dreaming of such a thing from those whose interest he had invariably been forwarding in every respect, was much mystified at this ingratitude, but sent his aide de camp to the officer-on-guard, desiring him to go immediately and demand the keys and if they persisted in refusing them, to break open the doors and place a guard there, at the same time to place an English flag on its cupola. This was actually done to the mortification and chagrin of these interested malcontents.'[4]

'A SINGULAR MIX' 87

The conquest of the Town House was a clear indication that the Castle would brook no display of independence from any of Cape Town's disloyal citizens. Under the Batavian administration such divisions were reconciled, not only by the replacement of the British administration with a Dutch government, but also in the recognition of a distinct status and identity for Cape Town. Commissioner de Mist, the Batavian government's representative at the Cape, proposed the diminution of central government control over the day-to-day affairs of the town by the establishment of a town council (Raad der Gemeente) exercising wider powers of local government and elected by all town burghers who paid a minimum amount of tax. And in an elaborate ceremony held in 1804 he led a procession from the Castle to the Town House and presented the Burgher Senate with Van Riebeeck's coat of arms for the town, which was now to be called Riebeeckstad, 'to remember in gratitude the first founder and governor of the colony'.[5] The celebratory dinner which followed this ceremony of Dutch commemoration was a notable contrast to the fracas over the king's birthday in 1798. Toasts were drunk to 'The burghers of the City ... All in power ... Commerce and Navigation' as well as 'the brave Van Riebeeck, may his memory never be forgotten by an ungrateful posterity'.[6] For the first time Cape Town was being recognised as the 'founding city' of the colony, as more than a mere headquarters of government or market for farm produce.

The ceremony was, however, also a celebration of the Dutch roots and character of the town. Although Van Riebeeck's emblems long formed part of Cape Town's coat of arms, the name Riebeeckstad did not survive as 'the English continue to call [the town] simply Cape Town'[7] and did so after their resumption of control in 1806. The elected town council was never established and instead the Burgher Senate, successor to the VOC system of burgher councillors, continued. It had powers to levy market dues on produce brought from rural areas and a water tax, to regulate building, see to fire precautions, and ensure the cleanliness of sewers and drains and of the water supply. Its remit also extended to the care of the poor, the arrest of vagrants, supervision of schools and, in the broadest charge, 'to attend to the morals of the inhabitants'. But the Burgher Senate lacked the financial resources to do much about even the poor state of the town's main streets and was dependent on government bank loans for its regular administrative costs.

In 1826 a government commission reported that it had found 'great abuses and irregularities' in the functioning of the Burgher Senate, including financial mismanagement and corruption, incompetence and lack of accountability.[8] British residents of Cape Town also complained that it was dominated by Dutch burghers and that its rating system discriminated against them: 'the Dutch proprietors are spared, and the English loaded'.[9] It was abolished in 1827 but nothing was put in its place until the establishment of a municipality in 1840. Cape Town thus came under the direct rule of the colonial administration for 13 years, much to the frustration not only of its Dutch leading citizens, who were deprived of their local representation, but also of British immigrants, who found no equivalent to the traditions of local government they had known at home.

The 'Singular Mix'

Between the end of the eighteenth century and the 1830s, Cape Town experienced major changes. From being a backwater of the VOC empire, it became the capital of an expanding British colony. New garrisons, administrators and immigrants altered the character of its population; slavery declined and was finally abolished. As a result, early

'To the brave Van Riebeeck, may his memory never be forgotten by an ungrateful posterity.'
Toast of the Burgher Senate, 1804

nineteenth-century Cape Town was by no means a homogeneous community. Robert Semple, son of a Boston trader, who inevitably made comparisons with the newly independent Americans, observed in 1803 that 'as yet the people of the Cape are only about to assume a character. They are neither English, nor French, nor Dutch. Nor do they form an original class as Africans, but a singular mix of all together which has not yet acquired a conscience, and is therefore almost impossible to be exactly represented.'[10]

Semple's observation was restricted to white colonists. When the identities and experiences of all the town's inhabitants are considered, Cape Town's social and cultural diversity is even more apparent. As one German visitor commented in 1838, 'there are probably few cities in the world which, within so narrow a space, could show a greater variety of nations than Cape Town does.'[11] Widely differing identities divided the town's population by class, wealth, religion, gender and ethnicity.

In 1820, 90 per cent of the free white population of the town was still of Dutch or German origin.[13] The terms of surrender, in both 1795 and 1806, guaranteed the property and status of the town's inhabitants and the Dutch burghers had no cause to leave. They continued to be employed in a range of occupations that differed little from those

CAPE TOWN'S POPULATION, 1795-1840

Although total figures for the permanent population of early nineteenth-century Cape Town show a relatively static picture, they belie some important changes of composition and status. Slave numbers steadily declined (with final emancipation in 1838), but free black numbers rose accordingly. After 1836, free blacks, ex-slaves and Khoi were all described as 'coloured' in the records. The number of whites rose, partly as a result of natural increase but also because of the arrival of new immigrants from Britain. Troops temporarily garrisoned in the town added to the total population.[12]

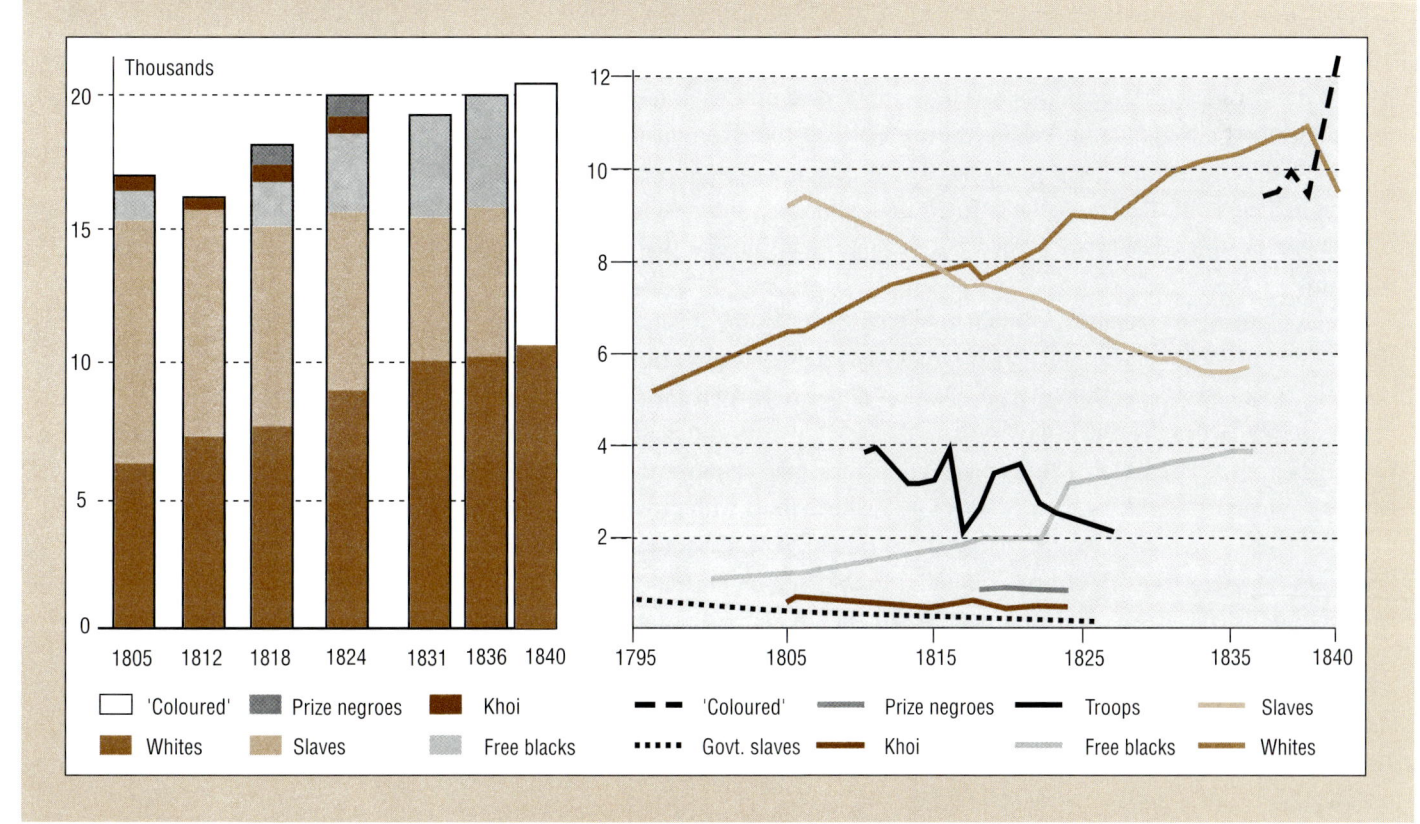

'A SINGULAR MIX' 89

Mrs Barker's retail store in a house at the corner of Burg and Castle streets, 1832. Drawing by D'Oyly. (CA A2998)

Shop windows only appeared in the Heerengracht in the late 1830s. This illustration by Johan Schonegevel was drawn *c.* 1850. (William Fehr C79)

of the preceding century and included both artisans and professionals. Boarding-house keeping and the hiring out of rooms, an important source of income in the VOC era, especially for widows or single women, remained a thriving occupation, aided by the influx of newcomers and visitors to the town in the early British period.

A large number of Dutch residents were listed in 1820 as retailers. Although some continued to sell a wide variety of goods from their homes as in the previous century, the more specialised retail store began to emerge in the early nineteenth century. In 1809 the Burgher Senate decreed that trading hours were to be from sunrise to 11 a.m. and from 3 p.m. to sunset.[14] Display windows began to be used only from the 1830s, which is doubtless why Edward Blount, visiting the town in 1820, could comment that, in comparison with Britain, Cape Town was marked by 'an absence of shops which brings the process and bustle of trade more immediately under the eye … business is transacted in warehouses or stores, as they are termed, but a stranger may imagine that none is going forward'.[15]

Some occupations remained entirely monopolised by Dutch inhabitants in 1820, such as the market gardeners and agriculturists who retained control of the remaining farms in Table Valley. Since Roman–Dutch law continued to be used and Dutch was still the main language of the courts until the late 1820s,[16] all the advocates and procurators of the town in 1820 were Dutch-speaking. In the medical field, however, the new administration attempted to restrict the practice of medicine to those with professional training. As a result many who had practised medicine under the VOC without formal qualifications now worked as apothecaries. After 1815 the medical profession at the Cape was boosted by the arrival of British doctors although there was also a small elite of Dutch and German Capetonians who had been professionally trained.[17]

For Company employees the political changes made a greater difference than for the burghers. But although the VOC garrison and senior administrators left in 1795 and their Batavian counterparts only stayed for a brief three years in 1803–6, many of the more junior clerical employees of the Company remained. The British were eager to

Dr Louis Liesching visiting a patient. The artist, Charles Cornwallis Michell, entitled this picture 'Mr Van der Bile and Dr Leeching'. Liesching, son of an apothecary who had come to Cape Town in 1787 with the Württemberg Regiment, had been sent to Göttingen University for medical training. He was one of the few local doctors whose qualifications were approved by the British authorities. (MuseumAfrica 55/923)

save costs by employing locals who were 'active, useful and who discharged their duty faithfully',[18] and their offer of increased pay proved a further inducement.[19] The continued use initially of Dutch alongside English as a language of local administration and justice meant that Dutch speakers were still in demand and clerical posts could provide a steady income and career for them and their offspring. As a result, over three-quarters of Cape Town civil servants in 1820 were from Dutch families. Government service could be something of a family business. The three sons of Adriaan Cruywagen, who had been a VOC official, worked as clerks in the Secretariat, the Council of Justice and Orphan Chamber.[20]

In the 1820s the situation did begin to alter with the appointment of more British officials when administrative reforms increased the use of English law and language. By

CORRUPTION IN HIGH PLACES

The level of corruption in Cape Town's administration may be judged from one historian's account of Sir John Truter, who 'was the President of the Orphan Chamber, a body with considerable funds at its disposal. In this capacity he agreed to lend himself and his family some 51,000 rix-dollars though he must have known that he never could – and, indeed, never did – repay them. Any anxiety which Sir John might have felt on this score was no doubt considerably alleviated by the thought that he was also President of the Court of Justice and thus empowered to deliver the final judgement on any case that might be brought against himself!'[21]

(SAL PHA)

'A SINGULAR MIX'

Troops on the Parade Ground, c. 1826, from George Thompson's *Travels and Adventures in Southern Africa*, London, 1827. (CA M455)

the 1830s there were complaints of 'the partiality of the English Governor to the English and [the] exclusion of the Dutch from office'.[22] Nonetheless, leading figures in the administration of this period were of Dutch origin, such as Johannes (later Sir John) Truter, who was secretary of the Council of Justice under the VOC and subsequently fiscal and chief justice under the British.

In place of the Dutch garrisons came a sizeable detachment of British soldiers and the presence of the Royal Navy, for this was the period when a British imperial army and navy were growing in size and presence in the Indian Ocean. In the aftermath of the British take-over in 1795, three artillery companies and a cavalry regiment (making some 5000 troops in total) as well as a large detachment of about 3000 seamen were stationed in and around the town. Numbers fell after control was formally ceded to the British in 1815, but in the 1830s there were still over a thousand troops garrisoned in Cape Town, most of whom had spent some period of service in conflicts with the Xhosa in the eastern Cape.[23]

Accommodation for so many soldiers in the early years of British occupation presented a problem. The partly completed VOC hospital continued to be used as a barrack, an arrangement which became permanent when the Somerset Hospital was built at Green Point in 1818. Some of the VOC storehouses were also converted into barracks.[24] Officers initially rented rooms in private houses, especially in Plein Street and Berg Street near the barracks, although by the 1820s this was no longer necessary.[25] Many troops in the 1790s were housed in temporary tents in Rondebosch during the summer and at a camp which became more permanent at Wynberg, since it 'forms a healthy situation for troops, and a good military post between the two bays'.[26] The experience of 1795 had revealed the need to be able to defend Cape Town from the direction of False Bay.

The fleet was initially based in Table Bay but was transferred to Simon's Town in 1813. Its area of control included both the Atlantic and western Indian oceans, covering St Helena, Mauritius and Madagascar. During Napoleon's exile on St Helena some of the Cape squadron was permanently transferred to the island, and after his death in 1821 the naval station at Simon's Town was reduced in size to a single frigate and six brigs. Its main function was to patrol the waters of the region for slavers.

The presence of so many soldiers and sailors had a considerable impact on the town. Military and naval consumption of beef, flour and wine matched that of the rest of the population and food prices soared as a result.[27] Grain and wine farmers of the hinter-

Khoi soldier, drawn by Lady Anne Barnard. A special Khoi regiment, which had been formed by the Dutch and bore the brunt of fighting at the Battle of Muizenberg, was barracked at Rietvlei (near modern Milnerton) until 1811 when it was moved to Grahamstown. (CA E2986)

Naval Mutiny

One reason for housing troops at Wynberg in the 1790s was to remove them from the 'tamperings' of a mutinous navy in Table Bay. In 1797, mutiny broke out at the British naval base at Spithead against low pay and appalling conditions of service. The Cape fleet followed the example. Officers were lured aboard one vessel, where they were seized and held prisoner. The mutineers demanded that the officers be court-martialled for maltreatment of their crews. The authorities played for time and indeed went through the formalities of a trial of one captain, although when he was acquitted sailors attempted to storm the Castle in protest and 'drunkenness and riot increased'.[28] Some alarmed citizens evacuated the town and it was only after several days that order was restored with the support of the Wynberg artillery and the threat of blowing up the rebel ships. Four of the leaders of the mutiny were hanged and others were imprisoned in the Castle, where Lady Anne Barnard took pity on them and 'found myself ... made a culprit of for dropping a bag of oranges into their very hot quarters in a sultry day ... poor things ... they eat them up skins and all. But I received a message from the sentinel immediately after to let me know that if I ever did so again, the General must be informed of it.'[29]

D'Oyly's drawing of inebriated sailors paying their attentions to local women. (MuseumAfrica 74/2539/17)

land found it difficult to keep up with demand. Brandy was in short supply and by 1801 bread had to be rationed.[30] The price of eggs increased fivefold 'only because the English soldier would not have eaten his breakfast without two or three of them'.[31] The Wynberg innkeeper's proximity to the military encampment turned him into a wealthy man overnight.[32]

Those who supplied provisions benefited greatly; those who paid for them complained bitterly of inflated prices. New forms of enterprise emerged. Dutch inhabitants observing British soldiers 'who were generally Scotsmen, carrying away the sheep and bullocks' heads to make soup, inquired if they made use of that part of the beast; and finding this to be the case, they immediately set a price upon them, at first about a penny a piece; but this was soon increased to a shilling or two'.[33] It was perhaps this new-found prosperity, recalling the heady days of the early 1780s, that led the Dutch Baron Nahuys to comment in 1806 that 'the inhabitants of the Cape, merchants by nature and set on gain, finding themselves much happier and richer under British rule than under the Dutch, will continue to prefer the former to the latter as long as affairs continue in the same way.'[34]

The presence of troops and officers again tipped the demography of Cape Town heavily in favour of males. Lady Anne Barnard commented in 1798 that 'our officers have of late been marrying the Dutch Frows at a great rate'. In 1801, when the British handed over the colony to the Batavian administration, a number of Scottish soldiers who had married local wives, 'thinking their greatness and situation were to last for ever', were dismayed to be sent to India or Ceylon.[35]

While most of the officers were 'persons of education who had been to the wars in the Indies and in Egypt ... the pick of the British army',[36] many of the rank and file were recruits from the poorer sections of British society. A high proportion came from the Scottish Highlands, Ireland and northern England. The navy also recruited a number of Hindu Indian crewmen, or 'Lascars', who as vegetarians looked forward to periods in dock at Cape Town where fresh fruit and vegetables could be obtained.[37] A few West African naval crewmen applied for their discharge after the end of the Napoleonic Wars in 1816 and were granted small plots of land at Simon's Town;[38] some soldiers also bought their discharge and stayed permanently in Cape Town. But for the most part soldiers and sailors formed a large and heterogeneous floating population in the town.

Other newcomers to Cape Town in the early nineteenth century came to stay. In the ward returns of 1820, there were 757 people of identifiably British origin.[39] Some of these had arrived during the first British occupation and stayed on, particularly those who had married local wives. Many were young men in search of a new life: over half of the British names listed were of unmarried men, and there were three times as many British adult males as females, in contrast to the more even sex ratio among the Dutch inhabitants. Although there was no planned emigration scheme like that to the eastern Cape of the 1820s, a good number of British people found their way to Cape Town of their own accord.

According to a German observer of Cape Town in 1838–9, 'the majority among the [British] immigrants are craftsmen or working class'.[40] Many were part of the diaspora spreading throughout the British colonies in the aftermath of the Napoleonic Wars, of people fleeing from the poverty of their homelands, especially from the western Scottish Highlands, southern Ireland and parts of England beset by agricultural depression.[41] The Irish were a particularly distinctive community. In 1823 and again in 1840 shiploads of Irish immigrants arrived in the town. By the 1830s the crowded and impoverished

Occupations of Capetonians, 1820

This list of occupations of Capetonians in 1820 is taken from the returns of wardmasters who walked around the houses in their wards recording details of occupants.[42] It includes tenants and family members, not just heads of households, and is thus a much fuller record than the printed street directories, although there are still gaps. The figures for females and widows are a subset of those for the Dutch, Germans, the British, and free blacks.

Cape Town baker with a dog cart, drawn by D'Oyly. (MuseumAfrica 74/2539/49)

	Dutch/German	British	Free Blacks	Female	Widow
Administrative					
bookkeeping	8				
govt admin	142	42	1		
nightwatch	20				
port offices		2	1		
postmaster	1	1			
sexton	3				
translator	3	1			
Professional					
advocate	8				
apothecary	10	2			
doctor	11	6			
horse doctor	2	1			
judge		2			
Malay priest			2		
military	2	2			
musician	6		3		
notary	4	3			
predikant	5				
procurator	4				
school teacher	27	7		4	
sewing school	7	1		4	4
solicitor		1			
surgeon	2				
surveyor	1	1			
Commercial and Retail					
agent	2	1			
auctioneer	8	1			
banking	4				
retail store	196	19	32	21	25
commerce	19	32			
beersales	1				
tobacconist	6		2		
wine seller	53	1			

	Dutch/German	British	Free Blacks	Female	Widow
Crafts/Skilled Labour					
artist	1				
baking	23	4	3	1	3
basket-maker	1		15	1	
blacksmith	7	2			
bonnet-maker	11			6	2
bookbinder	3	1			
brewing	2	1			
brickmaker	3				
butcher	13		2		2
candlemaker			12	2	
carpenter	137	26	10		
chandler		1			
charcoal-burner	1				
cobbler	74	8	12		
cooper	38	6	5		
coppersmith	8	1			
tailor's cutter	23	1	21		
distiller		1			
embroidery	31	3	3	30	7
glassmaker	2				
goldsmith	1				
gunsmith	5				
jeweller		1			
joiner	3				
mason	17	1	20		
matmaker			3		
miller	6				1
painter	16	3	10		
printing	2				
pump-maker	2	1	1		
saddler	14	3	2		
sail-maker	6	1			
sawyer	2	4			
seamstress	64	6	76	129	17
ship's carpenter	2	2			
silversmith	16	1	2		

94 Cape Town 1795–1840

Fishermen, seamstresses and laundresses, drawn by D'Oyly. (MuseumAfrica 74/2539/62)

An itinerant milliner, by D'Oyly. (MuseumAfrica 74/2539/12)

	Dutch/German	British	Free Blacks	Female	Widow
Crafts/Skilled Labour (continued)					
smith	38	6	1		
tailor	35	3	14		
tallow chandler	8		2		2
tanner	5				
thatcher			1		
tinker	1	3			
turner	7				
wagoner	21	1	2		1
watchmaker	14	5			
wigmaker	1		6		
Apprentice Craftsmen					
baker	3	1			
butcher	11				
carpenter	6	1			
cobbler	2				
cooper	7	1			
painter	1				
printer	1				
saddler		1			
smith	1				
tinker		2			
wagoner	1				
Farming/Market Gardening					
agriculture	14			2	
gardener	9	1			
Accommodation					
billiard house	2				
eating house	2	3	4		
hotel/innkeeper	4	2			
taphuis	14	3		1	
room hire	55	5		3	26

	Dutch/German	British	Free Blacks	Female	Widow
Service					
barber	8	1			
coachman	3	1	25		
cook	2	1			
horse hire	2	3			
slave hire	54			9	26
transport rider	8		3		
undertaker	3				
Unskilled Labour					
coolie			36		
domestics	20	6	20	21	
food hawking			31	15	
messenger	11	1			
midwife	3		4	5	2
servant	39	14	5		
shell collector				3	
stablehand	1	1	1		
stone-breaker	2				
laundress	72	2	101	165	10
wet-nurse	1		3	4	
Maritime					
sea captain	5	3			
boatman	32	7	2		
fisherman	92		65		
harpooner	1	2			
whaler			1		

'A Singular Mix'

area around Plein Street and Constitution Hill was informally known as 'Irish town' and became a source of much concern to the authorities, who complained that its inhabitants – 'mainly the lower Irish, intermingled with some English and Scotch' – lived in degradation and poverty, and were subject to drunkenness, 'orgies' and organised crime.[43] By the 1840s the area was losing its Irish character as freed slaves and other migrants from rural areas moved in.

But early nineteenth-century Cape Town did not offer poorer immigrants many opportunities for enrichment. This was still a town of small-scale craft workshops, service and retail, without large-scale manufacturing or industry. British immigrants with particular skills could establish themselves as bakers, cobblers, coopers, blacksmiths and saddlemakers, though in competition with local artisans.

Other immigrants with some capital could set themselves up in the ever-lucrative occupation of innkeeper or at least hire out rooms. Samuel Hudson, who came to Cape Town in 1798 as chief retainer to the Barnards, subsequently (and rather to Lady Anne's disapproval) 'established a good Hotel on the beach to be in fortune's way and by a turn of her whimsical wheel I believe is now a rich man & perhaps rather more respected than he is quite entitled to'.[44] But a number of single men and women had no such fortune and worked as domestic servants in the wealthier households of the town. The artist Thomas Bowler began his Cape career as manservant to Thomas Maclear, the astronomer royal, a position in which he did not distinguish himself and from which he was soon dismissed.[45] Not all were young and unmarried. In 1834 Lady Herschel engaged 'as monthly nurse an elderly English woman, married [to] a Scotch man who lived 14 years in Edinburgh and is just arrived in the Colony, on her way as she intended to a daughter in [New South Wales] but having been five months at sea between this and Leith she was so sick of shipboard, that she cast about her whether she might not remain here'.[46]

Women became increasingly confined to the private or domestic sphere. One marker of middle-class as opposed to working-class status was that women should not be in paid employment: this was in sharp contrast to Dutch Cape Town, where burgher women had played a key role in the economy. In the 1820 census, the only British women listed with occupations (16 in all) were seamstresses and domestic workers, clearly not of the middle class. By contrast 46 Dutch women were listed as owning retail stores. One of the few professions open to women was teaching, but then confined to infant schools.

'A Bengal Levy'

Not all British newcomers joined the lower social ranks. One distinctive group to make its presence felt from the early days of British occupation until the mid-nineteenth century was the 'Indians': British officers and administrators who served with the East India Company and, until the opening of the overland route via Cairo in the 1840s, passed through Cape Town on their way to and from India. The first British administrators depended heavily on the expertise of those with Indian experience. Lady Anne Barnard commented in 1798 that there were 'so many Indian men of some ability residing [at the Castle], so we have a Bengal levy every morning at breakfast the individuals of which are closetted and pour the riches of their knowledge and experience on [Governor Macartney].'[47]

Many 'Indians' came in the subsequent decades for health reasons: 'on a decay of health, the Indians usually resort to the Cape, before they are reduced to the absolute necessity of abandoning their post and going to Europe'.[48] The expression 'Cape doctor',

> 'I have engaged as monthly nurse an elderly English woman, married [to] a Scotch man who lived 14 years in Edinburgh and is just arrived in the Colony, on her way as she intended to a daughter in [New South Wales] but having been five months at sea between this and Leith she was so sick of shipboard, that she cast about her whether she might not remain here'.
>
> Lady Herschel,
> 11 July 1834

Some 'Indians' on leave in Cape Town brought their servants with them. This watercolour by W.R.H. shows several on the Parade Ground. (© The Brenthurst Press ART. 231)

'Indians' on their way to the governor's reception in 1833, drawn by D'Oyly. (MuseumAfrica 74/2539/59)

referring to the gusty south-easter winds, was first used by 'Indians' in Cape Town, who compared its climate favourably with the humidity of Bengal.[49]

The 'Indians' were not universally popular, for they made British Capetonians uncomfortable by comparing the town unfavourably with Calcutta, the metropole of the East India Company. John Fairbairn, editor of the *South African Commercial Advertiser*, was incensed by a report in a Bengal newspaper in 1830 that Cape Town 'boasts the anomalies of a College without professors, a Theatre without actors, an Exchange without commerce, and a Bishop without a church'.[50] On the other hand William Bird, customs controller in Cape Town, was more appreciative, stressing that their greater education, experience and intellect gave them the right to criticise, while their contribution to Cape Town's social activities was considerable.[51] Many were socially well connected, coming from aristocratic ranks, and they had a major impact on the construction of British 'society' in the town. A number belonged to the social coterie around Governor Lord Charles Somerset and were chiefly observed at the racecourse.

Not all 'Indians' came to Cape Town for leisure or health cures. Captain Harington, who had served with the East India Company in Bengal, became a prominent Cape Town merchant – he built Harington House and Harrington Street is (mis)named after him. C.S. Pillans, a purser with the East India Company, settled in Cape Town in 1823 and became a founding partner of the Thompson & Pillans trading company, while James Sedgwick, another East India Company officer, became one of Cape Town's leading wine merchants.[52]

'A SINGULAR MIX' 97

Expanding World Trade

During the early nineteenth century, the focus of British trading and imperial interests shifted from the Atlantic to the Indian oceans as Asia became an increasingly important market and provider of raw materials. Cape Town was well positioned to benefit from this development. After 1806 both the number and the geographical range of shipping which called in at Table Bay increased markedly, en route especially to India, South-East Asia and the new Australian colonies.

In contrast to the eighteenth century, when most ships were calling for provisioning only, in the early nineteenth century more were coming to Cape Town to sell their cargoes and, increasingly, to buy local staple products for sale elsewhere. Timber was imported from Port Jackson, tobacco and cinnamon from Ceylon, and cloth from Madras. A regular charter owned by Shortt & Berry traded Cape wine, dried fruit and other provisions for Javanese teak and flooring tiles in Batavia.

The weakening of French power in the south-west Indian Ocean after the Napoleonic Wars gave Cape Town access to the profitable trade in Mauritian sugar and Réunion coffee. Bread made from Cape wheat became a staple food for Mauritian plantation slaves. St Helena was largely dependent on Cape Town traders in the early nineteenth century, and the exile of Napoleon on the island from 1816 until his death in 1821 gave a small boost to local demand for produce.

(CA A2996)

In the 1820s the coastal trade to Plettenberg Bay and Algoa Bay, the Albany settlement in the eastern Cape, and the new settlement at Port Natal provided opportunities for enterprising traders. By the 1830s, an increasing number of vessels were based in Cape Town, an indicator of the growth of locally based trading and merchant interests.[53]

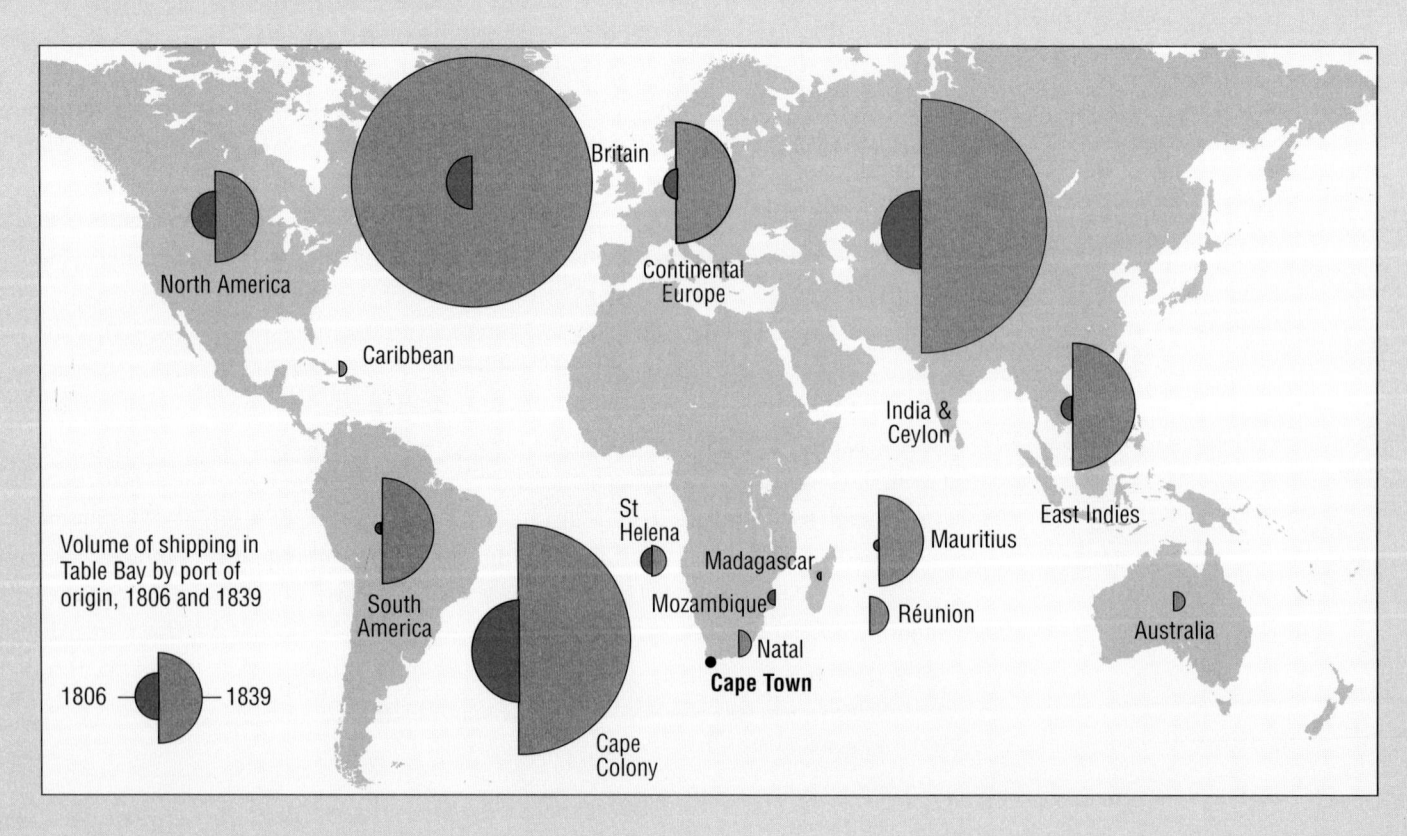

98   CAPE TOWN 1795–1840

TRADE AND COMMERCE

The occupations of men like Harington, Pillans and Sedgwick were indicative of the expanding opportunities for trade and commerce which attracted those with some capital resources to the town during the early nineteenth century. British merchants, backed by metropolitan capital resources, arrived in Cape Town from as early as the 1790s, drawn by the potential profits of the trading network in the region.[54] Many of them were part of the considerable Scottish mercantile diaspora of the early nineteenth century, which created sizeable Scottish communities in places as far afield as Buenos Aires, Cape Town and Toronto. During the first British occupation the slave trade proved one of the most profitable areas of private enterprise: the Scottish merchant Alexander Tennant imported slaves from the Mozambique Channel and West Africa. After 1806, although internal trade and retailing in Cape Town continued to be dominated by Dutch citizens, the growth of the import and export trade came to be closely associated with an embryonic British merchant community.

Cape Town's export trade received a major boost with the introduction in 1813 of preferential tariffs for Cape wines exported to Britain. In 1820 wine formed 62 per cent of the value of Cape exports.[55] The sale of wine from the farming districts to Cape Town was always a profitable trade, firmly in the hands of local families: 53 out of the 54 wine merchants in Cape Town in 1820 were Dutch. But the growth of the export market enabled British newcomers with commercial links and resources in Europe to capitalise on these new opportunities, among them John Collison & Co., which set up as a branch of the London-based family firm Collison, Starkey & Co. It was established by John Collison, who arrived in Cape Town in 1815, acting initially as general dealer and subsequently as shipping agent, owner of St Helena Bay fisheries and Swellendam farm land. On his return to England in 1827 he handed over control to his brother Francis, who was immediately elected to the Commercial Exchange, opened a new brandy distillery and brewery, took his seat as the only English member of the Burgher Senate and became a founding director of the first insurance company in 1831.[56]

Although the impetus for this commercial activity came from British newcomers, many of the most successful of them established close links with the local Dutch elite, for 'to succeed in commerce at the Cape in the early years of British rule one needed, not just sufficient capital, acumen and good fortune, but also the ability to straddle the worlds of old and new Cape Town'.[57] Such connections were both economic and personal. Although the expansion of vineyards in the decade after 1813 was primarily financed by mortgages to the government-controlled banks and by Dutch wine merchants, several British export firms also provided capital to Boland wine farmers. By the 1820s, most British merchant houses were also investing in land, especially in the Overberg and the eastern Cape.

Some of the most prominent British merchants were aided by their links through marriage to the wealthiest Dutch families of the town. Hamilton Ross, who had arrived with the Scotch Brigade in 1796, allied himself in a spectacularly scandalous way by eloping with Catherina van den Berg, the daughter of a VOC official turned meat contractor. John Ebden married into the van Reenens, one of the most successful private merchant families of late-VOC Cape Town.

Yet much of this mercantile activity was based on shaky foundations. Crop failures in the early 1820s, the decrease of the St Helena garrison after Napoleon's death in 1821 and the ending of preferential wine tariffs in 1826 led to a number of insolvencies.

Preparing wine barrels for shipping. Drawing by D'Oyly. (MuseumAfrica 74/2539/70)

Export trade from early nineteenth-century Cape Town offered wealth only for the fortunate few. In practice most trading in early British Cape Town still remained local and retail, with the more assured markets of the local garrison and population providing the most stable, if less spectacular, means of profit. As a result of inflation, the fluctuating market in property and an unstable currency (the rix-dollar fell dramatically in value and sterling was not introduced until 1832), many early British settlers went bankrupt.[58]

Although the British merchants were still a relatively small and financially vulnerable community, they nonetheless started to make claims to status and power within the town. In 1817 they founded a Commercial Exchange, which initially met in a coffee shop in Berg Street. In 1822 a grand new building in neoclassical style was erected for the Exchange on the Heerengracht side of the Parade Ground. Many Capetonians derided the pretentiousness of a building which was as much a symbolic statement of merchant self-importance as a practical necessity: 'no plan could be too magnificent for the

CONTRASTING MERCHANT FORTUNES

JOHN BARDWELL EBDEN

One of the most successful self-made British merchants in Cape Town, Ebden was shipwrecked in Table Bay on his way to India in 1806. He was initially employed as a clerk in the naval victualling office but soon set up his own business exporting wine to the Mascarenes in exchange for Mauritian sugar and Réunion coffee; subsequently he expanded his trading links to Ceylon and New South Wales with the aid of family connections in London and the support of his wife's family in Cape Town. After a period consolidating his capital in London, he returned to Cape Town in 1825 and shifted his concerns away from trading in wine (which no longer had the protection of British preferential tariffs) to wool. He also established the first local joint-stock private bank, the Cape of Good Hope Bank, in 1837. In later life he played an important role in the development of railways, steam navigation and diamond-mining and took an active political part, being a nominated member of the Legislative Council in 1834 and a member of the new representative government in 1854. He died in 1873.[59]

John Bardwell Ebden (CA J7835)

EDWARD HANBURY

Not all British immigrants in search of trading profits were as successful as Ebden. Edward Hanbury arrived from London with his wife and family in 1819, in the hope that his London connections would help to establish him as a ship chandler and then successful merchant in a town which seemed to offer great opportunities. He began by opening up a general store at 23 Berg (now St George's) Street, but soon ran into difficulties. To survive he needed to keep a wide general stock, since specialised retailing was little developed in the town. But his British suppliers were irregular, and he was unable to keep a large enough stock to satisfy shifting local demands. Imported shipments were not always a good idea: special cloth was ruined by a leakage of linseed oil and a consignment of 104 dozen bottles of beer was found smashed on arrival. Coal from Newcastle was delivered at the beginning of the Cape summer. Expensive cargoes of cut glass, cutlery and ladies' caps failed to appeal to local tastes or pockets. He had some lucky strikes, such as the arrival of an umbrella cargo in the middle of stormy weather, but soon found that most Capetonians preferred to buy at auction sales on the Parade Ground than in retail stores. He had some success in exporting wine, as well as tallow, horn and even flamingo feathers, but the depression of the 1820s hit him hard.

His attempts to recover losses by entering into partnership with an eastern Cape immigrant ended in disaster when his partner disappeared with the capital. When in 1825 his London suppliers abandoned him for Hamilton Ross as their Cape Town agent, he finally went bankrupt and died five years later. His widow opened a small haberdashery and drapery store in Hout Street – an adequate means of income, if a far cry from the riches Hanbury had expected for his family.[60]

The Commercial Exchange, from George Thompson's *Travels and Adventures in Southern Africa*. (CA M671)

rising self-importance of the Cape merchants, and the Exchange was erected on a scale ridiculous if compared to the required purposes.'[61]

However, the Exchange did become the centre in the 1820s and 1830s of a mercantile pressure group which reflected the frustration of many of the wealthier newcomers at their exclusion from local power and, after the abolition of the Burgher Senate, at the complete absence of local government. From 1825 members of the Exchange were supported by the London-based Cape of Good Hope Trade Society, which petitioned the Westminster government on their behalf on such matters as the establishment of a private bank in Cape Town, the improvement of harbour facilities, the replacement of the rix-dollar with sterling, and the ending of slavery. The *South African Commercial Advertiser*, Cape Town's first newspaper, was strongly backed by the Exchange and its editor, John Fairbairn, was a leading member.

Such campaigns were not always successful, as the removal of protective tariff support for Cape wines showed. A new stone jetty was started at the end of Bree Street, 'a crazy structure of very bad access',[62] but was never completed and lack of funding pre-

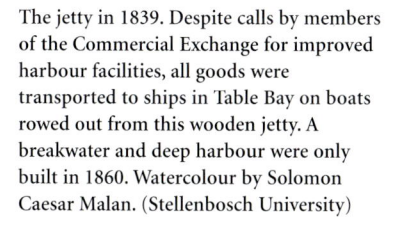

The jetty in 1839. Despite calls by members of the Commercial Exchange for improved harbour facilities, all goods were transported to ships in Table Bay on boats rowed out from this wooden jetty. A breakwater and deep harbour were only built in 1860. Watercolour by Solomon Caesar Malan. (Stellenbosch University)

'A SINGULAR MIX' 101

vented the building of a proper breakwater until the 1860s. Moreover, the government remained opposed to private banks until the late 1830s. But a major victory was scored when in 1827 a cargo of tea ordered from London by the Cape Town firm Borradailes, Thompson & Pillans was impounded by the local customs as transgressing the tea monopoly held by the East India Company. The Commercial Exchange protested loudly and succeeded in having the cargo released. Such actions gave rise to a strong sense of local mercantile identity which laid the basis for the 'self-conscious, organised social and political power bloc' that Cape Town's merchant class were to form in the mid-nineteenth century.[63]

The mid-1830s saw a recovery of trading prosperity. The level of imports and number of merchant ships entering Table Bay increased markedly (from 262 in 1830 to 506 in 1839),[64] leading one visitor in 1838 to comment that 'it is surprising how Table Bay has gained in liveliness through the almost daily arrival of ships and how the number of vessels from all nations has increased at the anchorage'.[65] A major impetus was provided by the payment of slave compensation money in the form of British government stock to be redeemed in London.[66] Many Cape Town merchants with London connections acted as agents for Cape slave owners, and provided imports in exchange. J.B. Ebden accepted transfer of compensation claims as payment for merino sheep he had imported from New South Wales. Alternatively, claims were processed at profit by power of attorney through local merchant houses. And a number of Cape Town merchants, themselves slave owners, were able to realise the capital they had invested in their slaves.

The 1830s also marked an economic upturn for the predominantly Dutch local traders and retailers. The impetus for this was provided in part by the ending of slavery, which not only brought compensation money into the town from Britain, but also turned slaves into wage-earning artisans and hence direct consumers. The end of the decade also coincided with something of a building boom in the town, stimulated by the influx of freed slaves from the surrounding countryside, which gave a boost to local craftsmen and retailers. As a result, an increasing number of local Dutch townspeople had money to invest, and several local joint-stock companies were established. The stimulus derived from the influx of compensation money also led to the establishment of Cape Town's first private bank, the Cape of Good Hope Bank (with Ebden as its chairman), and a number of insurance companies. In 1838 the Board of Executors opened to cater for the increasing number of Cape colonists seeking profitable local investment. Although this boom was to be temporary, the bases of Cape Town's commercial and financial infrastructure were being laid.

'We are Free Today'

The most striking change in the character of Cape Town's population in the early nineteenth century was the steady decline in the number of slaves and the emergence of alternative kinds of labour. From a total of 9367 in Cape Town in 1806, slave numbers almost halved to 5550 by the time slavery was abolished throughout the British empire in 1834. Whereas two-thirds of the town's burghers in 1731 had slaves, this was only true of a quarter of the households in 1820.[67]

How are we to account for this? Part of the answer lies in the ending of the external slave trade: in 1807 the British parliament outlawed the further importation of slaves into its colonies. But the ending of imports is not a complete explanation. No less than 2894 slaves were sold from Cape Town to the rural districts between 1816 and 1834 – many of them to the vineyards during the boom in the wine trade of the late 1810s.[68]

My mother asked a Coloured girl to go on an errand for her, she said "No, I won't, we are free today."
John George Steytler,
1 December 1838

THE GOVERNMENT SLAVES

The Company slaves (now called 'government slaves') were little used by the British administration. Many were sold to private individuals in 1810, while the 200 slaves remaining in the Slave Lodge were moved out to rented accommodation in the town and subsequently to new premises in the Company gardens. Old and infirm, they were finally freed in 1827, some years ahead of other slaves in the colony. The Slave Lodge was converted into government offices, housing the Supreme Court and Post Office. Today it is the Cultural History Museum.

The Slave Lodge converted into government buildings, as seen from the Company gardens in H.C. De Meillon's drawing of 1832. (CA M469a)

An itinerant vegetable hawker, drawn by D'Oyly. Many hawkers were slaves who returned part of their earnings to their owners. (CA A3012)

The threat of sale 'up-country', which was used by urban owners to disobedient slaves, became a real possibility in this period.

Slavery in an urban context was very different from that of the rural areas. Slave numbers also fell because of the changing character of the population and economy of Cape Town. Many urban newcomers lacked the resources to buy slaves at a time when external supplies were cut off and prices high. In 1820, only 13 per cent of the British inhabitants of the town were slave owners. Those Capetonians with the largest number of slaves were the agriculturists and gardeners whose labour pattern matched the rural areas, or wine merchants with similarly close links to the vineyards. Innkeepers and those who rented out rooms usually kept some domestic slaves, and artisans and craftsmen often had a slave or two working for them. But many of the occupations which the wealthier immigrants entered, such as the merchants or professionals, had less use for slave labour.[69]

In place of buying slaves, an increasing number of early nineteenth-century Capetonians hired them. The 1820 wardmaster returns list the chief source of income of 54 people as 'slave hire'. All were Dutch, and 35 of them were widows or single women. Most had inherited slaves for whom they had no direct use themselves. Slave hiring was a preferable system for many employers who required labour for fixed contracts. This was particularly true of builders and painters who hired labour for specific tasks.

'A SINGULAR MIX' 103

The availability of casual work in the town also encouraged the growth of the *coelie geld* system. 'Sometimes a slave is permitted to hire himself; that is, to work for whatever master he chooses provided he bring home every night a certain stipulated sum of money.'[70] Slaves granted a 'coelie ticket' by their owner could seek their own work and thus effectively enter the casual wage-labour market of the town. Mr Haupt, owner of the slave Gerrit, complained in 1830 that 'It was at the request of Gerrit himself that I got a "coolie ticket" for him. He gains by it at the rate of 2 rix-dollars per day out of which he should have paid 6 skillings per day to me but is now considerably in arrears.'[71] In effect, slavery was giving way to forms of wage labour in Cape Town several decades before formal emancipation in the 1830s.

Hiring out also added to the degree of social autonomy which Cape Town slaves asserted outside the homes and workshops of their owners. Semple described [Green] Market Square as 'the place of resort for the slaves, who assemble sometimes in such numbers as to fill a great part of the square ... the portico of the Stadthouse ... may be called the slave's portico; for here, when unemployed, especially in rainy weather, or

An abolitionist drawing of a Cape Town slave auction, published in 1824. The scene evokes outrage by depicting a hardened auctioneer and bidders and by contrasting the misery of the slave mother and child with the baby folded to its mother's bosom in the foreground. (SAL, *New Monthly Magazine*)

towards the close of summer evenings, they assemble together in groups and talk over the hardships of a life in slavery.'[72]

Hiring also increased social contact between slaves and free labourers in the workplace, for many employers hired free blacks and immigrant workers as well as slaves. There is evidence that some owners were content to allow their slaves to live in their own accommodation, often with partners, provided they continued to pay their *coelie geld*.

This close association of occupation, residence and marriage blurred the legal distinction between slave and free. It is thus not surprising that slaves who had obtained access to economic and social independence in this way sought to obtain legal freedom. Between 1808 and 1834, 1656 Cape Town slaves were manumitted.[73] A large number of manumissions came after the passing of Ordinance 19 of 1826, which permitted slaves to purchase their own freedom if they could raise the required amount. Such an option was usually open only to men who did 'coelie work', since female slaves tended to work in domestic labour where earnings were not so readily available.

But there were other ways by which female slaves obtained freedom. Many were pur-

---

'Just before the English got possession of the Cape, and when it was generally thought the French would be before-hand with us, the slaves who carried the sedan chairs, of which no lady is without one, used very familiarly to tell their mistresses, "We carry you now, but by-and-by it will be your turn to carry us."'

John Barrow, 1806

Slave Bids for Freedom

The people who responded most readily to talk about liberty were the slaves themselves. Barrow, a British official in Macartney's administration, discovered how French revolutionary notions had affected slave opinion in the 1790s:

'The Dutch use little prudence or precaution with regard to their domestic slaves: in the same room where these are assembled to wait behind their masters' chairs, they discuss their crude opinions of liberty and equality without any reserve; yet they pretend to say that, just before the English got possession of the Cape, and when it was generally thought the French would be before-hand with us, the slaves who carried the sedan chairs, of which no lady is without one, used very familiarly to tell their mistresses, "We carry you now, but by-and-by it will be your turn to carry us."'[75]

In 1808 the slaves Abraham and Louis (the latter a Mauritian slave who had already gained much independence from his owner by working as a tailor and living separately with his free wife) were talking with two Irishmen who often sought food and company with them at Louis's house in Strand Street. James Hooper, an Irish ship captain's servant, had been stranded at the Cape and had no fixed abode while Michael Kelly was a sailor discharged from the East India Company, who lived at the military hospital and sometimes obtained meals from Louis. They informed them that 'there were no slaves in their country but that every person was free'. As the evening wore on, they decided that they should take action to liberate those unjustly held in slavery at the Cape. Although the Irishmen later backed out, they all set off for the Swartland, Louis passing himself off as a 'Spanish captain', dressed in a 'blue jacket with red collar and cuffs, a large and small sword, a new hat, two gold and two silver epaulets, and some ostrich feathers'.[76] They were accompanied by a Mozambican whom Louis had hired as a 'coelie boy' for 2 rix-dollars a day, and Adonis, a slave who had run away from his owner because he had failed to catch any fish. They visited over thirty farms and persuaded some 330 slaves to join them in a march on Cape Town, stating that they 'would hoist the bloody flag and fight themselves free, and that then the slave girls could in their turn say *jy* to their mistresses'.[77] But the slave invasion of Cape Town was halted by militia at Salt River. Most of the slaves were sent back to their owners' farms, while 16 of the leaders were hanged.[78]

'A SINGULAR MIX' 105

chased and then manumitted by lovers or partners. Indeed the large majority of manumissions before Ordinance 19 were of women. Once free, men and women often saved up to redeem their relatives, especially their children. The mother of an infant slave owned by the merchant Hamilton Ross paid him £15 in 1827 to buy freedom for her daughter.[74] The psychological importance of such self-emancipation is shown by the fact that in the last decade of slavery 37 slaves of 65 years or older purchased their own freedom. As Rogers, the government-appointed protector of slaves, commented in 1830: 'I have known many instances of slaves on the verge of the grave praying to be emancipated that they may die free.'[79]

The frequency of slave manumissions explains why the number of free blacks increased so markedly: tenfold, from 352 in 1770 to 1896 in 1822, and then doubling in eight years to 3538 in 1830. The close association of free blacks and slaves was marked; their occupations were very similar. Of the 569 free blacks whose occupations were listed in 1820, 25 per cent were craftsmen, 18 per cent hawkers, porters and servants, 18 per cent washerwomen and laundresses, and 12 per cent fishermen. There are also numerous examples of slaves and free blacks who lived together in the same household, and who may well have formed parts of extended families. For instance, in 1799 the free black Baatjoe and his wife lived in a house in the crowded quarter by the waterfront,

Jan Persent, who was captured by Portuguese slavers in Mozambique and landed at the Cape as a prize negro, photographed in 1916 at Elgin. (*Cape Times Weekly*, 21 April 1916)

Emancipation Day

As the bells struck midnight on 1 December 1834, bonfires were lit on Table Mountain and Signal Hill and fireworks were set off over the harbour to celebrate the formal ending of slavery. The *Commercial Advertiser* reported with relief that although the new 'apprentices' 'of all ages and both sexes, promenaded the streets during the day and night, many of them attended by a band of amateur musicians ... their amusements were simple and interesting, their demeanour orderly and respectful'.[83]

The most enthusiastic supporters of emancipation among Cape Town's citizens were the 'Noble Britons', as Fairbairn described the merchant community. In the evening of 1 December, a celebratory dinner was held at the St George's Hotel where the guests, chiefly merchants, 'in true English fashion expressed their gratitude for this crowning mercy'. Toasts were drunk to the 'Champions of Emancipation' (who, with considerable imagination, were deemed to include not only Wilberforce but also Homer and Milton), to the 'King and people of England' and, more significantly in terms of the diners' own interests, to the London-based Cape of Good Hope Trade Society.

I'Ons's allegorical picture of 'The freed slave' drawn in 1840. The figure wears shoes – a marker of freedom – and carries a copy of the Abolition Act in his right hand. (SAL PHA: Slaves)

The first of December continued to be marked as an anniversary. In 1836 'about 15 hundred children with their teachers were marched in procession through the streets of Cape Town under their respective flags, & then met in a field belonging to Government House where they had sandwiches and plum cake.'[84] For many decades afterwards, the first of December was commemorated by the descendants of Cape Town's slaves. In 1886 Omaar Hendricks, a dockworker, drank with fishermen at the Queen's Hotel because 'we were keeping up the first of December', and well into the twentieth century 'each year on December 1 ... the washer-women of Platteklip [the stream from Table Mountain used by washerwomen since slave days] made merry with song and dance under the trees'.[85] However, by then most celebrations of 1 December had become eclipsed by the New Year festivities.

106 CAPE TOWN 1795–1840

Katie Jacobs, a 90-year-old resident of District Six, was interviewed in 1910 for the *A.P.O.* newspaper about her early life as a slave. After emancipation, she worked for a series of farmers and then moved to Cape Town and settled in District Six where, she complained, 'the electric trams pass my door from early morning until late at night'. (SAL INIL 11810)

ANNO TERTIO & QUARTO

GULIELMI IV. REGIS.

C A P. LXXIII.

An Act for the Abolition of Slavery throughout the *British* Colonies ; for promoting the Industry of the manumitted Slaves ; and for compensating the Persons hitherto entitled to the Services of such Slaves.   [28th *August* 1833.]

together with 'Fettong, slave of Juffrouw de Wit with his free black wife Silvia; Fortune, slave of Heer Flek; Fortune the free black; Alida a free-black; Rosina van der Velde, with a little boy and a girl; Prejab, slave of Prejab the free black, and his wife, 3 boys and a girl; January slave of Van Echte, Achilles, slave of Juffrouw Bateman, and Alson of Batavia, a free black, all of them fishermen, coolie porters and washerwomen.'[80]

The existence of a community which was so closely linked in occupation and kinship with slaves does much to explain the blurring of boundaries between slave and free in the decades before formal emancipation. On the other hand, there was also a free-black elite that was far removed economically from slavery. Indeed a number were themselves slave owners. Jan van Bougies, imam of the 'Palm Tree' Mosque, owned 16 between 1816 and 1834.[81]

The gradual erosion of slavery in Cape Town thus pre-dated formal emancipation. There was also a growing recognition by some urban employers that forced labour was less profitable and flexible than wage labour. This was in line with sentiment in Britain, where calls for the replacement of slavery by wage labour were grounded on economic rationality as well as moral force. These ideas were echoed in the columns of the *South African Commercial Advertiser*, which called in the 1820s for a process of gradual abolition. But Cape Town never developed a fully fledged abolitionist movement. The closest it came to an organised concern about slavery was the Cape of Good Hope Philanthropic Society, founded in 1828, with members drawn from the leading merchants and professionals of the town. The Society purchased the freedom of 126 slave children but was hardly radical in its thinking or methods. It disclaimed all intention of discussing the question of general emancipation and consciously avoided antagonising slave owners.[82]

In the event, general emancipation was decreed from London to take effect on 1 December 1834, but in ways which conciliated both slave owners and merchants. Compensation was to be paid to all registered slave owners, albeit by bills of credit in London. But more significantly, the Act's title also stated its purpose as 'promoting the Industry of the manumitted slaves'. Industry meant continued work as labourers. Slaves were to remain 'apprenticed' to their owners for a further six years (subsequently reduced to four) in order to provide a period of adjustment towards a wage-labour system for their owners (now termed 'employers'), although the right of physical punishment was transferred from the employer to new magistrates specially appointed from Britain to oversee the transition.

The apprenticeship system, which lasted from 1834 to 1838, ensured that emancipation made little difference to the daily lives of most of Cape Town's freed slaves. They were still obliged to work for their employers although, as before, men were often able to live and to earn with a high degree of independence. But what was new was the resentment which many apprentices felt at being kept in bondage after 1 December 1834. The 'spirit of insubordination', claimed one owner in 1835, 'was increasing'.[86] Some apprentices deserted their owners, arguing that freedom was theirs by right. Others refused to work under the same conditions as those of slavery, demanding wages, free time or a reduction of their workload. Leentje, owned by Otto Landsberg of Shortmarket Street, was brought to the magistrate for her 'insubordination' since emancipation day, and told him that 'she did not care for anyone, nor for the Tronk [jail], nor for any punishment' and that 'if she should stay in the Deponent's house a day longer she was certain she would hang herself'.[87]

On 1 December 1838, when apprenticeship ended, there were, as one Capetonian

'A SINGULAR MIX'   107

George Duff's painting of a Cape Town procession on the anniversary of slave emancipation. (MuseumAfrica 71/534)

later remembered from his childhood, 'a number of processions of Coloured people ... parading Cape Town, singing a Dutch song in which every verse ended "Victoria! Victoria! Daar waai de Engelschen vlaag." My mother asked a Coloured girl to go on an errand for her, she said "No, I won't, we are free today."'[88] According to one observer, the apprentices left their former employers on that day 'as if by arrangement'.[89] In practice this meant that many came from the rural hinterland to Cape Town in search of a new life. During the apprenticeship years, the Cape Town magistrate noted that 'most of the apprentices who run away from the country districts take refuge in Cape Town, to elude the search of their employers'.[90] In the town they were more easily able to conceal themselves in a place where there was a sizeable free-black population. This migratory process from countryside to town intensified after the end of apprenticeship. However, given the lack of skills or (usually) contacts in the town, most of the rural newcomers found it difficult to obtain employment and shelter. The *Ware Afrikaan* newspaper reported in early 1840 that 'an immense number of the late slaves have been, ever since their freedom, herding together in idleness and filth.'[91] Some work was obtained on the brickfields near the Castle, but wages were low and employment took place on a casual day-to-day basis. Similarly, some female migrants found domestic work, often replacing the urban female slaves who left domestic servitude after emancipation to set up their own households.

The freed slaves found themselves also in competition with a number of other labourers who had made their way to Cape Town in the early British period, for Cape Town employers had responded to the erosion of slavery by turning to other sources. One was a direct substitute for the slave trade. During the Napoleonic Wars, 27 ships belonging to both French and Portuguese slavers were intercepted in waters around the

Cape between 1806 and 1816, and their slave cargoes declared to be captured 'prizes' forfeit to the Crown. Over 2000 slaves, the large majority from Madagascar and Mozambique, were then indentured for a period normally of 14 years as 'prize negroes'. A number were taken by the army and navy and some were employed by the government, but the majority were allocated to private colonists and worked in circumstances which differed little from those of slavery itself. A disproportionate number were allocated to British residents, especially civil servants, merchants, retailers and businessmen; a few were allocated to free blacks, some of whom were themselves ex-slaves.

Although prize negroes were supposed to be offered instruction and training, in practice they were treated in the same way as slaves and their 'apprenticeship' meant little more than enforced labour. They were certainly in no more favourable an economic or social position in 1838 than the ex-slave 'apprentices' and in the post-emancipation period they merged into the labouring classes of the town. Most became casual workers although some entered into further contracts. Some may have established contact with a further influx of prize negroes from Mozambique and Madagascar who arrived in the colony from 1839, this time captured from Portuguese and Brazilian slavers.[93]

Under a proclamation of 1809, all Khoi in the colony had to be contracted to employers, whom they could not leave without a pass. In consequence 'vagabond' Khoi in the vicinity of Cape Town were arrested, placed in the Slave Lodge and forced to labour on public works projects for two months.[94] Over 100 male Khoi in 1820 were contracted as butchers' assistants, wagon drivers and carters, while 314 Khoi women were employed in domestic work.[95]

Ordinance 50 of 1828 encouraged the shift towards contracted wage labour in the town. It stipulated that workers were free to enter into contracts of between two months and a year, and were obliged to receive pay. While accommodation and clothing could also be provided, 'no liquor or tobacco shall be admitted as payment of money due as wages'. A number of Khoi, former prize negroes and free blacks entered into such contracts, mainly as herdsmen, house servants, wagon makers, butchers and gardeners, and freed slaves (now described as 'free people of colour') added to their numbers after 1838.

A further addition to Cape Town's workforce in the late 1830s was the presence of

Khoi hawkers in Cape Town in the late 1830s. Drawn by D'Oyly. (William Fehr B23)

SKELETONS FROM THE *PACQUET REAL*

On 18 May 1818 the Portuguese slaving brig the *Pacquet Real* was wrecked in severe storms in Table Bay. It was carrying 171 slaves from Mozambique to Salvador in Brazil. Some 25 bodies were washed ashore and hastily buried on ground near the Fort Knokke fortification. The surviving slaves were indentured as 'prize negroes' in the colony.

In the early 1950s, railway workmen digging at the site uncovered a number of skeletons, which are now in the South African Museum and have been analysed by anatomists and archaeologists at the University of Cape Town. Some of those buried without coffins had teeth which were 'decorated' by deliberate chipping to points in the custom of the Maconde, Yao and Macua of eastern–central Africa. Isotopic bone analysis also showed that they had lived primarily on a diet of sorghum, millet and maize of the kind used in that region. Skeletons found in nearby coffins showed no such teeth markings and bone analysis revealed a diet of predominantly European grains. It thus seems highly likely that the former are skeletons of the *Pacquet Real*'s drowned slaves.[92]

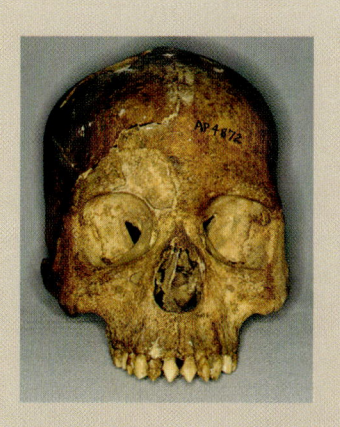

Skull with pointed maxillary incisors. (G. Cox, 'Skeletons found near the site of Fort Knokke', fig. 20)

'A SINGULAR MIX' 109

'The White Cattle Market'

Over 700 British children were brought to the Cape between 1833 and 1841 to work under indenture to local employers. They were part of a scheme organised by the Children's Friend Society in London, which sent 'surplus' poor and vagrant children from England's crowded city slums to colonies such as Canada, Australia and Mauritius. But the majority went to the Cape at a time when slave emancipation made many colonists keen to obtain new labourers. Most worked for farmers, but a number were taken by Cape Town employers. From the start the scheme was controversial. Capetonians feared, sometimes correctly, that they were taking young criminals into service. The first children to arrive were housed together with former government slaves and were made to line up in front of would-be employers in a process that was described as a 'white cattle market' and smacked strongly of slave auctions. A number of children deserted from their employers while others wrote home complaining of maltreatment. An uproar ensued in abolitionist Britain when the system became popularly associated with slavery, and support for the scheme dwindled.

The project had been strongly backed by John Fairbairn, advocate of slave emancipation, who believed that it would give English vagrant children an opportunity for a better life. However, its fate indicated that a society emerging from slavery was ill suited for free workers. The children sent to Australia and Canada fared considerably better.[98]

(C. D'Oyly; MuseumAfrica 74/2539/6)

Mfengus, who had been 'driven from Natal' to the eastern Cape. Although the way in which they came to the town is not known, a small community of between 20 and 40 were established in 'six or eight huts ... near the foot of Table Mountain' in 1839. Some worked at the town prison, but the majority, according to one visitor in 1839, were 'employed for rough work in the harbour'.[96] Their presence prefigured the later migration of eastern Cape workers to the docks in the mid-nineteenth century.

A number of apprenticed workers in Cape Town in the 1830s were white. Between 1817 and 1823 parties of British workers were brought to the Cape as indentured servants. Most were destined for the eastern Cape, but some got no further than Cape Town. The first party to arrive was brought by Benjamin Moodie; on arrival in Cape

D'Oyly's drawing of 1832 entitled 'Discussing the news of the day' depicts working-class white and black Capetonians talking together and engaged in the same occupations. The men carry fishing rods while the women hold baskets and pails. (MuseumAfrica 74/2539/62)

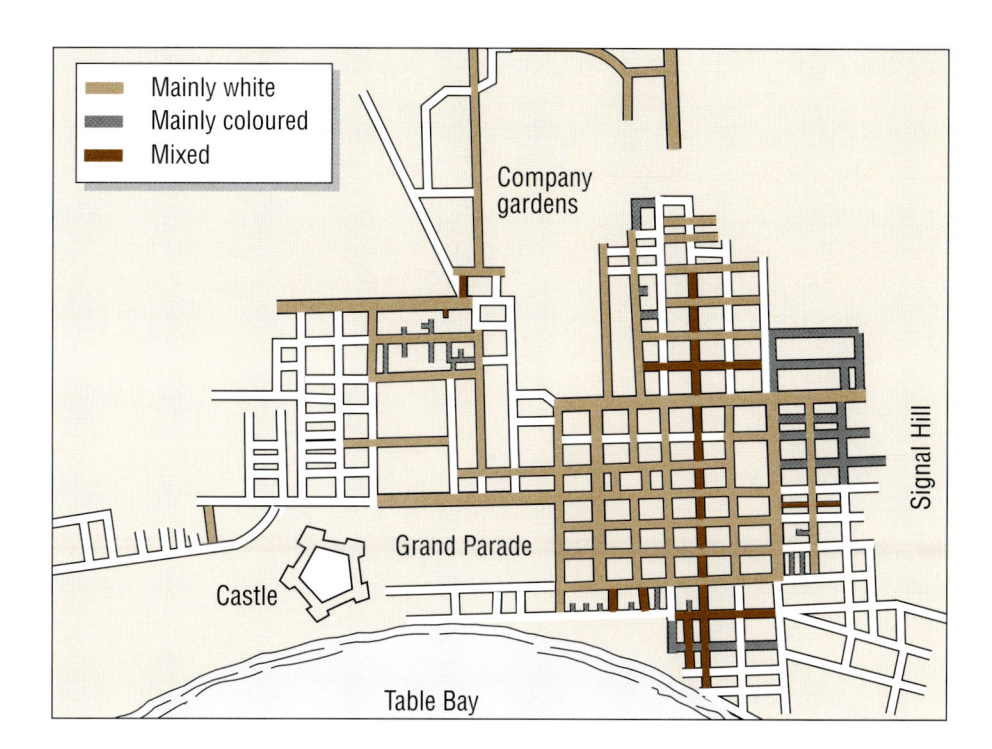

Racial patterns of residence in Cape Town in the 1830s. (After S. Judges, 'Poverty, living conditions and social relations')

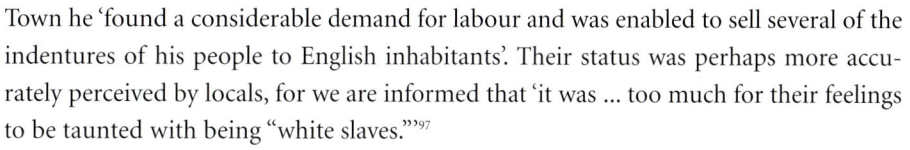

D'Oyly's 'Scene in the Herengraght' emphasises the racial divide between the white middle-class family and their black servants. (MuseumAfrica 74/2539/15)

Town he 'found a considerable demand for labour and was enabled to sell several of the indentures of his people to English inhabitants'. Their status was perhaps more accurately perceived by locals, for we are informed that 'it was ... too much for their feelings to be taunted with being "white slaves."'[97]

There was no fixed association of race and occupation in the 'singular mix' of early nineteenth-century Cape Town. This was especially true for its artisan and labouring classes, whose ranks were swollen by poorer British immigrants, especially those of Irish origin. Free-black and Dutch names featured equally in many artisan occupations and a sizeable number of messengers, servants and laundresses were of Dutch origin. And yet the large majority of the professional and administrative classes of the town were white. There was no formal segregation of residence and the poorer parts of the town were inhabited by people of many ethnicities: Sydney Street in 'Irish town', for example, was described in 1838 as a place 'where many low Irish and coloured people reside'.[99] But there was a growing tendency for some streets and parts of the town to be associated with primarily white or primarily 'coloured' residents, and it was comparatively rare for households to include both white and coloured residents (apart from live-in coloured servants in white households), even where the street itself was mixed.[100]

While white and black servants could be employed in the same household, the very fact that Lady Herschel found it noteworthy to comment in a letter of September 1834 that her racially mixed servants socialised together, indicates that it was seen as unusual: 'I have been fortunate in getting a nice white girl like Sarah to attend Carry and Bella [the Herschel children], so that in proof of the assertion (rather in contradiction) that white & black – slave & free would not mess together, the three women in my nursery now eating at one table are white, free half coloured & a coloured slave.'[101]

The racial supremacy of white slave owner/employer over black servant/slave had long been a feature of Cape Town households; 'no nursery tale exaggerates the inborn aversion a white has to a black,'[102] stated Lady Herschel of the town's employer classes. But the erosion of slavery in the 1820s and 1830s did little to help such a situation. Now that the VOC's legal categories of free–unfree and burgher–free black were removed,

'A SINGULAR MIX' 111

new means had to be found by the town's elite to maintain their exclusivity. Whereas earlier practices could, for instance, exclude slaves and free blacks from the theatre, give authorities the right to search free-black homes, and impose separate fire-watching duty on free blacks rather than burgher militia service, by the 1830s such categories were no longer applicable.[103]

Instead, the census records after 1836 started classifying Capetonians as 'white' and 'coloured'. Although middle-class white Capetonians tended to distance themselves from the 'labouring classes' rather than from 'coloureds', it was increasingly the case that their identity was also racial. The debates around the ending of slavery were not often explicitly racist, but it was a British immigrant, one 'Jones of Bloemhof', who opposed the abolitionists by arguing that 'Negro' slaves were 'half-reasoning brutes' whose enslavement was justified on the ground that they were a racially inferior species.[104] At the same time those whose class position clearly contravened the association of whiteness with social position, such as Irish labourers and domestics or the British 'white slaves', found themselves stigmatised.

Two Towns

The 'singular mix' of the population of Cape Town was reflected in its physical appearance. Early nineteenth-century Cape Town still had a very Dutch appearance. Edward Blount commented in 1821 that 'an Englishman is reminded that he is not in his own

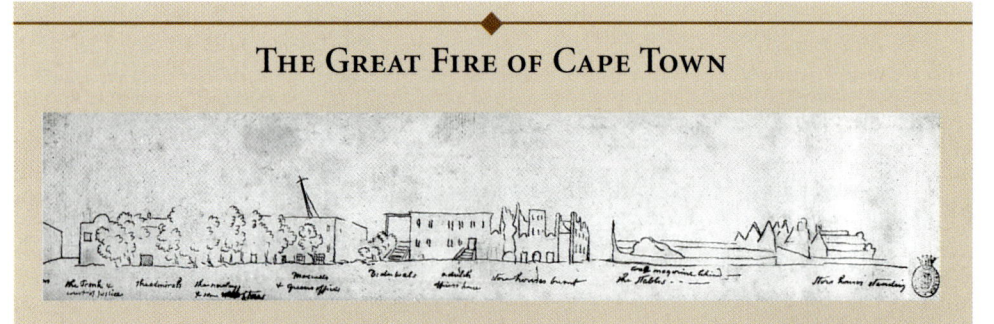

The Great Fire of Cape Town

Lady Anne Barnard's sketch of the storehouses burnt down in the fire of 1798. (SAL INIL 7057)

On 23 November 1798, Major-General Dundas was installed as new governor of the Cape. Late that evening the town was 'thrown into the greatest consternation' by a fire along the shore side of the Parade Ground which engulfed the cavalry stables. It was soon spread by a strong south-easter wind to the East India Company warehouses and a number of private dwellings and threatened the jail and Customs House.

Samuel Hudson helped to carry out the customs registers and papers onto the street. Soldiers looted the stores' brandy casks even 'while the roofs and floors were in a falling state and every aperture red with conflagration ... and these wretches blowing the flame away while they quafd the almost boiling beverage'. Hudson enjoyed some of the roasted salt pork found among the ruins two days later. Damages were estimated at over £4000.

Many believed that 'this dreadful and all consuming conflagration' was the result of arson intended for the barracks. Although a subsequent inquiry concluded that the cause was accidental, nervous Capetonians continued to believe as late as the 1830s that slave runaways were behind the fire.[106]

The fire had some practical effects on Cape Town's architecture. Not only were the Company stores and stables rebuilt, but regulations were issued forbidding new thatch roofs and ordering wooden shutters to be mounted on the insides of windows, since it was believed that fire could easily spread from one outside shutter to the next.[107]

The fish market in 1832, drawn by D'Oyly. (CA A3131)

The New Market in the early morning, painted by Leon Sabatier. (William Fehr C17)

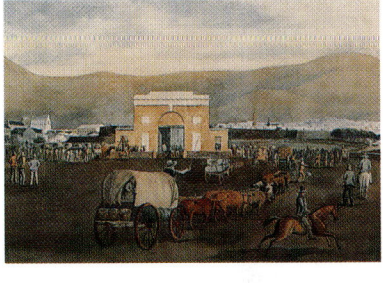

Public auction in the Heerengracht in 1832, drawn by D'Oyly. (MuseumAfrica 74/2539/54)

country by the white-washed houses, the want of pavement and flags [paving stones] in the streets and a few other peculiarities'.[105]

But the period did see a bid to refashion Cape Town's main streets in a style thought to be more appropriate to a growing commercial centre rather than a rural market town. Specialised retail stores appeared, especially around Greenmarket Square, on the previously prestigious and residential Heerengracht, and at the lower end of Bree Street. Some of the canals, which smelt in summer and attracted mosquitoes, were filled in and the main thoroughfares paved. In 1831 lamps were introduced to Berg (modern St George's) Street and soon appeared in the other main streets of the town.

Great concern was taken to banish disorderliness from the streets. A campaign was waged in the 1820s to eradicate pigs and stray dogs who 'live and grow fat on the offal of the fish market and of the butchery; and after a nightly repose ... rush tumultuously at dawn to the sea shore with the cry, but not the melody of a pack of hounds'.[108] As visiting farmers driving their ox wagons through the town were held largely responsible for the degeneration of the streets, in 1819 a new market was set up at the point where the 'Great Road' (later Sir Lowry Road) from the hinterland met the Castle. Here farmers were obliged to sell their produce, thus keeping them outside the centre of the town. The less disruptive vegetable market continued to take place in Greenmarket Square, while the fish market remained a lively trading place down by the shoreline.

The coexistence of old and new was visibly demonstrated by the building of the Commercial Exchange, symbol of the pretensions of the new mercantile class: it faced the Parade Ground, the exchange market of Dutch Cape Town, and the Heerengracht, where public auctions were still regularly held.

British newcomers also started to shape their homes to suit their own style. The British army officer Robert Percival, writing as early as 1804, commented: 'many new houses were erected by our countrymen, who came out here to settle on commercial business or in the service of our government. Those houses are handsomely built after the English style of brick retaining the natural colour, which is certainly much better on many accounts than having them whitened; a custom that in the hot season produces an insufferable glare.'[109] Even though many houses retained their Dutch exteriors, British styles and fashions were beginning to emerge inside. As early as 1799 Samuel Hudson could write: 'Houses which so lately were crowded with the heavy Dutch furniture now have the light elegant appearance of a London residence, everything seems new modelled English fashions ... marbled chimney pieces, polished stoves, English carpets, mahogany furniture of every description takes place of the heavy cumbrous antique conveniences of 1790.'[110]

114　Cape Town 1795–1840

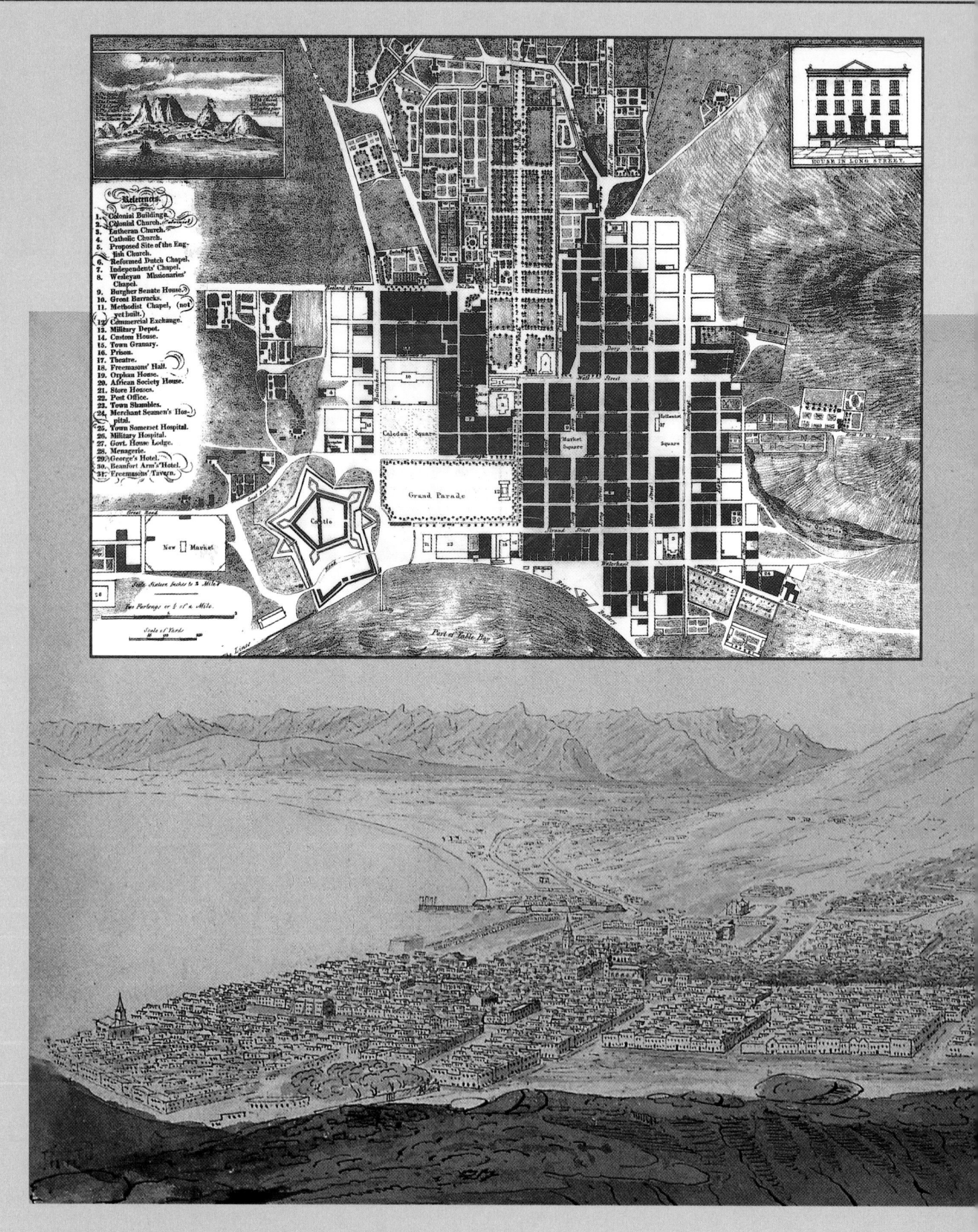

A Panorama and the First Surveyed Street Map of Cape Town

This map drawn by George Thompson in 1826 was the first properly surveyed street plan of Cape Town. The grid plan of streets inherited from the early VOC layout is still evident. (Thompson, *Travels and Adventures in Southern Africa*, London, 1827)

The panorama of Cape Town from Lion's Rump was drawn by F.B., an unknown artist, on 18 June 1832. Clearly visible are the new market place beyond the Castle and the Catholic chapel on the outskirts of the town. There are few tall buildings (the tower of the Lutheran Church in Strand Street stands out over the rest). The public spaces of the Parade Ground and the market squares are clearly demarcated.

Although there was some new building by the New Market and towards Green Point, no major physical expansion had taken place since the eighteenth century. Farms and open spaces still surrounded the town. Most people still lived in the tightly packed streets of the old centre, hemmed in by the surrounding mountains. (© The Brenthurst Library ART.324/8)

St George's Church under construction, *c.* 1833. Although the site alongside the Company gardens in Wale Street had been earmarked for this purpose as early as 1821 and was marked as such on Thompson's map of 1826, the church was opened only in 1834. This painting by J.C. Poortermans shows the water channels running down the side of Wale Street as well as the unpaved road. It contrasts strikingly with Thomas Bowler's depiction of the same spot in the 1860s (see pp. 184–5). (CA E4371)

The new St George's Church, opened in 1834, was modelled, as frequently in British colonial outposts, on the neoclassical style of London's St Pancras Church and St Martin-in-the-Fields. Painting by W.H.F. Langschmidt. (William Fehr CB25)

St Andrew's 'Scotch' Church, completed in 1829, copied the classical revivalist designs of the Glasgow architect 'Greek' Thomson. Watercolour by De Meillon. (William Fehr C84)

A house in Castle Street, drawn in 1841, shows the blend of Dutch stoep with Georgian window frames, chimney pots and tile roof. (William Fehr GH81/3)

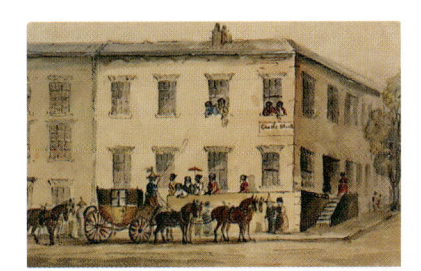

The stoep, 'a custom of Dutch origin ... unfortunately however of late finds less imitation in the increasingly predominant English style despite its being a suitable and beneficial institution in the prevailing climate', according to Ferdinand Krauss in 1838.[111] Large glass window frames replaced small shuttered windows, plastered ceilings succeeded open beams, and thatch roofs gave way to tile. A common new feature of house interiors was the division of large rooms with multiple functions into separate drawing- and dining-rooms. This often required the building of new interior passages and staircases and sometimes an additional storey. Staffordshire porcelain replaced Oriental ceramics at the dinner parties of the wealthy, where the new habit of seating men and women alternately round a formal table was known as 'dining promiscuously' by Capetonians more used to the eighteenth-century habit of family eating.[112]

Some Cape Town British settlers went to great lengths to reshape their houses into a more British form: '[Our house] has undergone a thorough repair. We have built three new rooms upstairs and knocked the dining room and drawing room into one, built a new breakfast room, stable, coach house and a forage room, turned other rooms into store room, pantry and kitchen, also a new staircase and entire new roof of English slates. Our old breakfast room is turned into a dining room, and all but two rooms are ceil[ing]ed. You would not know the house again if you were to see it.'[113]

Sir George Yonge had the interior of Government House radically altered to match the aristocratic households of Regency London, so that, in Lady Anne Barnard's words, 'instead of finding a dirty old house with a perpendicular staircase, up which Lord Macartney [the previous governor] hopped, gout and all, like a parrot to its perch, he will find rooms well painted & prepared with paper of my Lady Yonge's own choosing ... an excellent staircase the fellow of Lady Buckingham in St James Square; instead of gardens productive only of weeds, his are now full stockd with everything – fish ponds, made at an expense – we shan't talk of that now ...'[114]

WYNBERG

By the 1830s Wynberg was developing as a distinct community. Its origins lay in the 'garrison village' which grew up around the military camp of the late 1790s; it was particularly popular with the 'Indians'. By the 1820s, as tradespeople and speculators began buying land in the area, including many British artisan immigrants who aspired to property ownership, the village lost its military character. In the 1830s and 1840s a number of free blacks also obtained plots here as well as in the nearby areas of Plumstead and Diep River.[115] The influx of slave compensation money gave a boost to property development all along the Liesbeek and adverts for divided property holdings appeared in the press particularly in 1838 and 1839.[116]

Catherine Cloete's pencil drawing of Wynberg in 1853. (SAL INIL 7096)

'A SINGULAR MIX'   117

SIR JOHN WYLDE'S DRAWING-ROOM

D'Oyly's illustration of 'Music in a drawing room' depicts the interior of Sir John Wylde's Hope Street house in 1832. It is a striking example of the influence of British Regency style on Cape Town houses. In the distinct drawing-room the floral wallpaper, elaborately draped curtains, edge-to-edge carpeting, fireplace and hearth rug, Grecian sofa, chintz upholstered armchairs and thin-legged tables are all features which would not have been found in eighteenth-century Cape Town homes.[117] The picture was drawn at the height of a scandal in the town. Sir John Wylde's daughter (possibly the figure playing the harp) was believed to have given birth to an illegitimate child and there were suggestions of incest. D'Oyly's image of domestic bliss may have been intended to contradict such gossip. Certainly it gave his choice of subject a particular interest.[118]

(CA A3100)

Many of the wealthier British newcomers built residences outside the centre of town in areas previously occupied by market gardens and farms. Some of the largest houses were erected along the road to Green Point while villas in Newlands and Rondebosch were also becoming fashionable. Edward Blount described the road from Cape Town to Wynberg in 1821 as 'lined on either side with the villas of the merchants and more opulent tradesmen of the town, who drive their buggies to and fro like our London citizens and repose from the fatigues of the day in these rural retirements. The houses have large gardens and vineyards attached to them, with here and there a few acres of arable and pasture land.'[119]

From the 1780s, when the presence of foreign troops raised demands for accommodation in the city, wasteland on the slopes of Signal Hill had been parcelled out in plots for housing construction in the area that was to be known as the 'Bo-Kaap'.[120] As early as 1800 it appears that a number of free blacks were living there, and the first mosques and

Rustenburg, the country residence for Dutch governors at Rondebosch. In the early nineteenth century a number of similar villas were built by the mercantile elite on the road to Wynberg. Drawing by D'Oyly. (CA A3046)

A sketch from sea, made c. 1840, of the land on the Atlantic coast, later known as Green Point and Sea Point, which was beginning to be developed for residential housing. In 1813, 28 plots on the lower slopes of Signal Hill were sold for private development. The merchant Pieter Woutersen and the attorney Jacobus Wessels built large residences, David Kuuhl opened a retail shop and pottery kiln, while Charles de Villet, a Frenchman who had arrived in Cape Town in 1803 and ran a shop in Long Street that boasted a stuffed hippopotamus and mermaid, set up a new menagerie with a lion and lioness, rhino, zebra and leopard. In 1835 Judge William Menzies bought the old Society House at Sea Point and converted it into a private residence. (UCT BC923 C1)

madaris (Muslim schools) were established in this part of the town. But it was not until the 1840s that speculative building really got under way both here and on the other side of the Castle in District Six. In the early nineteenth century, most of Cape Town's population still lived in the old centre of the town.

In Cape Town in 1820, three out of every four inhabitants were tenants. Owner-occupancy tended to dominate in the commercial and wealthier districts, such as the Heerengracht, the upper ends of Strand and Wale streets, and Green Point as well as a number of residences in Long, Castle, Hout and Longmarket streets, but the poorer districts around the waterfront, Constitution Hill, Roeland Street, and the lanes and alleyways between the main thoroughfares were almost all owned by landlords. Some of the *steegs* (alleyways) were owned entirely by one person. Many of the 'hire houses' that filled the *steegs* were in an appalling condition as their chief function was 'for the pur-

The Port Office along the shore was surrounded by the cramped housing of this poorer part of the town. Drawing by D'Oyly. (MuseumAfrica 74/259/5)

'A SINGULAR MIX' 119

The water pump at the top of the Heerengracht, 1833. Pumps were a centre of social life for Cape Town's poor, as hours were spent collecting this vital commodity. A mass of municipal regulations dealt with the management of these sources of water, regulating the size of the vessels which might be used, the hours the pumps were open, and the use made of them. Drawing by D'Oyly. (William Fehr B72)

pose of yielding to the proprietor the greatest possible amount of rent'.[121] The practice of subletting was also widespread: 'houses comprising only 3 or 4 rooms are often let and sublet to 5 or 6 families or persons: 2 or 3 distinct parties frequently occupy one small room ... the chief renter of the house loses all control over his lodgings.'[122]

For Cape Town was rapidly becoming two towns. Behind and between the neat grid of streets of the colonial town was a maze of *steegs* – lanes, alleys, squares and culs de sac. Although some parts of the town were particularly crowded, such as the area behind the fishing beach at Roggebaai, even the more prestigious areas contained slum properties. In many places every square foot of spare ground was filled with shacks and sheds housing people and their livestock. They were crammed also into the basements and cellars of the old houses. In 1840 'even stables, cellars, and holes under stoeps ... [were] in many instances let as human habitations ...'[123] Squatting was already a common problem. An area 'behind the R.C. Chapel' (the neighbourhood of Constitution Hill) was 'covered with hovels'.[124] In 1829 a group of people had been found 'sleeping (as is their habit) near one of the Batteries', because of 'their being without home or employment'.[125] Deaths from exposure were by no means unknown.

This was not a town of tenements though some were built later on. But living conditions could be appalling. Most houses were small. Ventilation was often inadequate or, in the cellars, non-existent, so that 'the smoke finds its way out – either through the door – or the flooring of the room above'. There was no sanitation. In the absence of any 'expedient for draining off the filth' it might be 'left to putrify' in a yard or allowed to 'meander across the street'.[126] Inspectors in 1840 reported 'in several cases quantities of rotting fish and human excrement in the very sleeping apartment'.[127] Such examples may have been extreme. But it was in general difficult for people to keep clean when the only water supply consisted of public fountains or the 63 pumps 'dispersed over the town'.[128] Although the old wooden water-pipes had been replaced by lead in 1799, none reached the poorer alleyways of the town.[129]

Poverty was becoming more visible in early nineteenth-century Cape Town. In part this was because of the migration of impoverished families from Britain and from the rural Cape hinterland, the increasing numbers of manumitted slaves, and the absence of regular employment for the town's labourers. But poverty is relative. There had always

'Even stables, cellars, and holes under stoeps ... [were] in many instances let as human habitations ...'
Wardmaster report for area around Longmarket Street, 1840

Cape Town was a harsh place for the old, the sick and the poor in the first decades of British rule. Drawing by D'Oyly. (MuseumAfrica 74/2539/47)

been Capetonians with few resources. It was the emergence of a new middle-class elite in the town that highlighted the existence of the poor. Poverty presented a challenge for those who wanted Cape Town to be a model of colonial prosperity and order.

There were many references by the 1830s to the difficulties of survival. On an income of 1s 6d a day a single man could live in a 'poor but respectable house' but must 'be content to eat *bakfish* and rice, six days out of seven'.[130] The minimum income for a family, to cover basic food, fuel and rent, was 6d per person per day.[131] Many families struggled to obtain this. Because much employment in Cape Town was casual, income might be intermittent. On the other hand, many people supplemented their incomes by working at more than one job. In addition, often more than one member of a family worked. J.H. Lesar, who owned a fish-curing business, employed over 100 people, 'chiefly consisting of the wives and children of the poor fishermen'.[132]

Victorian investigators recognised the links between poverty and ill health early in the century. Sickness reduced the incomes of the poor, driving them further into destitution and making them still more susceptible to disease. In 1839, when a severe measles epidemic struck the town, killing an estimated 1500 people,[133] the *Commercial Advertiser* commented on the 'squalid poverty' of many of the victims and warned of the 'danger to which ... their crowded and destitute condition' exposed them, should 'a visitation of a more deadly character, pestilence, small-pox, or cholera ... fall upon us'.[134] The warning was borne out when smallpox broke out the following year. Its incidence in the slums was at least double that of the more affluent parts of the town. Ward 13, a developing area around the New Market on the outskirts of the town with 'very few narrow passages and lanes', had a case rate of only 5 per cent and a mortality rate of 0.6 per cent compared with Ward 1 on the foreshore, where about 34 per cent of the population were affected and at least 3 per cent died.[135]

Smallpox was a dramatic pointer to the state of Cape Town. But what killed its inhabitants more regularly was the endemic diseases of the pre-industrial town such as dysentery and diarrhoea in various forms, pulmonary complaints and intermittent epidemics of fever. Diphtheria, whooping-cough, scarlet fever, measles and rheumatic fever were also common killers amongst those who were debilitated by poverty, although Cape Town escaped cholera and major typhoid epidemics at this stage.

The average life expectancy at birth in the 1830s ranged from 23 to 40 years. Some groups may have been particularly vulnerable. A visitor to the Cape commented of Mozambique porters that 'strong though these men are, they seldom live beyond thirty years with this sort of labour'.[136]

Cape Town was a harsh place for the old, the sick and the poor in the first decades of British rule. The system of poor relief administered in the VOC period survived: in 1820 several houses in Pepper Street were occupied by those in receipt of maintenance from the 'church fund', and there was an orphanage in Long Street. Benefit societies for specific communities were established. In 1820 the St Andrew's Friendly Society was founded to provide relief and medical aid for the Scottish community and in 1829 the St Patrick's Society was set up to accomplish the same for the Irish. In 1843 St Stephen's Church, with a congregation mainly of ex-slaves, counted 880 members who subscribed from 6d to 1s a month to cover the cost of medicines in time of sickness and a burial grant in the event of death.[137]

The strongest philanthropic impetus came from the missionaries and evangelicals. In their view, care of the soul was closely allied to the relief of suffering: philanthropy was an expression of piety, benevolence a moral obligation. The Ladies' Benevolent Society

'The greatest number of ... cases of [smallpox] infection and death was of course found in the narrow lanes and alleys.'
Wardmaster report for area around Barrack Street, 1840

The Long Street orphanage, photographed in the 1870s. (CA J76)

was founded by Jane Philip, wife of the Congregationalist minister and missionary John Philip. Its aim was 'to alleviate [through monetary aid] the sufferings of deserving persons ... they have also procured work for others and thus freed the public from many calls on their liberality'.[138] It was often concerned with the 'genteel poverty' of immigrants who had been 'plunged into unlooked for calamities'.[139] Fundraising was initially confined largely to a female management committee and money was solicited from the respectable elite of the town.

But only a tiny number of Cape Town's poor benefited from such public philanthropy. Most could find institutional aid only at the prison or the hospital. Retirement being an unfamiliar concept, the aged were expected to support themselves until they were too sick or too physically handicapped to do so. Elderly ex-slaves were particularly unfortunate, for they often had no resources and no family. Many ended their days in the Pauper Establishment, where life was bleak and basic. Even a request for some snuff to make life more tolerable was spurned by the government with the request 'to cease any further representations on the ... subject'.[140]

The Somerset Hospital became the catch-all for Cape Town's indigent sick. This hospital had been founded in 1818 by the remarkable Dr Samuel Bailey as the first civilian hospital in Cape Town. Funded by private subscription, built on the margins of the town on the road to Green Point, it was implicitly intended for the outcasts of society – merchant seamen and slaves, paupers and 'lunatics'. Understandably it did not prosper in parsimonious Cape Town and in 1821 Bailey was forced to sell it to the Burgher Senate, which removed Bailey and his English staff. In the hands of the Burgher Senate, as Dr James Barry, the colonial medical inspector, later complained, the hospital became an institution controlled by foreigners, a lunatic asylum, an almshouse and an abode for the menial servants of the Burgher Senate.

The old Somerset Hospital, built in 1818. This photograph was taken in 1934. (SAL, *Cape Times*)

Dr Samuel Bailey (1778–1864)

Dr Bailey's career typified the uncertainty of life for the rising middle classes in early British Cape Town and illustrates the allegiances of the enlightened reformer of the day.

Bailey had been a naval surgeon, his service including a spell on Nelson's flagship. He had retired on half-pay to Cape Town in 1814 as 'surgeon and man midwife'. He was integrated into local society by his marrying first a Dutch woman, Hester Aletta van Reenen, and secondly Rebecca Manuel, the widow of a German immigrant.

An energetic reformer, he founded first the Somerset Hospital and subsequently a Merchant Seamen's Hospital close by. Both were financial failures but he eventually

'Dr Bailey on his rounds.' (SAL INIL 6899)

became part of the colonial establishment after 1827 as a member of the Colonial Medical Committee and surgeon to the Town Prison, the House of Correction, the Pauper Establishment and the Vaccine Institution in addition to running the Somerset Hospital. He also became Cape Town's district surgeon. For all this he was paid £300 a year. His private practice included a position as surgeon to the Good Hope Fire and Life Assurance Society.

Typical of middle-class reformers, Bailey was member of a host of societies, in his case the South African Medical Society, the South African Literary Society, the Temperance Society and the Committee for the Encouragement of Juvenile Emigration.

Bailey died at 86, beloved, said his obituary, by the poor and needy sick of Cape Town.[141]

'Going to the Protestant Church', drawn by D'Oyly in 1833. Before the opening of St George's Church in 1834, the Dutch Reformed church was also used for Anglican services. (William Fehr B71)

~
RELIGIOUS AFFILIATIONS IN CAPE TOWN, 1841
~

The VOC's opposition to any religious practice apart from Reformed Christianity was removed in the early nineteenth century. Estimates made of the religious affiliation of the inhabitants of Cape Town and its surrounding area in 1841 thus show a considerable diversification since the eighteenth century. (The descriptions used are those of the original source.)[142]

Dutch Reformed	15,000
English Episcopalians	4,200
Scotch Presbyterians	750
Lutherans	1,800
Roman Catholics	676
Protestant Dissenters	2,069
Mahomedans	6,492
Heathen	1,541

The Roman Catholic chapel in Harrington Street in 1833. The chapel drew many of its members from nearby 'Irish town' and from Scottish and Irish troops in the garrison. Drawing by D'Oyly. (CA A3011)

RELIGION

One indicator of the increasing heterogeneity of Cape Town's population was the profusion of religious bodies and activities. While the Dutch Reformed and Lutheran churches retained sizeable followings among the Dutch and German inhabitants, new Christian denominations emerged at this time, each catering predominantly to new ethnic groups: English Anglicans, Irish Catholics and Scottish Presbyterians. By the 1830s, the Anglican congregation of St George's Church was over a thousand strong. According to one German observer, the association of the Anglican Church with the British establishment was such that 'a large proportion' of the Dutch and German inhabitants 'seem to regard it as refined to visit the English church as well'.[143]

The presence of Scottish regiments gave impetus to the holding of Presbyterian services by 1813, and this, together with a growing number of Scottish immigrants to the town, led to the foundation of St Andrew's 'Scottish' Church in 1827. One English visitor admired the building but thought the preaching of its minister 'so metaphysical that he is scarcely intelligible; and this, to an English ear, is increased by his strong Scotch accent and manner. His sermons consequently require a great effort of the attention.'[144] When the legal term of apprenticeship for former slaves ended, the church made a concerted effort to attract converts and by 1841 some 134 ex-slaves had been added to the church roll.[145]

Both Scottish and Irish troops were the mainstay of the regular Catholic masses held at a chapel in Harrington Street from 1822. There was no permanent priest and not until Bishop Patrick Raymund Griffith arrived from Ireland in 1838, setting up a Catholic Academy and founding St Mary's Cathedral, was Catholicism firmly established. Most of the names listed in the first church census of 1838–42 lived in the 'Irish town' areas around Plein Street and Constitution Hill. The early Catholic Church served a distinctly poorer community than other denominations, although not exclusively so: the colonial secretary Christopher Bird was a Catholic.[146]

The rise of evangelicalism, both in its Dutch Pietist form and in such denominations as the British Congregationalists and Methodists, prompted a new interest in missionary work. In 1799 the Zuid-Africaans Genoodschap (ZAG) was established in the town with the aim of converting slaves and other 'heathen'. However, the ZAG did not meet with wholehearted support from the main Reformed congregation. It had difficulty in finding a missionary leader and for a long time was forced to meet in private houses, subsequently renting rooms at the corner of Hout and Long streets. But by 1804 it had managed to raise sufficient funds to open a chapel in Long Street 'for the Christian instruction of slaves', although objections from the Reformed Church meant that it was not permitted to describe itself as a formal congregation.[147]

The London Missionary Society, representing the evangelical thrust of a variety of 'dissenting' churches in Britain, was established in Cape Town in 1811 under the leadership of the Rev. George Thom.[148] In 1822 it opened the Union (or 'Independent') Chapel in Church Square, which was run on Congregational lines. Its members were predominantly English in origin, and the only coloured members were their servants. A Sunday school was set up and included a number of coloured children, but continued conflict with the ZAG prevented any evangelising of slaves and the focus of attention was directed instead at convicts, the poorer immigrants and their illegitimate children. A particular concern was the free-black fishermen of Roggebaai in the 1830s; the Union Chapel also held services in Malagasy at this period for some of the 'prize negroes'. By the time of emancipation, the LMS was concerned at the lack of proselytisation among the freed apprentices, many of whom were turning instead to Islam.

The rapid growth of Islam was one of the most striking features of early nineteenth-century Cape Town. Although Muslims had formed a significant part of the Dutch settlement, it was only in the early British period that a distinctive and sizeable Muslim community began to be visible. From less than 1000 in 1800, the number of Muslims in Cape Town grew to 3000 in 1822 and then doubled to over 6000 by 1840.[149] This growth was the result not just of natural increase, but of conversion, especially among the slave and labouring classes of the town. Several commentators at the time believed that this was because owners neglected the religious instruction of their slaves. The Earl of Caledon, the governor, commented in 1808 that many of the slaves who had been imported from Mozambique in the preceding decades, 'arriving here in total ignorance, and being permitted to remain in that state ... for the most part embrace the Mahomedan faith'.[150]

But to view Muslim conversion as solely the result of a lack of missionary effort on the part of Christians is to ignore the very real social as well as spiritual benefits that Islam offered to its adherents in early nineteenth-century Cape Town. The Muslim community transcended divisions of class, if not race, and was marked by an increasing number of institutional structures which gave support and identity to its members, both slave and free.

Although there had been Muslim slaves, exiles and free blacks in the town from the seventeenth century, this sense of community only began to emerge markedly in the late VOC period. The growing toleration of the authorities partly explains this: although 'the Dutch certainly did not welcome Islam neither did they try to destroy it'.[151] There is evidence that celebrations of the Prophet's birthday and the end of Ramadan were held in the homes of free blacks in 1772.[152] By the 1790s regular Friday prayers were being conducted in the stone quarries at the foot of Signal Hill.[153]

A key figure in the development of Islam at this stage was Imam Abdullah ibn Qadi Abd al-Salam (known as the 'Tuan Guru' or 'Master Teacher'). He was banished to Robben Island from Tidore in 1780 for conspiring with the British against the Dutch. While incarcerated there, he wrote *Ma'rifa-t al-Islam wa al-Iman* (Manifestations of Islam and the Faith), an explication of the law and practices of the Ash'ari creed of

Thomas Baines's painting of the interior of St George's Church, *c.* 1845. John Fawcett, who lived in Cape Town for eighteen months in 1835–6, admired the new 'handsome building' though was less impressed by the preaching of its minister, which 'is, I regret to say, uncertain and often unsound'. There were a thousand seats, of which some 300 at the back were reserved for the poor. (MuseumAfrica 39/51)

Sunnism, which stressed acceptance by faith of Allah's will in the world – a creed particularly suited to the experience of exiles and slaves.[154] It also included discussion of amulets and sacred cures, thus combining philosophical teaching with the more secret and mystical faith that had developed amongst Cape Town's underclass when the open practice of Islam was forbidden.

Tuan Guru's teaching and philosophy were to provide the basis of Cape Islam until the mid-to-late nineteenth century, for he presided over the shift from a hidden and mystical form of Islam to a more open and public practice of the faith. After his release in 1792 he set up a *madrassah* (religious school; pl. *madaris*) at his house in Dorp Street, where the Qur'an was recited and Arabic taught.

As yet, none of this had secured approval from the authorities. But in 1797 the new British administration gave permission for the conversion of a warehouse in Dorp Street into the Auwal Mosque with Tuan Guru as imam. In 1804 the Batavian government guaranteed religious freedom in a desire to co-opt the growing numbers of Muslims into a special artillery unit to defend the Cape against British invasion, and granted land on the slopes of Signal Hill for a Muslim cemetery. By 1824 there were two mosques, five smaller prayer rooms and four *madaris*; by 1832 the number of Muslim schools had increased to twelve.[155] The Dorp Street *madrassah*, which had 372 slave and free-black pupils by 1807 and almost 500 by 1825, 'initiated a prolific process of literacy among Cape slaves'.[156]

Greater freedom of religion after the end of VOC restrictions accounts for this emergence of open Islamic practice. But there is no doubt that slave and free-black conversions were the prime cause of expansion. Some of the reasons related to legislative restrictions. Slaves, forbidden to marry under Christian rites until 1823, were able to obtain recognition of their unions under Islam. Male Muslims could take several wives and several female slaves obtained manumission through conversion and marriage to such men.[157] But there were more direct reasons for conversion. Although some Muslims were themselves slave owners, the Muslim community nonetheless offered slave converts an equality of status otherwise denied to them. The increasing freedom of social contact between slaves and free blacks explains the identity of interests of which Islam was a clear marker.

As the bonds of direct control under slavery slackened, access to Muslim meetings and services increased. By the mid-1830s, former slave owners found it difficult to restrain their Muslim apprentices. A number absented themselves on Fridays without permission and insisted on observance of the Ramadan fast. At the celebration of Eid in 1835, many apprentices ignored the protest of their owners and went to the Muslim 'priests' and houses owned by free blacks.[158] January, an apprentice who had constantly absented himself from his owner since 1 December 1834, was brought before the authorities in February of the following year because, although he had been 'brought up in the Christian religion ... [he had] latterly chosen to turn Malay'. When refused permission to attend 'the Malay Church' on Fridays, he replied defiantly that he would 'run away instead and his Master might make a convict of him'.[159]

Some of the distinctive features of Cape Islamic practice may have resulted from the

The interior of the Auwal Mosque, Cape Town's oldest mosque. This photograph of the decorations for the Prophet's birthday was taken in 1961. (*Cape Argus*)

An 1884 engraving of a Cape Town *khalifa* ritual. The depiction was much influenced by late-nineteenth-century white prejudices that Muslims were alien, fanatical and potentially dangerous. (SAL, *The Graphic*)

Cape Town's second mosque, known as the 'Palm Tree Mosque', was founded in a Long Street house bought by Frans van Bengal and Jan van Bougies in 1807. They led a breakaway from the Auwal Mosque after Jan van Bougies failed to secure succession as imam to Tuan Guru. Jan was a freed slave and Arabic teacher who appears in the records as a tallow chandler and 'Malay priest'. Rivalry between the two congregations continued into the 1830s, with the imams of each claiming senior status. Jan van Bougies died in 1846 at the age of 112. (CA E2956)

large number of slave converts. The medium of instruction and of the early manuals of ritual was Melayu, the lingua franca of the islands of South-East Asia from which many of the slaves came, although at a later date use was made of Afrikaans, of the form coming into wide use among Cape Town's labouring classes, albeit written in Arabic script. The *ratiep* or *khalifa* rituals, in which skewers were pierced into the flesh of entranced worshippers, owed much to Hindu-influenced practices of South and South-East Asia, as did the *rampi-sny*, the cutting of orange leaves by women on the Prophet's birthday. Both were recorded by observers in Cape Town in the late eighteenth century.[160] The *barakat* tradition of taking food to those who could not attend special ceremonies may also have derived from the large numbers of slaves who could not obtain their masters' permission to go in person.

Islam was not yet apparent in the architecture or spatial layout of the town. Mosques still looked like ordinary houses and minarets were only added in the mid-century. Although a number of Muslim free blacks were beginning to concentrate in the area later known as the Bo-Kaap, many Muslim slaves were scattered across the town before emancipation. But what was becoming distinctive was a Muslim style of dress, which almost all visitors remarked on and many artists depicted. The *toedang* conical straw worn by men over the red *kopdoek*, and the *kaparring* wooden sandals, had originated in South-East Asia, but by the 1820s they were becoming broader markers of Islam, being also adopted by African converts.[164] Imams and those of higher status wore turbans.

The use of South-East Asian dress and language (namely Melayu) by many Muslims led outsiders to misname them 'Malays'. This generic term was used in the East Indies to

---

THE EMERGENCE OF AFRIKAANS

Many different languages were heard in the streets of nineteenth-century Cape Town. Alongside Dutch, German and many varieties of English, Melayu was spoken – a lingua franca for slaves and free blacks. There are clear signs that a local creole was developing, influenced by this medley of languages, which was to become known as Afrikaans. Dutch visitors began to comment on the distinctiveness of the language they heard; van Burgst disapproved in 1806 of the habit of leaving Dutch children in the care of slave nurses, from whom, 'besides acquiring a number of bad habits, it learns to speak a Dutch bastard language which it always retains'.[161] By the 1820s the Netherlands-born court interpreter commented that this language, 'entirely new to me', not only was spoken by the lower classes of the town but 'is not entirely strange to even the more civilised of the Christian and leading classes'.[162] Although 'pure Dutch' continued to be taught in Cape Town schools and was used in writing by the urban elite, it is clear that Afrikaans was triumphing in the streets and homes of the city.

Afrikaans had replaced Melayu in the Muslim *madaris* by 1815. The earliest written Afrikaans texts are Muslim student notebooks and ritual manuals, written in Arabic script but phonetically reproducing the sounds and words of the spoken language.[163]

Pages from a student notebook written in a mixture of Arabic and Afrikaans. A transcription of the first sentence reads: Allahoemma iejakana' aboedoe – *Jaa Allah vier oeai [= 'U'] a-leen iek maak 'iebaadat* (O Allah, for thee alone do I worship.). The italicised phrases are in Afrikaans. (A. Davids, 'The words slaves made', p. 20)

'A SINGULAR MIX' 127

refer to those who spoke the trading lingua franca of the whole region (and was not limited to the modern state of Malaysia). But in Cape Town the term 'Malay' conveniently ignored the fact that the Islamic community comprised people from a wide variety of ethnic origins. Moreover, the label reflected a transfer by many white Capetonians of negative images and fears previously associated with 'dangerous' and 'untrustworthy' slaves and exiles of South-East Asian origin. Thus Samuel Hudson confidently believed that 'Malays ... can administer poison in such a way as to destroy the health, without occasioning death for many months or even years',[165] and a certain Colonel Blake regaled an admiral's dinner party in Simon's Town in 1837 with stories of strange deaths caused by 'Malay poisoning pins, hair, nail pairings vomited in a ball'.[166] A more positive image held by white Capetonians of the 'sober Malay' was only to emerge later in the nineteenth century, although earlier fears still lay just below the surface.

Muslim figures, painted in the 1830s. The man wears a *toedang* and the woman a red kerchief *woelsel* or *kopdoek*. The *toedang* was worn by both men and women in the East Indies, but appears to have been used only by men at the Cape. This type of headgear was noted by visitors from as early as 1772 as a marker of Islam. Watercolour by W.Huntly. (© The Brenthurst Press ART.84/2)

Middle-Class Identities

During the VOC period, status was largely a function of rank within the service of the Company. Although the emphasis shifted with a growing sense of burgher self-identity in the late eighteenth century, Dutch Capetonians still tended to define themselves by rank or inherited status rather than individual attributes.

High society under the British in the 1790s, and under the governor Lord Charles Somerset up until the 1820s, was not dissimilar. The elite consisted of high-ranking army and naval officers and the upper echelons of government service. Such positions were largely confined to men of aristocratic birth and connection. However, this group remained a tiny sector of the town's population, and had little identity with the colony itself, being dependent for their social position on occupations which did not form an integral part of Cape Town. The army was only temporarily garrisoned there and aristocratic appointments to high government office were no longer guaranteed after the 1820s.

According to Edward Blount, who visited Cape Town in 1820, the army and government elite were 'nearly all that there is of gentility in Cape Town society'. But he also identified a second grouping within 'the respectable part of the inhabitants': the merchants.[167] The members of the mercantile and commercial British community which emerged in this period were not part of aristocratic circles, and were excluded from political power. But their economic independence and sense of difference both from the aristocratic leanings of the Somerset government and from the labouring classes of the town gave them an identity that began to find powerful expression from at least the 1820s, particularly after Somerset's removal. They may, in other words, be loosely described as Cape Town's first 'middle class'.

Middle-class identity was expressed through a variety of means. In contrast to Britain, involvement in trade and commerce was no barrier to social acceptability, although Blount despised the fact that the 'merchants' included 'a vast number of the lowest order of money-getters'.[168] Indeed, trade was almost a prerequisite, for financial independence was essential, as was ownership of one's own home. Markers of middle-class status included the employment of servants and the possession of such items as carriages and pianos.[169] Many immigrant artisans and small-scale retailers aspired to own property as soon as possible to denote their new social status, although the economic uncertainties of the 1810s and 1820s meant that a number failed to retain their status and bankruptcy brought social disaster.[170] Financial instability was a concern to all middle-class Capetonians. Turns of fortune could be swift and dishonouring. When

Lord Charles Somerset on horseback. (MuseumAfrica 66/1909)

The Union Chapel Group

The most prominent representatives of the world-view of Cape Town's new middle class formed a small but influential group that centred on the Congregational Union Chapel and were bound together by close family connections. They were strongly influenced by liberal ideas.

John Philip, founder of the Chapel, is better known for his influence as a humanitarian on the eastern Cape frontier, but he was also a notable presence in Cape Town, where he was involved in a range of educational and reformist activities. His son-in-law John Fairbairn was editor of the influential and often controversial *South African Commercial Advertiser*, which propounded the values of a new age. Merchants were also an integral part of the Union Chapel community. John Harfield Tredgold, a chemist, was a founder of the Commercial Exchange and one of the managers of the Cape of Good Hope Savings Bank. Ralph Henry Arderne cut short his voyage to Australia at the Cape, where he already had family connections, for his sister had married a missionary on the eastern frontier. Through this link he had an introduction to Dr Philip. He made a fortune in the timber trade, and a substantial amount of his wealth was invested in property, some in District Six. He was director of the Equitable Fire Assurance Company, a director of the Tramway Company, and one of the managers of the Botanic Gardens. Other notable figures of the Union Chapel congregation included Thomas James Mathew, a cooper; James Cameron, 'zealous friend of the missionaries' who was also a member of the early Board of Commissioners; and, at a later date, the brilliant, diminutive Saul Solomon, 'the member for Cape Town', printer, newspaper proprietor and Cape Town's most distinguished parliamentary representative and leading mid-century liberal.

'The respectable part of the inhabitants may be divided into two classes: first, the military … and, secondly, the merchants; a most comprehensive word; among whom are to be found a few men, who might rank with that class on the Royal Exchange; and a vast number of the lowest order of money-getters.'
Edward Blount,
1821

W.G. Gadney, treasurer of the South African College, was forced to turn his Sea Point home into a lodging-house after a business failure, his neighbours were horrified. And to impugn a 'gentleman's' financial soundness without good reason could be cause for libel action.[171]

The culture and society which Cape Town's new middle class developed were thus bourgeois rather than aristocratic. Their status was reinforced through the churches they attended, through the schools, organisations and institutions they founded, and through intermarriage. Although closely linked to their British roots, by the 1830s many members of Cape Town's middle class were beginning to identify more closely with the colony. A new generation was growing up which was permanently settled in the town and had no direct experience of Britain. The values they held were closely associated with those of the Enlightenment and the commercial class that was emerging in Britain at the time, forged in the context of the market economy. In place of notions of status and birth, inherited patronage and privilege, they emphasised self-made qualities achieved through education, hard work, Christian devotion (often of an evangelical nature), and a sense of moral responsibility. Property and education defined access to this middle class.

Middle-class activities were highly gendered. This was a male domain, and middle-class women were expected to confine themselves to the home and family. In VOC Cape Town, as we saw, burgher women had played an important economic role at a time when trade and retailing were mainly carried out from their homes. But in the early

Charles Bell's depiction of his uncle, the government secretary Colonel John Bell, at his home in 1832 represents the idealised middle-class gendered division: men read books and newspapers while Bell's wife makes lace. (Library of Parliament A.Pic.Mend.37624)

nineteenth century these activities moved outside the domestic sphere. The male-dominated Commercial Exchange and the club became centres of public economic life. Although women continued to be important in the work performed by the slave and labouring classes of the town, especially as laundresses, seamstresses and domestic servants, the new middle class frowned upon the notion of female paid employment. The organisation of households and control over the domestic sphere became the major pre-occupations for many middle-class female Capetonians. Some were less than enchanted with such a role, even if social pressures and economic vulnerability gave them little opportunity to escape. As John Fairbairn's wife Eliza wrote in 1838 to her friend and confidante in England, 'there is a sad feeling of stern reality creeps over me sometimes as I ask myself – *is this the all of life*.' Two months earlier she had complained that 'Mr F does nothing but go to sleep when he comes home or sigh and groan over the sins of mankind. I have heard folks talk about the *self dependent mind*, I wonder where it is to be found.'[172]

Right into the twentieth century, however, the wives and daughters of the evangelical reformers played a more prominent role in the public life of the town than other Cape Town women, even if they were not to acquire financial independence. As the 'moral guardians of the family', women were considered to be particularly suited to dispensing charity in its various forms, public and private. Many missionary wives and daughters worked as teachers or ran the business of the mission. These were working women in every sense of the word, although their position was unacknowledged and usually unpaid. Mrs Jane Philip (née Ross) was 'the linchpin of the female church community of Cape Town'. As the wife of the minister of the Union Chapel, she was the centre of a hospitable domestic circle. She was a founder member of the Ladies' Benevolent Society and, in 1831, of the Bible and Tract Society, distributing religious literature to the poor; she also played a prominent role in establishing mission schools in Cape Town. Unusually, she was paid for the bookkeeping that she did for the London Missionary Society, work customarily done by men. But there was no guarantee of financial or intellectual freedom for women even in this family. Her daughter Eliza (who later married John Fairbairn) was forced by her father to give up her ambition to become a teacher since she would fail to gain the social virtues desirable in a young woman. 'You are still

'There is a sad feeling of stern reality creeps over me sometimes as I ask myself – is this the all of life.'
Eliza Fairbairn, 1838

A Library and a Museum

The Literary Society was responsible for the library, housed in the Commercial Exchange, which incorporated the former Dessin collection and supplemented it. Thus, 'besides an over-abundantly rich collection of scientific works on any subject, ... [the library] contains a substantial amount of fiction from contemporary literature, and offers the citizen many a satisfying leisure hour by displaying all Cape newspapers and numerous English journals and periodicals.'[174] The Society also opened a museum to replace the 'menagerie' in the old Company gardens, which by 1800 was 'nearly without inhabitants, a few secretary birds, a pair of ostriches ... a beautiful lion and lioness that have had young several times but from some mismanagement the female has invariably destroyed them'.[175] Whereas the Dutch governors had kept a motley collection of stuffed animals in the Government Guest House,[176] the new museum was an altogether more ordered affair, organised according to the classificatory principles of early nineteenth-century scientific thought. It contained 'a valuable, rare, and beautiful collection of the animal, mineral and vegetable world'.[177] Representation of the human world was less clearly organised: items in the collection included a Mahratha suit of armour given by visiting 'Indians',[178] and, as an ominous indicator of the way in which indigenous South Africans were becoming objects of scientific rather than human interest, 'a Hottentot woman's skin stuffed'.[179] In the early 1830s, the museum was moved to new premises in Looyer's Plein (near Stal Plein) and became one of the tourist attractions for visitors to the town. However, entrance was by special permission and charges were made. By the late 1830s some of the collections had been removed and the remnant were housed out of sight at the South African College.[180]

in want of that nameless ease, that self command, that light society, that grace in company and in conversation which give to Woman her liveliness, her Empire.'[173]

Middle-class men placed a particularly high value on a culture of literacy. While they encouraged a basic education for the poor, their notions went much further. In clubs and coffee houses, reading and language societies, through lending libraries, theatres, journals and newspapers, they propagated their ideas on the right ordering of the colonial world.

In 1824 a meeting at the Commercial Exchange established a Literary Society to encourage interest in scientific and cultural matters. Although its constitution forbade discussion of the controversial topics of politics, religion and slavery, it met with great opposition from Governor Somerset, who opposed any forum which might criticise authoritarian rule. It was only in 1829, after Somerset's removal and some administra-

George Greig's bookshop and printing works, where the *South African Commercial Advertiser* was published. Drawing by De Meillon. (William Fehr C83)

'A SINGULAR MIX' 131

tive reforms, that the South African Literary and Scientific Institution was created. This began the publication of the *South African Quarterly Journal*, presenting papers on matters of scientific and cultural interest.

But the main manifestation of this movement for public debate and education was the establishment by the printer and bookseller George Greig of the first private and independent newspaper, the *South African Commercial Advertiser*, in 1824. It declared in its launching prospectus: 'as a free diffusion of knowledge is the grand means of giving a tone to society, by elevating its morals, and promoting a taste for literature, we look to the more enlightened part of the community; in the confident hope that they will not allow this, the first attempt to establish a medium of general communication in a British Colony, to fail for want of that support which the well informed, the intelligent, and the patriotic, are alone able to afford.'[181]

The theme of advancement of civilised learning was one which the *Advertiser* constantly stressed. It advocated all the concerns of the new liberalism of Britain's commercial classes, transferred to a colonial setting: free trade; the replacement of slavery by free 'wage' labour; self-help and social responsibility. It did much in the process to foster a sense among the town's elite of their role as the harbingers not only of social and cultural advancement, but also of political leadership. John Fairbairn became its editor (and sole proprietor after 1835). One of his main goals was to demonstrate the enlightened maturity of the town's leading citizens in order to encourage the metropolis to consider granting a measure of responsible government to the Cape, a government which they would then lead.

Such notions were not welcomed by the Cape's autocratic administration under Lord Charles Somerset, a man who represented the older aristocratic order and had little sympathy with enlightened ideas of public debate, rationalism and representative government. Somerset's attempts to censor the *Advertiser* led Fairbairn to suspend publication and the paper was closed down completely in 1826. But after the governor was replaced by an administration rather more sympathetic to new ideas, the paper was re-established. As a result of pressure from Fairbairn and his supporters (mostly members of the Commercial Exchange) a press ordinance was enacted in 1829 guaranteeing the right to an independent press. Other newspapers emerged, representing different interest groups in the colony, most notably *De Zuid-Afrikaan*, which appealed in the tenser years of the 1830s to Cape Town's Dutch-speaking community.

Although becoming more locally rooted, the identity of this new middle class was still strongly British in a town whose white inhabitants were still overwhelmingly of Dutch descent. The urban Dutch elite were not at all averse to co-operation with the British government; as we have seen, many retained positions of power within it. But at the same time, as one observer commented, while 'the employees in the civil service conformed, at least outwardly, to the peculiarly English formalities', they also 'retained the customs of their forefathers', continued to use the Dutch language and 'did not change the overall tenor of their traditional way of life'.[182]

However, this was to change. As the German visitor Krauss observed of the mid-1830s, some of the younger Dutch Capetonians 'approached the English national character more and more … it became the rage to copy everything English and to adopt the manner of life of their fellow-citizens, which trend was of course strengthened by frequent contact with them. The considerable importation of English goods and the growing number of all sorts of craftsmen enabled them to follow this fashion and to furnish their homes in the English style. This, however, was not enough; they lived in the English

John Fairbairn (CA E365)

JOHN HERSCHEL

Cape Town's most distinguished man of learning in the 1830s was the astronomer Sir John Herschel, who came to the colony in 1834 to document the stars of the southern hemisphere. Not only did he greatly improve the facilities of the observatory which had been established in 1820 on the outskirts of the town (from which the suburb of Observatory derives its name), but he also measured the tides, collected and classified plants and insects, was president of the South African Literary and Scientific Institution, examined students at the South African College in mathematics and, for good measure, commented on Sanskrit articles for the *Journal of the Asiatic Society of Bengal*. He returned to Britain in 1838.

OPPOSING REFORM

(Library of Parliament)

Not all middle-class Capetonians supported reform. *De Zuid-Afrikaan* newspaper was founded in 1830 and was initially edited by the teacher and playwright Charles Etienne Boniface. It was intended to challenge the sentiments of the *Commercial Advertiser*. Boniface's successor was the attorney Christoffel Brand, who had studied law in the Netherlands, where abolitionism had taken little root. Brand became the defender of Cape slaveholders against the *Commercial Advertiser*'s abolitionism, telling a mass meeting in 1832 that 'our slaves are better off, yes much better off, than many free British citizens',[186] and leading the campaign for adequate compensation.

Boniface was also the author of *De Temperantisten*, described as 'the first published and oldest original drama extant in South Africa', and set in Cape Town in the 1830s. It was a satirical parody of the humanitarian movement, with scenes alternating between hypocritical meetings of the Temperance Society, led by thinly disguised caricatures of John Philip (Dominee Humbug Philipumpkin) and John Fairbairn (Sir John Brute), and street scenes of drunken, quarrelsome and criminal Khoi.[187]

---

manner, spoke nothing but that language, and even went as far as to feel obliged to go to the English Church as well.' As a result, 'there was considerable improvement in social contacts on both sides ... and it happened not infrequently that an Englishman chose his bride from among the pretty Cape girls'.[183] Cape Town was not yet a British town, but some younger members of its leading Dutch families were moving away from the ethnic identities of their parents.

The literary and educational activities of British Capetonians were paralleled by those of the Dutch. In 1803 a small group of intellectuals influenced by the Enlightenment founded a Cape Town branch of the Genootschap van Kunsten en Wetenschappen, onder de zinspreuk 'Tot Nut van 't Algemeen' (Society of Arts and Science under the motto 'For Public Welfare'). The goals of this Society, founded in Holland in 1784 'for the public instruction of all classes', were explained at the first meeting held in the Town House: 'the instruction of youth, improvement of agriculture and the encouragement of the arts and sciences'. In addition to opening a school, the Society also began publishing in 1824 its own journal, *Het Nederduitsch Zuid-Afrikaansch Tijdschrift*, edited by Abraham Faure, minister of the Groote Kerk, which called for recognition of the Dutch contribution to the Cape. In 1830 the leading Dutch intellectuals of the town established the Maatschappij ter Uitbreiding van Beschaving en Letterkunde (Society for the Expansion of Culture and Literature) and it set about preparing a history of the colony that would fully reflect its Dutch origins and traditions.[184]

In the late 1820s and 1830s new policies challenged more overtly the position of the Dutch elite in the town. The Burgher Senate was abolished in 1827, and at the same time English was made the sole language of administration. The civic power of the Dutch elite was thus destroyed and some Dutch-speaking officials, such as the attorney-general Daniël Denyssen, were forced to retire. Monopolies were removed in the meat, wine and baking trades, on which the economic prosperity of many leading Dutch Capetonians was based. By the mid-1830s tensions between Dutch colonists throughout the Cape and the British administration had risen considerably as a result of the emancipation of slaves and the veto over vagrancy legislation, and men such as Fairbairn and Philip were despised as the harbingers of social anarchy. In 1836 Fairbairn and his wife were physically attacked on the Grand Parade by a Dutch farmer incensed by his abolitionism.[185]

Although these tensions were most apparent in the rural districts of the colony, they did lead to an urban reaction and a resulting sense of Dutch identity, based not so much on the landed elite of the past but rather on the Dutch urban intelligentsia. New publications appeared such as *De Zuid-Afrikaan* newspaper, the weekly *De Verzamelaar* edited by the Amsterdam-born J.S. de Lima, and the *Kaapse Cyclopedie*. All contained articles emphasising the link with the Netherlands, although overt opposition to British rule was censored by the editors. The *Tijdschrift* in particular expressed alarm about the increasing domination of the English language and English customs.

In these circumstances, English–Dutch tensions in the town grew. John Fawcett, who was in Cape Town in 1835, commented that 'exhibitions of hatred' occurred: 'speak of the emancipation of the slaves; the Dutch are in arms. They go forth blustering in words of violence and wrath.'[188] And yet this anti-liberal Dutch intellectual movement of the 1830s was not a Dutch (or Afrikaner) nationalist movement calling for separation from the British connection, but rather an appeal to be treated equally as citizens of the colony.[189] By the 1840s its impetus had declined, largely as the fears of social upheaval subsided in the wake of emancipation, and both Dutch and British Capetonians united in their opposition to convict labour and in their call for self-representation.

'A SINGULAR MIX'

MOULDING THE CITIZEN

The columns of the *South African Commercial Advertiser* were filled with ambitious plans to remodel the town so that it might become an efficiently run, commercially oriented capital, worthy of self-government.[190] Just as the streets and public places of the town had to be cleansed and regulated, so too did its population. Ignorance, poverty, disorder and crime needed to be eradicated. Imbued with a zeal for the righteousness of their own vision of the world, Cape Town's elite sought to mould all its citizens by methods which rather uneasily combined encouragement of self-discipline and coercion.

The early nineteenth century saw a profusion of schools established in the town, although many of them were short-lived. Most numerous were private schools, of which there were some forty (often only existing for a couple of years) between 1814 and 1826.[191] The Tot Nut van 't Algemeen Society School had a precarious existence. It was opened in 1803 in New Street (now Queen Victoria Street) and provided a training in Dutch that differed from the curriculum of the church-dominated schools in the town, including for instance commercial subjects. In the 1820s it seems to have disbanded, but it was re-established in 1831, stressing both Dutch and English as well as mathematics. Other schools included the Classical and Commercial Academy founded by Fairbairn and Pringle; this opened in 1823, offering an education along the lines of an English grammar school. It had only 36 pupils at most, and incurred considerable displeasure from Governor Somerset, who accused it of teaching the 'most disgusting principles of Republicanism'.[192]

Although many British middle-class Capetonians aspired to send their sons to school back in England, calls were made in the late 1820s for a local secondary school with firmer financial support and appealing to both the Dutch and English sectors of the population. As a result the South African College was opened for the first time in 1829. It was initially supported entirely by public subscription, although a special ordinance of 1837 guaranteed government backing. The school was considered by 1840 to provide adequate grounding 'for academic studies in Holland or England'.[193] By this stage there were also more Dutch-speaking pupils, not only from the town: 'the more affluent resi-

The South African College was initially located in the Orphan House in Long Street before moving in 1841 to a new site at the top of the Company gardens. (William Fehr C96)

C. C. Michell's watercolour entitled 'A dancing class at the Cape' satirises a Dutch family giving private dancing lessons to their children. (MuseumAfrica 55/920).

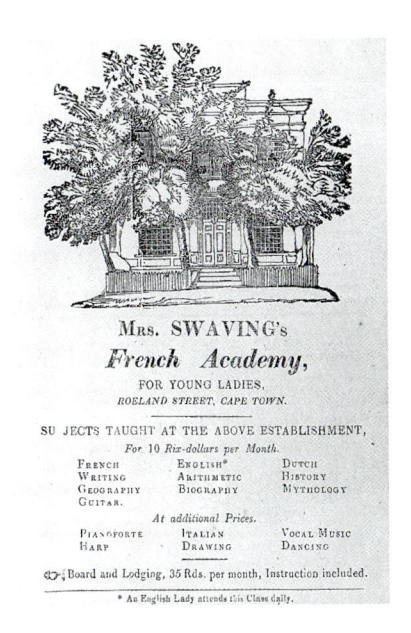

Mrs Swaving's French Academy offered private schooling for 'young ladies'. Mr Swaving ran a parallel institution for the 'young gentlemen' of the town. (*South African Directory*, 1831)

dents of remoter districts are also sending their sons to town in order to attend this establishment, which has not always turned out to the satisfaction of the parents and the advantage of the sons, since the young people find too many distractions in city life'.[194] It was doubtless to discourage such indulgence that the school included 'two places of confinement ... an "upper" and "lower" prison, the latter known as the "Black Hole,"' into which some pupils were placed until 9 p.m. each evening for a fortnight on bread and water.[195]

These higher-level educational establishments were restricted both by class and by gender. For girls there was no equivalent, and the daughters of Cape Town's elite were often educated privately by teachers of languages, drawing, music and embroidery. There were ten such establishments in the mid-1820s.

Although some basic education in reading and writing was provided for government slaves from 1810, the education of the lower classes was left primarily to philanthropic and missionary institutions. The ZAG and the LMS missionaries as well as the Islamic *madaris* had provided basic literacy classes for adults to enable the reading and recitation of scriptures, although it is uncertain how much further such reading abilities went. The ZAG school for slaves had over 187 students in 1813, meeting on Wednesday and Friday evenings, as well as 32 boys and 75 girls who attended a Sunday school.[196] Clearly the focus was primarily to counteract the influence of Islamic teachers. In 1830 an interdenominational missionary committee established a number of infant schools. They were divided into 'upper' and 'lower' schools, the latter explicitly for the children of slaves and the 'poorer classes', which contained 'every cast of complexion from jet black to perfect white'.[197] Instruction in the 'lower' school was aimed at teaching each child 'the duty he owes to God, and his master, and render him a good man, a faithful servant and in both characters a blessing to the community.'[198] One teacher showed pupils a bunch of unripe grapes and, after establishing that it was unwise to eat them, continued to describe the way in which vines should be planted and pruned. A subsequent class focused on 'the operations of ploughing, sowing, reaping, binding, carting, threshing,

'A SINGULAR MIX' 135

George Angas's depiction in 1848 of a 'Malay school' romanticises the exoticism of the *madrassah*. (Library of Parliament A.Pic.Mend.18507)

sifting, kneading [and] baking' as the 'staff of life' for future employment.[199]

Most working-class pupils proceeded no further than this, although there were a few opportunities open to them. The two government-sponsored free schools in Bree and Keerom streets had between them over 600 pupils, and there were also eight mission schools for older boys in the town by 1839. A school of industry funded by the Ladies' Benevolent Society was opened in 1824 for girls between 5 and 12 years 'whose parents are destitute of the means of procuring them other instruction'.[200] Education 'suited for their station in life' was provided and consisted of reading and writing as well as needlework and sewing. This had a dual purpose since 'plain work is taken in at a very moderate price, the profits arising from it contributing to the support of the school'.[201] By the late 1820s daughters of free blacks and slaves were being admitted. There were also a few Muslim girls, despite the strong evangelical Christian emphasis of the school, a factor which may well point to the relative lack of schooling for females in the *madaris*.[202]

Social Control

In the 1820s and 1830s it seemed to many middle-class Capetonians that Cape Town's labouring classes were getting dangerously out of control. The 'moral panic' about the criminality and depravity of the lower orders, which had seized the middle classes in Britain as well as the British in India, found expression also in Cape Town.[203] Although slavery and forced labour were deemed undesirable in a model commercial town, there was great concern that reform and regulation would be essential if they were to be replaced by a diligent, hard-working wage-labour force. The removal of forced apprenticeship for the Khoi after 1828 and the imminence of slave emancipation in the early 1830s brought such concerns to the fore. A petition to the governor, signed by 79 inhabitants of Cape Town in July 1834, demanded a law to control vagrancy which

> besides giving better security to life and property in this colony, [will] raise the coloured classes in general from that state of moral degradation wherein so many are still to be found, and to support the virtuous and industrious man as much in his noble efforts to promote his state and situation, as to create a dread in the knave, sluggard and vagrant; or at least curb his evil dispositions and intentions, and by so doing to afford, even to the greatest objects of evil and malicious intentions and acts through the threat of the law, an opportunity of returning from their erroneous path and to become virtuous and useful members of the community.[204]

Such sentiments expressed the fears and stereotypes of Cape Town's propertied classes. John Fairbairn had been no less strident in his views that 'a thousand complicated levers are requisite to elevate the barbarian to the rank of civilisation'.[205]

When the lower orders failed to conform to middle-class notions of self-discipline, regulation and the law took over. The old Dutch system of the burgher watch and *caffers* was replaced in 1825 by a new municipal police force under the control of an ex-army officer, Baron Charles de Lorentz, who styled himself 'the Baron'.[206] Until 1840 the number of constables rarely exceeded 20. Recruits were not easy to find, since the duties were unpopular and the pay poor (£45 per annum for an ordinary constable). Most were British soldiers who had bought their discharge. Training was poor and discipline lax; absenteeism and drunkenness were a constant problem and in one month alone in 1826 nine constables were dismissed.[207] Those who were unmarried were housed, in barrack style, either at the prison or at the new police station in Greenmarket Square.

In general it was the labouring classes who felt the brunt of the police's presence. The most common charges brought against the poor reflected the definitions and perceptions of unacceptable behaviour held by the ruling elite. Drunkenness, public disorder and contravening municipal regulations were common offences against the order of the streets, while petty theft and housebreaking threatened the propertied. Exaggerated fears at a time of social transformation in the 1830s led one judge, when sentencing a group of apprentices to transportation to New South Wales for receiving stolen goods, to claim that he 'knew of no town in His Majesties dominion where stealing was as numerous as in Cape Town'.[208] The targets of the law were also by the 1830s coming to reflect ethnic stereotypes. Shock at the arrest of two white burglars in 1830 led the *Cape of Good Hope Literary Gazette* to comment: 'The depravity of the coloured part of the population of this colony has long been bitterly inveighed against ... Heretofore, when a store has been robbed, suspicion immediately fixed itself on the Malays; if a sheep or horse were stolen, the thief could have been no other than a bushman; or if a garden were stripped of its fruit, some of the neighbouring slaves were doubtless the aggressors, but on either of these occasions no one ever dreamt of a white man being capable of such an act of atrocity.'[209] Propertied white men, that is. The Irish were held to be drunkards and, as in the eighteenth century, disorderliness was a frequent cause of complaint against soldiers and sailors.

There was some change in the forms of punishment: this reflected the trend away from retribution to reform of the offender that was emerging in post-Enlightenment

---

'Besides giving better security to life and property in this colony, [a vagrancy law will] raise the coloured classes in general from that state of moral degradation wherein so many are still to be found.'

Petition of Cape Town residents, July 1834

Western Europe. Although Cape Dutch laws were largely preserved after the British take-over, the use of torture to extract evidence and more painful forms of public executions were swiftly ended. The man responsible for breaking limbs hanged himself for 'fear of starving for want of employment' when he heard that breaking on the wheel had been abolished.[210] Hangings still took place but outside the jail rather than at the entrance to the town, and the bodies of the condemned were no longer left on public gibbets.

Instead of mere incarceration, habits of 'diligence' were to be instilled in the prisoners. Those sentenced to hard labour were sent to a convict station on the Cape Flats and chain gangs were a regular sight on the road-building projects there and on the Hottentots Holland passes. The use of the treadmill as an additional means of punishment was thought to induce habits of discipline and 'the education of the muscles' since (as Fairbairn put it) 'mere imprisonment without labour ... ruins the industrious habits both of the mind and body of a common labourer where such habits have been formed; and where the prisoner has always been an idle dog, he is turned adrift after the period of his confinement ten times more the child of idleness than before.'[211]

The reality was rather less idealised. The main town jail in Strand Street was overcrowded and hardly a model of enlightened penal policy. M.D. Teenstra, visiting it in 1825, 'witnessed the most appalling scenes'. These included 'practically nude' Khoi and slave prisoners, some chained and 'treated worse than animals', the whipping of a female slave with 39 lashes 'at the request of her owner', and

> the treadmill where ten or twelve slaves, dressed merely in breeches, were undergoing punishment. This is the severest form of punishment. The wheel itself has the shape of an oblong cylinder, six or seven yards in length and two yards in diameter, around the outside of which 24 strips of wood, ten to twelve inches wide, are fitted, on which the victims tread with their feet to keep the wheel in motion. A policeman, a callous, unkempt ruffian, kept guard over them. The prisoners are subjected to this form of torture from dawn till noon, and again from one o'clock to sunset, by which time they are reduced to a state of helpless exhaustion.[212]

Moreover, since the treadmill was hired out to contractors who used it for grinding corn to make the town's bread, it was necessary to keep it constantly turning. 'To find the

'Mere imprisonment without labour ... ruins the industrious habits both of the mind and body of a common labourer where such habits have been formed; and where the prisoner has always been an idle dog, he is turned adrift after the period of his confinement ten times more the child of idleness than before.'
South African Commercial Advertiser, 13 April 1831

Strand Street jail, next to the Customs House. Drawing by De Meillon. (CA E3983)

138 CAPE TOWN 1795–1840

Robben Island

Robben Island was used for a variety of functions in the early nineteenth century: whaling station, lobster fishing, stone quarry, and hunting ground for pheasants and quail. But its main purpose continued to be a place of incarceration. A new prison was constructed in 1808, replacing the delapidated Dutch buildings.

The island was a place of banishment for those excluded from the town. Among them were quarantined arrivals suspected of smallpox, (in 1815) a group of Khoi women with venereal disease, and (in the 1820s) several 'lunatics' from the Somerset Hospital. But the majority of inhabitants were prisoners, many sentenced to hard labour on the quarries. The greater number were Khoisan, accused of crimes ranging from cattle theft to assault on farmers. There were also court-martialled soldiers awaiting transportation to New South Wales. In addition the island was used to exile captured opponents from the eastern Cape frontier conflicts, such as the Khoi leaders Hans Trompetter and David Stuurman, and Makhanda, the Xhosa warrior-prophet who led the Gcaleka and Ndlambe attack on Grahamstown in 1819.

Chief Maqoma and his wife, banished to Robben Island for murdering another chief who refused to take part in the 1857 Xhosa cattle-killing. (SAL INIL 24159)

After an escape bid in 1820, when some prisoners got away in boats used by fishermen, outsiders were excluded from the island and security was tightened. Complaints of the superintendent's cruelty (lashing prisoners with whips soaked in urine) led to some reforms and improvement of conditions in the later 1820s. Prisoners were to receive religious instruction and, after 1825, were given small amounts of pay for extra work.

In the 1840s convicts were used extensively for road-building and other public works and fewer were sent to the island. Instead, a hospital was opened for 'incurable cases', including 'lunatics', 'lepers' and the chronically ill who were too poor to maintain themselves. The leper institution was only closed in 1931.

Xhosa chiefs who resisted the British in the 1850s were banished to the island, included those who were believed to have encouraged the cattle-killing of 1857.[214]

---

required number of offenders the police are in the habit of seizing any drunken or brawling Hottentots or slaves found on the streets, particularly on Saturday and Sunday nights, to do the work.'[213]

Leisure

The differing ways in which Capetonians entertained themselves provide a good measure of the diverse ethnic, gendered and class identities that existed in this period of transition. Although the culture and leisure of the town's inhabitants in the VOC period were by no means homogeneous, in the early nineteenth century the divisions of leisure experience and expression became both more complex and more entrenched.

The stress on rank and status that had accompanied the social gatherings of the VOC elite was perpetuated by the British governing class that succeeded them. Although Anne Barnard was concerned to bring together the Dutch and British at her monthly Thursday afternoon soirées and her evening dances, she was equally determined that social distinctions and rank must be maintained. When asked by the governor for advice about who should be invited to a state ball at the Castle in 1799, 'I recommended all the garrison and every Dutch person who had been in the habit of attending the levees and balls in the Dutch time, which was making them draw their own line – I knew the folks here are critical respecting ranks and proud to a great degree.'[215] She strongly disapproved of a wedding party offered by one Dutch inhabitant, at which rank and status

DINNER AT GOVERNMENT HOUSE

Something of the social circle that surrounded the governor is indicated by surviving guest lists kept by Governor Bourke's wife for the 97 dinner parties she organised at Government House in 1827–8. Army officers and their wives were the most frequent guests; Indian officers passing through Cape Town were invariably invited. High-ranking officials of the government administration were also regulars. Lower-ranking army officers and civil-service employees were also sometimes included, but private citizens formed only a small percentage of the guest lists. It seems as if the army and civil service maintained a social distance from the merchants and commercial citizens of the town.[217]

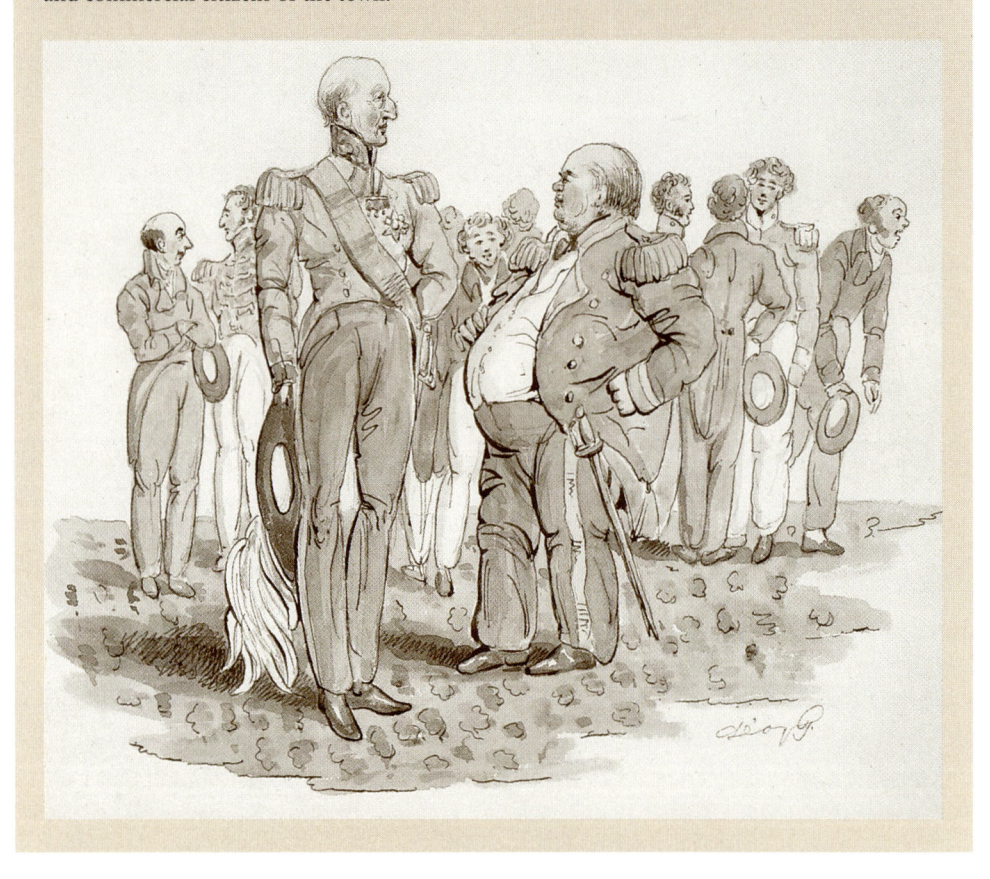

Governor Sir Lowry Cole talks to a portly naval officer at a Government House reception in 1833. Watercolour by D'Oyly. (MuseumAfrica 55/21)

were flouted: not only were some invitations sent out in a suspiciously 'Jacobin' style of address 'to Citizen this – Citizen that', but a major of the Castle regiment 'was just beginning to dance with the daughter of the family when he saw standing above him General Dundas's cook just ready to lead off'.[216]

The aristocratic background of the army and naval officers, the 'Indians' and the leading administrators was emphasised in the introduction at the Cape of that quintessential pastime of the British landed gentry – the hunt. From their first arrival at the Cape, British regimental officers hunted buck on the Cape Flats, although they were disappointed to find this 'very indifferent sport; for though the game is plenty, the country is unenclosed, and the glorious difficulties and dangers of the chase are wanting ... the horsemen ... are occasionally precipitated into deep holes, formed by the ant-eater and other animals, and may return covered with the sandy honours of the field.'[218] By 1806, many of the steenbuck had been hunted out and the British had to make do with jack-

140   CAPE TOWN 1795–1840

als.²¹⁹ By the early 1820s, hunting parties for wild foal and antelope were being organised during the 'shooting season' from 1 December to 30 June. The venues extended to Saldanha Bay and sometimes further afield; 'in these the Indians, being unoccupied, take the lead.'²²⁰ Attempts were made to breed hunting hounds locally, although the prevalence of distemper was 'one sad alloy to the pleasure of sporting'.²²¹

The British army officers also introduced horse-racing to Cape Town. Two main meets a year were held in the 1790s, with prizes raised by subscription. They proved so popular that the Dutch inhabitants commented that the British 'preferred racing to dancing'.²²² There were inevitably contemptuous comments about the poor breeding of Dutch horses, and a number of racers were imported from India in an attempt to improve the local stock.²²³ Regular races were held at a course on the outskirts of the town at Green Point. By the 1820s, 'cups are awarded and the betting is brisk. The meeting usually lasts two to three days, impromptu field sports following the racing and a great ball crowning the whole festival. To reduce the weight of the horses and jockeys – the latter usually slave lads – both are sweated down before the race. The Governor, Lord Charles Somerset, who loves racing and also enters horses, is said to be a bad loser but a good winner, acting most generously on the latter occasion.'²²⁴

Certainly such meets were places for the town's elite to see and be seen: Lady Anne Barnard was dismayed to find that gossip was circulating about her at one race meeting.²²⁵ But in contrast to the social exclusivity of hunting, they also attracted other inhabitants of the town, in addition to the slave jockeys. Garrison soldiers made or lost up to a year's pay by gambling at the races and a man like Samuel Hudson, who had arrived in the colony as a personal servant, was a regular attender.

If army officers and civil servants found their entertainments at government banquets and the hunt, the town's civilian elite created their own leisure spaces. The eighteenth century Dutch practices continued: men and women made separate visits in the mornings, spent the afternoon sleeping and the evening house-calling or gathering socially on stoeps; to these were added dancing parties, which became fashionable from the late 1770s. But such activities were derided by newcomers used to a more cultivated environment. De Jong complained in 1793:

I have never known any people to eat more heartily, drink more heartily and sleep

Carrying a jockey to the races, 1833. By D'Oyly. (MuseumAfrica 74/2539/67)

Visiting friends on the stoep in the late afternoon. By D'Oyly. (MuseumAfrica 74/2539/80)

'A SINGULAR MIX' 141

so much. By 11 p.m. all houses are shut up – many of them by 10 p.m. Some men get up at 6 a.m., but most women seldom before 8 a.m. In the morning the men visit each other for a glass of wine; at midday they eat until 1.30 p.m., then go to sleep at 2.30 p.m.; not just a little nap but completely undressed and they stay in bed until 4, sometimes 5, during which time no-one may speak a word. After this the women get dressed and appear. This goes on from Monday to Saturday, each day just the same. There are no coffee houses, newspapers or public amusements.[226]

The British army officers in 1799 'all to a man united in reprobating the dullness and dreariness of the place'.[227] This was the response of outsiders who were not part of the social network of the town and so were excluded from its prime activities, which took

THE ADVENTURES OF TOM RAW AT THE CAPE OF GOOD HOPE

(SAL AQ821 DOY)

A satirical impression of a Cape Dutch drawing-room from *Tom Raw, the Griffin ... A Burlesque Poem in Twelve Cantos*, published in London in 1828 and written and illustrated by Charles D'Oyly.

Tom Raw is a naive young English recruit to the East India service. On his way to India he stops in Cape Town (noted for its 'monstrous bays and monstrous vrows or women') and is entertained at the home of 'Herr and Madame van der Sluggenbottom'. He is squeezed between Madame Sluggenbottom ('twenty stones at least') and her neighbour who are 'talking in broad Dutch', is overwhelmed by the 'pungent flavour of Dutch pipes and undigested fumes of potent gin', and burns his shins on the coals of their foot-warmers.

This satirical image reveals British stereotypes and caricatures of the Dutch inhabitants of Cape Town. D'Oyly was a member of the Bengal civil service who spent a year in Cape Town in 1832–3. Many of his other drawings are more realistic, giving a lively impression of the people and scenes of the town. A number of them have been used in this chapter.

142 CAPE TOWN 1795–1840

> 'Company, dancing, and the theatre are to the taste of all ... the habits of the Dutch and English are not as yet sufficiently amalgamated to allow them to associate in the same free manner as is usual with individuals of a common stock.'
>
> William Bird, 1820

place in the confines of private homes. William Bird commented in 1820 that although 'company, dancing, and the theatre are to the taste of all ... the habits of the Dutch and English are not as yet sufficiently amalgamated to allow them to associate in the same free manner as is usual with individuals of a common stock'.[228] In contrast to the daily pattern of Dutch Capetonians, 'The English follow precisely the same mode of life as at home; – dine late; go to bed late; and get up late; drink Port wine and bottled stout; wear narrow-brimmed hats; and walk in the noonday sun. This attachment and close adherence to national habits, in defiance and contempt of all local customs, is characteristic of the English, wherever they are found.'[229] But as time passed, the British also established their own domestic society, which mirrored that of Dutch Cape Town: even the ever-active John Herschel found the habit of an afternoon nap 'irresistible',[230] and receiving callers and returning their visits became a major occupation for the Herschels.[231]

But new leisure spheres also began to find expression. In contrast to the public display of physical prowess in the hunt, the duel or the races, men from the new middle classes of the town focused rather on the club, where the concerns appropriate to intellectual character and public action could be developed. The club was an exclusive leisure space – entirely male and, unlike the popular culture of the tavern, confined to a leisured elite. Membership of the Harmony Club in the Heerengracht was restricted to 'the principal functionaries, merchants and others of the respectable part of the community'. New members had to be proposed by existing ones and were only admitted on general ballot; 'it was a great favour to a young man to gain admittance.'[232] The club included a billiard room and card tables as well as a room 'set aside for conversing, smoking and the reading of newspapers'. Conversation was 'mostly about commercial matters',[233] although Barrow was somewhat scathing about the intellectual pursuits of its members: 'a club called the Concordia recently aspired to a collection of books, but the pursuits of the principal part of the members are drinking, smoking and gaming'.[234]

Other clubs catered for different sectors of the town's leisured classes. The Africa Club was mainly for officers of the garrison and subscription fees were high. Here there was less pretence to enlightened conversation and reading: 'there were here to be found two billiard tables, a whist club and conveniences for other games of skill and chance; and these I have reason to believe were the cause of throwing many of the members into distressed circumstances, while they enriched others.'[235]

An innovation in this period was the theatre. In the eighteenth century plays had been performed and watched by soldiers in a large room set aside for this purpose in the military barracks. The practice, which was continued well into the nineteenth century by British officers, was described by Lady Anne Barnard as 'good innocent fun and much

The garrison players in the variety of roles presented during the 1850 season. (CA E3913)

'A SINGULAR MIX' 143

Freemasonry in Cape Town

Freemasonry was closely linked to the Enlightenment. Many Patriots in the Netherlands were masons. The first lodge was established in Cape Town in 1772 and attracted support from Patriot sympathisers. It faced opposition from the established church as well as from the authorities, who urged 'men not to join an order that put forward equality as one of its maxims lest it should injure their standing in the estimation of others'. Numbers were few although in the mid-1790s masons hired rooms in Plein Street for meetings. The Batavian government gave a boost to freemasonry, Commissioner de Mist being a leading member in the Netherlands, and a new building for De Goede Hoop Lodge was completed in 1803.

Freemasonry was also gaining popularity in Britain at this time, and many army officers and administrators were masons. Regimental lodges held their own meetings, and some high-ranking British officials became members of De Goede Hoop Lodge. However, in 1811 a new lodge was opened under the English masonic constitution; it tended to attract members from immigrant retailers and traders. In 1821 The Hope Lodge was established with the backing of the mercantile and administrative elite. Many of its devotees were also members of the Commercial Exchange. Although at first it had cordial relations with De Goede Hoop Lodge, by the early 1830s strains between Dutch and British in the town had an impact on masonic affairs. At a dinner at De Goede Hoop Lodge in 1843, Dutch members were reported to have turned their glasses over and shouted 'No, No' when a toast was proposed to the Queen. The news spread through the British community as evidence of anti-British sentiment among the Dutch.[236]

The Dutch journalist Joseph de Lima in Masonic regalia. (CA M605)

more harmless than horse racing or drinking'.[237] 'Morgan of the Madras Cavalry' acquired quite a reputation as a star actor by 1810,[238] and in 1835 officers from the garrison gave a performance of David Garrick's bowdlerised Shakespearian adaptation, *Katherine and Petruchio*, together with *The Haunted Inn* and *Bombastes Furioso*, for the benefit of the charity schools.[239]

But theatre also found a civilian home. In 1800 the British governor Sir George Yonge formed a committee that presided over the building of Cape Town's first proper theatre, the African Theatre, in Hottentot (later Riebeeck) Square. Amateur companies – German, Dutch, French and British – provided the actors, who played only for charity. They were mostly men: Anne Barnard's refusal to take women's parts on a public stage had set something of a precedent of propriety. But a Mrs Kinniburgh apparently became the first British woman to perform at the African Theatre in 1807, and Dutch women were performing for the Africander Amateurs by 1810. Audiences were not always attentive and frequently talked through the performances, although 'when they saw a person smoking on the stage, they were reminded of their favourite occupation, and the sight provoked loud laughter and applause. From that time, desiring to take advantage of the public's taste, the actors introduced a few persons into each play produced by them who had to smoke pipes.'[240] Entertainments soon varied widely, from plays, usually with songs between each act, to the likes of a 'Turkish ballet', whistled English folksongs and dancing on stilts.

The coexistence of English and Dutch theatre groups emphasised the linguistic divide of the town. Charles Boniface, editor of *De Zuid-Afrikaan*, wrote a number of

Lady Anne Barnard's drawing of the African Theatre. (CA AG15691)

Dutch plays for public performance, and a Dutch children's theatre, Tot Oefening en Smaak, was started by the journalist J.S. de Lima.[241]

The African Theatre was initially confined to the elite: 'all boxes – no pit – each box to cost £24 per annum and to hold 6 subscribers, for twelve nights only, consequently it is too dear a plan to suit the pockets of subalterns'. Such exclusion was prompted by the fear that a theatre would 'render the younger branches of the Public Service indolent, dissipated and intractable, in place of active, industrious and obedient; by encouraging profusion the parent of profligacy; and by filling the settlement with all the refuse of the Green Rooms and foyers of Europe.'[242] But by 1804 a pit had been added. Admission to this part of the theatre cost 2s 6d, thus opening the theatre to some of the lesser ranks, though still ensuring that the majority of Cape Town's population would be excluded. Ticket pricing and a subscription-list system were two ways that social divisions could be reinforced in theatre seating arrangements.

But by the 1820s – partly because admission to the pits was now two rix-dollars (less than a shilling) – it seems that these means were not enough and the theatre was threatening the social hierarchy of Cape Town's classes. More direct methods of exclusion were implemented. Colonel Bird reported in 1822 that 'none of doubtful appearance are admitted to those seats in the theatre where, by their behaviour they might put modesty to the blush'. And in 1829, racial exclusion was introduced. After a fight, 'all slaves and free blacks' were barred from attending, and two years later three policemen were still on duty during performances to 'keep all black boys out'. Ironically the African Theatre was subsequently turned into a mission church for emancipated slaves and its windows were stoned by infuriated citizens who had lost a place of entertainment and disapproved of a 'slave church'. The church was named St Stephen's, after the saint who was martyred by stoning.

The need to exclude the undesirable was also marked in the public leisure spaces of the town. Governor Yonge attempted to close the government gardens to the general public altogether, but when this caused an outcry he consented to permit entry to all, provided that strollers wrote their names in a book kept at the sentry box at the entrance.[243]

'A SINGULAR MIX'

The middle classes take a Sunday afternoon stroll in the Company gardens. The purpose was primarily social – to see and to be seen. Note the prevalence of top hats, markers of male status, and the absence of lower-class Capetonians. Drawing by D'Oyly. (MuseumAfrica 74/2539/51)

But while the elite of the town were carving out new leisure spaces of their own, the popular culture of the majority of its inhabitants continued to thrive along lines which had been long established. As in the eighteenth century, the presence of large numbers of troops in the 1790s and 1800s gave a strongly masculine character to this culture, centred as it was around the tavern and the barrack room. Anne Barnard lamented in 1797 that 'for want of better society ... the garrison were much given to drinking and gaming'.[244] Attempts were made to limit access by troops to the town's taverns during the naval mutiny of 1797, but this proved a temporary and highly unpopular measure.

Drink was an important source of income in the town at every level of society, from the 54 wine merchants in 1820 to the 'smuggling houses' where people could buy drink when the licensed premises were closed, 'more especially on Sundays'.[245] Alcohol was cheap and easily available: not ale and beer, which were relatively expensive, but wine

The Parade Ground was a locality which accommodated the racial, class and gendered divides of Cape Town. D'Oyly's picture entitled 'Sunday evening on the Grand Parade' shows a busy scene of strollers of all classes and races with a military band playing in the background. (MuseumAfrica 74/2539/48)

George Duff's painting of Dock Road *c.* 1845 showing a number of taverns. (CA M466)

'The Cape wines and brandies are so attractive to the generality of mechanics, that not one in twenty can resist their seductive influence. Clever artisans exist a few years in a state of constant and wearying excitement from liquor, and are then transferred from the hospital to the churchyard ...'

J.E. Alexander, 1838

and Cape brandy, with spirits at 3d a half-pint. Many of the Irish labourers who had been imported in 1823 were reputed to have died of Cape brandy by 1829.[246] Immigrant artisans as a whole were considered to be vulnerable: 'The Cape wines and brandies are so attractive to the generality of mechanics, that not one in twenty can resist their seductive influence. Clever artisans exist a few years in a state of constant and wearying excitement from liquor, and are then transferred from the hospital to the churchyard ...'[247]

Alcohol dulled pain and provided relief from the unremitting monotony of poverty and overcrowded homes. Labourers were often paid at drinking places, to the extent that Ordinance 93 of 1832 forbade such practices on pain of a £5 fine.[248] Above all, at drinking houses Cape Town's poor could relax. When the authorities tried to forbid skittles in drinking houses on the grounds that it encouraged gambling, there was indignant protest that people 'should be deprived of every opportunity for amusement during their few hours of leisure'.[249] 'The melancholy, brooding, over-legislated, over-taxed, working population of this impoverished capital' needed some form of recreation, it was asserted, and the pubs kept them off the streets.[250]

In the eyes of the middle classes, Cape Town's poor were a 'mass of Drunkards, which our canteens nightly vomit forth'.[251] Canteens were regarded as 'mere receptacles of vice, and dens of thieves', 'pigsties which ought not to be allowed to exist'.[252] Undoubtedly drunkenness existed on a large scale in Cape Town. A Cape Town doctor claimed that 'There were hundreds of tipplers in this town, who would take offence at being called drunkards; who began with their *soopie* in the morning – took wine at breakfast, wine at dinner, wine at supper, and then their *soopie* again', and suggested that there were some people who were continually not quite sober.[253] Travellers were appalled: 'I had ever thought that drunkenness had in India reached the summit of its destructiveness but I had yet to see a still more awful display of its alarming, lamentable, and debasing

'A SINGULAR MIX' 147

effects as exhibited in South Africa', wrote one.²⁵⁴ In 1831 John Fairbairn, with the support of Samuel Bailey of the Somerset Hospital, established a Temperance Society to counteract the 'dreadful effects of intoxication', but its efforts came to little and by 1835 it had disappeared.²⁵⁵

Some popular social occasions were specifically intended to facilitate contact across divides of class, race and gender. Bird described in 1822 how

> while the public and private balls of the upper classes are going on, there are continual dances amongst the other orders, denominated rainbow balls, composed of each different hue in this many coloured town. The females are chiefly slave girls of the first class, and girls who have acquired their freedom; and amongst the men are seen officers, merchants and young Dutchmen. It cannot be pretended that these meetings add to the morals of the town.²⁵⁶

'The South African besetting sin', by D'Oyly. To middle-class eyes, Cape Town's poor were a 'mass of drunkards'. Wine was relatively cheap and dulled the pain and misery of poverty. (MuseumAfrica 74/2539/30)

But other recreations remained confined to the town's labouring classes. Gambling, card-playing and cockfighting, for which 'all the blacks and slaves of every nation here have an extravagant passion', continued to be found in 'every bye street or retired corner of the squares, even in the sands of the outlets or environs'.²⁵⁷ Cockfighting for gambling purposes was a popular male pastime that had been transplanted from the East Indies. In fact, inability to pay gambling debts was one cause of enslavement in some parts of the eighteenth- and nineteenth-century Indonesian archipelago.²⁵⁸ Robert Semple came across a 'a great crowd of slaves ... principally Malays' at a cockfight held at the Lion's Rump quarries: 'Loud shoutings, a mighty bustle and the crowd fluctuating to and fro, like an immense wave of the sea, indicated that some spectacle highly interesting ... was exhibiting. All the upper side and borders of the quarry were full of slave spectators who testified by their eager gestures and the clapping of their hands how deeply they were interested in what was going forward.'²⁵⁹

And one visitor in 1806 described how cocks were 'commonly armed with artificial spurs, and are seldom separated until one of them receives the mortal blow'. After the match, gambling with dice followed, which led the visitor to comment that 'among the ['Malay'] slaves a wild gambling spirit is universally predominant, and is carried to excess, that not only do they cheerfully risk every farthing they possess, but the very clothes upon their backs'.²⁶⁰ Such activities in the open streets met with official disapproval: the slaves at the 1806 cockfight posted lookouts to warn of the approach of the street patrols.

Dancing was another popular pastime for both male and female slaves and free blacks, who were often accompanied by musicians from Madagascar and Mozambique. In contrast to the dances of the elite or the 'rainbow balls', such dancing took place in the open. William Bird noted in 1822:

> although a few of these dances take place every night, yet the grand display is in the outskirts of the town, to which the black population rush, on a Sunday ... the Sunday dance is accompanied by native music of every description. The slave boys from Madagascar and Mozambique bring the stringed instruments of their respective tribes and nation ... the love of dancing is a ruling passion throughout the Cape population in every rank but music, though a pursuit favoured by a small part of the society, is here a passion with the negro alone.²⁶¹

'Loud shoutings, a mighty bustle and the crowd fluctuating to and fro, like an immense wave of the sea, indicated that some spectacle highly interesting was exhibiting. All the upper side and borders of the quarry were full of slave spectators who testified by their eager gestures and the clapping of their hands how deeply they were interested in what was going forward.'

Robert Semple, 1805

Charles Bell's depiction in 1840 of ex-slaves dancing to the music of drum, seaweed horn and *ramkie*. The *ramkie* was an instrument which was probably brought by slaves from Malabar where it had been adapted from Portuguese stringed instruments. Cultural transfers across Cape Town's mixed slave and free-black population were numerous. The original of this picture was destroyed by fire at the University of the Witwatersrand in the 1930s. (P. Kirby, *Musical Instruments of the Native Races of South Africa,* Johannesburg, 1965, plate 71b)

'DESTINIES OF AN EMPIRE'

All dancing on Sunday 10 September 1837 was halted by receipt of the news of the death of the monarch William IV. On Monday, 72 minute guns were fired from the Castle 'morning and evening' and the town was placed in formal mourning.[262] The following week an address to the new queen, Victoria, was laid out for signatures at the Commercial Exchange. Assuring the new sovereign of the 'fidelity and devoted attachment' of the citizens of Cape Town, it applauded the forthcoming 'perfect Freedom' to be attained 'by all ranks and classes of your people' as well as stressing the role that a self-governing Cape could play in the 'great destinies of an Empire which penetrates and occupies a most influential station in all the great divisions of the globe'.[263] Such patriotic sentiments, applauding the end of slavery and presented at the mercantile heart of the town, did not find universal acceptance: two months later the *Commercial Advertiser* reported that, 'if not numerously it was most respectably signed – which was much better'.[264] Middle-class British Capetonian notions of 'respectability' and mercantile self-assurance had only partially asserted themselves over the 'singular mix' of the town. But during the long reign of the new queen, Cape Town was set to become an unambiguously British colonial place.

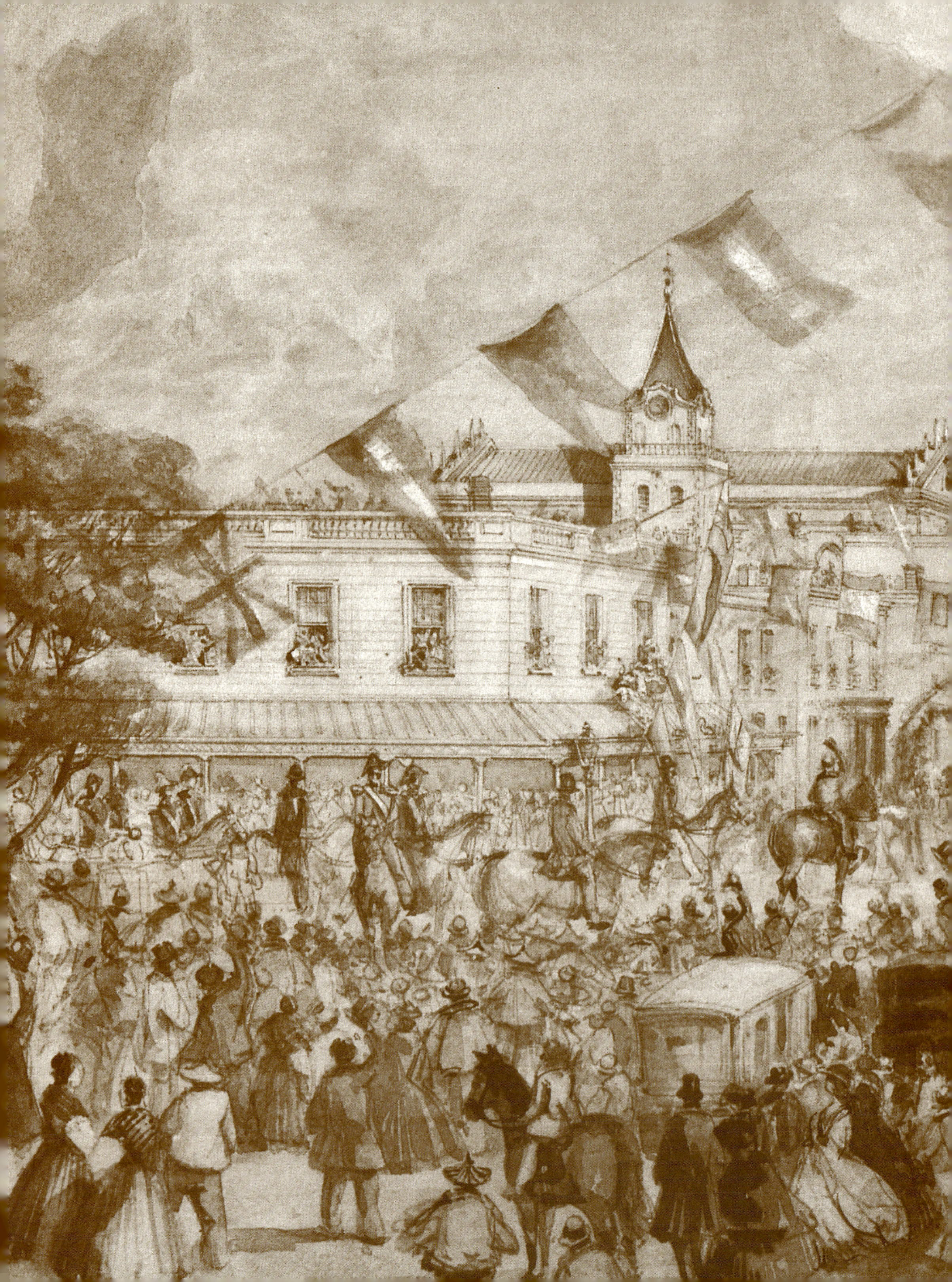

CHAPTER FOUR

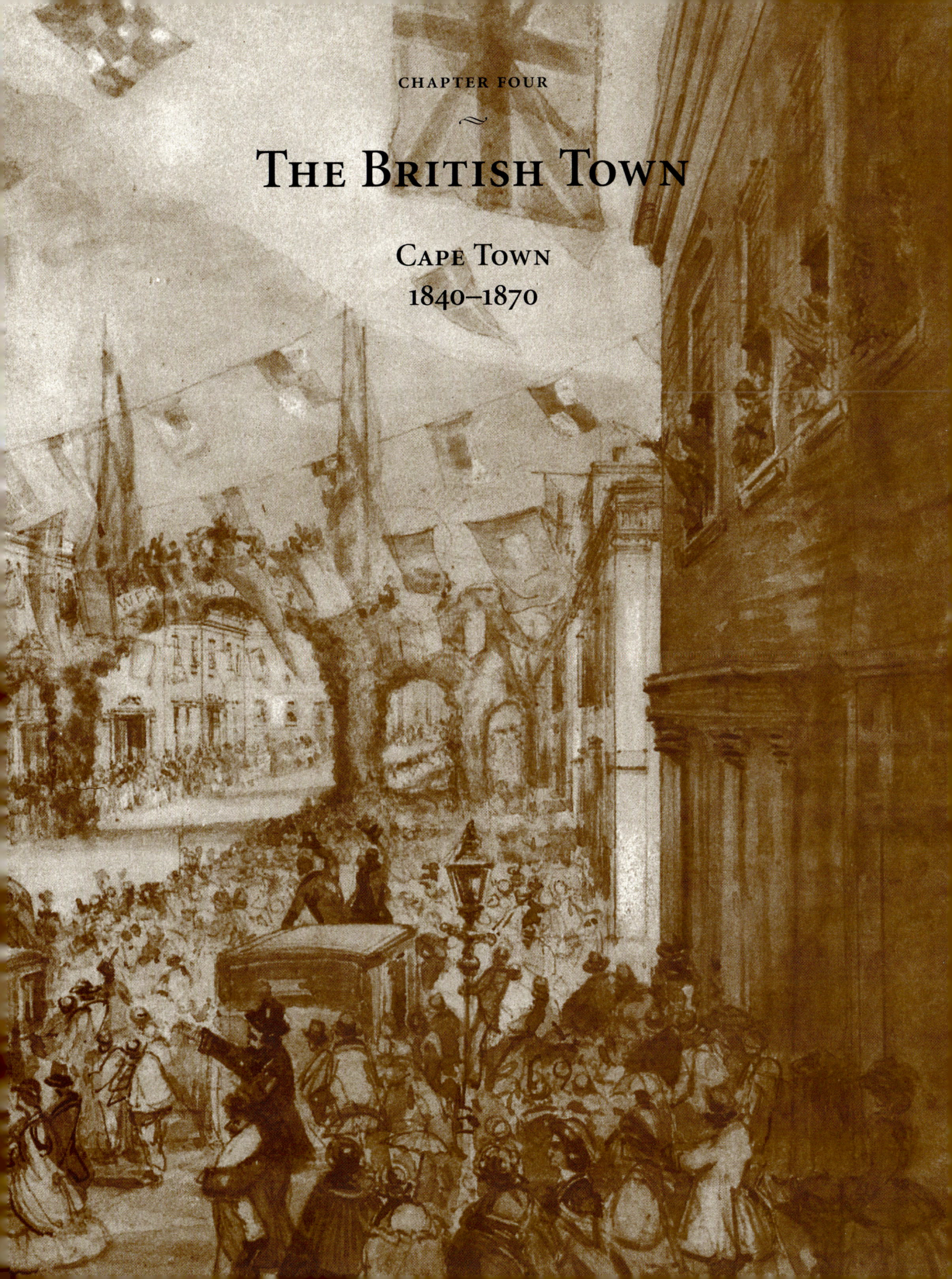

The British Town

Cape Town
1840–1870

AN explosion of sound heralded sunrise on 15 May 1863. The bells of all Cape Town's churches were ringing. They announced the start of a day of extraordinary celebration to mark the wedding in Britain of the heir to the throne, Prince Albert.

The central event of the day was the Grand Procession, at once entertainment and a symbol of social order in the town, led by a band and the military, the ultimate guarantors of order. In the wake of the soldiers trooped municipal councillors, followed by members of parliament, civil servants, foreign consuls, and directors of banks and institutions. Then came the schools and, after Education, Thrift and Prudence in the form of the benevolent societies, tailed by the Dignity of Labour in hierarchical order – artisans, labourers, a life-boat crew, seamen, fishermen, boatmen and the fire brigade. Bringing up the rear was a carnival parade: floats included 'Britannia in triumphal car attended by Tritons', 'Lady Godiva', 'Knights in armour', the giants 'Gog and Magog', 'Bacchus and Bacchanals' and 'Jack-in-the-green'. A motley throng of men dressed as clowns, chimney sweeps, harlequins and varlets made fun of the crowd. Winding its way slowly through the main streets, the procession started and finished on the Parade. 'The whole of Cape Town' watched or performed, and people from the country increased the audience, who 'cheered and yelled almost to madness'.

Afterwards came the feasting. The schoolchildren were fed in Greenmarket Square, in the centre of which was a 'lofty flagpole … bedecked with evergreens to remind one of a Maypole'. Members of the fire brigade were treated in the Town House and Breakwater workmen at Mr Fuller's store. Other workmen, artisans, seamen and soldiers, together with 'the poor', were entertained on the Parade. There a whole ox was roasted on a spit. After the first slice was ritually tasted by the governor, the meat was then distributed with copious amounts of free wine. When lunch was over the Parade hosted 'rustic sports' – climbing the greasy pole, catching the pig with a greasy tail or wheelbarrow races – and athletics. After watching for a while, the governor and 'elite of the city and neighbourhood' repaired to a marquee in the Botanic Gardens for a late but splendid subscription lunch. In the evening, the gardens – illuminated with lanterns – became the venue for a fête and 'fancy fair', with boxing, marionettes, a mock Chinese astrologer and Christy-minstrels. Bonfires were lit on Lion's Head, Lion's Rump and Robben Island. At 10 p.m. there were fireworks on the Parade, while a Grand Masquerade Ball commenced at the circus.[1]

The 1863 parade, like the Jubilee parades of 1887 and 1897, was highly organised, the order of appearance of its huge cast determined by the municipal and festival committees which represented the political, economic and social elite of the town. This was less an exercise in popular sovereignty, like parades in the United States, than a ritual display of rank. Control was vested in the city's resident magistrate, Colonel Hill, the local lord of rule rather than misrule. For all its carnival component, it was 'dominated by planning and respect', confirming the existing social order.[2] Yet the parade had to satisfy the entire city and the marching units revealed much about group identity, reinforcing structures of class, gender, occupation and religion.

Seen through the eyes of young Eliza, a black schoolgirl from St Matthew's mission at Keiskammahoek in the eastern Cape, the rituals were less impressive:

Yesterday was said to be the wedding-day of the Great Son of Victoria, but it was not really the day of his marriage, for he had been married some time. The thing first done was arranging the children of the schools and I was there too. All walked

Previous pages: The joyous celebrations of 17 September 1860 when young Prince Alfred visited Cape Town – captured here by Cape Town's most assiduous mid-century artist, Thomas Bowler – were typical of patriotic imperial commemorations. (CTCC)

Traversing the main streets in procession not only displayed the nature of urban social order; it also described the emerging central business district, the area in which much of the city's wealth was accumulated. The Grand Parade, scene of the feasting of the poor, was the regular venue for military reviews before the seventeenth-century Castle, bastion of European rule, while on Greenmarket Square, where the schoolchildren dined, stood the focus of municipal government, the Town House. The Botanic Gardens, location for both subscription dinner and fancy fair, had originally been the VOC's vegetable garden, the raison d'être for the city's existence.

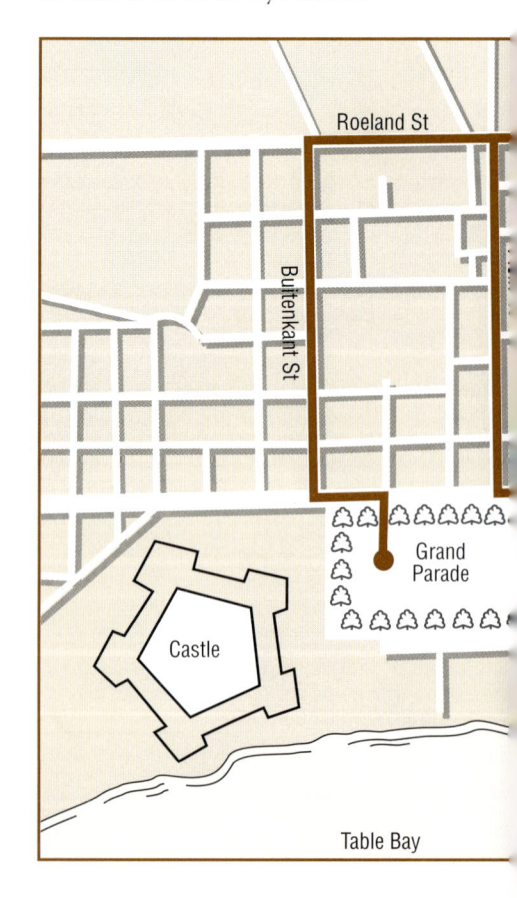

in threes, going from one street to another. When we left the school-house we took up our station on an open piece of ground, other people climbed on the houses, and others looked from below. On one house where we were standing there was a figure of a man like a king, a red cloth was put as if it were held by him, it is called in English a flag. Amongst all of us there were flags of different beautiful kinds, we stood there a great while, till we saw a multitude of soldiers and their officer and little chiefs and different sorts of people; one set wore clothes all alike, another had different clothes and ancient hats which were worn by the people of that time. All these now went in front, a very long line, then followed the ranks of another school, and we came after them. When we had finished going through many streets, we went to stand in another open spot of ground. All the time we were walking we were singing the song of Victoria. And there we saw the Governor and his wife; we all saluted.[3]

The 1863 festivities affirmed a social order which had many continuities through to 1900. While the city's elite was wholly white, black and white intermingled among the lower orders. But there were some features of the 1863 celebrations that were less likely to appear towards the end of the century: among the participants in the athletics was Simeon, 'a Kafir', who won one race and came second in two. Black and white sportsmen were not yet segregated, and the society as a whole was more open than it would become in later decades.

The British Town

By the middle of the century Cape Town had become an identifiably British colonial city. English was generally accepted as the medium for public discourse. In government, business, school and even the church the British dominated. In 1837, 12 of the 22 Dutch Reformed ministers at the Cape were Scots. 'The earlier part of the nineteenth century can be described in terms of the rise of British hegemony in colonial society,' writes one historian.[4] If so, dominance was not maintained through force of numbers, for in 1865 only 4500 of the 15,000 white residents had been born in Europe. It was through education and high culture, as well as commerce, that they asserted their social position.

Men dominated this world although a few women established a recognised place in the society. Social mobility was tolerated by the ethic of 'self-improvement' and the door was not entirely shut to the working classes. Barriers were, however, much more difficult for black people to breach, an indication of the limits to an open society in mid-century Cape Town.

British ascendancy in the town was established partly through education. Schools proliferated, not only for the middle classes but also for the poor. From the Scots superintendent-general of education through to the ill-paid teachers of the schools of industry or model infant schools, the majority of teachers were British. The systems they employed, whether it was 'Bell's system' or the 'monitorial system', were based on British methods, requiring the use of British textbooks, the singing of English songs and the learning of English verses. Although in the mission schools children learnt little more than the three Rs, it was here that British culture was transmitted to the emergent urban proletariat.

One indication of the success of formal education was literacy rates. According to the 1875 census about 50 per cent of the Cape Town population could read. Most of these were white people but statistics for coloureds were misleading since many Muslims read

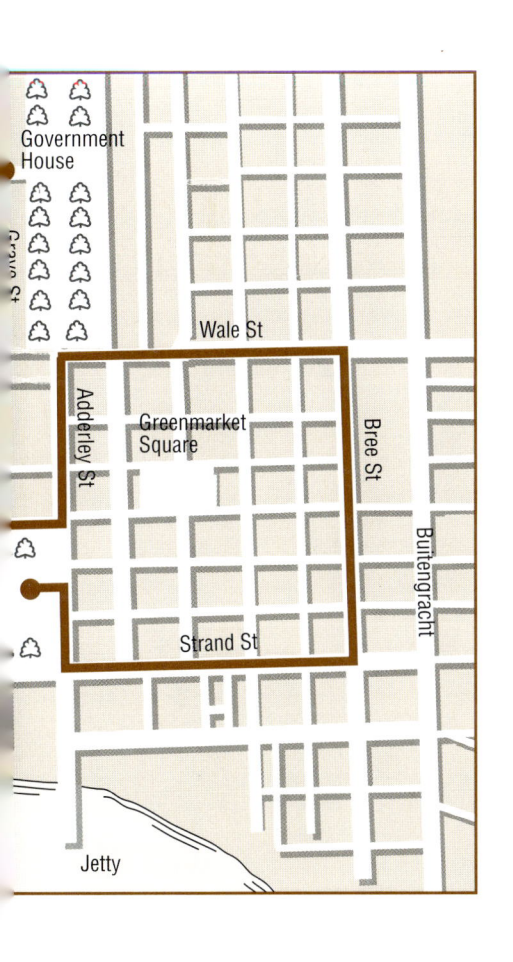

A.S. Robertson's substantial premises on the Heerengracht suggest that trade as a bookseller could be lucrative in the mid-nineteenth century. Robertson's standing in the local British community was further enhanced when he succeeded John Fairbairn as the second chairman of the Mutual Life Assurance Society of the Cape of Good Hope (later known as the Old Mutual) in 1850. In the foreground is the Wynberg omnibus and on the right 'Old Moses', one of Cape Town's 'characters'. (MuseumAfrica 312)

Arabic, a language which was not regarded as a measure of literacy. The press was another ingredient of a literate culture. In 1857 there were four newspapers published in the town; a year later there were eight, two Dutch and six English, with a combined circulation of about 3500, although many more probably read the papers than bought them. There was also a thriving book trade. In 1875 Cape Town boasted 5 booksellers, 41 male and 5 female book-binders, 121 printers and compositors, and 9 newspaper proprietors, editors and publishers. Of the publishing firms Saul Solomon's company, with its lucrative government printing contract, was the largest, with over 300 employees at its height.

Apart from the newspapers, there was one major attempt to instil a local literary culture through the kind of monthly periodical so popular with Victorians: the *Cape Monthly Magazine*. This was a journal of miscellaneous essays, edited by Roderick Noble. First launched in 1857, it died out in 1860, to be resuscitated in 1870. The *Cape*

RODERICK NOBLE

Roderick Noble (1829–75) had emigrated to Cape Town from Scotland in 1850 in an attempt to recover from a 'pulmonary condition'. He taught initially at Dr Changuion's school where he learnt Dutch, before moving on to the South African College. Although he was not an original thinker, his students testified to his ability to excite his pupils. His typical programme for the day indicates his wide range of interests. At 9 a.m. he was at the College lecturing on England's novelists or theologians; at 10 he would be teaching on the constitutional history of the British empire. By 11 he would be at a public meeting, taking prolific notes and returning to the College at 12 to give a dissertation on the philosophy of Dugald Stewart or another of the luminaries of the Scottish Enlightenment. In the next hour he would turn to the teaching of science – astronomy, zoology, geology, electricity, magnetism or heat. At the end of the day he would visit the Public Library or the Commercial Exchange while the evening would be spent at a public meeting, Bible union or ball.

In addition, Noble attended parliament regularly and made a point of meeting any notables visiting Cape Town. Apart from his teaching activities he was a prolific journalist, editing a number of papers at different times. Noble died in 1875 at the age of 46.

(SAL INIL 1045)

154   CAPE TOWN 1840–1870

In the 1860s the South African Museum was housed in the South African Library. The collection which Layard built up, intended to provide something for everyone, was an eclectic assortment: 'A cast of a famous Victorian nude statue known as "Bayley's Eve" separated the geological collection from the shells. Between two of the bird cases stood a "beautiful working model of a cathedral erected in Jamaica by Mr. Calvert." On the floor underneath a model of a railroad lay a Stapelia from Namaqualand which Layard had to admit was decaying. A case contained "a mixed assortment of birds' eggs, Egyptian and Greek relics, casts of celebrated men and lastly an interesting relic, an embroidered Greek jacket worn by Lord Byron, preserved by an old and faithful domestic, now, like his master, where the weary are at rest"' (A.C. Brown, *A History of Scientific Endeavour in South Africa*, Cape Town, 1977, p. 63). (CA AG1874)

Monthly Magazine was an ardent propagandist for middle-class values, covering such topics as the need for local medical training, Cape Town's water supply and recent scientific developments including Darwin's theories, of which the *Cape Monthly Magazine* was cautiously supportive.

By the 1850s the South African Literary and Philosophical Society (formerly the Literary and Scientific Institution) had faded from the scene, and the libraries and scientific bodies were emerging as the main centres of high culture in the town. The South African Public Library, established in 1818, acquired a new building in 1860 – opened in one of the many ceremonies attended by the young Prince Alfred, Queen Victoria's 15-year-old midshipman son. The Royal Observatory, with Thomas Maclear as the astronomer royal, remained a significant institution of scientific endeavour while the South African Museum, in a state of decay in the 1840s, was revitalised by E.L. Layard (brother of the Egyptologist) when he was given the task, in 1854, of looking after the museum. His hours of work at the Colonial Office, from 10 a.m. to 4 p.m., left him with enough spare time to prepare a catalogue of South African birds, the first comprehensive study, published in 1867.

Although the working classes rarely penetrated the Public Library, in 1853 a second Mechanics' Institute was started in Cape Town to provide facilities for their self-

THE BRITISH TOWN   155

Lucy Lloyd

The long life of Lucy Lloyd (1834–1914) illustrates the nature of the space which existed in Cape Town for the genuinely intellectual. Although a woman, Lucy Lloyd started with two advantages: she was the daughter of a clergyman and was well connected – after her mother's death she was educated privately by her uncle, Admiral Sir John Dundas. Both factors provided a potentially cultivated environment.

In 1862 Lloyd's sister married the German philologist Dr Wilhelm Bleek, then curator of the Grey collection in the South African Public Library. In the mid-nineteenth century philology was at the forefront of intellectual advance. Recognising his sister-in-law's ability, Bleek employed her initially as a copyist and translator of Italian. When he developed an interest in Khoesan languages, he was quick to realise that she had a better ear than he for grasping their tongue. Together they recorded the Khoesan language, folklore and religious beliefs. After Bleek's death in 1875, Lloyd continued the work independently. The Library also invited her to complete Bleek's inventory of the Grey collection (at half Bleek's salary).

Lloyd played an active role in the South African Folklore Society and in 1879 helped to establish the *Folk-lore Journal*. For about fifteen years, from the mid-1880s to 1905, financial constraints forced her to live in Europe but she returned in her old age to Cape Town and her local ethnographic interests.

(SAL PHA)

---

improvement. Located in the Town House, it contained a small library offering books on science, history, travel, theology, poetry and fiction, as well as a number of monthly and weekly periodicals. Membership fluctuated from about 60 to 180 and it survived for some eighteen years, serving a core of immigrant artisans.

Art, as much as literature or science, was a means both of maintaining and of displaying British hegemony. Two artists active in Cape Town pictured in their work contrasting aspects of the mid-century town. Thomas Bowler (1812–69) was the epitome of the successful immigrant. After leaving Thomas Maclear's service he turned to art. A friend of the evangelicals, Bowler presented in his work an image of Cape Town that was orderly and tranquil. His vision of the post-emancipation coloured class was one of industry, progress and self-improvement, catering both to his liberalism and to the tourist market.

Charles Davidson Bell (1813–82) presented a very different face of Cape Town. His depictions of Khoi revelry showed drunk, dissolute, indolent and violent subjects, anarchic scenes of men and women fighting, of women fighting with women, and even of children torn between aggressive and riotous parents. In his classic painting, 'Jan van Riebeeck meets the Hottentots', Bell encapsulated the settler interpretation of colonial history in a single image. Here the imposing central figure of Jan van Riebeeck is flanked by a trader, a preacher and two soldiers, representing the agents of European civilisation in Africa. These heroic civilisers confront a miserable clutch of Khoikhoi, seemingly already conquered and dispossessed of their lands. This most famous of Bell's works – and an enduring image – won first prize at a fine arts exhibition in Cape Town in 1861.[5]

Yet, if this was an era of British hegemony, the Dutch in Cape Town were more

Charles Bell's anti-evangelical stance was captured in this scene of drunken Khoi. (UCT Bell Heritage Trust BC 686 C8)

L.ᵗ Williams. 4. M.ʳ Hertzog. 5 Gibbs. carpenter. 6. Kirke. soldier. 7. Policemen. keeping the ground.
ors. 10. Members of an Extra-provisional-deputy-superintendent-opposition-sub-committee of the
of the Ecclesiastical Courts of the Dutch Reformed Church. Cape Town. Cape of Good Hope

The Royal Observatory was the site of the most advanced scientific endeavour in mid-century Cape Town. In this 1837 watercolour by Maclear's young assistant, Charles Piazzi Smyth, Maclear is establishing a surveying baseline on the Grand Parade, 1050 ft long, marked at each end by a cannon. (SA National Cultural History Museum)

resilient than historians of Afrikaner nationalism have acknowledged. They adapted themselves to British commercial and political practices and reshaped their identity as they moved further away in spirit and mores from a Holland that had changed considerably from the pre-Napoleonic country they had known under the VOC.

How do we define this group and how did they define themselves? A significant proportion of the Dutch elite had been thoroughly assimilated by 1840. Josias Cloete of Constantia, born under the VOC, rose to become a general in the British army. A generation later, the businessman J.G. Steytler sent his children to be educated in Britain and retired there himself for a number of years. Who would deny that Andrew Murray jun., married to Emma Rutherfoord of Cape Town, was Cape Dutch? How would one describe J.S. de Lima, a Portuguese Jew, or the French-born Etienne Boniface, or Antoine

THE BRITISH TOWN 157

Changuion, all regarded as founders of the modern Afrikaans language? At the other end of the social scale, Cape Town's coloured prostitutes were also categorised at the time as 'Afrikander' and often spoke only the *taal*. And what of the 'Cape Malays' who wrote the *taal* in Arabic? The Cape Dutch in Cape Town (now sometimes calling themselves Afrikaners) illustrate the point that ethnic identity depends on self-perception. Their numbers can only be roughly estimated but it is probable that they still formed the majority of whites in 1865.

Economically the Dutch flourished under the British as they could not under the monopolistic and moribund VOC. Many were slave owners themselves and they profited even from emancipation. The fortunes of Dutch businessmen in Cape Town had been laid during the 1830s and 1840s when they acted as moneylenders to their compatriots on the security of slaves. Cape Town's Dutch slave owners were not neglected when compensation was paid. P.M. Brink and J.J.L. Smuts were both members of the slave compensation board while Smuts, acting with Hamilton Ross, was an agent for the payment of compensation money, along with Servaas de Kock and J.H. Hofmeyr.[6]

Slave compensation money was frequently invested in property to house the newly liberated population. The brothers J.H. and J.A.H. Wicht were outstanding examples of moneylenders turned slum landlords. J.A.H. Wicht also reinvested slave compensation money in business. Of the six companies formed in 1838, three were dominated by Dutch shareholders – De Protecteur Fire and Life Assurance Co. (chairman, J.H. Hofmeyr), the South African Bank (chairman, F.S. Watermeyer) and the Board of Executors (chairman, the Hon. H. Cloete). The improved financial status of these Dutch businessmen gave them a sound economic basis for their bid for political power in succeeding decades. To judge from the records of such institutions as the Board of Executors, 'old' Cape Town families like the Hofmeyrs and the Hiddinghs retained their economic position in the town into the twentieth century. The first English-speaking chairman of the Board of Executors, the lawyer W.E. Moore, was appointed only in 1903, at which time the directors were still substantially Dutch-speaking.

By the 1830s a new Dutch intelligentsia was emerging which challenged British cultural hegemony. Sophisticated immigrants like Boniface, de Lima and Changuion enriched the cultural life of the town but they were European interlopers. A more significant figure in this process of adapting and shaping identities was Christoffel Joseph Brand. His first names indicate his divided heritage, for he had been named after his godfather, Joseph Banks, the renowned English naturalist who was a friend of his father's. Brand was educated in Leiden and Edinburgh as an advocate, but despite a successful career he did not become a judge, partly because of his insolvency in 1848. Never fully anglicised, he was one of the founders of *De Zuid-Afrikaan* and became its second editor. Strongly opposed to emancipation, he also engaged vigorously in the struggle for parliamentary representation working, ironically, with his former opponent, John Fairbairn. In 1854 Brand became the first speaker of the Cape parliament.

Brand's career illustrates the extent to which Dutch legal men in Cape Town, from Sir John Truter onwards, absorbed British legal and constitutional values. *De Zuid-Afrikaan*, despite its opposition to aspects of British rule, saw British authority as 'synonymous with civilized progress and order'.[7] Just how pervasive these views were can be seen in the continuing presence of the Dutch in Cape Town's legal fraternity, assured as they were by the continued use of Roman–Dutch law, which was less accessible to immigrant British legal men. In 1820 there were 95 Dutch and 28 British professionals in all in Cape Town, and in law 18 Dutch and 5 British; both judges were British but all the

---

EARLY PHOTOGRAPHY

Photography was relatively slow to develop in South Africa. The first professional photographer, Carel Sparmann, set up shop in Cape Town in 1847. It was fitting that the first photograph in South Africa should have been of the Royal Observatory (below), taken in February 1843 by Charles Piazzi Smyth. Early processes limited the illustrations to still studio portraits and stationary objects and it was only in the 1880s that subjects began to achieve some of the liveliness found in paintings and drawings. But photographers were even more selective of their subject matter than artists and ignored many facets of Cape Town life, particularly the growth of District Six and the lives of the poor.

(Oxford Museum of the History of Science)

Christoffel Joseph Brand (1797–1875) (CA AG7383)

The Cape Town Dutch newspapers always had a vigorous circulation in the country districts. This drawing by Charles Bell illustrates the point that news reached the illiterate population as well. (SAL A.Pic.Mend. 23)

Josephus Suasso de Lima

(CA E311)

*J*osephus Suasso de Lima (1791–1858) epitomised the cosmopolitan character of mid-century Dutch Cape Town. Of Portuguese–Jewish descent, educated in Holland where he converted to the Dutch Reformed Church, de Lima came to the Cape in 1818. His appearance was eccentric, his private life unconventional, and his financial dealings erratic. His main claim to fame was as a pioneer author of Dutch literature at the Cape but for Cape Town his importance lies in his almanacs, more detailed than the official directories, and including backstreet lanes not usually listed. Although his almanacs were confined to the economically active, he claimed for his 1855 edition that he had 'not left unvisited a single house, situated in any nook or corner, street, gracht, lane, passage, court or yard'. In Elbow Lane he noted nine Chinese – by name, Asat, Ajoet, Akon, Ajie, Ajoen, Akan, Atjung, Alok and Atjong.

advocates were Dutch. In 1847 there were 185 professionals of whom 108 were British and 77 Dutch. Of these, however, 32 Dutch and only 15 British were in branches of the law.

Brand stood between two worlds. If he was enlightened on issues of representation, his views on race and labour were conservative. Within the Dutch Reformed Church, however, he ranked as a 'liberal' for having embraced the ideas of German scientific rationalism. These were anathema to many of the DRC ministers, trained as they still were in Holland, and they rejected 'liberalism' in favour of the confessional Dutch Reveil movement, which was a reaction against such thinking. In effect the influence of the Reveil movement isolated the mass of the Dutch population in Cape Town from the modern ideas which were integral to British middle class values. Indeed, if the gulf between the British and Dutch widened in the 1850s in Cape Town, it had as much to do with the different intellectual influences permeating the two societies as with policies of anglicisation. For under British rule the Cape Town Dutch enjoyed greater political liberties, greater prosperity, better educational facilities and a freer church than they had under the VOC.

A Trading Economy

In the 1820s Cape Town had seemed to British immigrants to suffer from a thoroughly stagnant economy. A 'waveless calm, that slumber of the dead' was the description of the energetic young journalist John Fairbairn.[8] Yet in the next twenty years Cape Town acquired the elements of modern capitalism, including a private commercial bank, the Cape of Good Hope Bank, in 1837.[9] The motive force behind this expansion was British imperial enterprise even if sources of capital remained largely local. By 1838 private joint-stock companies had proliferated and the Dutch presence in local commerce had also expanded.

This was an economy which was still based mainly on agriculture. Although the wine industry of the western Cape was under pressure, the expansion of the merino wool industry from 1846 reinforced the alliance of Cape Town merchants with the colonial farmers. The boom only ended in 1859 when overseas wool prices collapsed. Wool farming was an Eastern Province industry: by 1860 the volume of trade passing through Port Elizabeth was greater than that of Cape Town. But by this time Cape Town commerce was ubiquitous, spread through the agency of insurance companies and investment,

JOSEPH BARRY

Joseph Barry (1796–1865) was one of the most successful Cape Town merchants to corner a place in the wool trade. The firm was founded in 1834 in partnership with Barry's nephews. Barry's marriage to Johanna van Reenen gave him extensive farming connections in the Overberg. He handled the family estates and even issued private banknotes. He promoted superior merino sheep farming by offering favourable terms of trade and providing prizes for good-quality wool. He took shares in sheep farms himself. On the Breede River Barry built up a successful little port. Between 1847 and 1860 the company handled more than £2 million of wool sales. The Barrys also represented the Equitable Fire Assurance and Trust Co., the Mutual, and De Protecteur throughout the Overberg. Barry wealth was reinvested in the powerful Cape Town Railway and Dock Co., and the London and South African Bank.[11]

(SAL PHA)

both private and formal. Western Cape merchants 'became financiers and bankers to the first generation of eastern Cape sheep farmers'.[10] The fruits of this were to be seen in Cape Town where, by 1860, there were five local banks with a total capital of £494,000, and thirteen non-banking joint-stock companies, mainly insurance and trust companies.

One should not, however, exaggerate these developments. Cape Town held little attraction for overseas investors. But Capetonians themselves could not resist a promising opportunity. Gold had recently been discovered in California and in Australia, and Capetonians succumbed in the 1850s to 'gold fever'. Despite the collapse of the first Namaqualand copper company by 1848, favourable surveying reports led to a 'mania of speculation' in Namaqualand copper shares after 1853. The boom lasted for nearly 18 months. Over 22 companies were formed and £70,000 invested, often by people of very limited means, including 'apprentices and errand boys not out of their teens'.[12] Most lost everything and even merchants like Maximilian Thalwitzer were declared insolvent. It was a hard-earned lesson for Cape Town.

The town suffered partly because it was so badly served by existing legislation. The Dutch legacy in mercantile and company law was weak and little in the way of English practice had been introduced. But the Namaqualand copper débâcle hastened changes. Companies acquired a corporate legal identity and shareholders came to be protected. Most important of all was the passing of the Joint Stock Companies Limited Liability Act of 1861.[13] These reforms made the Cape a more attractive field for investment. In 1861 the London and South African Bank was formed as the first imperial bank operating in South Africa. The Cape Town Railway and Dock Company, established in 1855, also with overseas investment, brought substantial sums of money into the town.[14] Thus when diamonds were discovered in 1868 a capitalist infrastructure already existed which

The growth of the wool trade, 1848–1860, by weight (x 1000 lb) and value.

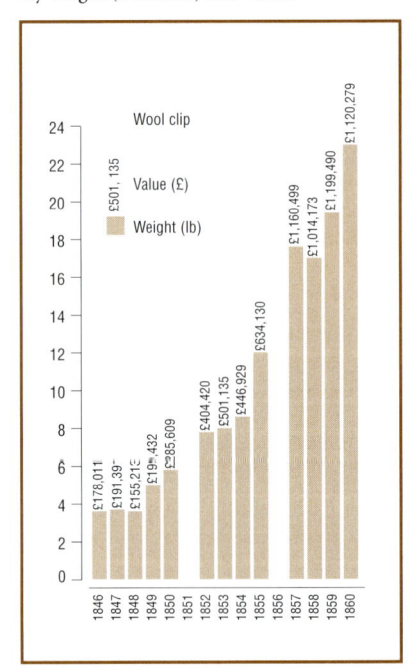

Year	Value (£)
1846	£178,011
1847	£191,39-
1848	£155,21-
1849	£19-,432
1850	£285,609
1852	£404,420
1853	£501,135
1854	£446,929
1855	£634,130
1857	£1,160,499
1858	£1,014,173
1859	£1,199,490
1860	£1,120,279

made the development of the fields much more viable. Such changes should be kept in perspective, however. Cape Town was no El Dorado for European or imperial investment, and growth remained moderate.

A strong military presence continued to influence the Cape Town economy. An increase in the garrison, as a result of war on the eastern Cape frontier or in India, had a substantial short-term effect on local prosperity. Between 1825 and 1838 government military expenses brought over £340,000 worth of currency into circulation in the colony compared with £254,000 as a result of private imports, including slave compensation money. Much of this cash found its way into the pockets of Cape Town traders. Similarly the Indian Mutiny of 1857 brought a minor boom to Cape horse-breeders, introducing over £400,000 into the colony and leading to a spending spree on carriages, pianos and fashionable clothes and furniture.

The middle of the nineteenth century saw a global revolution in communications. From the beginning of their rule the British had recognised the importance of communication as the Dutch had never done. Roads formed the 'sinews of empire', enabling first the military and later the settlers to exert control over the African wilderness.[15] As early as 1801 a regular weekly wagon between Cape Town and Simon's Town had been instituted. By 1806 a postal service, mainly on horseback, had been established throughout the colony. Before 1830 wagons (4500 in number in 1821) still had to struggle up the steep and dangerous route over the Hottentots Holland mountains east of the Flats. In that year the opening of Sir Lowry's Pass greatly eased contact with the interior. Behind many of the improvements in communication was John Montagu, the colonial

LADIES' MINING COMPANY

This parodic advertisement for Namaqualand mining spoke worlds about gender and class attitudes, epitomised in the pathetic figure of 'Queen Rebecca', a well-known Cape Town 'character'. (UCT Macmillan)

"Several young ladies, who have made a tour to Namaqualand (in imagination), are desirous to make known their discoveries to the Wives and Daughters of their fellow-citizens of all classes.

The scheme on which they purpose to commence their work, will be, not only as avowedly honest and safe as many of those started before, but the Projectors assure their Sister-citizens, that they know as much of the NAMAQUALAND METAL (Brass) as many of those who have previously projected Mining Schemes. There will be no need of either Tramway or Railway for bringing their Metal from the Country, and its value is so well known to Speculators, that the Projectors feel no analysis of Samples is necessary. It is proposed to issue THREE MILLION SHARES, at A SHILLING each. Sixpence to be paid previous to any information being given of the Whereabouts of the Mines, and the other sixpence when the Mines produce anything beyond the first Sample. The Directors will be appointed previous to the First Meeting taking place (as is usual); and no old Women or Apprentices will be allowed to have any Share in the undertaking. If all the Shares should be taken up before Applications can be sent in from the Country, the Original Proprietors will not hesitate to issue a few Extra on their own responsibility.

Some excellent hands at 'Stagging' are engaged, and nothing will be left undone that legitimate trading in Mines will admit of. The First Meeting will take place on ROBBEN ISLAND. QUEEN REBECCA is engaged to propose the First Resolution.

Offices: Kable Court
Treasurer: Agnes Stretchem
Solicitors: Mesdames Fleece'em and Do'em
Secretary: Sarah Scrip"[16]

secretary. A key feature of Montagu's public works programme was the 'rehabilitative' use of convict labour. To achieve his ambition of a trunk road between Cape Town and the Eastern Province, a hard road across the Cape Flats was his first objective. By 1845 this was completed, 'hard' in more senses than one for the men who built it.

But for individuals regular and comfortable travel remained the preserve of the wealthy who could afford their own carriages. Only when local roads were improved did a public transport service become viable. In 1830 the 75th Regiment built a road to Green Point. Access to the Atlantic coast was further improved when the road over Kloof Nek to Camps Bay was started in 1848. By this time the Salt River had been bridged, at last providing an approach to the town from the Flats during the winter rains. The first regular horse-drawn omnibus ran from Cape Town to Wynberg in 1836, 'a handsome covered wagon' carrying about eight passengers.[17] It was sorely needed. By 1859 there were four competing companies, William Cutting running the most popular service. Valuable though it was, fares, at 1s 6d from Cape Town to Wynberg, were well beyond the daily budget of most people, and it was horribly uncomfortable in Cutting's 'broken-down' omnibuses, which 'jog and jingle into town every day, over dislocating roads and at eight miles an hour'. To 'neutralise' the dust from the south-easters, passengers habitually wore their oldest headgear, keeping their best hats for their arrival – one old lady emerging in Cape Town 'like an elderly butterfly, quite spruce and gay'. Omnibuses were surprisingly egalitarian: inside 'you may meet fat Malay matrons, jammed side by side with unctuous officials', while outside might be found a judge or bishop side by side with clerks or publicans – 'we are not at all exclusive'.[18]

Improved communications were not confined to roads. The year 1860 brought the first telegraph line between Cape Town and Simon's Town, erected by the Cape of Good Hope Telegraph Company. By 1863 Cape Town was also linked telegraphically to Grahamstown. Similar rapid links with the outside world had to wait for the laying of submarine cables – in 1879 between Durban and Aden and in 1885 between Cape Town and Europe.

Locally, the coming of the railway proved more revolutionary. The Cape Town Railway and Dock Company built the first stretch of line to Eerste River in 1862; Wellington was reached the following year. The Wynberg Railway Act of 1861 incorpo-

John Montagu (1797–1853) was an energetic but controversial figure. With a background as one of the most brutal administrators of Van Diemen's Land (Tasmania), Montagu arrived at the Cape in 1843 and 'set to work without delay, defining departmental responsibilities, remedying existing evils and supplying necessary services' (*DSAB*, vol. 1, p. 554). His achievements ensured his respect amongst earlier historians, but more recent academics have pointed to his corruption and dictatorial methods. Capetonians detested him. (CA M481)

The hard road across the Cape Flats greatly eased contacts with the interior. (UCT Bell Heritage Trust BC 686 C5)

P.C. Trench, an 'Indian', produced a series of paintings depicting Cape Town transport at mid-century. Here the Victoria coach, which operated between Wynberg and Cape Town, speeds briskly downhill. (CA)

In this watercolour J.C. Poortermans depicted a substantial mid-century Cape Town with a graceful terrace of houses on Sir Lowry Road opposite the New Market, energetic workmen, quarrelsome sailors and the Swellendam mail. (MuseumAfrica 1034)

In 1853 the first adhesive stamp, designed by Charles Bell, was introduced at the Cape. This was a minor revolution, transforming postal communication.

rated a new company and the Wynberg line was opened on 19 December 1864. It was wonderfully fast compared with Cutting's omnibus service – 18 as opposed to 8 miles an hour – and was smooth and comparatively clean. It was also exclusive: the middle classes could now travel first-class, avoiding the 'mal-odorous nurses reeking with cocoa-nut oil, who almost poison our merchant princes'.[19] It was not surprising that it attained instant popularity with the latter.

The railway age also introduced Cape Town to industrial dispute. 'Navvies' were imported from Britain to build the railways,[20] and almost immediately Salt River gained a reputation for industrial unrest. In 1861 a 'navvies' war' erupted when the railway contractor E. Pickering fell out with the company building the Wellington railway. Employees, deprived of their pay, took sides. Well primed with beer from the local hostelries, they fell upon one another, derailing the railway engine 'Wellington' in the process. Fighting, which went on for several days, only ended when Pickering reached an agreement with the company.[21]

As crucial as the railways were advances in shipping. On 13 October 1825 the *Enterprise* entered Table Bay after a remarkably short journey of 58 days from Britain.

THE BRITISH TOWN 163

The iron coaling station, built in 1847, symbolised the arrival of the industrial revolution in Cape Town. Not only did it store coal for the production of the new source of energy, steam, but its construction introduced new technology. It was built of galvanised iron, prefabricated in Britain and sent out to the Cape. Coaling became one of the major occupations in Cape Town. (SAL, *Illustrated London News*, 21 January 1854)

The *Enterprise*, entering Table Bay in 1825 (SAL, *SA Illustrated News*, 21 June 1884); and the *Bosphorus*, the first mail steamer to reach Cape Town, on 27 January 1851 (William Fehr C19).

What made the difference was the use of steam to power the ship. No longer did vessels have to lie motionless in the doldrums, waiting for winds to carry them on. Not everyone was delighted by this development, for the early steamships were extremely dirty. Lady Duff Gordon refused to travel on a steamer, 'for they pitch coal all over the lower deck, so that you breathe coal-dust for the first ten days'.[22] But increased speed, regularity and spaciousness soon transformed even steerage passages. In 1857 the Union Steam Ship Navigation Company obtained the contract to run a regular mail service to and from Britain. The uncertainties of contact with home, and the anxious wait for the next ship and a supply of post, which had been such a feature of expatriate life, were now over.

The volume of shipping in Table Bay also expanded. Not only was there a greater increase in tonnage, but a great variety of countries came to be represented. Although British ships still predominated, those of other European nations grew markedly in number, and the local coastal trade became a significant feature, with 154 ships regis-

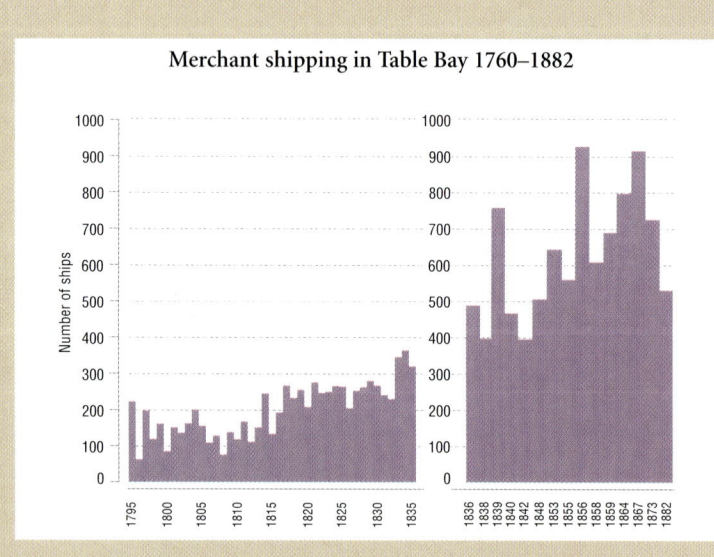

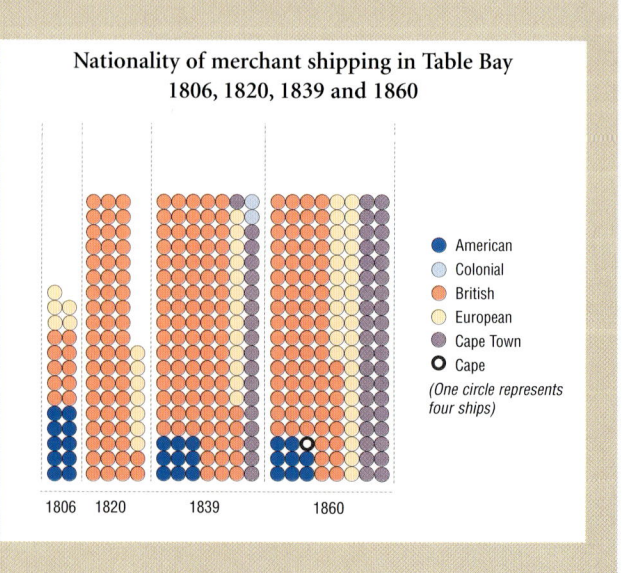

SHIPPING IN TABLE BAY

Merchant shipping in Table Bay 1760–1882

Nationality of merchant shipping in Table Bay 1806, 1820, 1839 and 1860

- American
- Colonial
- British
- European
- Cape Town
- Cape

(One circle represents four ships)

164 CAPE TOWN 1840–1870

tered in Cape Town itself in 1860. Most of them traded up and down the coast, particularly for guano from nearby islands, timber from Knysna and Plettenberg Bay, copper ore from Port Nolloth and Hondeklip, and wool from Port Elizabeth and East London. Others travelled further afield, bringing coffee from Rio de Janeiro and sugar from Mauritius.

Many of the 470 ships that traded with the town in 1840 were continuing to other destinations, but Cape Town was a sufficiently large town to make it worthwhile to offload some cargoes. In addition to the wide range of 'sundries' brought primarily on British vessels, Cape Town regularly received coal from Wales and northern England, mules and horses from Montevideo, deals (cheap pinewood) from Sweden, as well as immigrants from Britain and Germany. At the same time it continued to be a port of call for provisioning only, for some 30 per cent of shipping. These included ships taking emigrants to Australia and New Zealand, Indian and Chinese indentured labourers to Demerara, Welsh coal to Shanghai, and Burmese teak and China tea to Britain. In addition to merchant shipping, 21 French naval vessels arrived between January and July 1860 transporting troops to China and New Caledonia.[23]

Despite the increase in shipping which the widening trade network brought, Table Bay remained an uncertain refuge. The toll of wrecks rose steadily, increasing demands for better protection. But the engineering problems in providing a secure harbour in an exposed bay were considerable. The solutions were also expensive with estimates up to £300,000, a very large sum when the total colonial revenue was only about £750,000 in 1860. Before Montagu's reforms put the colony on a sound financial footing in the 1840s expenditure on this scale was inconceivable. Even after the Cape's finances improved, the British Colonial Office had too little faith in the future of the colony to sanction loans of such a size. In the end a harbour had to wait until the colony acquired greater control of its affairs in 1854.

Yet representative government by no means solved the problem. A jealous Eastern Province was reluctant to see money spent on a harbour which would strengthen Cape

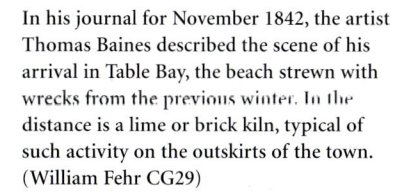

In his journal for November 1842, the artist Thomas Baines described the scene of his arrival in Table Bay, the beach strewn with wrecks from the previous winter. In the distance is a lime or brick kiln, typical of such activity on the outskirts of the town. (William Fehr CG29)

THE BRITISH TOWN 165

Commencement of the Breakwater by H.R.H. Prince Alfred, Sept 17, 1860

On Monday 17 September 1860, in squally weather, 20,000 people assembled on the shoreline near the Chavonnes Battery to witness a ceremony that symbolised British power at the Cape. Flags fluttered above them. Ships and fishing boats of all kinds drew close. Just after two in the afternoon, Sir George Grey, 15-year-old Prince Alfred and a retinue which included the Xhosa chief Sandile and the first black Presbyterian minister, Tiyo Soga, arrived. 'God save the Queen' was played. After a brief religious service, the prince tipped the first load of stones into the bay to start the breakwater. A royal salute was fired from the Chavonnes Battery. The men-at-war in the bay fired more salutes and the bands played 'Rule, Britannia'. (SAL INIL 6453)

Town's economic ascendancy. The energetic governor Sir George Grey had no such inhibitions, however. With his support a viable plan was drawn up in 1858 by John Coode, an imperial engineer. Even so, the proposal might have been blocked by unhappy Eastern Province MPs had it not been for Grey's brash ingenuity. When he announced in July 1860 that the harbour plans would be implemented, the pill was sweetened for the Easterners by the decision that Prince Alfred would launch the scheme. Loyalty and the Victorian love of ceremony persuaded the Easterners to acquiesce.

In every way, building the harbour was the single largest enterprise the colonists had ever undertaken. It was technically difficult, involving a broad-gauge railway to carry stone from the quarry to the breakwater, new blasting techniques and diving machines, cranes and steam machinery. Labour costs were also a consideration. The anti-convict agitation of 1849 scuppered any idea of using imported convicts but colonial expansion and conquest meant that increasing numbers of local San and African prisoners became available, to be housed in the Breakwater Prison, which was custom-built for the pur-

Thomas Andrews, appointed resident engineer, conceived the idea of building a breakwater using rock scooped out of the shore, thus creating a basin for the dock at the same time. (William Fehr E45)

The harbour altered the character of Cape Town's waterfront economy. Contract migrant labourers from the eastern Cape, employed by entrepreneurial contractors like A.R. McKenzie, replaced the self-employed boatmen of the early nineteenth century. (SAL, *The Squib*, 10 June 1870)

Long Street in the Mid-nineteenth Century

(William Fehr CD115)

This street scene, on the corner of Long and Bloem streets, is 'probably the most detailed and interesting Cape streetscape from the middle of the nineteenth century'. It shows many of the features which struck visitors so forcibly. Although so close to the commercial heart of the town, this is a residential scene. Only the buildings on the far left and right suggest a British or industrial presence.

Recently studies have commented on the way in which artists in mid-century, catering to a tourist market, presented Cape Town as an orderly town, the streets clean and tidy, the poor absent or neat and busy. There are elements of this image-making here but the picture is still instructive. Cape Town had developed little since the beginning of the century. The *gracht* (canal) in the foreground was not yet covered over. The street was not paved and the water carrier was a common presence as pumps were still the main source of household water.

A washerwoman, that archetypal Cape Town figure, carries her load in the background. On the left was the home of the Rev. Leopold Marquard, a German missionary, then attached to the Dutch Reformed Church, working amongst the convicts of the Amsterdam Battery. On the right was the home of Christian de Kock, a baker. The Muslim figures in the foreground may well have been residents of the street, for central Cape Town was not entirely segregated racially or socially.

At 59 Long Street, the address traditionally associated with the house on the right, lived in 1855 Chrisje, widow; Pietje, greengrocer; Izak, coolie; Danie, coolie; Jeriem, mason; and Philida. A Marquard descendant recalled that in the old slave quarters behind were later two 'hire houses'.

The Cape Town depicted in this picture by W.H.F. Langschmidt confirms, then, the impression of a town in which social relationships were more open than they would become by 1900.[24]

THE BRITISH TOWN 167

pose. As the resident engineer explained, 'I think if you were to bring seven hundred or eight hundred free labourers into Cape Town on these works it would upset all the arrangements of trade. We should have men asking for higher wages, strikes taking place from the knowledge that the works must be executed rapidly and that we are entirely dependent upon them.'[25]

The Robinson Dry Dock was started in 1867 at the west end of the Alfred Basin. A patent slip, also for ship repairs, was laid at the east end. To coax additional funds out of a reluctant parliament the Table Bay harbour commissioners laid on lavish entertainments, finishing with a grand 'tiffin', at which parliamentarians were feasted with wine, chicken, tongue, turkey 'done to a turn' and ham 'juicy and sweet'. The well-fed MPs succumbed. On 17 July 1870 Prince Alfred, now the Duke of Edinburgh, returned to preside over the official opening of the harbour.

The Alfred Basin was completed just before South Africa's economy was transformed by the discovery of diamonds in 1867 and gold in 1886. As a result of the mineral revolution, the South Arm and the Outer Basin were added before the turn of the century. By 1905 the breakwater had been extended and the Victoria Basin constructed. With some difficulty Cape Town harbour was able to cope even with the excessive demands of the South African War.

Prosperity was not immediately obvious to Cape Town's visitors at mid-century. To the cultivated Lady Duff Gordon in 1861, Cape Town was, notwithstanding its natural beauty, depressing: 'beyond words untidy and out of repair'. The Dutch buildings were 'very handsome and peculiar, but are falling to decay and dirt'.[26] This was not how locals saw it. Cape Town seemed to them a place of substance. W.H. Rabone, founder of the *Graaff-Reinet Herald*, described the town in 1853 as 'not only substantial, but in many parts noble, containing fine shops and warehouses, and public buildings which indicate such good taste in the designers. Many parts are enlivened with trees, and the public garden and botanical garden are especially attractive …'[27] In the mid-Victorian period the centre of town was substantially transformed. For reformist British residents this project of rebuilding the city acquired great symbolic significance, for what they envisaged was a town in which 'the old Dutch city was to be reincarnated as the city of rational British commerce'. Indeed, already by 1858 Cape Town, 'with its omnibuses, cabs and elegant shops, [was] gradually partaking more of the character of an English city'.[28]

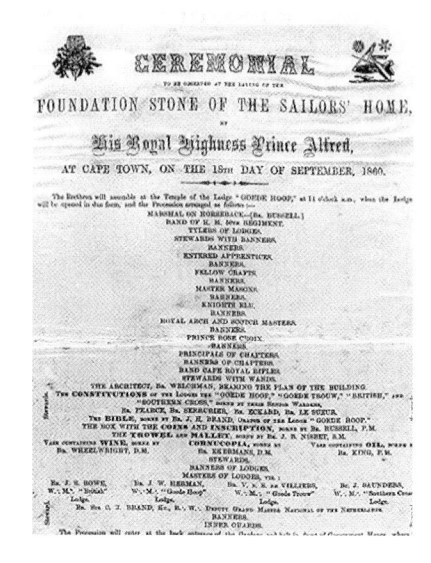

The creation of British Cape Town was attended by regular ritual. The Freemasons usually played a prominent part. Here ceremony joined with Freemasonry ritual in the laying of the foundation stone of the Sailors' Home. (UCT BC2 B1)

This view of Adderley Street in the 1860s shows a town which was still dominated by Dutch buildings. (CA AG13449)

The Old Mutual building in Darling Street, designed by T.J.C. Inglesby, was one of the earliest to have glass-fronted shop windows. He also favoured the palazzo style with its array of arches, a fashion which reached Cape Town in the 1860s. (CA AG8237)

Although change was slow, new materials and techniques came in time to alter the physical character of the city. Governors were important patrons of architecture. For Sir George Grey public buildings had a moral virtue. The governor, it was noted, 'considers that the display of correctness and taste of design in Public Buildings of a town have an influence, by no means to be neglected, on the taste of the inhabitants and encourages improvements in the erection of private edifices'.[29] Willing to fund 'finery' on public buildings, he also saw a public building programme as a means of introducing skilled artisans into the colony. But it was the great merchants who influenced town architecture most. After the 1850s they began to put money into buildings which reflected their status and values. Already in 1842 the first plate-glass shop window, belonging to Mrs Graham, was installed. Two years later the satirical journalist 'Sam Sly' admired the bril-

---

THOMAS INGLESBY

TJC Inglesby (1832–89) was the first major Cape Town-born architect. After serving an apprenticeship with his father, an 'artificer' in the army, Inglesby started out on his own in 1851. He was a mason for St Michael's Roman Catholic church in Rondebosch in 1853–6 but his first big contract was the Mutual Life building in Darling Street in 1862–4, then the largest in Cape Town.[31]

He went on to build the General Estate and Orphan Chamber in Adderley Street in 1865. Other buildings which he designed and built were the South African Fire Insurance, the Odd Fellows Hall, and Stuttafords. In the 1870s he obtained much government work, including the new Post Office in 1874, and the Registry of Deeds. In 1873 he built the South African College school and the Standard Bank in Adderley Street in 1882–3, followed by the Queen's Hotel in Sea Point and the Lock Hospital behind the Roeland Street jail. He died at the age of 57 in 1889, having served, amongst other activities, as mayor of Cape Town in 1885.[32]

liant effect of plate-glass windows and mirrors in a new shop at 28 Heerengracht.[30] The rebuilding of Adderley Street started with a minor economic boom in the early 1860s.

Prior to the 1830s there had been few professional architects in Cape Town. In the late 1840s P. Penketh was still the only private architect; but by the 1860s their number had risen to seven.[33] Although in 1865 building and its related occupations were still mainly in the hands of local coloured craftsmen, it was the immigration of skilled artisans that made possible the use of new techniques like the ornate plastering of Victorian buildings.

More striking was the rapid development on the fringes of the town, where property speculators built with little regard for hygiene or quality. The last of the undeveloped inner-city blocks was sold in 1879. Terrace housing, almost unique in South Africa to Cape Town, was particularly popular amongst speculative builders since it made optimum use of the ground space. Speculation was the name of the game, for builders were untrammelled by municipal regulations until 1861. Without any master plan, they could, and did, lay out streets and buildings as they wished. District Six was a typical result. R.W. Murray complained: 'Houses of all shapes and sizes were built, without any drainage being thought of, much less provided. The population grew, and had to be provided for in the way of house room. People built where they liked and how they liked, with no object but that of rent.'[34]

J.W. Glynn started his portfolio with property in Harrington Sreet and a block to the south of Roeland Street. He left his name in Glynn's Square and Glynnville Terrace, a middle-class development. Another speculator was the docks contractor, A.R. McKenzie. He acquired large portions of the last inner-city lots. By the 1890s he was concentrating in two areas, around Prestwich and Alfred streets on the waterfront near his business premises, and in the Gardens around Wesley Street where he lived. Unlike some of the other speculators, McKenzie did not confine himself to working-class housing. He owned two substantial terraces, Shamrock Terrace in Somerset Road and the Avenue alongside the Botanic Gardens, both built in the early 1880s. In 1896 he possessed 130 dwellings in all.

The most prominent of all Cape Town's speculative builders was the Wicht family. J.A.H. Wicht owned 145 houses by 1850, while J.U. Wicht had 30–40 and J.C.Wicht 11, all mainly in a band starting at Napier Street and ending in New Church Street. Here J.A.H. Wicht had about 40 houses with 19 in Buitengracht Street and 7 in Buiten Street. He also had 17 in Vandeleur Street and interests in District Six. By the early 1860s the family holdings had increased. J.A.H. Wicht now had 340 houses, of which about 106 were in District Six. He had been building at least 20 a year for the last decade. J.U. Wicht now owned about 40, all on the west side of the town, while J.C. Wicht had 80. All told, this made a family group of 460 houses. Typical of these properties was 'Sebastopol', nicknamed in reference to the notorious London tenements, consisting of a row of small, two-storeyed houses in Bree Street. Without water supply, sanitation or much refuse removal, such places were overcrowded and squalid in the extreme.

After J.A.H. Wicht's death in the 1860s, the estate devolved on his children, C. and A. Wicht, who themselves had some 325 houses. These increased after the boom of the 1870s. By 1880 C. and A. Wicht owned 375 houses worth about £60,000 according to the municipal valuation, mainly in District Six. In the 1890s they began to sell their holdings and by 1896 they had a combined total of less than 70 houses.[35]

In 1862 William Barclay Snow was commissioned to produce the first survey of Cape Town buildings. (CTCC)

In 1845, when Thomas Bowler painted the Town House, the administrative heart of Cape Town had changed little from the eighteenth century. Only the Thatched Tavern on the left had altered, losing its gable and thatch. Greenmarket Square was still a site of informal trading.
(MuseumAfrica 64/776)

The Evolution of a Municipality

The middle decades of the nineteenth century were a period of transition for Cape Town. The changes were marked less by outward signs in the buildings and people than by a slow revolution in institutions, administration and economy. The town achieved maturity when it was finally granted municipal government in 1840. In the colony as a whole authoritarian imperial control gave way to local institutions based on a qualified non-racial franchise. In 1854 the Cape received representative government, with an elected lower house, the Legislative Assembly. In 1872, with the granting of responsible government, the Legislative Council was also brought under colonial management. These changes had real meaning for Cape Town, which was deeply embroiled in the early struggle for independence. Despite resistance from the Eastern Province, Cape Town became a capital city in its own right, asserting its identity as the home of parliament.

Between 1827 and 1840 Cape Town had existed in a municipal limbo at the same time as business and trade were growing steadily. But neither merchants nor businessmen were content to leave all political control in the hands of an autocratic government. To men like John Fairbairn local government was also a training school for an efficient central government, a step in the direction of representation, and he and like-minded reformers agitated for a municipal council. For this reason, the struggle for local government in Cape Town and the struggle for representation in central government became fused in the 1830s and 1840s.

Cape Town's first municipal ordinance, promulgated in 1839, was a failure. It was described by William Porter, the newly appointed attorney-general, as a 'beautifully bungled piece of legislation' whose regulations were 'exquisitely Pickwickian, and amused me by their solemn folly'.[36] When it was disallowed, Porter produced a new ordinance intended to balance executive and legislative power. This 1840 ordinance set up a two-tier system. At the first tier was a board of wardmasters, 96 in all, representing the 48 wards into which Cape Town was divided. They were elected by householders, defined as renters or proprietors of any house of a yearly value or rent of at least £10. On this basis 10 per cent of Cape Town's population of 22,000 qualified. One striking

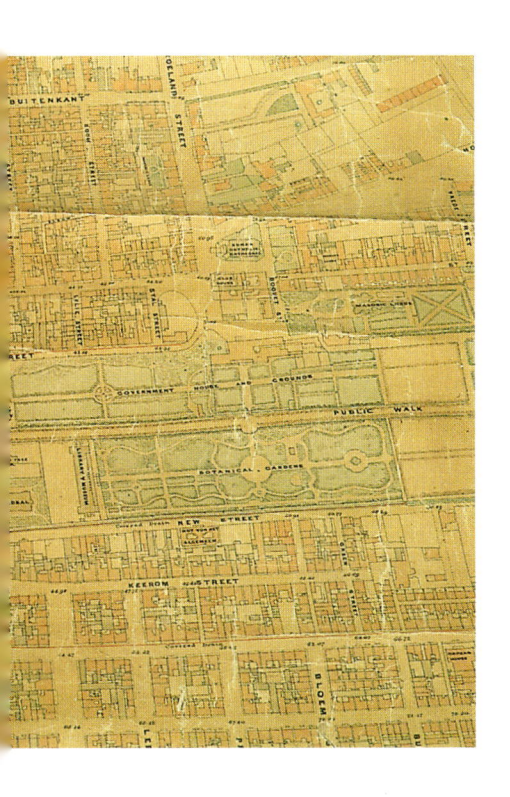

THE BRITISH TOWN 171

The provision of gas was a private rather than a public service. The Cape of Good Hope Gas Light Company, founded in July 1844, was one of Cape Town's first major industries, existing until 1996. The works were situated on the seaside end of Long Street. As it provided gas for street lamps, the company grandly proclaimed its aim to be not mere pecuniary gain, but the improvement of the moral and social fabric of the town. Painting by Thomas Baines. (William Fehr C56)

difference between the 1839 and 1840 ordinances was that women were specifically excluded from the definition of householder in 1840. Only in 1867 was the system of wardmasters abolished, when the town was formally divided into the districts which gave District Six its name. At the second tier, executive power lay in the hands of a board of twelve commissioners, proprietors of landed property of over £1000 in value. In 1842 only 326 men in the town qualified. One feature of Cape Town municipal government was the role of public meetings. If the two boards disagreed, a meeting of householders would be convened to decide on the points of difference. Final decision, however, lay in the hands of the governor. These public meetings remained a feature of local government in Cape Town into the twentieth century.

The 1840 ordinance has been much debated. Hailed at the time as a victory for 'liberalism', later critics considered that it entrenched privilege; 'it put corruption on a legal basis' was one comment.[37] It is certainly true that nineteenth-century legislators accepted the need to protect status and hierarchy. And in a small town, where skills and resources were limited, 'jobbery' was difficult to avoid. There seems little doubt, moreover, that the early municipality was often amateurish in its proceedings and incompetent in its management of town affairs. The energy of wardmasters soon declined. The *Cape Town Mail* described them as 'a set of mere drones' with a few exceptions and within a short time the press was commenting on the 'thin attendance' at meetings.[38] By 1843 it was difficult to make up a quorum to pass estimates. With this decline in diligence on the part of public representatives went public apathy at elections. By 1848 it was reported that commissioners were nominated merely by 'a couple of idlers'.[39] The indifference of the residents gave the municipal commissioners a relatively free hand in administering town affairs and ample opportunity to promote their own propertied interests.

In the first five years of municipal government the council had to place the administration on a firm footing. One legacy of the past was the anomalous position of the police. In 1838 the new governor, Sir George Napier, arriving in the Cape, had been dis-

This lively Poortermans watercolour of 1840 shows the reformed police lined up outside the Wale Street police station, once the home of the Brand family. (MuseumAfrica 1214)

mayed at what he found and the police were reformed under Ordinance 2 of 1840, modelled anew on the London Metropolitan Police. Although the municipality contributed to their upkeep, the police fell under the Colonial Office. Amongst their stated functions was the duty 'to prevent, abate, and suppress all such nuisances and offences' as defined by the municipal regulations. For their part the wardmasters, anxious to cut costs, considered the police a cheap and convenient means of enforcing municipal regulations. But the police, although still headed by the ageing and incompetent Baron de Lorentz, were now under the control of Inspector John King, a dynamic officer personally selected by Napier's friend Colonel Rowan of Scotland Yard. King did not take kindly to this undignified interpretation of police duties; at the same time the municipality resented paying for the upkeep of a force over which it had no control. The quarrel dragged on for months until towards the end of 1844 the municipality was forced to take responsibility for the private contractor who cleaned the town.

The presence of commissioners and wardmasters implied the existence of a class hierarchy in Cape Town. This has attracted the attention of historians partly because an analysis of their social composition helps illuminate the unprecedented opposition generated in the town by the proposal that Britain introduce convicts to the colony – an occasion when Cape Town municipality virtually represented colonial opinion for a short time. In addition, such an analysis enables us to explore the relation between wealth and power in the town at a time when 'ownership of property became the key to local political influence'.[40]

Obvious differences in wealth distinguished the commissioners from the wardmasters. The latter could best be described as petit bourgeois rather than middle class. About one-fifth were professional or commercial men; the rest were tradesmen, shopkeepers, artisans and craftsmen. There was some social mobility: between 1840 and 1854 12 of the 56 commissioners began their careers as wardmasters. The wardmasters saw themselves as the natural representatives of the small man and fought fiercely over the

The Mercantile Elite versus the Rising Commercial Class

Hamilton Ross (1774–1853), a member of the Legislative Council, was typical of the older mercantile elite, mainly British, whose companies were based on metropolitan capital. They were often politically conservative, collaborating with the colonial government. Where such merchants invested in property, it usually consisted of offices in St George's or Adderley Street, the commercial centre of the town, or stores or warehouses on the waterfront. Most of the merchants had global connections. In 1855 the bulk of Ross's fortune of £55,000 consisted of his import–export business (£37,000). About 15 per cent of his assets (£8000) were derived from fixed property, mainly his two estates, Sans Souci in Claremont and Mount Nelson, his town house at the top of Government Avenue.

Hamilton Ross (CA AG2331)

J.A.H. Wicht, linen draper and ironmonger, represented the rising commercial class. He derived a quarter of his estate, valued at £122,000 in 1867, from stock-in-trade and promissory notes. The bulk, over £55,000, came from his extensive property holdings. While the elites had considerable liquid assets, Wicht's bank balance of £3000 was relatively small, suggesting that most of his profits were promptly reinvested in property. Nor was this the only source of wealth derived from property. In 1867 a quarter of Wicht's estate was made up of bonds, mortgages and debentures; in other words, he was financing mortgages on the household property of others.

---

years to prevent tenants from bearing the brunt of municipal rates. Incompetent they may have been, and their policies undoubtedly inhibited improvements to the town, but their existence guaranteed some voice for Cape Town's less wealthy residents.

By the 1840s the older mercantile elite, often with links to the mother country, was giving way to an indigenous commercial class of professionals, wine merchants, shopkeepers and leading Dutch businessmen, closely aligned to Cape Town municipality through which they agitated for representative government. Their financial origins often lay in the profits of emancipation. They also acquired a reputation for jobbery. H.C. Jarvis used his position as chairman of the commissioners 'more for the sake of the political advancement of himself and his friends than for any other object'. Such owners of property were extremely reluctant to bear the full burden of Cape Town's rates and much of the town's financial history consisted of attempts to force tenants to contribute. Yet the two groups, the older merchants and emerging commercial class, had much in common and their interests often overlapped. Family ties, friendship and religious association crossed the boundaries of the economic divide in this small community. By the late 1840s the merchant elite, particularly the British, had all but disappeared from the ranks of the commissioners, disillusioned apparently by the growing radicalism of the municipality.

But conflict between wardmasters and commissioners, Dutch and English, conservative and liberal, dissolved in the late 1840s over the issue of representation in central government. For the British townsfolk, through the mouthpiece of the *South African Commercial Advertiser*, this was the moment when they began to define their colonial identity. As early as 1825 Fairbairn proclaimed, 'Whatever we are, whether born in the Northern or the Southern hemisphere, in England, or in Africa, if we have made Africa our home, and feel a common interest in the prosperity of the Colony, we are all

Africans'.⁴¹ To Fairbairn differences between English and Dutch had virtually disappeared by 1848: 'Their interests are identical, and cannot be separated, or opposed to each other, without equal injury to both. By local intermixture, by intermarriages, and by connexions in business, these two classes have, to a great extent, lost their original distinctions, and the educated, well-informed and well-disposed sink them entirely, without an effort, in the ordinary affairs of life'.⁴² Yet there was ambiguity in their construction of a colonial identity. While representative government was considered the goal of a civilised country, progressive Capetonians, Dutch as well as British, continued to look to Britain and its institutions as models of an enlightened society. The umbilical cord was not yet cut.

Almost from its inception Cape Town municipality took a lead in representing colonial political opinion. As early as July 1841 councillors presented a petition to the Queen for the 'boon' of representative government. Above all, they resented the failure of government to show a return on taxes, for the bulk of colonial revenue was absorbed by salaries, pensions and the expenses of government departments. By 1847 relations between town and government were at a low ebb, not least municipal relations with the colonial secretary Montagu. Lack of finance for the harbour was a particularly touchy issue. Growing resentment led to the stirring of a 'vital spark' in the minds of Capetonians. 'We are no longer clods of clay, ready to receive and retain the impress of the leaden hand of power,' Changuion proclaimed. The day to fight for the privileges which were 'the inalienable property of every British subject' was dawning.⁴³

Then in 1848 the British government announced that it would send out convicts to

In an extraordinary feat of endurance, on 4 July 1849 Capetonians stood the entire day in the pouring winter rain listening to speeches protesting against the importation of convicts. Thomas Bowler, identifying closely with colonials, depicted a scene of respectability, prosperity, racial harmony and industry rather than riot. (CA)

the colony. When the governor Sir Harry Smith informed the Legislative Council of this on 8 November 1848, there was consternation. To colonials the attempt to turn the Cape into a penal colony was demeaning, threatening their claims to respectability. On 18 November one of the 'largest and most respectable public meetings ever held in Cape Town' assembled to protest against the move. The municipality assumed the leadership in the campaign against the introduction of convicts. On 5 April 1849 colonists signed a pledge not to receive or employ any convicts. The agitation gathered further momentum with a massive public meeting of nearly 7000 inhabitants on the Grand Parade on 19 May. The spirit of accord that prevailed indicated 'a remarkable degree of co-operation' between English and Dutch.[44] Another meeting on 31 May led to the formation of the Anti-Convict Committee to co-ordinate public protest. Initially dominated by the merchant elite, its membership included several municipal commissioners and such political allies as John Fairbairn and F.S. Watermeyer.

The municipality worked closely with the committee, using the Town Hall for its meetings, while wardmasters collected subscriptions for an indemnity fund to compensate those who might suffer financially because they had kept the pledge. When in June 1849 an Order-in-Council arrived declaring the Cape a penal settlement, the Anti-Convict Association, as it now called itself, launched a new pledge, amounting to a social and economic boycott of anyone who assisted in landing the convicts or who supported, housed or employed them. On 4 July another mass meeting was held 'of all ranks and classes', who braved the pouring rain for seven hours.[45] Merchants and commercial men were united in their opposition not only to the convicts but to the collaborative part played by the Legislative Council. Colonial nominees on the Council, present and future, were added to the boycott.

The agitation took on a radical dimension not seen in Cape Town politics since the Patriot movement. The result was a rift between the Government House party and its supporters, including reluctant establishment figures such as Bishop Gray, on the one hand, and the 'Ultras' led by John Fairbairn, on the other. When the *Neptune* sailed into Table Bay on the evening of 19 September, the Town House gong was sounded and the wardmasters toured their wards to ensure that householders complied with the pledge. Angry inhabitants collected at street corners and meetings were held in all parts of the town. A vigilance committee was dispatched to Simon's Town to ensure that the convicts would not be disembarked.

By this time the municipality was functioning to all intents and purposes as an alternative government. At the height of the agitation, however, a split occurred in the ranks of the protesters between moderates and radicals. Moderates, drawn largely from the merchant elite, believing that Sir Harry Smith would honour his assurance that the convicts would not be landed, called for everyone to resume their normal occupations. 'Ultras' proposed suspending all intercourse with the colonial government. When this line was endorsed by a public meeting on 28 September the moderates resigned from the Association. From then on the affairs of the Association were dominated by John Fairbairn and his followers including H.C. Jarvis and other members of the commercial class. For the next few months the Association reigned supreme. Shops were closed, business was suspended and Cape Town became a ghost town. Some who attempted to supply the government suffered severely, notably Joseph Norden, who was attacked by a mob and left semi-invalid; he was also expelled from his office as commissioner. Finally Britain yielded and on 21 February 1850 the *Neptune* sailed for Van Diemen's Land.

In April 1853 a new constitution was promulgated at the Cape, introducing repre-

(UCT BC 225)

Although the convicts suffered severely from their long stay in Simon's Town where the *Neptune* was anchored, many of them – Irish rebels imprisoned because of their own struggle for independence against the British – sympathised with the colonial cause. The young convict John Mitchel wrote in his diary, 'I was delighted to find the colonists so determined to resist the abominable outrage attempted by "Government" – that they were completely in the right and hoped they would stand out to the last extremity.' (J. Mitchel, *Jail Journal*, Glasgow, 1914, frontispiece)

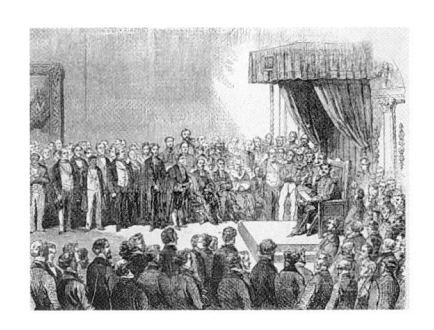

Having no building of its own, the early Cape parliament met in the banqueting hall of the Freemasons' Good Hope Lodge at the top of Grave (later Parliament) Street. Representative government altered Cape Town's status. It became at once an imperial and a national capital. Eastern Province MPs were forced reluctantly to spend long weeks in the town. (CA M579)

sentative government. It was hailed with jubilation as a 'new era' in Cape affairs. The *Cape Town Mail* congratulated the town on a victory for open government, responsible to the community, over selfish opponents who had no permanent interest in the colony.[46] For Fairbairn Capetonians were no longer the same people. They had undergone a spiritual revolution 'which enables them without anger or fear, with loyalty and self-respect, calmly to take their place as equals amongst, and as fellow heirs of Freedom with the proudest, most enlightened, and the most powerful people on earth'.[47]

The first parliament of 1854 was dominated by the Cape Town-based 'popular party' headed by Fairbairn. Five years later, in 1859, old divisions re-emerged. While the town's Dutch candidate, Mr Louw, urged 'the Africanders' to oppose the English, the British campaign was marked by a strong undercurrent of anti-Dutch feeling. Apart from Louw, who came second, and Saul Solomon (third), two Cape Town merchants, J. Stein of Hamilton Ross & Co. and J.D. Thomson of Thomson, Watson & Co., were elected to the Legislative Assembly. To the journalist R.W. Murray, this was a victory of the conservatives and of corrupt government. In 1854 they

> had not the shadow of a chance of getting a candidate returned for four years, nor would they at the end of that time, but that in 1858 it was discovered that the Constitution Ordinance had no bribery clause, and the merchants on the discovery of that, to them cheering fact, resolved to make a push for it. They had the wealth, and as Cape Town votes were as purchaseable as snoek or rice they in 1858 succeeded in getting Mr. John Stein, of Hamilton Ross & Co., returned to the Legislative Council at the head of the poll ... This was followed by the return of Mr. J.D. Thomson, of the firm, Thomson, Watson & Co. to the House of Assembly ... The popular party was nowhere from that time. The return of members for Cape Town and the Western Province fell completely into the hands of what was called the Conservative party ...[48]

The reality for Cape Town was that its days as representative of the colonial nation had ended. For after the early 1850s urban interests were to take second place to agricultural concerns in the public affairs of the colony.

The Reshaping of Cape Town Society

In 1865, when the first official census was taken, the Cape Town municipal population stood at 28,400, with a small preponderance of females. Whites, at 15,100, slightly outnumbered 'Other' at 12,400, with 628 'Hottentots' and 274 'Kafirs' making up the rest. The great majority were locally born, with only 4600 from Europe and 536 born 'elsewhere'. Although the single largest component was in the age-group 21–39 (9000) – the wage-earning population – this was a young city with 9700 under the age of 14. Only 1700 were over the age of 55.[49]

Such figures failed to disclose the continuing ethnic diversity of the town, reinforced by Cape Town's place in a cosmopolitan British empire. There was a substantial influx, unheralded and unacknowledged, of black immigrants in the early 1840s. Most were 'prize negroes' taken from illegal slavers by the Royal Navy; they were brought into the colony and 'apprenticed' to local employers. From 1840 possibly 3000 arrived. Their numbers dropped off sharply at the end of the decade and the last to end his apprenticeship was 18-year-old Charles Boyle of Claremont, freed on 27 May 1856. Most assimilated readily: some converted to Christianity and a number were educated in

The *Gentoo* Immigrants

The experience of Mary Cowie, who emigrated to the Cape in 1851 as a domestic servant, gives us a glimpse of the underside of Cape Town life. Cowie – probably Irish, certainly Catholic – was sent to the Cape by the English Fund for Promoting Female Emigration. But the *Gentoo*, on which Cowie sailed to the Cape, brought scandal to the colony, for the captain and surgeon failed in their duty of protecting the 45 young women in their care. Freed from restraint, the immigrants spent their nights in dancing and their days in the arms of the sailors, it was reported.

Their reception in Cape Town was bleak. The Emigrant Depot was deserted when the women arrived and there were no facilities for them while they looked for employment. Mary Cowie eventually found work as a nurse to the children of the Rev. Mr McElroy but, just before the family embarked for India, she was arrested for theft and sentenced to two years in the House of Correction. It was a grim experience. Worst of all was the unrelieved tedium, for the prisoners had no recreation or exercise. Their days were spent picking oakum or coir, washing or doing needlework. Mary Cowie was probably a thief and a prostitute, but she had little hope of recovering her reputation in a small colonial town which was even more censorious than Britain and where she was known to the attorney-general, the chief justice and the chief of police, amongst others. Yet she had a resilient spirit and she was one of the few women to complain about conditions at the House of Correction and the behaviour of the matron, Mrs Quinn. 'I was kept my full 2 years for I told them I speak of the vile doings, the matron out all day for pleasure and Balls & routs until four o'clock in the morning with the Corporals & Sargeants of the Gallant 73 – a prison no one can call the place it is a den of Infamy. I have plenty who will come forward and Solemnly did give my word to a poor creature that was flogged the day before she died that I should speak about her ...'[52]

After her release Cowie disappeared from the record, presumably to join the prostitutes of Keerom Street who danced to the tunes of the 'Malay' bands. She was certainly not unique. Lady Duff Gordon reported of another group of domestic workers, sent to Cape Town by Angela Burdett-Coutts, England's heiress philanthropist, that 'what in London is called "a pretty horsebreaker" is here known as one of "Miss Coutts' young ladies."'[53]

The old granary in Buitenkant Street served for most of the nineteenth century as the House of Correction, Cape Town's women's prison. (CA J77)

English and Dutch at the 'negro school' in Papendorp. A few retained a distinctive identity as 'Mosbiekers'. In Archdeacon Lightfoot's congregation at St Paul's in Bree Street some still spoke their own language at the end of the 1850s.[50]

Black St Helenans were another group to enter Cape Town in the 1840s. Colonial employers found them less conveniently docile than the prize negroes, for they 'assumed an air and tone of independence unsuited to their condition' and 'an unbecoming impertinence and restlessness of all wholesome control'.[51] St Helenans continued to trickle into the colony for the rest of the century, encouraged by their most famous compatriot, Saul Solomon.

British hegemony in the town was strengthened by sponsored European immigration, particularly since a colony in control of its own affairs was much more willing to invest in white immigrants, ostensibly to provide new labour skills. Between 1845 and 1873 several state-aided schemes brought British settlers to the Cape. Women were prized especially, both as domestic servants and for their reproductive capacity. While many prospered, others drifted into Cape Town's underclass. In an age of mass emigration of poverty-stricken peasants, the Irish, arriving as dock labourers or domestic servants, acquired a particularly disreputable name for drunkenness and fighting, a stigma which they carried with them from Britain.

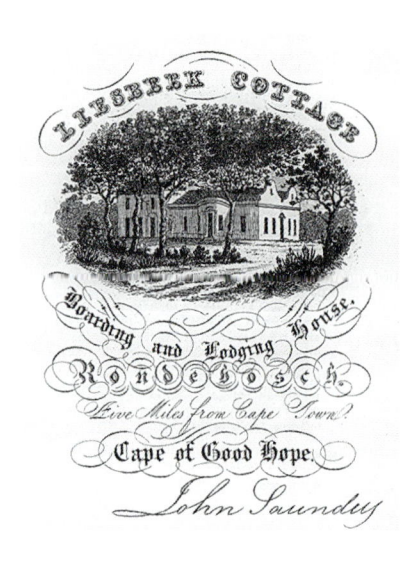

*At the Tavern of the Seas, the provision of accommodation continued to be an important occupation, one of the few avenues of employment for women. (*Cape of Good Hope Almanac*, 1846)*

Early photographs of artisans are rare. The first shows two 'Malay' skimmers (plasterers) with the tools of their trade. There were 79 coloured painters in Cape Town in 1865. While their wages might be good, employment was often intermittent. (UCT BZE 86/18 (18)) Two white carpenters are also pictured with their tools. Their Scots allegiance is proudly displayed in their tam-o'-shanters. (SAL PHA)

In 1865 just over 9000 of Cape Town's population were officially in paid employment, while nearly 7000 women were designated as non-earning females. Trade and commerce (1400) and the category of 'manufacturers, mechanics and artificers' (3200) absorbed the great majority of the employed. A surprisingly small number claimed to be labourers – just under 1000 – but to this has to be added 2300 in domestic service and about 500 boatmen, fishermen and stevedores. Just over 1000 fell into the elite category of the professions, the civil service and the navy, including 16 Muslim 'priests' and 12 coloured midwives. Although the census indicated distinctions between white and coloured, racial differences were not as extreme as they would later become, except in commerce and the professions. In the category of skilled artisans there were about 1200 coloured men and 1600 whites. Differences certainly existed – 135 white blacksmiths as opposed to 49 coloured, or 122 white printers compared with 24 coloured – but in such skilled occupations as carpenters, coopers, saddlers or shipwrights numbers were roughly equal while coloureds predominated in building and tailoring. Gender differences were far greater, women being confined to a very limited number of occupations, particularly if they were coloured: for them there was little beyond domestic service, washing or dressmaking.

But census categories belie a more complex reality. By 1865 occupations in Cape Town began to show the same intriguing diversity that existed in mid-Victorian London. Despite the difference in size the two cities were oddly comparable in so far as both were sites of craft workshops rather than great industrial factories. The diverse and varied jobs followed in the town were a marker of poverty in the pre-industrial economy, for every tiny specialism, however poorly remunerated, had to be protected and cherished as a source of income. Although Cape Town had no Mayhew to delineate its occupations, the 1865 *Cape of Good Hope Almanac* included grave-diggers, a sugar-boiler, lamplighter, net-maker, wool-presser and two tidewaiters.

Wages varied but certain patterns were consistent. White labourers and artisans were almost invariably paid more than blacks: in 1858 white day labourers earned 3s 2d a day and coloureds 2s 6d. 'Journeymen tradesmen' were considerably better remunerated at between 5s and 6s a day without food while domestic servants earned between £1 and £2 a month all found.

Cape Town was not a healthy town. Self-government brought few sanitary improvements, and by the late 1850s the town was in a lamentable state. Above all, before the era of dam-building, water was in desperately short supply. Allegations mounted of bad smells, the wretched state of the streets and filthy gutters. Packs of stray dogs foraged through the town, 300 of them destroyed in October 1858 alone. Neither the colonial government nor the municipality was prepared to invest in sanitary services. The inevitable result was a mounting mortality rate to which wealthier Capetonians could close their eyes since it went largely unrecorded.

Although government was moribund, the elements of a new reform movement were emerging. In the first place a press came into being that purveyed urban crisis as social drama. The *Cape Argus* had been started in 1857 by Bryan H. Darnell and R.W. Murray as a newspaper which would be 'as welcome in the family circle as in the merchant's office'.[54] It rapidly replaced the ailing *Commercial Advertiser* (now the *South African Advertiser and Mail*) as the leading Cape Town newspaper. Owned by the prominent Cape liberal, Saul Solomon, from 1860 and edited by the Rev. Thomas Fuller, once a Baptist minister, from 1864, it mixed crusading zeal with a shrewd commercial eye to the value of representing the slums as the source of colonial depression. Over the years

In a somewhat down-at-heel Longmarket Street in 1875 signboards indicated a variety of retail businesses including a pantechnetheca (defined in the dictionary as a furniture warehouse), a jeweller on the left and, further down on the same side, the West of England pub. (UCT Macmillan)

This intriguing drawing by R. Krynauw shows Abraham de Smidt, the assistant surveyor-general, and Krynauw at Krynauw's house in Wandel Street in October 1870, negotiating with striking porters, who were unwilling to accept the wages offered for a surveying expedition up Table Mountain. (A. Gordon Brown, *Pictorial Africana*, Cape Town, 1974, p. 184)

Murray ran several series of articles on 'The dwellings of the poor', 'Our lower ten thousand' and 'The back slums', graphically describing such places as Sebastopol and attacking slum landlords like Messrs Wicht, Glynn, Smuts and Higgs.

In addition, a more powerful Anglican establishment strengthened the Christian provision of care for the poor. Thomas Fothergill Lightfoot arrived in Cape Town in 1858, having been inspired by Bishop Gray to undertake mission work in South Africa. He was the first of a long local line of reforming Anglican clergy. Attached to St George's Cathedral until 1880, when he moved to St Paul's in Bree Street, he devoted his life to mission work amongst the urban poor.

Epidemic disease finally brought about the establishment of a charitable medical dispensary in 1860. Yet the Free Dispensary (the 'Free Expenses') was not entirely free. To guard against abuse by the 'undeserving' poor, a system of 'lines' was introduced whereby patrons could recommend patients. Prescriptions were 9d unless patients were too poor to pay. The Free Dispensary was an instant success, catering within a short time for

The Rev. T.F. Lightfoot. (SAL PHA)

'The real value of the pamphlet lay in its compilation of statistics related to the epidemic, which made a unique contribution to the development of public health reform in the Cape' (Naudé, 'Free Dispensary', p. 73). By commissioning the project the Free Dispensary demonstrated its value as a monitor of health conditions in Cape Town.

Despite its imposing appearance, the New Somerset Hospital, like its predecessor, was relegated to the margins of the town. In the foreground is a wide-gauge railway used for building the new harbour in the 1860s. (UCT Macmillan)

about 10 per cent of the town's population. The Dispensary committee reports provided the most regular monitor of living conditions in Cape Town and became a crucial instrument for reform. Very soon the Dispensary was acting as the main agent for relief in times of hardship.

When a fever epidemic, described as 'analogous to the low fever of famine years, in Ireland and other lands',[55] broke out in 1867 it was the Dispensary that drew attention to the mounting toll of the disease and called for official action. The death rate escalated as the temperature rose, 58 dying in the last week of September, 54 in the first week of October. The Dispensary estimated that about 1000 people died of fever in the 27 weeks of the crisis, a mortality rate of 20 per cent. The condition of the town became a public scandal. Comparison of the statistics compiled by the signalman on Lion's Rump, who could see most of the funerals taking place in the Somerset Road cemeteries, with those provided by the Town House suggested that doctors knew of only about half the deaths occurring in the town. The Rev. Thomas Fuller called for more accurate data: 'if a medical officer is to work efficiently, he must have social statistics for his guidance. He must be able to know and to report the weekly number of deaths in the town. As it is, we can only make the most random guess at the state of public health.'[56]

The most modern care available for the poor in the town was provided by the New Somerset Hospital, opened in 1862, and inspired by Florence Nightingale's ideas on hospital design. Its prominent position on the seashore and its castellated parapets embodied Sir George Grey's belief in the moral value of public institutions. Although by no means everyone admired this 'abortion of a building' it offered better accommodation for the sick poor than Bailey's old hospital, which now became in essence Cape Town's poor house. Robben Island, designated for the chronic sick poor as well as lepers and 'lunatics', also supplied health services: it was desperately overcrowded despite attempts at reform.

But in the mid-nineteenth century the Cape government had neither the resources nor the willingness to provide more than the most elementary care for the poor. Traditionally this had been the role of the church. Mission institutions in particular increasingly through the century, established self-help organisations like the friendly societies. Mutual benefit societies also created a partial net against illness and accident. Such institutions as the Mutual Life Assurance Society (later the Old Mutual), started in 1845, catered mainly for the middle classes. The very poor could depend on few resources but their own to survive.

For female lepers on Robben Island, events such as this Christmas party early in the twentieth century were rare events which relieved briefly the monotony of their lives. (CA J6356)

A severe depression starting in 1863 forced Cape Town society to reconsider its attitude to the poor, perhaps because of the unusual presence of unemployed British navvies who, in Britain, would have had recourse to the Poor Law. It was these workmen who 'knew that the poor had a right to relief', unlike the coloured poor who looked first to their friends and then 'suffered in silence', as the Anglican dean observed.[57] For the first time limited relief work was provided – quarrying stone at 6d a day. Private donors opened a soup kitchen. But debates about poverty and its solutions were rudimentary and Capetonians readily accepted the argument that need was superficial and temporary. The *Cape Argus*, describing an early meeting of the unemployed, set the tone which was to be maintained until the end of the century: 'There was no end of coolies and Malays; the loafers who hang about the corners of streets, and who make the Gardens their favourite beat, mustered in full force. The morning being wet, a considerable number of masons and carpenters, who would otherwise have been employed, went to swell the numbers.'[58] This recession of the mid-1860s was relatively short-lived, with protest and relief confined largely to immigrant workers,

These Breakwater prisoners were some of those who had been imprisoned as a result of rebellion against colonial control. (SAL Ethnological album (Auckland))

182   CAPE TOWN 1840–1870

Robben Island

If the Cape escaped the stigma of a penal colony in 1848–9, this was not true of Cape Town. Starving and rebellious Xhosa from the eastern Cape, San hunter-gatherers, diamond smugglers, lepers and 'lunatics' were all incarcerated in the institutions built in the environs of the town during this period. Robben Island had been a place of imprisonment from the earliest days of settlement. In the middle of the nineteenth century conquered Xhosa chiefs were confined there, as were lepers, 'lunatics' and the chronic sick poor. The distinction between disease and crime was often blurred in these places of incarceration, lepers, for instance, being deprived of their right to vote while on the Island.

Langalibalele, chief of the amaHlubi, was held as a political prisoner on Robben Island. He was later to be remembered in the name of Langa township on the Cape Flats. (CA M1061)

Men serving hard labour building the breakwater. (T.M. McCombie, *Ten Pounds and Ten Days*, Glasgow, 1883)

but it did set the pattern for the management of poverty into the 1880s.

Roeland Street jail, opened in 1859, was another of Sir George Grey's crenellated public institutions, a moral statement built to the most modern design in which total surveillance was the object. On the other hand, the Breakwater prison, built specifically to house convicts working on the breakwater, put into practice Montagu's belief in the rehabilitative value of hard work. Only a small proportion of prisoners in these jails were local Capetonians. Crime in Cape Town remained moderate, often drink-related, confined largely to the poor – a tally of petty theft and public nuisance rather than violent crime. Sentences were harsh – Mary Cowie received two years for stealing a few shillings' worth of goods. Hard labour, often spent building colonial roads, was the usual

THE BRITISH TOWN

punishment for men except for those who were too unfit to serve such sentences.

To the British middle classes in Cape Town the lives of the poor remained alien and distasteful. Although she regularly ministered to the respectable poor of Rondebosch, Mary Maclear's views, confided to her diary, were probably typical of her class. An expedition from the Castle to Zonnebloem in 1862 took her through District Six: 'a tedious journey through one of the district outskirts of the Town, open gutters beside the streets & between the houses, & sometimes from under the doors filled with offensive black sluggish stuff, idle people at most of the doors & windows, or lounging about dirty & vacant, surely they are not in any want, or they could not be so idle; perhaps it is because they don't care to be clean that they seem to have nothing to do!'[59]

In a remarkable article on 'Our lower ten thousand', the *Cape Argus* used the gender-laden metaphors of Victorian England to contrast rich and poor, black and white. The scene described a paterfamilias and his daughter attending a ball at the Commercial Exchange: 'with light shawl, carefully gathered round the fair shoulders, and the white dress held up from municipal impurities, the Belle of the evening makes her way, clinging to papa's arm, through the crowd of half-lighted swarthy faces on either side, and hears behind her strange guttural expressions of admiration, as the delicate feet, encased in white kid slippers, twinkle up the steps, and vanish within the entrance.' The girl, the reporter suspected, was barely conscious of the watchers and hardly cared but 'these are actually fellow-creatures with ourselves'.[60] This scene, and the journalist's perceptions, said much about identity in mid-Victorian Cape Town, as well as about notions of gender and class. The delicacy of the girl, dressed in white – a protected insider – is contrasted with the darkness and 'guttural' crudity of the admiring watchers – excluded outsiders. But identity in the town was constituted by other beliefs and actions as well, of which religion was a significant component.

Mid-century Cape Town could be described as a religious society. A high proportion of the inhabitants participated in religious ceremonies. Amongst the white middle classes church attendance was a mark of respectability. Mission endeavours, from St Stephen's Dutch Reformed church for ex-slaves to the work of Canon Lightfoot, attempted with some success to impose the same values on the poor. Islam appeared to be growing. Probably only the rare freethinker or the heathen poor did not attend church occasionally, and even the latter almost certainly had some form of religious conviction. But the impress of religion went further, for it shaped the moral world of colonial society and was an integral part of ethnic identity in Cape Town. Belief in mid-nineteenth-century Cape Town was reinforced by the expansion of religious institutions, from the Dutch Reformed and Anglican churches to Islam. This did not occur without conflict, and religious disputes formed almost the bread and butter of Cape Town lawyers at this time. In most cases authority and doctrine were both at issue.

In 1848 Robert Gray arrived in the colony to take up his appointment as the first Anglican bishop of Cape Town. His election should be seen in the context of the Tractarian movement in England, which Gray admired, and which emphasised the spiritual life of the church. As a result there was a deliberate effort to increase the number of colonial bishoprics by new establishments, among them the diocese of Cape Town. Prior to Gray's arrival there were only six Anglican clergymen in the town, five 'isolated and introverted' churches including St George's, and a military chapel. By the time Gray died in 1872, however, in addition to several new churches, the administrative and educational foundations of the church had been firmly laid in the colony. Above all, urban mission work had become a feature of Cape Town Anglicanism. But Gray's episcopacy

St George's Cathedral, described by Ronald Lewcock as 'undoubtedly the most perfect building in the pure Greek style ever erected in South Africa', and much admired when it was built, was despised by the mid-Victorians. 'The church itself is a huge whitewashed barn, with a tower like a succession of blacking bottles standing one on each other's shoulders in regular acrobatic style. Beyond a few mural tablets there has been no attempt at ... any of the usual architectural accessories of a place of worship' (Lewcock, *Early Nineteenth Century Architecture in South Africa*, pp. 264–5). Watercolour by Bowler. (William Fehr C37)

St Saviour's, Claremont (1853), designed by Gray's indefatigable wife Sophy. (UCT Macmillan)

rang with controversy over the introduction of the synod as a form of church government, and over church doctrine, which ended with Gray's excommunication of Bishop Colenso of Natal. At St George's Cathedral Gray resisted the influence of the 'Indians' who 'regarded the church as their own private preserve' and who with 'their long purses and pious purposes are the pest of the place'.[61] The Indians epitomised to Gray a church that expressed worldly rather than spiritual power. The contrasting architectural styles of St George's and Gray's personal foundation of St Saviour's in Claremont reflected the old and new religious attitudes.

Education lay at the heart of Anglican reform. For the middle classes church schooling was provided by the Diocesan College ('Bishops'), founded in 1849, and its female counterpart, St Cyprian's, founded in 1871. Zonnebloem College, the 'Kaffir College',

THE BRITISH TOWN 185

'In Cape Town rather than of Cape Town', Zonnebloem College set out to transform Xhosa pupils into black English gentlemen and women. As Janet Hodgson has described it, life was strictly regimented, ordered by the ringing of a bell. As well as English and religious instruction, boys were taught the 'discipline of honest industry', while the girls cleaned and cooked. Initially housed at Bishop's Court, the school was transferred to Zonnebloem on the outskirts of the town in 1860. The pupils had mixed feelings about the move: Zonnebloem was 'a beautiful place to look at, but it is not a very pleasant place to live in', wrote one in a school composition. It was 'very windy' but it was 'a good place to look at the ships in the bay'. (CA AG13389)

By the 1830s the congregation of the Groote Kerk had reached 5000 and they could all no longer be accommodated. The church was rebuilt, re-opening in 1841, and a second church, the Nieuwe Kerk (see above), was erected in Bree Street. Both featured a mixture of classical, Gothic and Egyptian elements, only the baroque tower of the old church surviving as a reminder of an earlier style. (CA E1892)

encouraged by Sir George Grey as part of his civilising mission, was designed to imbue the children of African chiefs with Western values. It was the education offered by church schools which also attracted Cape Muslims in the 1850s. Early proselytising work began at Protea (Bishop's Court) in the suburbs and at the North Wharf at the waterfront, later spreading to District Six, where St Mark's mission was established.

Urban mission work provided an outlet for some of Britain's surplus single women. Mary Arthur started an orphanage in Roeland Street in 1862, later moving to Granite Lodge in Harrington Street. In 1868, in the wake of a movement to reintroduce sisterhoods in the Anglican Church, a group of young women were recruited for Cape Town by Gray. This small community developed St Michael's home for orphan boys and a 'refuge' for 'penitents' (prostitutes). The driving force behind much of the urban mission work was the desire to reclaim Cape Town's poor from Islam, but it was also part of a larger movement to inculcate Western values, to create a 'respectable' poor. Through dress, a time discipline, basic literacy, and drill and games a church-going urban working class was being forged.

Like the Anglican Church, the Dutch Reformed Church expanded greatly during the middle years of the century, with six congregations in Cape Town by 1875. Most of these, such as the Ou Kerk of Hanover Street (founded in 1867), were mission institutions, ministering to the poor. This in itself reflected changes in the DRC, which had previously taken little interest in such activity. By 1874 there were over 1000 pupils in four DRC schools in Papendorp, Roggebaai, Buitengracht and Hanover Street.[62] Leopold Marquard, recruited from the LMS, was the church's first official missionary, ministering in Cape Town to the prisoners at the Amsterdam Battery.

Like the Anglican Church, the DRC was riven by strife as it grew. 'Liberalism' was one source of tension. A second source of conflict, cutting across these divisions, was the use of English. For many of the Cape Town Dutch families attachment to the DRC was virtually their only remaining tie with their Dutch past and Dutch had become a foreign language. Such people pressed for English services, which started at the Groote Kerk in 1862, continuing into the twentieth century. Yet C.J. Brand, a religious 'liberal', and the

The dress of this trio and the very act of being photographed suggest that they had some status within their community. (UCT Macmillan)

The interior of the Chiappini Street Mosque in 1894. (CA M998)

The reception in 1862 of Abu Bakr Effendi in Cape Town. (SA National Cultural History Museum)

Scots-born Ds. William Robertson fiercely resisted such a move even while the conservative Ds. Stegmann used English willingly. Religious revivals in 1860 and 1875, led by Andrew Murray jun., strengthened the spiritual life of the church, and contributed as well to the foundations of modern Afrikaner identity in Cape Town.

The position amongst the town's Muslims was not dissimilar. By mid-century Islam was an officially recognised religion in the town, if not socially accepted by the white middle classes. In 1840 there were only two fully constituted mosques in the Bo-Kaap district. By 1860 this had grown to five, while Claremont's first mosque was constructed in 1854. The most prominent mosque was the Jami'a Mosque, the so-called Queen Victoria Mosque, in lower Chiappini Street, built in 1850. It was the first mosque to be erected on land granted by the government for such a purpose, and was sanctioned in a deliberate attempt to secure the loyalty of the 'Malay Corps' during the frontier war of 1846. Lady Duff Gordon was quick to note how this alliance was reflected in the building itself: 'A large room, like a country ballroom, with glass chandeliers, carpeted with common carpet, all but a space at the entrance, railed off for shoes; the Caaba and the pulpit at one end; over the niche, a crescent painted; and over the entrance door a crescent, an Arabic inscription, and the royal arms of England!'

In the early part of the century Cape Islam was still somewhat isolated from the mainstream of Islam though emancipation and greater prosperity made pilgrimage to Mecca possible for a few. Lady Duff Gordon struck up a friendship with an ex-slave, 'Abdul Jemaalee', who was, he confided to her, now worth over £5000; his son was a student in Cairo after spending several years in Mecca. The introduction of a steamship to Zanzibar further improved contacts between Cape Town and the Islamic world. By the 1860s teachers reportedly came from Arabia and India to work in the town.[63]

This did not mean that Cape Town Muslim society was harmonious. Disputes over the appointment of imams were common, partly because they were so central to Muslim life. The imam 'was not only the leader of the congregation and its spiritual head, but acted at times as its official spokesman, its adviser, its guide in social life, and the central figure around whom the entire congregation revolved.'[64] The Palm Tree Mosque in Long Street was the site of conflict for years, eventually prompting a Cape

THE BRITISH TOWN 187

Dutch sympathiser, P.E. de Roubaix, to intervene. He appealed to the Turkish government, through British offices, for assistance. As a result, in 1862 Abu Bakr Effendi arrived in Cape Town, supported financially by the Ottoman government, to provide new leadership to Islam in the town.

Abu Bakr Effendi's personal life, by no means smooth, was indicative of the continuing permeability of the colour line in Cape Town. His first wife, Rukea Maker, was reputedly the daughter of an English woman and a Cape Muslim man. When the marriage disintegrated, Effendi married again, this time, it is said, to the daughter of a Yorkshire shipbuilder. In the long term Effendi's greatest contribution was probably the writing of the *Bayan al-Din*, a religious text, in Afrikaans, written phonetically in Arabic. The unusual orthographic techniques he adopted provide a rare example of the sound of spoken Afrikaans in mid-century Cape Town.

Effendi's arrival in Cape Town proved a mixed blessing for Cape Muslims. An energetic and learned man of Kurdish origin, he brought the Cape into closer touch with the wider Islamic world. But he also introduced doctrinal disputes, for, although a Sunni Muslim like the local religious, he was an adherent of the Hanafi school of thought, which followed different practices from the local Shafi'is. His ruling that snoek and crayfish were *haram* (unacceptable for Muslim consumption) ran counter to local culture, and in 1869 an unsuccessful petition requested Effendi's removal from the Cape. Doctrinal disputes of this kind continued to smoulder throughout the nineteenth century, and were only partially resolved with the establishment of the Muslim Judicial

Another result of the modernisation of Islam in Cape Town was to be seen in the more conventional construction of mosques, which now acquired minarets from which the imams called the faithful to prayer. A minaret was added to the Jami'a Mosque in Chiappini Street after 1914. (CA M999)

The Confederate raider *Alabama* (depicted here in Table Bay by Thomas Bowler) was remembered in the best-known of the Muslim *ghommaliedjies*. (William Fehr C20)

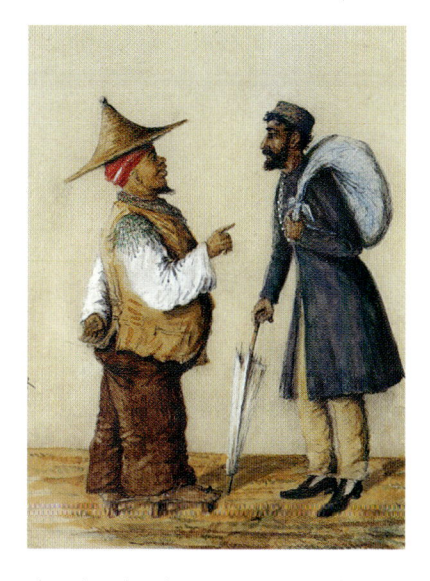

'Snoek and rice' was sometimes used as a metaphor for Cape Muslims. In this watercolour by W. Ritter, the dress of the two figures captures the conflict between the old and new styles of Islam at the Cape. The man on the left, dressed in traditional costume, is a fisherman and snoek eater, while the one on the right, dressed in fez and black coat, carrying a bag of rice over his shoulder, symbolises the Ottoman influence. (William Fehr GHV 87/15)

Opposite: The Malay Corps setting out for the eastern Cape. Their participation in the frontier war of 1846 contributed to the formal recognition of Islam by the Cape government. Drawing by Charles Bell. (UCT Bell Heritage Trust BC 686 C37)

Council in 1945. Controversial he might have been, but there seems little doubt that Effendi injected fresh life into Cape Islam. Muslim schooling expanded and children were attracted from Christian mission schools. Under his influence there was an increase in religious services and Cape Muslim men altered their style of dress, abandoning the conical hat for the fez, a feature of Ottoman Islam. A stronger feeling of brotherhood was engendered amongst Muslim boys, as Anglican missionaries testified bitterly, and conversion to Christianity practically stopped.

Cape Islam existed as a subculture in the town, proud and self-sufficient, but despised or looked down upon by other residents. Lady Duff Gordon was quick to grasp these nuances. On one occasion, after watching a funeral, she was assured that her presence was welcome: 'A white-complexioned man spoke to me in excellent English (which few of them speak), and was very communicative and civil. He told me the dead man was his brother-in-law, and he himself the barber. I hoped I had not taken a liberty. "Oh, no, poor Malays were proud when noble English persons showed such respect to their religion. The young Prince [Alfred] had done so too, and Allah would not forget to protect him. He also did not laugh at their prayers, praise be to God!"'[65] It was plain that Muslims were well aware of the suspicions they aroused and were sensitive to them. Offered a cough medicine by Abdul Jemaalee, Lady Duff Gordon drank it reluctantly only after she had been assured that Muslims did not poison Christians. 'They also possess the evil eye', Lady Duff Gordon noted drily, 'and have a talent for love potions. As the men are very handsome and neat, I incline to believe that part of it.'[66]

In the 1841 count of religions in Cape Town Jews did not appear, although individual Jews had lived in Cape Town since the days of the VOC. But by 1841 there were enough Jewish settlers, including such prominent merchants as the Mosenthal brothers and Benjamin Norden, to provide a *minyan* (religious quorum). At the end of 1841 a permanent congregation was created, the Society of the Jewish Community of Cape Town, Cape of Good Hope (Tikvath Israel). The arrival in 1859 of the Rev. Joel Rabinowitz as rabbi revitalised the town's community. A synagogue was completed in 1863. Young, energetic and capable, Rabinowitz threw himself into the task of organising the scattered communities throughout the colony. Generally Judaism was well integrated into Cape Town life. Most of the early Jews were English immigrants, already thoroughly assimilated into British society, and many were wealthy men, of standing in the town. Moreover, their numbers were small. Influence and status ensured that anti-semitism, where it existed, was low-key. To all intents, up until the 1880s, Jews formed an integral part of the local elite of Cape Town.

THE BRITISH TOWN

Leisure also reveals much about society and its changes over time. The celebrations of 15 May 1863 described at the beginning of the chapter were a dramatisation of patriotism, with British symbols abounding. It was also a visible manifestation of patriarchy, class and ethnic identity. There was little place in the celebrations for women, except as onlookers. The Platteklip washerwomen and domestic workers were absent from the procession. Certainly there was no place for the prostitutes, who would have been to the fore in a Brazilian carnival. Men played the women's parts in the carnival, including a 'veiled' Lady Godiva. Because the parade was almost entirely confined to white middle-class men, only they were licensed to take part in this 'rite of inversion'; the exceptions were the giants Gog and Magog – two large labourers recruited from the breakwater. The entertainers at the fancy fair, including the Christy-minstrels, were also pale males of the middle class – the part of the Chinese astrologer being taken by the editor of the *Cape Argus*, while the 10s admission to the ball ensured that it was exclusive.

Yet the day was also a 'carnival', suggestive of the reversal of hierarchy and licensed spontaneity. The float of Bacchus and his Bacchanals gave the stamp of approval to the use of alcohol and this message was reinforced when free wine was dispensed on the Parade. There were also echoes of older European festivities. Most British immigrants would have recognised the figures in the carnival parade, which they would associate with the old occasions of fun and frivolity 'back home'. Shrove Tuesday, May Day, Midsummer and saint's days were traditionally in Europe occasions for rites of inversion or licensed debauchery – gambling, drunkenness, sexual promiscuity – associated with the carnivals, sports and fairs that accompanied them.

In mid-century Cape Town was still small, a place where it was only a slight exaggeration of D.P. Faure's to recall that 'everybody knew everybody else, or were acquainted with them'.[67] This may help to explain why many leisure activities appeared so inclusive of the city's social spectrum. A typical occasion was the capture in Table Bay of the Yankee ship *Sea Bride* by the *Alabama*, a Confederate raider, in August 1863: 'over the quarries, along the Malay burial-ground, the gallows hill, and the beach, there were masses of people ... ladies waved handkerchiefs from Green Point villa windows [and] ... people watched from the roofs of houses'.[68] A strong north-wester kept the *Alabama* in Table Bay for several days, and many Capetonians, 'rich and poor' alike, went to visit her in 'whatever boats they can'. 'Everybody' was allowed on board, and they went 'everywhere ... even up the rigging'.[69] The occasion was recorded in paintings, photographs, print and a *ghommaliedjie* that survived into the twentieth century, 'Daar kom die Alibama, die Alibama die kom oor die see'.

It was the casual or seasonal work of mid-century Cape Town that enabled so many inhabitants to enjoy the *Alabama*. In poor weather fishermen would not have ventured to sea and so in the winter of 1863 they could visit the warship. Self-employed workers could decide for themselves when to take time off. The fact that many people had control over the rhythm of their work, and were largely free from the hostile surveillance of employers, explains the emergence of cultural forms associated with particular occupations, like fishermen's songs or the washerwomen who kept up the commemoration of 1 December with their own 'song and dance under the trees' at Platteklip Gorge.

Low levels of literacy in the town meant a highly visual and oral popular culture crucial not only in entertainment but also in communicating social knowledge. Plays and pantomimes taught history, politics or morality. For instance, the play *The Snake in the*

John Fairbairn's offices decorated in celebration of the departure of the *Neptune* after Capetonians had refused to allow the disembarkation of convicts in 1849. (Library of Parliament)

At the Races

'Fox'- (jackal-) hunting was confined to the elite, but horse-racing was patronised by rich and poor alike. In the 1850s trotting matches for 'heavy' stakes were common on the Wynberg Road between the George Hotel and Rathfelder's Inn. But the most popular occasions were undoubtedly the spring and autumn races on Green Point Common. All along the finishing straight were 'the coaches of the rich, the wagons or carts of those less favoured by fortune, cabs, drags, charabancs, all filled with people who meant to make merry and did so'. Gambling on the horses was supplemented by gambling on games such as 'pea and thimble', 'under and over' and 'crown and anchor'. Swing-boats and coconut shies added to the attractions, and the sense of festivity was enhanced by itinerant musicians. The races were often rowdy, a police presence being required, but they survived because they were patronised by the rich and influential. These were opportunities for wealth to be displayed. At the same time the elite maintained their social distinction through separate seating facilities, which were kept even more exclusive after racing started at Kenilworth in 1882. Class and ethnic distinctions could lead to violence: at one Green Point race meeting 'a hundred Irish navvies declared war on all Malays, who to escape destruction fled homeward over Signal Hill'.[70] Yet such multi-ethnic events could also instil a sense of belonging to a common Cape Town, Cape or British colonial society. Drawings by Charles Bell.

(© The Brenthurst Press ART.179/8)

Grass, or Clouds in Holland and Sunshine in South Africa (1867) was one of the first popular attempts to tell the story of Dutch settlement. Signs and emblems advertised shops or politicians. Illuminations informed people about notable events of the day, like the British victory over the Boers at Boomplaats in 1847 or Queen Victoria's Jubilee in 1887. A light in a window on certain occasions demonstrated patriotic enthusiasm; failure to provide one could lead to broken windows. Along with illuminations and the iconography of dress, civic and religious processions were some of the ways in which illiterate and literate citizens could learn the structure and ideologies of Cape Town and Cape society, and see them reinforced. Singing expressed 'shared interests and values':

Misleadingly entitled 'The Tom Tom dance' – in fact 'gom gom', referring to the drum – this watercolour by Charles Bell, which illustrates 'Mozambiekers' and others of mixed race, imputed an African origin to the *ghomma* drum. (UCT Bell Heritage Trust BC 686 C14)

the coolies, some eighty or a hundred of them, who had been coaling a steamer, were brought back to shore in a large cargo boat, and as the boat was being slowly rowed over the dead calm blue waters, in which it was mirrored, the leader, generally a clear tenor, would strike up a few bars, after which the whole company would fall in, a chorus of stentorian voices resounding over the Bay, entrancing in its grandeur and with thrilling effect ... [The best singers in the world] never moved me as these swarthy coolies, begrimed with coal dust, chanting their vespers in the twilight on the still waters of Table Bay.[71]

The theatre also played its part in shaping social identities. Ethnic identity, or ethnic hostility, was encouraged by English and Dutch theatre companies. The Aurora group of Melt Brink consciously strove to keep the Dutch language alive in Cape Town in the 1860s by staging poetry readings and drama. President Brand of the Orange Free State, son of C.J. Brand, was a frequent patron when in town. When Brand attended a performance in 1869, he was greeted by the Free State anthem. The highlight of the evening was *De Moord van Dingaan aan Pieter Retief* by H.W. Teengs.

A wide variety of entertainments catering for differing tastes, from the popular to the high-brow, was staged at a host of venues in the town, from refurbished wine stores to the Drury Lane Theatre, Constitution Hill (founded in 1848). These included circus acts like the spectacular 'Battle Jump and Somersault over a company of thirty soldiers, with fixed bayonets, and firing at the same time'.[72] There were life-sized 'automaton' or puppet shows, and 'novelties' such as Monsieur Verreaux's Cabinet of Froglands, which had the frogs arranged as 'Artillerymen at Practice, Billiard Players, Intemperates'.[73] In the 1840s and 1850s at least some of these entertainments were open to all who could afford them. Equestrian displays were particularly popular among 'Malays'. They could be viewed at Severo's Italian Circus in the middle of Buitenkant Street, where prices ranged

'An interesting feature at the Theatre is the Malay audience to be seen every evening in the gallery, and sometimes in the pit, keenly attentive as they are to the proceedings on the stage and interested in the action of the play' (*Cape Times*, 3 August 1877).
Drawing by V.R. Glynn, 21 June 1878.
(© The Brenthurst Library ART.388/2/60)

192 CAPE TOWN 1840–1870

The foundation members of the 'Aurora' drama group were all members of Die Genootskap van Regte Afrikaners, which promoted the early Afrikaans language. Here Piet Koster, Johan van Heerde, G. van Heerde and W.G. Combrink enjoy a convivial meeting. (CA E3902)

Sefton Parry, who 'established professional theatre in South Africa', opened the Theatre Royal in 1860 on the corner of Caledon and Harrington streets. The governor's box was surmounted by the royal arms and 'splendidly decorated'. The grand entrance opened into the boxes, separated from one another by damask curtains; the pit, divided into stalls, was 'neatly and comfortably cushioned' (Fletcher, *Story of South African Theatre*, p. 90). (SAL INIL 1778)

In 1875, at the Bijou Theatre in Plein Street, the impresario Disney Roebuck employed 'a band of coloured boys picked from the streets of Cape Town' to play Ashanti dancers and singers in *Brown and the Brahmins*. On this the first occasion that black actors had been used in South African theatre, their 'extravagant contortions of body and limb and grotesque action' created a sensation in Cape Town. (Fletcher, *Story of South African Theatre*, p. 99)

from 4s to 1s, or at the slightly more expensive Mr McCollum's Circus at Roggebaai.

Sefton Parry's up-market Drawing Room Theatre in the Commercial Exchange (founded in 1855) was more exclusive. But seat-pricing rather than racial exclusion seems to have been the accepted means of ensuring social exclusivity at mid-century. In 1858 Mr English, 'the celebrated comic vocalist' from Sheffield, lampooned Cape Town institutions, personalities and events at the New Music Hall in Buitenkant Street. This venue had 280 'reserved seats' and 150 in 'the gallery', each section with its own entrance and 'refreshment room'.[74] Theatre galleries – 'the gods' – often had only basic seating, as a young African visitor from Lovedale College in the eastern Cape reported to his school: 'I was among the rowdies and low characters of Cape Town, who had gone to pass their time in the gallery of the Theatre Royal. With the majority of these present, the lower the tone of the play the better it took, and the higher the tone was raised, I fear, the less paying it would become to the managers.'[75] The gallery of the Good Hope Theatre, opened in the 1880s, was 'often packed with enthusiastic Malays'.[76] Here Jongie Siers and Hadji Mohamet Dollie persuaded the impresario Disney Roebuck to hold a benefit performance for sick and wounded Muslims of the Turkish Army who were fighting the Russians: 'The pit was filled with gaily dressed Malays, men and women, amongst whom the turbanned priests were conspicuous. The gallery was packed with Malays and they seemed thoroughly impressed with the beauties of *The Lady of Lyons* and enjoyed the humour of Terry O'Rourke in *The Irish Tutor*.'[77]

Annual holidays were often an expression of Cape Town's unique identity. The most popular were probably New Year's Day and the Queen's Birthday, officially held on 24 May. On New Year's Day and 'Tweede Nuwejaar' business was suspended, and 'the streets of the city presented a deserted and solemn appearance'.[78] On New Year's Day in 1866, 'Along Sir Lowry Street pass the never-ending succession of English, Dutch, Bastards, Hottentots, Mozambiques, Kafirs, Malays ... listen to the song which they [a group of Malays] are setting up, and say whether you have ever heard anything more dismal, discordant, ear-splitting.'[79] The colours of 'Malay' dress were 'wonderful'. The variety of wagons included the splendid vehicle of a merchant adorned by a crest 'strongly suspected not to be registered at the Herald's office'.

Ghommaliedjies, literally 'drum songs', were originally slave songs. They had formed part of the licensed festivities surrounding the annual slave holiday at New Year and

THE BRITISH TOWN 193

continued to be performed by their descendants into the twentieth century. A male would sing a verse, and the rest of the group would join in with the refrain. The lyrics occasionally referred to historical events, persons and places. More often they were satirical and lewd – frequently lampooning female employers or fellow 'Malays' such as those who 'tried for white' – and parodied respectable Dutch or Afrikaner folksongs. Sometimes violence towards the subject of satire would be imagined or threatened.

Hoor wat sê die mense	*Listen to what the people are saying,*
Kanal dorp se mense:	*The people of Canal Town [District Six]:*
...	*...*
Maar Aderjan bly nie hier nie.	*Aderjan cannot stay here.*
Wat word dan van my?	*What will become of me [Aderjan's lover]?*
Die nonna wat die bolla dra	*The lady with the bun [Aderjan's employer],*
Laat sy in die taaibos lê.	*Let her lie in the thorn bush.*[80]

The singing of *ghommaliedjies* was not confined to Muslims. Together with street parades they became part of a coloured working-class culture that cut across religious divides. One Tweede Nuwejaar in the 1880s a Scotsman noticed 'Coloured people' near Somerset West on their way back to Cape Town from the Strand. They had 'imbibed freely, and are quarrelling, drinking, singing and shouting rough jests'. Some were 'dancing in the grass to the music of an old concertina, or the strains of some ditty sung by themselves ... they are celebrating their emancipation from slavery or serfdom some half-a-century ago'.[81] *Ghommaliedjies* and the 'picnic songs' of Dutch burghers developed in symbiosis, like the Afrikaans language they shared. As *moppies*, or satirical street songs, *ghommaliedjies* were frequently heard, if infrequently understood, by white Capetonians after emancipation. D.P. Faure remembered that in the 1850s 'small parties of Malays, about eight or ten in number, slowly strolled up and down the streets singing the most sentimental Dutch songs in perfect time and harmony'.[82]

New Year's Eve street parades may have existed by 1823. By the 1870s paraders were formed into singing and sporting clubs distinguished by different costumes. In 1871 the *Cape Argus* reported that 'one or two bands of music paraded through the streets, but there was no disturbance or disorder of any kind'. Two years later, the same paper complained that 'the dreadful dissonant Ethiopian clamour was never louder, and we should imagine the returns of the sale of malt and other liquors showed ... an improvement'.[83] By the mid-1880s, if not before, the New Year street festivities had taken on a form closer to that of the 'Coon Carnivals' of the twentieth century. The number of paraders had increased, their costumes had become more outrageous, and parading now flowed over from New Year's Eve to New Year's Day:

> The frivolous coloured inhabitants of Cape Town ... [went] ... about in large bodies dressed most fantastically, carrying 'guys', and headed by blowers of wind and players of stringed instruments, who evoked from their horrible monsters the most discordant and blatant noises that ever deafened human ears. At night time these people added further inflictions upon the suffering citizens of Cape Town in the shape of vocalisation, singing selections from their peculiar weird music, with variations taken from 'Rule, Britannia' and the 'Old Hundredth'. They also carried Chinese lanterns and banners, and as they proceeded through the streets playing their discords, beating the drum, singing and shouting, and the strange glinting of

Guy Fawkes was still enthusiastically commemorated in Cape Town in the 1880s. 'Oulap vir die guy, asseblief' was the local version of 'Penny for the guy'. Celebrations at the Grand Parade or the quarry at the top of Strand Street were enlivened by fireballs, 'collections of old rags, dipped in paraffin and bound with wire. You lit one, and with the long wire attached, swung it round and round, and let go' (UCT BC 230 M. Leendertz, 'The vanished city'). (UCT Macmillan)

the combined light from the street lamps and the Chinese lanterns fell upon their dark faces, they seemed like so many uncanny spirits broken loose from – say the adamantine chains of the Nether world.[84]

Christmas in Cape Town was largely a family and church affair and was 'lightly regarded at the Cape', compared with New Year's Day, which was 'shared by all creeds and colours'.[85] However, Christmas Eve was the occasion for street parades by 'Christmas choirs' – bands of Christian coloured people, soliciting alms for their church. On Christmas Eve in 1857 'various instrumental bands played suitable musical selections ... [It was only] towards morning, [that] the peregrinations of those who had so welcomed the reappearance of Christmas, were concluded.'[86] Christmas was also a time of charity. Special meals were often organised by various institutions for the poor of the city. On 22 December 1859, children from the Anglican mission schools of Protea, Claremont and Newlands marched with flags and banners to Bishop's Court for 'a feast'.[87]

While Whitsun was celebrated with races on the Grand Parade or 'traditional' English sports such as climbing the greasy pole and wheeling barrows, the first of December celebrations were mostly confined to ex-slaves and their descendants. Sometimes employers like Mrs Langham Dale contributed. 'I made a plum pudding for the servants and Papa gave Solomon a bottle of ale.'[88] The *Cape Argus* lamented that the nature of celebration was left to the emancipated: 'it is discreditable to the English section of the Cape community to concede to the Malays the celebration of Emancipation Day', which the paper perceived to have 'degenerated into a Bacchanalian orgy of the emancipated'.[89]

Working-class culture was rooted in the realities of an everyday life of toil and hardship. In the numerous canteens of the Tavern of the Seas – there were about 100 licensed and 300 unlicensed 'smuggling houses' in the mid-1840s – working-class immigrants and itinerant soldiers and sailors rubbed shoulders with the local underclasses. Cock-fights were organised along with gambling and the popular game of skittles. Chess, dominoes and billiards were alternatives in superior establishments, some of which even stocked periodicals for literate working-class customers. In other places prostitution and dancing went hand in hand: 'Jack appears on the scene, and ... there is a tuning up of squeaking fiddles, a fluttering of nasty finery, a display of leering, tipsy nymphs, and as the glasses go round ... Jack in all his glory, reckless of money, reckless of the nature of this fun, leads the wild "tarantule," while the fumes mount higher and higher.'[90]

Particular class, gender and ethnic identities were affirmed in different canteens. In the 1850s and 1860s Frenchmen gathered at Louis Mahe's smuggling house in Hanover Square; Africans met weekly at 'one of Mr Glynn's houses'; 'low and abandoned women' were admitted to a canteen in Glynn Square because otherwise they broke its windows; and 'coolies' gathered at the London Tap in Buitengracht Street when weather prevented work.[91] This culture was largely male and unapologetically escapist, which partly explains the political apathy in Cape Town. Alcohol, like dagga, created a sense of well-being, but it was also cheaper than most non-alcoholic beverages, and water was in any case often contaminated.

Dancing halls, like those in Constitution or Chiappini Street in the 1880s, were frequented by soldiers, sailors and prostitutes. Men of all classes attended Cape Town's 'rainbow balls' in the mid-nineteenth century; alarmingly for middle-class Cape Town, so did their washerwomen and domestic servants, some whom were 'white'. But at least one dance hall, the Caledonian close to the Castle, paralleled the white exclusivity of

---

'Jack appears on the scene, and ... there is a tuning up of squeaking fiddles, a fluttering of nasty finery, a display of leering, tipsy nymphs, and as the glasses go round ... Jack in all his glory, reckless of money, reckless of the nature of this fun, leads the wild "tarantule", while the fumes mount higher and higher.'

Cape Times,
26 June 1876

many Cape Town institutions by the 1880s. According to one frequenter it was for 'brown' people only.[92] 'Here is a tall Damara woman, her soapstone pipe still in her red, fez-like headgear, circling in the arms of a diminutive Cape Boy, a Malay cab driver, as white as Abdol Burns [a local Muslim figure] ... here are white women alas! and all shades and all sorts of men from the swart Ethiope to the white loafer-criminal.'[93]

Poorer Capetonians took their leisure on their stoeps and streets. On summer nights in the middle decades of the nineteenth century 'small parties of Malays strolled up and down the streets singing the most sentimental Dutch songs in perfect time and harmony', while others sang 'at their open windows'.[94] People like 'Goma' Domino, Achmat Africa and Lanie Abdol drank, danced and played the banjo in front of their homes in Herman Lane off Buitenkant Street in the 1880s. Such songs, learnt in mission schools or at parades and in music halls, often had European or American origins. As a professional singer from Scotland observed, 'the latest success of the concert-room is reproduced immediately in the streets of the Malay quarter'.[95] Popular imported songs included 'My grandfather's clock', 'Ta-ra-ra-boom-de-ay', 'Daisy' and 'After the ball was over'.

Children played in the streets. In Keerom Street in 1860, 'A crowd of boys assemble from the neighbouring alleys and proceed to mark out the road for their game. They take water from the gutters in shells or tin boxes ... and make lines in the dust by dropping the water over it. One long line runs up the centre, the gutters are considered the sides, and the whole space is divided by transverse lines into a double row of square spaces. There will be six or eight of these pairs of square plots, and at the top the centre line is prolonged into a representation of a flag-staff, with a large banner attached to it.'[96] This game looked to the observer like a cross between hopscotch and 'prisoner's base'. Girls sometimes joined in, 'shouting and yelling, and obstructing the street by playing different games'.[97] Other popular games were racing sticks or reeds in gutters and a form of 'pitch and toss' in which coins had to be thrown into a hole and the most accurate player scooped the pile. Many street games involved gambling: John Johannes was one of a group of young boys playing cards outside the barracks for 1s 2d stakes each in 1862, while in 1876 12-year-old Abdol Boollah gambled on the success of his reed in a gutter race. Both ran the risk of harsh punishment by the reform-minded authorities.

Emerging notions about appropriate leisure pursuits, disseminated from Britain, were slowly diffused to the lower classes, transforming older pursuits. These ideas were influenced by Victorian views on health, evolution and competition, and shaped by rapid industrialisation and imperial endeavours. For men, a range of new or reformed outdoor pastimes was offered as an alternative to gambling and drinking. Football, cricket and mountaineering were first associated with the British public schools and universities. They went with a new conception of masculinity as strong of body and pure of heart. Men should be their natural selves – 'loyal, brave, and active' – in contrast to 'spiritual, sensitive, and vulnerable' women, whose natural domain was the home.[98] The new sports were intended as an antidote to the physical perils of industrialisation and urbanisation. It was hoped that the young male body would be the site of innocent vitality rather than sexuality. In the process, codes were worked out, and by the 1870s the distinctions between rugby football and soccer had been defined. The way was open for competitive nationalism in sport, pseudo-Darwinian tests of national character.

In 1862 football, 'this manly English school-game', was played on Green Point Common between army officers and civilians, including the future Cape premier John X. Merriman. The game, 15 a side, was a mixture of modern rugby and soccer, with goalkeepers as well as 'scrimmages', similar to the Eton field game. The goals were placed 150

'Here is a tall Damara woman, her soapstone pipe still in her red, fez-like headgear, circling in the arms of a diminutive Cape Boy, a Malay cab driver, as white as Abdol Burns [a local Muslim figure] ... here are white women alas! and all shades and all sorts of men from the swart Ethiope to the white loafer-criminal.'
The Lantern,
28 June 1884

THE CAPE VOLUNTEERS

The military review on the Grand Parade, featuring regiments of the local garrison, was a reminder of British power. Young men from fashionable volunteer formations such as the 'Sparklers' (the Cape Town Cavalry) could preen themselves in uniforms costing over £100. In this painting Bowler illustrated the occasion marking the start of the building of the first railway in 1859. The first Cape volunteer force had been raised only a few years before, in 1855, and was renamed the Cape Royal Rifles in 1856. (SAL, *Illustrated London News*, 16 July 1859)

yards apart and the game lasted 105 minutes. It was declared a draw when the wind got up, giving the military too great an advantage. The return match, won 2–0 by the Army, was watched by 'a large party of ladies and gentlemen in carriages and on horseback, with a crowd of admiring spectators'. Two days later the Diocesan College played 'their first match' against the Army, in a type of football that eventually developed into rugby.[99]

Forms of cricket and football had been introduced to the Cape by the British Army early in the nineteenth century. By mid-century they were played regularly by civilian and soldier alike. In the 1860s cricket and football matches between civilians and the military were held throughout the week, at any time of the year. Such an ostentatious pursuit of leisure during 'working days' was a mark of social standing, a token of the newly desirable masculinity. Originally an elite affair, by the 1850s cricket was being organised by clubs in the southern villages involving white players of the lower ranks. In

Hamilton Sea Point Rugby Football Club (SAL Andersson album)

The Cape Civil Service Rowing Club, 1865. Contestants in the Cape Town regatta spanned the social spectrum. But only middle-class white men took part in rowing races, involving battles between the Civil Service, Alfred or Union clubs, or in yacht races. In contrast the shore-gig and sailing-boat races were lower-class affairs, more inclusive in terms of ethnicity, if not of gender. (UCT Macmillan)

1861 the game was introduced at Zonnebloem College and in 1866 the first eleven, including N.C. Mhala, Julius and Fandeso, beat the Reformed Club (mainly soldiers) at the Fort Knokke ground in Papendorp.

Cricket and football forged a sense of spatial community as players and spectators supported their own localities. The late 1850s saw cricket matches between 'Cape Town and the Royal Artillery', 'Cape Town and the Army against Wynberg and the Navy' and 'the Army and Navy against South Africa'. In 1862 an annual contest began between 'Mother Country and Colonial Born'. In what was perhaps the first international tour, a group of cricketers came to Cape Town from England in 1871 and suffered an innings defeat at the hands of the 'locals'.

Patriarchal views of gender ensured in mid-century that middle-class women's sport

'Bonnie Cloete, with Friday carrying her archery set.' (Kuttel, *Quadrilles and Konfyt*, p. 17)

was confined mainly to the home. Croquet and, later, lawn tennis were popular. Bonnie Cloete often competed at archery with friends 'on the great lawns of Newlands House' at about this time.[100] Dancing also provided a welcome opportunity for exercise. Fortunately Cape Town's topography and climate encouraged swimming, walking, riding, and climbing picnics on Table Mountain. According to mid-Victorian convention women had only their own company at places like Green Point beach. 'No mixed bathing in those days had ever been heard of,' Georgina Lister remembered, 'and the men kept far away, while the women bathed in the deep rock pools along the coast.'[101] Such privacy was rare. As 'A Lady' noted, 'The population of 30,000 is too mixed to make it safe for ladies to go about unattended; and one's motives are liable to misconstruction by the ignorant many.'[102] Emma Rutherfoord went riding either with her father or with his Malay groom; she preferred the latter 'as I like riding alone'![103] For the most part women of the middle class were confined to sedentary activities at home, to reading, music, games and conversation. Letter-writing sustained networks of friendship and information. Although servants created leisure time, preparations for entertaining could

THE PICTURESQUE PENINSULA

Rondebosch below the ramparts of the mountain. (CA J9734)

'*A* Lady', in the 1850s, was eloquent about the romantic combination of geology and botany: 'There is, for instance, the Devil's Peak – a perfect poem in itself ... It stands out boldly against the sky-line ... Its sides and gullies are full of proteas, heaths, and silver trees. Here cascades leap and bushes shiver, as the fierce north-westers crash down upon those heights, and make the foliage change from emerald to opal at every successive blast. At one moment its jagged crests are swallowed up in vapour, then a whirl of wind, and the fleecy masses are torn into shreds and sent howling over the precipices in tortuous eddies. Anon the whole mountain becomes deep purple as the sun is obscured, only to break out again into wealth of colour as the passing cloud has melted into thin air. Thus the mixture of clay, granite, and lichened stones, cropping out everywhere in those wind-tormented heights, is beautifully toned down and brought into harmony with surrounding objects, by the fusion and contrast of every tint of green and purple which bush, rock, or flower individually furnish.'[106]

still involve the mistresses in considerable labour.

Lower-class women had far less leisure. For many of them domestic chores were added to paid employment. For some 'home' was not even a place of safety. Francina Brill ran a greengrocer's shop and had eleven children, which would have left little time for leisure. But in addition she had an alcoholic husband who 'constantly' beat her.[104]

Suburban Domesticity

In the 1840s inner-city Cape Town was still the home of many of the older colonial families. On the fringes of the town they continued to live a semi-rural but formal life. Georgina Lister, who visited her de Smidt grandparents at 23 Somerset Road as late as the 1860s, later recalled the vegetable and flower gardens which surrounded the house. Behind the house were stables, a coach house and a cowshed, for her grandmother kept three cows, 'two Jerseys and an Alderney'; in an enclosed field the de Smidts grew fodder for the animals. On the other hand the dining-room was stately and ceremonious.

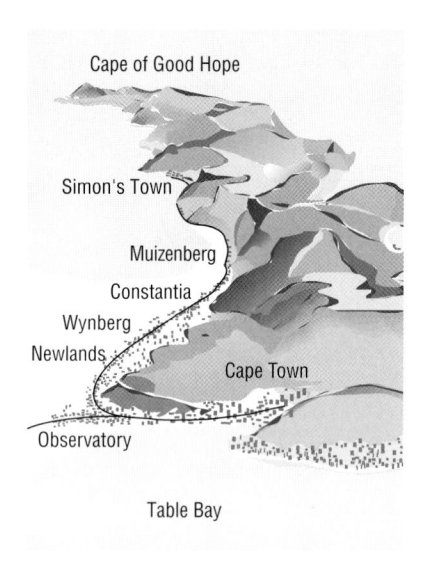

> The table was a long oval one beautifully polished, of course, as were all the chairs and other furniture ... The drawing room was big and square ... In it were a tall gilt-framed mirror over the fireplace with lustre candlesticks on the mantelpiece, a sofa and chairs and a large round table in the middle of the room spread with books and albums. In one corner stood an upright piano, a most decorative piece, high fronted with a pink fluted silk panel and carved woodwork and brass candlesticks which pulled forward when wanted ... In another corner was grandfather's lovely old writing bureau. It was made of some golden-tinted wood, very tall with a cupboard above and a desk to slide forward; there were drawers below, beautifully carved and on each of the doors a large shell in inlaid wood.[105]

It was the railway line which made suburban life a practical possibility in the middle of the nineteenth century.

By the 1860s this style of life had become outdated, confined mainly to the older Cape Town families, for the younger generation were moving out to the suburbs. The younger de Smidts, for instance, lived at Westerford and Groote Schuur in Rondebosch.

'The climate, cooler and more sheltered than Table Bay, was another attraction of the suburbs. A pleasant habitat was one of the necessary qualities of a gentleman's estate. By the 1830s upwardly mobile merchants had begun to express their newly acquired status in the form of landed property in the suburbs. From the 1860s the professional middle classes started building more modest country homes here. At the end of the century even clerks and minor civil servants were seeking out their rose-bowered cottages. Yet Cape Town suburbs were not entirely the preserve of the white middle classes, for coloured people also had homes in the lee of the mountain. They were integral to the functioning of the village communities, as independent artisans and as servants.

The history of the suburbs is also the history of land speculation in Cape Town. In the first part of the century James Maynard was the principal beneficiary in Wynberg. In mid-century Philip Morgenrood entrenched himself in the suburb in a similar manner. One of ten children, Morgenrood was launched in his career by his godfather, Philip Leeb, a general dealer in Strand Street. Through connections derived from his membership of the Lutheran Church, Leeb acquired an interest in Rathfelder's Inn in Diep River, belonging to a fellow German. This was only the start of Morgenrood's Wynberg affiliations, for after inheriting Leeb's estate in 1840, Morgenrood proceeded to invest extensively in Wynberg, financed by interest from bonds and rentals, as well as the general dealer's store. By 1877 he had extensive properties in Wynberg, as well as St James, Kalk

Kinship and Locality

Large families and kinship ties reinforced the British ascendancy in Cape Town. In 1831 Thomas James Mathew, a member of the evangelical Union Chapel, bought part of the farm Weltevreden in modern Claremont and built Harfield Cottage, 'a roomy single-storied building under a thatched roof'. In 1837 his co-religionist Ralph Henry Arderne followed. In 1845, at The Hill, he established a patriarchal estate with magnificent gardens. The second generation extended these Claremont connections. Henry Mathew Arderne, married in 1857, settled locally, as did his sister Elizabeth, who married Henry Knight Tredgold, an attorney, in 1861. They were joined in 1864 by Tredgold's younger brother, Clarkson Sturge Tredgold, who had entered Ralph Henry Arderne's timber business and married Susanna Arderne, residing in Palmyra House. Henry Beard, a photographer, married Joanna Arderne while her sister Lydia married John Christie, a grandson of Dr John Philip, both in 1865. By this time Henry Mathew Arderne was living in a cottage near The Hill, the Beards were living at The Firs, while the Christies settled in yet another house in the vicinity, The Wilderness. The youngest of the Arderne sisters, Marianne (May), married John Philip, grandson of Dr Philip, in 1867. They lived in yet another of Ralph Henry Arderne's houses.

Until mid-century, the religious centre of the evangelical community remained the Union Chapel, although the chapel was replaced by a grander church in Caledon Square in 1858. The position of the church, it was observed, was one of 'striking peculiarity' since so many of the members embraced 'much of the wealth, intelligence, [and] position in society'.[107] It was inevitable, however, that the extended family of Ardernes centred on The Hill in Claremont should prefer a church close at hand, and one was built there in 1877. Family pride was displayed in the Arderne coat of arms above the entrance door.

Financially and politically, few of the Arderne family achieved great wealth and status. They remained educated, middle-class, professional people, many retaining their close links with Cape Town into the late twentieth century.

Music, reading and needlework were acceptable occupations for middle-class women, evidence of which can be found in this domestic interior with its piano, needlepoint cushions and books. The closely confined hair and dark, sober dress also reflected the constraints on women's lives. (SAL INIL 22332)

Bay and Plumstead further south on the Peninsula.[108]

One feature of the early Wynberg development was its multi-ethnic character. The Dutch formed a continuing presence; some residents like Tennant and Maynard were British; Eggers, Ellert and Morgenrood were German in origin; yet others were free blacks or emancipated slaves. In general the holdings of the last mentioned were less substantial but they established family properties that remained integral to the Wynberg area for generations. When Jan Sintler of Klein Oude in Wynberg died, he left the estate to his common-law wife, Rachel van die Kaap. She later married Abraham Zasman, a carter, and the deeds were registered in his name, although part had been sold. The Zasman property became a Muslim enclave in the centre of Wynberg village. In 1838 in lower Wynberg Philip Ryklief, described in the *Cape Almanac* of 1830 as a free black and wagoner, bought land strategically placed on the Simon's Town road, originally part of the Rust en Werk farm. Ryklief was the son of an Englishman, probably called Ratcliffe, and Johanna Barbara, the daughter of Jan van Bougies and Samieda van die Kaap. Ryklief himself had married Sophia, whose mother was English and who was the stepdaughter of an imam of the Palm Tree Mosque in Long Street, Cape Town. Such family connections may have assisted Ryklief in his purchase but he was not the only free black to buy land in the area. Others included Jan van Mauritius, Hammat, Pedro, Abdol van die Kaap, O'Deane, Sarah Adams, John Rabboula (Rabullah) and 'Friday', listed in the 1830 *Cape Almanac* as a prize negro.[109]

In the suburban villas of the middle classes the Victorian domestic world was preserved. During the day the suburbs became the domain of the women. Here they exercised their petty control over children and servants, training both in the order and cleanliness essential to the smooth running of Victorian homes. Emma Rutherfoord's life at Herschel, the old Feldhausen estate, was busy and trivial.

> In the first place you must know I am the lady of the house, Mama having devolved all the cares of the housekeeping and servants upon me ... and then duly at 10, I go to inspect meat and bread, etc., and on Saturday make up and pay my

Elaborate attire marked the status of mid-Victorian women. Black dress and intricate lace caps were often the livery of widows but the serious expressions were a feature of early carte-de-visite photographs when subjects had to pose for a long time. (SAL PHA)

'In the first place you must know I am the lady of the house, Mama having devolved all the cares of the house-keeping and servants upon me ... and then duly at 10, I go to inspect meat and bread, etc., and on Saturday make up and pay my bills.'
Emma Rutherfoord, 1853

bills ... We usually walk in the mornings, and once or twice we have taken our sketch books and Lucy her work, and sat out the whole morning, Mama reading to us the life of Madam Guion ... At one we take our tiffin, or nearer two; then practising, work, reading and not infrequently returning or receiving visits, fill up the time till 5.30, dinner, talking round the fire, reading or work, till bed time.[110]

By no means all housewives were well organised. Mrs Maclear at the Observatory had 'no right order', but she was 'determined to learn the art & to watch more strictly in future'.[111] While some women were entirely satisfied with this life of incessant activity and trivial gossip, others were bored. 'A Lady' found the day in Wynberg 'dull and quiet' when the men had left for town.[112] Agnes Merriman was emotionally dependent on her politician husband. She recorded in her diary: 'At work on my altar cloth all morning. Jack out at 4.30 and with him for a ride on Flats. Wrote to B.B ...' (13 April 1876). 'Lazing about in the morning. At 2.30 to Botanical Lecture at College ... Met Jack at Newlands station and with him to call on Mrs — he stayed for Lawn Tennis' (26 April 1876). 'At home all morning – began and finished "Through the Mist" 3 volumes, stupid book. Jack out at 2 ... With him for long ride on Flats' (29 April 1876). When Merriman was away for extended periods she poured out her anxiety in a stream of letters and telegrams to which he responded with irritation. 'I received a long letter from you yesterday which to tell you the truth gave me great pain – the whole letter with the exception of a few lines is taken up with accusations and grumbling at me ...' (18 September 1877). 'I was surprised and shall I say not pleased at getting a telegram from you yesterday – what for – I have written every day and it only makes people snigger' (2 September 1881).[113]

Agnes Merriman's nervous boredom was part of a darker side to suburban women's lives. Although they rarely recorded their frustrations in detail, occasional fragments suggest the tensions that might exist. The Maclear home, for one, was not happy: Mrs Maclear was often lonely and exhausted. When she died, responsibility devolved on her daughter Mary through whose diary often runs a bitter thread.

> I don't care a bit about Meggie [her sister] misrepresenting myself or my actions, though I do really think I have been very kind to her, I have never let her words of hatred expressed towards me when we have been alone influence me in any way. They are all forgotten quite as much as before they were spoken they were forgiven & excused, but I do care about every syllable she has breathed against our dear darling Mama, whose sweet words to her used to seem to me as if they must be irresistible! & when I have seen Meggie scowl at her, & heard her muttered words of anger or scorn, it has seemed to me as if it could surely be like the bread cast upon the waters that would be found after many days, & that dear Mama's words – which were like the words of an angel – would though unseen & slowly yet imperceptibly & surely take root & blossom with beautiful fruit, – but I think Meggie was deranged, that sort of hard stony self will & passion whose effect, & want of reason are derangement – & though the very idea of such a thing used to seem to make her half wild with anger & bitterness, – she said last night when Georgie [her sister] spoke of her acts, & that they seemed like derangement – she said 'Yes – that she thought she was deranged!'[114]

Sexual passion was even more rarely displayed. Emma Rutherfoord's comments on

Agnes Merriman. (SAL PHA)

her future husband, Andrew Murray jun., after she had rejected his first proposal of marriage, hint at the difficulty which a young Victorian woman had in coming to terms with this aspect of her life. 'To tell you the truth so often almost unconsciously a sense of the depth & reality of Mr Ms piety & a consciousness of his originality & power of thought & mind strikes one fresh & then like a cold shudder comes that want of refinement of some sort, something I feel most painfully ... O I hope I shall soon forget.'[115] Usually these passions remained hidden within the bosom of the family. Occasionally, however, they erupted in scandal and divorce, especially when the wife was the erring partner, for 'an adulterous wife jeopardized not only an interpersonal relationship, but the very fabric of society'.[116] In the Victorian household the wife was possession as much as helpmeet, and an injured husband could, and did, claim restitution. When the wife of Charles Bell, the Cape surveyor-general who lived at Canigou in Rondebosch, committed adultery with an Indian Army doctor in 1850, Bell obtained custody of their 18-month-old daughter in two consecutive legal actions, and £500 damages from the doctor for the 'injury' he had inflicted.

Unequal yet vital partners in this domestic world were the servants. In 1865 there were 24,300 domestic servants in the Cape Colony, of whom less than 10 per cent were white, although in Cape Town the rate was higher, at 30 per cent. They were considered so essential that Emma Rutherfoord's marriage agreement stipulated that she 'should always be provided with at least two servants'.[117] In Cape Town their subordinate position was enforced in law through the Masters and Servants Act of 1855 and its amendments. Servants were bound by contract to their mistresses and broke them at the cost of a fine or prison sentence. Even the most generous employers took their servants to court.

The demand for servants was not the result of sheer laziness, for household work was exhausting. Victorian homes were stuffed and cluttered, cooking on coal stoves hot and tiring, and the laundering of quantities of starched, white linen an enormous task.

'To tell you the truth so often almost unconsciously a sense of the depth & reality of Mr Ms piety & a consciousness of his originality & power of thought & mind strikes one fresh & then like a cold shudder comes that want of refinement of some sort, something I feel most painfully ... O I hope I shall soon forget.'

Emma Rutherfoord, 1855

Large families and quantities of white starched linen contributed to women's domestic labour. (SAL PHA Pocock album)

Middle-class women often undertook much of the work themselves. 'Fatiguing work,' commented Mary Maclear, daughter of the inept housewife, when she spring-cleaned. On Christmas Day, 1861, Mrs Dale in Maitland 'made some more apricot jam ... then stuffed the sucking pigs [and] tied up the puddings. Then dressed baby and bestirred myself to get down to church ... we had about 35 to the tea.'[118] It was not surprising that she wanted help.

Sheer desperation may partly have accounted for the endless grumbles about the quality of servants at the Cape. All the same racism was often inherent in the relationship. Servants were insolent, a visitor complained. 'The black girls say they are quite as good as the white people, and will not take any "cheek" from their mistresses. They bring forward their taunt of equal rights, on every occasion.'[119] White servants, even the despised Irish, were usually preferred to local women. In the 1860s Lady Duff Gordon noted that 'emigrant ships are cleared off in three days and every ragged Irish girl in place somewhere'.[120] But liberally minded employers sometimes found coloured servants better than they had expected. Lady Herschel and Lady Duff Gordon both spoke well of their darker-skinned maids and Mrs Dale was surprised to find that coloured girls were preferable to whites, who wanted to go 'into town every week-end'.[121]

The social and racial hierarchy of the Cape was replicated in the home. The most responsible and best-paid positions, like that of housekeeper or cook, were usually reserved for whites, while housemaids would be coloured, preferably light-skinned. Like all women's work, domestic service was ill paid. In the 1830s Lady Herschel's nurse and housemaid were both paid £1 7s a month.[122] The housemaids at Rathfelder's Inn in 1862, both white, fared rather better at £1 15s and £1 10s.[123] Mrs Dale in 1852 paid her cook 25s, with 30s after three months if she were satisfactory. Men's wages were slightly better. Lady Herschel's groom earned £3 9s 6d and 'A Lady' paid hers £3 a month. The latter had to 'find' himself and support a wife and two children in addition, 'so that it is quite clear that he must be thrifty in his housekeeping'.[124]

Conditions of work created stress. Mrs Lancaster's maid got only three hours' holiday a month, received no visitors without special permission, was subject to a curfew

Women such as Dinah, the Pocock family's cook, held a position of standing in the household while the nursemaids had lower status and poorer pay. All were expected to conform to standards of respectability, neatness and cleanliness. (SAL PHA Pocock album)

THE BRITISH TOWN 205

from sunset to sunrise, and liable to instant dismissal if pregnant, drunk or guilty of other misconduct. She was also expected to inform on fellow domestic servants if she observed them transgressing 'the household rules'.[125] Apart from the long hours an alien culture was imposed on the servants, who were often country girls. In the Maclear household, once regulated, the maid rose early, tidied two rooms downstairs and three upstairs before breakfast, laid the table and served at table as well. She cleaned the silver and glassware and helped with washing dishes. 'In the afternoon there will be time for needlework. The servants have the evenings for their own needlework but of course are expected to be ready in case they should be wanted.'

Domestic servants entered the sacred heart of the Victorian family and their potential waywardness threatened its stability. Conscientious mistresses often saw their role as a civilising mission. Moral virtues had to be instilled. 'Three important points are *truthfulness, cleanliness, and obedience* ... Be always clean and tidy ... Be obliging to your fellow servants and ready to help one another – but at the same time your own work is your own particular duty and must not be neglected.'[126]

But the enforced intimacy was often another source of tension. While domestic servants rarely left a record of their lives, in Emma Rutherfoord's complaints one can glimpse a young woman watching from the outside the doings of her young mistress.

> We have a most horrid vulgar maid servant whom I almost think it contaminating to speak to, look at or even pass through the same room therefore seldom do ... I do not know any mean or vulgar trick she could not do. I hope she won't read this among others. She makes me savage watching all my proceedings. I actually caught her peeping through the keyhole the other day when Mr Hundersley called & Mama being out asked to see me. She evidently thought it very suspicious. Then when I am reading or writing etc., she comes peeping & peering, what for I can never make out.[127]

'In the afternoon there will be time for needlework. The servants have the evenings for their own needlework but of course are expected to be ready in case they should be wanted.'

Mrs Maclear,
c. 1835

Rites of Passage

The ceremonial rituals which attended rites of passage in mid-Victorian Cape Town accompanied the end of life as well, for rich and for poor. The funerals of public personalities were public spectacles. When C.J. Brand (Sir Christoffel) was buried in 1875 a funeral procession of three mourning coaches and sixty private carriages was led through the streets of Cape Town by members of De Goede Hoop Masonic Lodge dressed in full mourning regalia. The flags of the town were hung at half-mast and the bell of the Dutch Reformed Church tolled as the cortège wended its way to Somerset Road. Every member of a friendly society would expect that his associates would bury him with as much ceremony as possible. Indeed, such an injunction was often a requirement of membership. Muslims were adjured by their religion to carry their dead on foot to the cemetery. As long as Cape Town was a walking city, walking funerals were amongst the events that added colour and interest to the daily round. As a reforming British establishment attempted to impose order on Cape Town society in the decades following the mineral revolution, however, the customs of pre-industrial society would become the focus of conflict.

'I went in after the procession which consisted of a bier covered with three common Paisley shawls of gay colours ... They took the corpse, wrapped in a sheet, out of the bier, and lifted it into the grave, where two men received it; then a sheet was held over the grave till they had placed the dead man; and then flowers and earth were thrown in by all present, the grave filled in, watered out of a brass kettle, and decked with flowers ...' (Lady Duff Gordon, *Letters*, p. 35). (Library of Parliament)

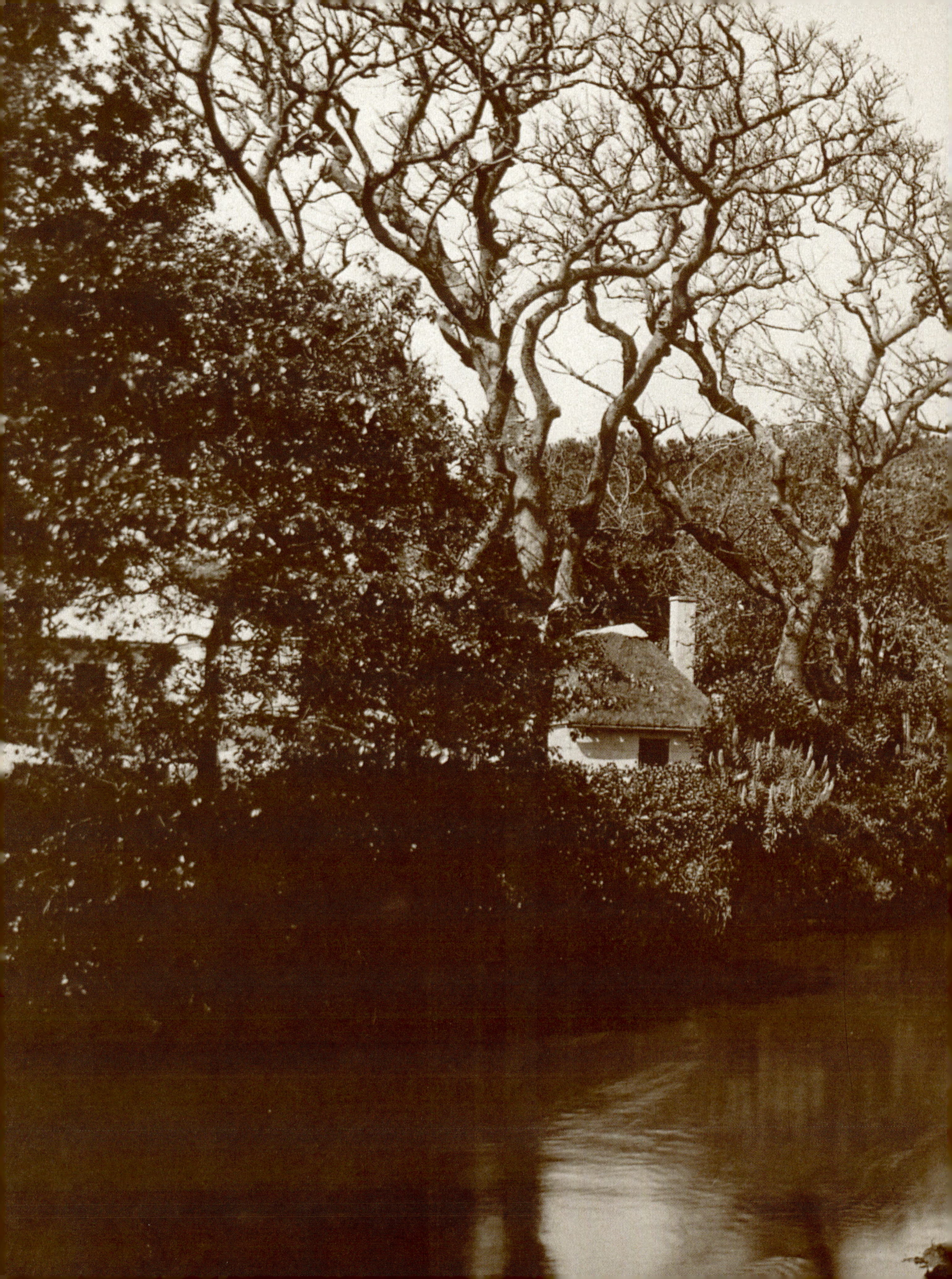

CHAPTER FIVE

THE SEARCH FOR ORDER

CAPE TOWN
1870–1899

AT the top of the steep slope of Longmarket Street, lying below Signal Hill, stood the white walls of the Tana Baru. Crooked tombstones inscribed in Arabic indicated that this was a Muslim burial ground. Above Somerset Road was the Anglican cemetery with tumbled urns and broken crosses, while in the Dutch Reformed graveyard family vaults lay cracked and broken, revealing their contents. Most dilapidated of all was the Ebenezer cemetery for the poor, where bones protruded from unmarked graves, to be chewed by roving dogs; an odour of putrefaction hung over the whole area.

On a warm January afternoon in 1886, just 17 days after the New Year celebrations, a procession of men bearing a small burden wound its way along Sir Lowry Road, through Darling and Shortmarket streets and up Longmarket Street to the Tana Baru. In their wake straggled some three thousand Muslims. Curious bystanders watched their passing. After the funeral a dozen policemen approached the mourners to take their names. The tension which had hung over the proceedings exploded into violence. Stones flew. 'Kill the *deeners* [police officials],' someone shouted. A policeman was stabbed and his jaw broken.

The riot ended after the commissioner of police addressed the Muslim leaders, but that afternoon a second burial took place. Again crowds assembled. 'I do not suppose there was a man, woman, or child who could walk, inside of their homes. They were either in knots at street corners, in groups in the streets, on their stoeps or on the house-tops, whilst on the wooden balcony of a Mosque-minaret a priest and his followers were looking down on the scene as if directing the defence of a beleaguered town.'[1] When the burial was over the people dispersed after setting up 'a ringing shout of triumph and defiance'. That evening the Volunteers were called up, camping on Green Point Common and mingling with the restive crowd the next day. Sixteen rioters were arrested and appeared in court a few days later. Most were middle-aged men, charged with assault and sentenced to two months' hard labour. Abdol Burns, singled out as the ringleader, was sentenced to an additional £10 fine. The magistrate castigated the police: 'It

Previous pages: This orderly silvan scene of the Liesbeek River in Newlands in the 1890s captures the rural dream cherished by British immigrants to Cape Town. But it also reflects the reality of an industrialising town: an independent young woman is using the most up-to-date technology; workmen are busy behind her with a traction engine; on the left is Ohlsson's Breweries, later to become the local headquarters of South African Breweries. (UCT Macmillan)

The Lantern reflected the views of those who saw the cemetery riots as a breakdown of law and order. On the left are the Volunteers, the Dukes and the Cape Town Highlanders, who were called out to put down the riot; on the far right is Abdol Burns, who was convicted as the ringleader. (SAL, *The Lantern*, 28 January 1886)

is my opinion that if they had not gone there there would not have been any misconduct on the part of the Malays.'[2]

This unprecedented violence of Cape Town's usually compliant Muslim population was the result of hotly disputed legislation, introduced in 1884 after a catastrophic smallpox epidemic two years earlier, to close Cape Town's insalubrious burial grounds. The reasons were sound enough: the town's appalling overcrowding and mounting mortality rates demanded urgent action. Mephitic cemeteries were an obvious target. But death is a rite of passage, deeply embedded in social custom, and Muslims were not alone in their desire to retain the old cemeteries. The Dutch were also unwilling to abandon traditional practices. While British residents viewed the Dutch family vaults with distaste, suggesting that it was a desecration of the dead to pile up bones in the vaults so as to make room for fresh coffins, to the Dutch they represented continuity: 'for us all to be buried in one place as a family was my chief reason for having it,' explained one of their number. Muslim burial sites had even greater sanctity, for it was in the Tana Baru that such revered figures as Tuan Guru were interred. More important, the Tana Baru was close enough to the town to permit mourners to carry the dead on foot to their graves. The difference between the Dutch and the Muslims lay in their responses to the interdict. When attempts to negotiate a compromise with the colonial medical authorities failed, the Dutch reluctantly gave way; the Muslims did not.

The 'cemetery riots' involved more than a clash of cultures. In advocating the closure of burial grounds the medical profession – the embodiment of modern scientific knowledge – offered a partial solution to rising mortality rates, for doctors in Britain's industrial cities had shown that disease could be reduced through cleanliness. Sanitation was a hallmark of imperial civilisation, a gospel carried to the colonies by British middle-class immigrants. The cemetery riots represented a clash between the forces of modernism, including an efficient but indifferent bureaucracy, and the communal values of pre-industrial societies. Beyond this went the question of power, of who had the means to enforce particular values and how. The disagreement deepened Dutch resentment of British control but the Dutch had a voice in parliament to express their opposition; the Muslims, on the other hand, driven by a stronger religious conviction, lacked the same platform to express their objections. In the last resort, they argued, religion was above the law, to be protected constitutionally if possible, unlawfully if necessary. Although middle-class reformers, backed by the Volunteers and the police, tasted victory in 1886, the battle was by no means won. Indeed the struggle to impose a new social order in Cape Town formed a dominant theme of the closing decades of the nineteenth century.

THE IMPACT OF THE MINERAL REVOLUTION

Twenty years earlier, in 1867, the colonial secretary Richard Southey had placed the first diamond found and identified in South Africa on the table of the Legislative Assembly in Cape Town. 'Gentlemen, this is the rock on which the future success of South Africa will be built,' he told the assembled members of parliament. Although at first people were slow to recognise the implications of the discovery, by 1870 Cape Town was in the grip of diamond fever. Men abandoned their jobs, their wives and children to seek their fortunes on the diamond fields. This find was the start of a vast transformation of South Africa that was to gain momentum with the even more significant discovery of gold in 1886. The 'mineral revolution' brought an influx of capital and people into the country and disrupted existing social patterns. In thirty years Cape Town underwent a metamorphosis from sleepy colonial backwater to thriving city.

Unlike the Somerset Road cemeteries, the Tana Baru remained in existence until well into the twentieth century. (CA AG9491)

The hope of finding riches enticed thousands of immigrants to South Africa. In 1875 Cape Town and the suburban villages had 45,000 residents. By 1891 the population had grown to 67,000 and by 1904 to 171,000. The outlying villages, negligible in 1865, became substantial municipalities. New suburbs sprang into being in Salt River, Woodstock and Mowbray. Woodstock (previously Papendorp) grew by a staggering 394 per cent, rivalling the Transvaal boom towns. People began to settle north and east, along Durban Road, around the Bay towards Blouberg, and into Uitvlugt forest station.

Immigration made Cape Town even more ethnically diverse than before. Jews, driven from Eastern Europe by poverty and pogroms, came to seek their fortunes on the diamond fields; after 1882 an even larger influx occurred. The number of professed Jews in the municipality of Cape Town rose from under 1000 in 1891 to over 8000 by 1904. Indians too began to make their presence felt: by July 1899 there were 600 Indians in the Cape Peninsula; already in the 1880s Indian corner stores had made their appearance. The Indians were by no means homogeneous: while the majority were Muslims, Pathans from the north-west frontier formed a small minority. Gujarati-speaking Hindus came

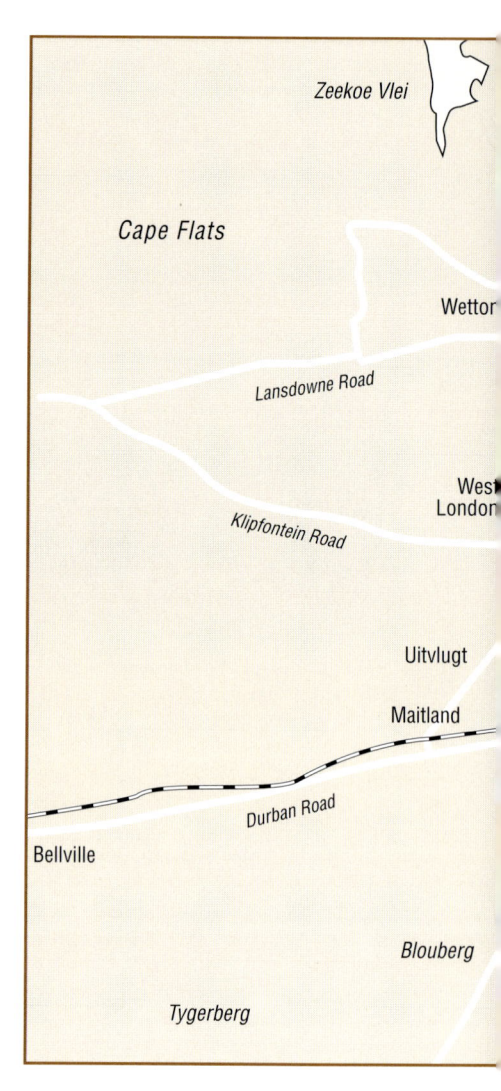

The growth of Cape Town in the late nineteenth century.

This boardgame, 'The journey from Genadendal to Cape Town', a form of 'snakes and ladders', which was printed at the Genadendal mission press in the 1860s, illustrated evocatively the tug of the town for the rural poor. By 1886 so many Moravians from the mission stations in the western Cape had moved to Cape Town that a church was established in District Six. (Genadendal Museum; photo by Rex Reynolds)

mainly from Broach and Surat; their number also included Tamils from the Madras Presidency and Bengali-speakers from eastern India.[3] By 1899 Africans were also a familiar presence in Cape Town, estimated at about 10,000. Their origins were as varied as the rest of Cape Town's population. At a baptism in the town on Christmas Eve, 1890, there were three Xhosa-speakers, three 'Shangaans', one 'Inhambane', one Zulu and one Mosotho attending the service.

Such immigrants added to the ethnic diversity of the town. All the same Northern European Protestants continued to be preferred by the white ruling class. A few German settlers were introduced by the government in 1876. On Wynberg's bleak and sandy flats at Philippi they struggled to survive, gradually establishing themselves as market gardeners. Most striking of all was the great influx of British settlers. In 1891, 17 per cent of the population of the Cape district was born in Europe; by 1904 this had increased to 27 per cent. In that year about one in seven Capetonians was British-born. The end of the century saw Britain's ascendancy more completely established when 'English' values came to dominate the town – in business, in the municipality, in educational and cultural institutions. In the colonial context 'English' identity had more to do with consciousness than birth, for it embraced Scots and anglicised Dutch. White skins, the English tongue and bourgeois values were the defining hallmarks.[4] Yet even among the British there was greater diversity than before. Though many of the immigrants were of the lower middle class – poorly educated clerks, unemployable at home – struggling to maintain middle-class values on labourers' salaries, others were working class. The latter introduced into Cape Town new skills and new forms of labour organisation.

Immigration transformed the gender and age profile of the city. In 1875 the ratio of men to women was roughly equal; by 1891 there were 2000 more men than women and by 1904 this had increased to 13,376. Cape Town had become once again a predominantly male city. It was also a young city: in 1891, 81 per cent of the Cape district's population was under the age of 40; 45 per cent was between 15 and 39 years – the economically active sector. Given these demographic features the authorities feared that a young, largely male city had the potential for social disorder particularly in times of depression. This was one reason for the attempts to create a more disciplined society in the last part of the nineteenth century.

Transformation in the city occurred within a new political context. By 1870 wealth and the spread of firearms were making the Cape increasingly unruly and expensive for Britain to control, not only on the diamond fields, but also on the eastern frontier. The British government was ready to offer self-rule. This prospect delighted middle-class Capetonians, not least because responsible government, based in Cape Town, might promote the interests of the western Cape above those of the eastern districts. Certainly once responsible government was granted in 1872, Cape Town profited wonderfully. The town became the linchpin of colonial communications as the government poured money into the harbour and railways. Between 1879 and 1883 alone, £450,000 was spent on the harbour. This gave the capital the edge over Port Elizabeth, an advantage that was reinforced by the extension of the western Cape railway to Beaufort West by 1880 and to Kimberley in November 1885. By 1884 Cape Town's ascendancy over Port Elizabeth was complete: it would be symbolically confirmed when the Standard Bank moved its headquarters from the eastern port to Cape Town in 1886.[5]

Merchants and businessmen flourished in this economic climate. The colony could now raise sizeable loans on the London market and Cape Town benefited from this bounty, to the tune of £1,350,000 between 1888 and 1899. New joint-stock companies

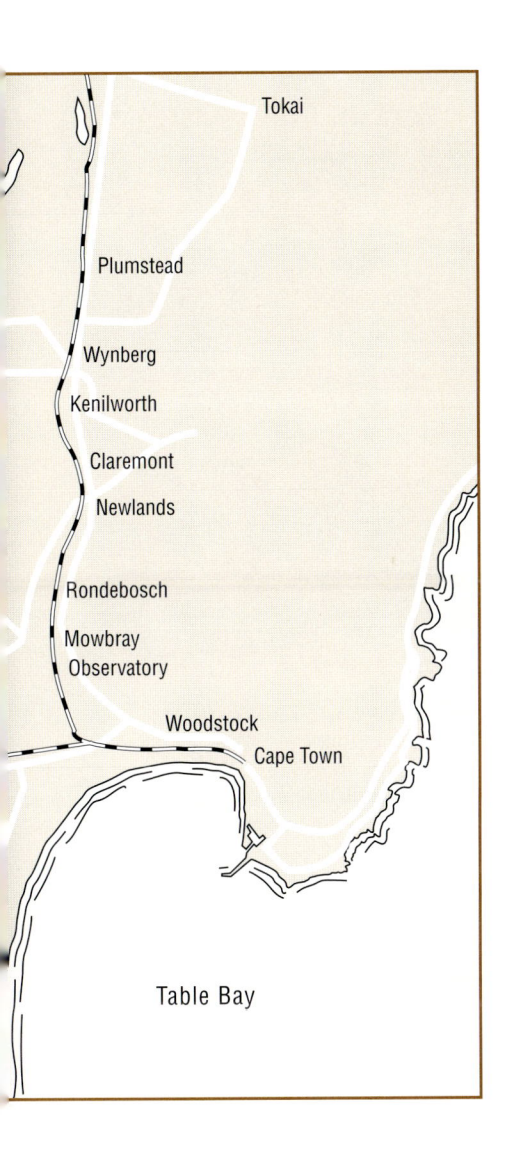

By no means everyone favoured responsible government. Here the monkey, Saul Solomon, 'the member for Cape Town', and the bear, Sir John Molteno, the first premier, are dancing to the tune of the organ-grinder, presumably the governor Sir Henry Barkly. (UCT Macmillan)

were floated and old ones revamped: their number doubled between 1875 and 1882. One innovation of the time was the considerable sum sunk into transport and electrification. In 1892 the Metropolitan and Suburban Railway Company constructed a line to Sea Point. The City Tramways Company was reborn in 1894 and by 1896 the first electric tram was trundling up Adderley Street, four years after a syndicate had been formed to supply electric light to the town. Electricity also made refrigeration possible. In 1893 fruit was first exported to Europe from the Western Province in refrigerated ships, marking the start of an important new industry in the region.

In transforming the physical face of Cape Town the architect Charles Freeman played a large role. Initially employed by the Public Works Department, for which he designed the General Post Office in St George's Street, Freeman was forced into private practice after a débâcle over the Houses of Parliament. Standard Bank and the second Stuttafords department store were both his work. As an architect Freeman was a man of his age, from the Central Methodist Church in Greenmarket Square, Cape Town's only example of High Victorian city church architecture, to his florid shops. He was quick to take advantage of new prefabricated techniques and became the local agent for MacFarlane's

In 1885 the tramway with its spanking horses was extended to Gardens but it was superseded in 1896 by the electric tram, which did much to help clean up Cape Town streets. (P. Coates, *Track and Trackless*, Cape Town, 1976, p. 62; CA AG2671)

ADDERLEY STREET IN THE 1870s

In the 1870s Adderley Street showed only a few signs of modernisation. The *grachts* had disappeared but the wide, unpaved street and low buildings confirmed the appearance of shabbiness which struck so many visitors. By 1873 the Gothic telegraph office no longer performed its original function. This 'Chinese Pogoda [*sic*], Dove-cot, Pepperbox ... that cost so much, was opened so ceremoniously ... With its wires snapped and *news* diverted into another channel, its stained glass broken, and boundary chains and links unfastened, its "*stop-clock*" always pointing to 3, and its cupola and general appearance faded and dusty, it looks as forlorn and wretched as a day after the fair, or a race-course or a watering-place when the run and seasons are over'.[6] Prominent on the right is Inglesby's Stuttafords building and in the centre the water fountain presented to Cape Town by the merchant-philanthropist and ardent advocate of temperance H.E. Rutherfoord.

(UCT Macmillan)

214　CAPE TOWN 1870–1899

Rebuilding Cape Town's Centre

Victorian taste and a new affluence transformed the centre of late-nineteenth-century Cape Town.

The Standard Bank. and the General Post Office. (SAL PHA)

Juta's bookshop, 1902. (SAL PHA)

The 'flat iron' building owned by Thomson, Watson & Co. (SAL INIL 17843)

Freeman's Central Methodist Church, Greenmarket Square. (CA AG1573)

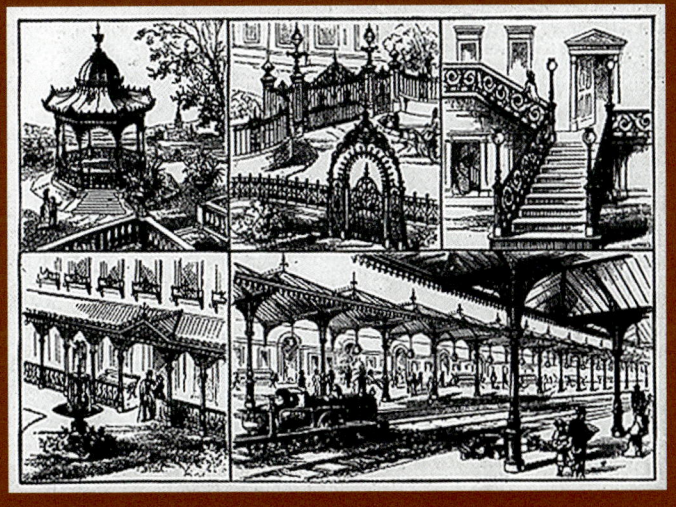

Unlike colonies such as Australia, the Cape had few iron foundries. Decorative cast iron was obtained by mail order. (*SA Review*, 1.1.1904, p.8)

The Search for Order

The Houses of Parliament

(CA M582)

decorative cast iron, which would embellish so many of Cape Town's buildings.

Cape Town was still dominated by the great merchants, now about 150 in number. In the last part of the century their low post-Georgian offices gave way to taller, exuberant Victorian structures, made possible by the steel frame and the lift, which was first installed in the new Stuttafords building in 1890. Ransome's 'flat iron' building at the bottom of Adderley Street, designed for the merchant house of Thomson, Watson & Co., with its corkscrew staircase, was one of Cape Town's more striking landmarks. Banks favoured a sober Renaissance style, intended to convey a message of solidity and reliability. The most splendid example of the genre was the Standard Bank building, whose dome above the columns and pediments was surmounted by the figure of Britannia. Shops could afford to be showier: Stuttafords and Garlicks were a riot of ornament. One of the most luxuriant was Juta's bookshop: in a niche at the top of the façade Shakespeare presided over a lavish display of moulding and ornaments.[7]

These imposing structures were emblematic of economic change. Where Stuttafords now stood had once been the site of the old Colonial Bank, one of the last of the local banks, which had been such a feature of the first generation of South African banking. In contrast the imposing Standard Bank, situated across the road, was the first truly national bank, financed by overseas capital. Similarly Stuttafords and Garlicks were no longer general dealers but department stores, using modern marketing techniques.[8] The upper end of Adderley Street was still primarily the site of political and religious authority. The

'The Cape Times *is flung into my yard every morning at six o'clock and I go for it, as "Contemporary History" is too exciting at present to wait until breakfast time. It is a comfort that what would reduce other men to despair only rouses Gordon to his best ... he is a man quite by himself with the courage of a lion.'*

Dr Jane Waterston,
1884

Charles Freeman won a prize of £250 for his plans for the Houses of Parliament. The foundation stone was laid in 1878 with much fanfare. The day was proclaimed a public holiday. The stone that was laid was a block of granite with 'AF 1875' inscribed on it in gold letters; in a cavity a glass tube was inserted containing specimens of coins of the realm with a parchment scroll of the names of the people present. Corn, wine and oil were poured on the stone by the masters of Masonic lodges and the building was blessed by the Anglican dean of Cape Town. Unfortunately building did not proceed smoothly. The foundations had to be laid deeper and the cost of construction doubled. Freeman was sacked. The final building, designed by Harry Greaves, cost £220,000 compared with Freeman's original estimate of £50,000. The new parliament building was eventually opened in 1885.

Groote Kerk and the Supreme Court building were unchanged, as was St George's Cathedral, but beyond them colonial control was now asserted in a stately Houses of Parliament, opened in May 1885.

The transformation of South Africa occurred at a critical moment in history. Britain was no longer the confident imperial power she had been at mid-century. Her industrial and imperial ascendancy was being seriously challenged by a united Germany and the United States of America. Not only were British industries ageing but strikes at the London docks in the mid-1880s did much to cause the British middle classes to view the urban masses with misgiving. This general apprehension gave rise to jingoism – a strident nationalism very different from the comfortable superiority of earlier imperialists. Colonials echoed similar sentiments and imperial exploits were followed closely in Cape Town. General Gordon's stand in the Sudan in 1884 aroused great enthusiasm, as Dr Jane Waterston described to a sympathetic correspondent: 'The *Cape Times* is flung into my yard every morning at six o'clock and I go for it, as "Contemporary History" is too exciting at present to wait until breakfast time. It is a comfort that what would reduce other men to despair only rouses Gordon to his best ... he is a man quite by himself with the courage of a lion.'[9]

Economic and social anxieties, disguised by this noisy nationalism, were also translated into biological metaphors. Influenced by Darwin's theories of evolution, the British middle classes feared that the 'unfit' denizens of the slums, breeding faster than their more worthy selves, would bring about the degeneration of the imperial race. The result, they believed, was a 'qualitative' decline in the British stock, which was failing to match 'the formidable Germans and Americans, or ... [even] the lowly Boers'.[10] Social imperialists saw the problem and its solution in imperial terms. 'Distress in London is not the distress of a great city – it is the distress of a great empire,' wrote the journalist Arnold White in his book *Problems of a Great City*.[11] White believed that the flight of poor people to the cities should be deflected to the colonies, thereby solving colonial problems as well. Whereas this solution provided expressly for those who had not yet 'degenerated', General Booth of the Salvation Army considered that even the 'submerged

This cartoon by H.H. Egersdorfer encapsulates late-nineteenth-century British xenophobia. The values of the honest British working man and the English squire are threatened by the thronging hordes of alien immigrants – Jewish, Chinese, Indian, Greek and Italian amongst others. (SAL, *The Owl*, 12 December 1902)

THE SEARCH FOR ORDER

tenth' could be relieved in the colonies. His book *In Darkest England and the Way Out*, advocating colonial emigration, became a bestseller after it was published in 1890.

Britons in Cape Town shared these apprehensions although their bogies were closer at hand – the Dutch, Asian immigrants, their own poor. Cape Town's 'mixed race' seemed particularly vulnerable to degeneration: to the Rev. James Mackinnon, for instance, sympathetic though he was to the plight of the only African student admitted to the Stellenbosch Dutch Reformed seminary, and then ostracised, the 'bastard Hottentots' of the western Cape were examples of racial 'retrogression'.[12]

At the Cape class prejudice, which had partly overridden racial intolerance in the first part of the century, gave way to increasing racism. By the 1890s racial anxieties added a new edge to the desire for British immigrants, as John X. Merriman explained to Sir Charles Mills, the colonial agent in London, in 1891: 'The whole question of getting an increase in our white population is at … once of the greatest importance and of such complication that it makes one despair. I have induced Sivewright [the minister of railways] to go in for Scotch plate-layers and gangers instead of the [Chinese indentured labour] we employ so largely …'[13] Female domestic servants from Britain were particularly desirable. Sir Charles Mills wrote wistfully, 'If only four or six were imported by the weekly steamer you would in a few years feel their effect upon the Census.'[14]

By the end of the century, legislation began to exclude 'undesirable aliens'. In 1902 an Immigration Act was passed keeping out those who could not write in European characters. Only after some struggle was Yiddish recognised as qualifying in these terms. Asians came under attack in 1906 when the General Dealers Act was introduced to protect the 'European trading class' from Indian competition. The Chinese were singled out more directly, for this was the age of the 'yellow peril', a threat which 'will … in time permanently spoil or wholly root out [South African] civilization. This is a danger which threatens all classes of our society, no matter of what descent or political parties of the past. Let us thus co-operate to keep that plague from our country.'[15] Gambling and crime were believed to be peculiarly Chinese vices. In 1904 a Chinese Exclusion Act was passed to keep out all those Chinese who were not British subjects. The few who were exempted were obliged to be registered and controlled. Yet the Cape was not unique in enforcing this legislation: Australia was equally anxious to preserve the purity of the white race and the southern United States provided a potent model of a segregated society.

At the same time the strident jingoism and assertive imperialism that marked the late-nineteenth century were propagated by a flurry of new daily and weekly papers in Cape Town. Among them the *Cape Times*, edited by the ex-missionary Frederick York St Leger, became the mouthpiece of the new imperialism. A host of satirical weeklies served the jingoism of the lower middle classes. Sometimes using outrageously racist stereotyping, *The Lantern*, edited by Thomas McCombie, and *The Owl*, founded by Charles Penstone, expressed their concerns.

As middle-class people became alert to the problems of poverty in their midst, lurid descriptions of slum life found fashion in the late-Victorian press. Deliberately dramatic and stylised, this slummer journalism became a means by which British immigrants at the Cape affirmed their English values and defined 'their ideals of community'.[16] Through a common literary language their English identity was mobilised to refashion Cape Town into a model society. Although the press used the rhetoric of enlightened reform, it was combined with such ethnic prejudice and class consciousness that the value of reform was severely vitiated. Cape Town's slummer journalists were neither as well known nor as well informed as their colleagues in Britain or Australia, but they had

'As for the ordinary relationships of social life, they are unknown, and the laws of common decency are set at utter defiance; indeed, anyone desiring to see life in about its lowest aspect could not do better than pay a visit, if he could summon up sufficient courage, to some of the horrible byeways which branch off from Waterkant-street, where a stream of moral pollution is constantly flowing.'

Cape Times,
8 January 1876

ample material. The world which they depicted appeared as alien as a foreign country. 'Yet in this city of Cape Town, proverbially one of the fairest and most inviting in the southern hemisphere, there are localities haunted by the dregs of society, which a respectable person would no more presume to visit than one would the purlieus of Ratcliff Highway in London, or Montmartre in Paris.'

Suffering and vice were in this view interchangeable. Poverty destroyed basic family life and opened the way to crime and degradation. 'As for the ordinary relationships of social life, they are unknown, and the laws of common decency are set at utter defiance; indeed, anyone desiring to see life in about its lowest aspect could not do better than pay a visit, if he could summon up sufficient courage, to some of the horrible byeways which

Coffee Lane in District One on the waterfront was typical of the impoverished *steegs* of the older quarters of Cape Town. (CA E7979)

THE SEARCH FOR ORDER   219

branch off from Waterkant-street, where a stream of moral pollution is constantly flowing.' The very air in these quarters was contaminated. 'It is a fact, that the condensed air of a crowded room gives a deposit which, if allowed to remain for a few days, forms a solid, thick, glutinous mass, having a strong odour of animal matter. A few drops of the liquid matter obtained by the condensation of the air of a foul locality, introduced into the vein of a dog can produce death; what incalculable mischief, therefore, must it not produce on those human beings who breathe it again and again, rendered fouler and less capable of sustaining life with each breath drawn.'

In this journalism women appeared degraded and dissolute, the antithesis of the chaste and passive creatures of the Victorian stereotype – from an old woman who was a 'bundle of filthy rags' to the mother with her 'troop of 'emaciated children', her swollen eyes betokening 'a recent pugilistic encounter', and 'unsteady gait'.[17]

This stereotyping of the poor acquired a distinctive racial dimension by the 1880s. Cape Muslims, previously seen as clean and industrious, were now depicted as independent (an undesirable trait to employers), dirty, lazy, profligate, ignorant and unruly. 'Disgusted citizen', writing to the *Cape Times* in March 1881, brought all these elements together in a diatribe: 'Malays' were 'a motley lot of blacks, half-breeds and Europeans'. They would only condescend to do four days' work per week, never saved, monopolised 'certain' branches of industry, were ignorant, could be bought at election time, and dressed like 'peacocks' though they lived at home like 'swine'.[18]

As the number of Africans in the town grew, white residents adopted the mentality of frontier settlers. Prejudice was influenced by the belief that African behaviour was hostile to, even subversive of, middle-class urban values. Africans were declared 'immoral' or 'indecent'; 'almost naked Kaffirs' were reported to be wandering about town and begging from the inhabitants, while African women produced reactions of 'annoyance and disgust'.[19] The growth of the city's African population increased the volume of morally outraged and fearful contributions to the English-language press. Reporting from Papendorp in September 1881, a correspondent of *The Lantern* found 'ten, twelve, or even more, natives ... in miserable, filthy, hovel homes and huts. Women half, and children wholly nude, tumble indiscriminately out and in, amidst an atmosphere reeking of profanity, drunkenness, and immorality.'[20]

Occasional assaults also provoked the perception of Africans as 'dangerous'. When an English carpenter was mugged in July 1881, the prosecutor remarked that 'since Cape Town has been flooded with Kafirs there was no safety in walking out after dark'.[21] What became known as the 'Kaffir problem' was chiefly a question of control – how to make Papendorp, where many Africans had settled, and Cape Town in general safe from the 'Kaffir' danger. The language employed was often drawn from scientific medicine – Africans were contaminated and contaminating, they were a source of infection, threatening the physical and moral health of the city.

New wealth and new imperial perspectives produced the demand for a new order in Cape Town. Although local institutions often acted as pressure groups, reform was also initiated from above, through the actions of an elite in parliament or of civil servants who believed that they held the key to the right ordering of society. 'Order' became a crucial concept. This society, young and male, often uneducated and – in British eyes – 'uncivilised', appeared potentially unruly. One function of reform was to impose controls which would make crowded urban life manageable. For many Capetonians, however, who were the object of reform, these ideas of right living were alien and unappealing. Yet they could not avoid their influence and an interchange occurred in which some

'The wretched old woman is engaged in preparing the midday meal, and what do you think it consists of? No less a savoury dish than snoek heads, about the nearest approach to substituting a stone for bread that one could imagine. Yet with a kind of garbage concocted of some dozen of these heads, nearly as many mouths have to be filled, and this, too, day after day, the only variation in the family diet being crawfish and rice.'
Cape Times,
8 January 1876

concepts were rejected and others absorbed and appropriated.

Parliament and the municipal council were both instruments of reform. There the black vote still had a limited reality although no black sat on either body. When responsible government promoted the Afrikaner Bond as a rapidly growing force by the 1880s, the black vote (suitably restricted) became for English speakers a counter to increasing Afrikaner political power. As the editor of the *Cape Times* rationalised in 1889, 'social separation does not involve the political extinction of the weaker race'.[22] Parliamentary candidates regularly included coloured men on their electoral committees. In the 1884 House of Assembly elections, Taliep Mohmoed, Gatiep Taliep and Achmat Effendi (all Muslims) formed part of the committee of the brewer Anders Ohlsson. His election pamphlets were translated into Arabic for the benefit of Muslim voters. The black vote was also considered worth buying. Potential voters were 'treated' in 1884 – 'the consumption of Ohlsson's beer on an unusually thirsty day was copious'.[23] Tenants or employees were particularly vulnerable to pressure. *The Lantern* reported that the leading dock agent, Andrew McKenzie, 'stood by the booth counting his workmen as they voted – there was moral if not legal coercion'.[24]

After the introduction of the secret ballot in the early 1890s, candidates adopted more subtle methods. In 1902 the department-store retailer John Garlick placed an advertisement in the *South African Spectator*, the city's first black newspaper, stating that he supported equal rights for 'all civilised people'.[25] If the black vote was courted, it was also manipulated. *The Lantern* suggested that black voters merely provided electoral fodder on polling day. 'Coloured men ... were met at the Town Hall by one of the candidates, who supplied them with printed voting papers, found if they were registered ... and then saw them conducted to the voting table where they deposited their ticket with no more conception of what they were about than if they were dumb animals.'[26]

Yet if the black vote still had a value, it was much circumscribed. In the last decades of the century the non-racial franchise was steadily eroded. In 1893 the government abolished Cape Town's 'plumping system', which had allowed each voter in the city four votes; these could be distributed in any combination among the candidates for four seats. The immediate aim of this step was in fact to prevent the election of a black candidate, Achmat Effendi. In general one can say that the rapprochement which took place between English and Afrikaner politicians in the early 1890s, when Cecil Rhodes wooed the Bond, came close to destroying the non-racial political tradition. In fact the Jameson Raid of 1896 probably preserved the non-racial parliamentary franchise by increasing tensions between Afrikaners and English.

In the 1880s and 1890s alteration to the municipal franchise also ensured British domination of local political office. Most dramatically, a municipal law of 1893 introduced multiple votes for property owners – the more valuable the property, the more votes the owner could cast. The beneficiaries were the English businessmen who owned valuable commercial real estate, rather than the Dutch inner-city residents and their coloured tenants, who now found themselves linked in an uneasy alliance. The existence of the plural vote did, however, make possible the candidature of a coloured butcher, J.C. de Jager, who in 1898 stood for District Six on a platform of fighting 'for the coloured class', excluding Africans whose competition for jobs he railed against. However, class was also an element in the election, for the coloured elite did not consider him sufficiently 'respectable' to represent them and he was defeated.

In the 1880s parliamentary legislation was passed to structure local administration more systematically. In the process haphazard local institutions were formalised. By

An election handbill of A.B. Effendi urged, in Arabic, 'Vote for Ohlsson, Plump for Ohlsson'. (J. Walton (ed.), *The Josephine Mill and its Owners*, Cape Town, 1978, p. 75)

Suburban town halls were the proud symbols of independent status. Both Mowbray and Rondebosch built halls after they became separate municipalities. (CA AG8159; J9740)

1902 there were ten municipalities in the Cape Peninsula (Cape Town, Woodstock, Green and Sea Point, Maitland, Mowbray, Rondebosch, Claremont, Wynberg, Kalk Bay and Simon's Town). A Divisional Council was responsible for the rural districts while the Table Bay Harbour Board had a separate jurisdiction. Camps Bay and Milnerton, still in the hands of property developers, formed incipient municipalities. All these bodies were fiercely proud of their independent existences, symbolised by the small, ornate town halls which sprouted in every suburb. Autonomy was hard bought, though, for the suburbs lacked the resources to service their growing populations. Constant water

The Cape Census of 1891

Statistics have never been an objective study. Although their collection is usually preliminary to identifying the ills of society, their real importance lies in their propaganda value. Counting means categorising, a Western mode of thought which in turn implies a hierarchy, from young to old, from superior to inferior. The way in which the Cape categorised its population tells us as much about the perceptions of the authorities as it does about the people themselves.

The year 1891 was chosen by Britain for an imperial census in which the Cape was to participate for the first time. Although the under colonial secretary Henry de Smidt wanted to know the size of the population, he had a second agenda – to discover 'how the European population has progressed, to what extent the aboriginal natives and other coloured races have increased, how many Indians, Chinese, and others of alien race have established themselves in our midst'.[27] His language was telling – Europeans 'progress', blacks 'increase', Indians and Chinese are 'alien'.

The Colonial Medical Committee in the 1870s was a Cape Town organisation. It included the sons of two of Cape Town's merchant princes, H.A. Ebden and W.H. Ross, as well as J.P. Landsberg, doctor to the Free Dispensary, P.G. Stewart, who practised in Rondebosch, and C.L. Herman, 'a fanatical Capetonian' and passionate supporter of the public health movement. (*South African Medical Record*, 12 July 1912)

shortages and rising mortality rates plagued them throughout their short lives.

At central government level the Colonial Office at the Cape was reorganised. The great reformer was Dr Alfred John Gregory, an autocratic, ambitious man with a mission – to give the Cape an efficient public health service in the British tradition. In 1891 the Colonial Office was divided into two branches, of statistics and health. The first colonial medical officer of health was appointed in 1893 and the next year a Births and Deaths Registration Act was passed. In 1897 the first effective Public Health Act was promulgated, putting considerable power into Gregory's hands. This gave the Cape the most advanced public health system in South Africa and contributed to the dominance of British culture in Cape Town. By 1903 the health branch of the Colonial Office had a staff of 16, almost all of whom were English-speaking.

Modernisation at the Cape was spearheaded by the medical profession, prompted by the shocking conditions in the town. Many medical men were immigrants lured from an overstocked profession at home. Colonial-born doctors, who also had to train abroad, imbibed the same sanitary values as their immigrant colleagues. Health was seen in moral terms – the dirty were also bad – and civilisation equated with a clean water supply. By the 1880s such sanitation rhetoric had become part of the common ideological currency of British imperialism. In Cape Town it was promoted too in the English-language press, which stigmatised opponents of reform as obstructionist, often in the most virulently racist terms.

In a rapidly growing town the need for reform became urgent. Cape Town in the 1880s was in a shocking state. Unrestrained winter torrents gouged out the roads and flooded homes, while the sand raised by the raging summer south-easterly winds enveloped the town 'in clouds of red dust, which, tearing round corners, sweep over the unwary pedestrian, speedily reducing him to a state of helpless and frantic blindness'.[28] Fortunately the 'Cape doctor' helped to purify the air of its noxious odours, for almost every activity in the town contributed to the offensive smell. Waste accumulated in the covered *grachts* and the resultant gases were released through 'stink traps', only too appropriately named. Human ordure, which was supposed to be collected in tubs, was frequently poured into the streets. Refuse and night-soil collection was, in any case, inefficient since the town council was constantly at loggerheads with the contractors it employed. Slaughtering was still carried on at the shambles below the Castle walls and

Even at the end of the century, after drainage had been improved, winter rains wrought havoc in Adderley Street. (UCT Macmillan)

fish was cured at Roggebaai: in both cases the result was nauseating. Animals roamed the streets and the superintendent of public works claimed scavenging pigs were being bred 'by hundreds' in District Six. Even street watering contributed to the aroma, for polluted seawater was carried by horse from Roggebaai to the upper parts of the town. To all this was added a chronic shortage of water. Everyone suffered – the military in the Castle next to the shambles, the patients in the Somerset Hospital where there was not even enough water in 1880 to cook their food, and government officials confined to offices next to unflushed water closets, who had to 'submit to the danger of inhaling the noxious stench'.[29] Most neglected were the back streets, the lanes and alleys of Ward 1 behind the fish market, in Ward 4 on the slopes of Signal Hill off Helliger Lane and Rose

Municipal failure to deal with Cape Town's sanitary deficiencies was a favourite subject for cartoonists. (SAL, *The Lantern*, 5 August 1882)

224   CAPE TOWN 1870–1899

Street, and the *steegs* between Boom and Barrack streets in Ward 10. District Six was an instant slum where houses were flung up hastily, uncontrolled by building regulations.

Despite these conditions demanding of attention, reform was slow. The main features of Cape Town government in the 1880s were lethargy and conflict. Meetings were sometimes abandoned for lack of a quorum. The Cape Town press ranted ineffectually about the 'grave-like torpor, a mouldering stagnation, a dream-like unsubstantiality about us, that is stamped on all our corporate life'.[30] Underlying the reluctance of the councillors to invest in sanitary improvements were several interrelated issues. Costly reforms would have to be paid for from the pockets of the ratepayers, hitting the property owners on the council particularly hard. Many of them were Dutch, still resident in the city. Strains of an emergent Afrikaner nationalism could be heard in their resistance to encroaching British reformers. But they also represented an earlier generation of business in the town, ousted by entrepreneurial immigrants. Their attitude to sanitation was old-fashioned, a view shared by English-speaking residents of the same vintage, like R.H. Arderne: 'I believe that any dirt is comparatively innocuous, and I believe it is the waste of water in all the little houses and alleys that has been the source of more annoyance than anything else can possibly be. When these people [tenants] had to go to the public pumps they did not waste water.'[31]

Opposition to the 'Dirty Party' was led by merchants resident in the suburbs. The vested interests of the 'Clean Party' lay in a thriving town which could be successfully promoted on the London bond markets. The neglected state of the town, as the Clean Party complained in 1881, threatened residents with an epidemic and prevented 'Strangers and Visitors remaining in this Town to the detriment of its Trade and prosperity'. By 1880 the Clean and Dirty parties were locked in mortal combat. In the 1882 election the Clean Party sent a spanking-clean 'Van of Progress' round the town with a band inside playing 'lively airs' in an attempt to garner votes. 'It was a smartly painted conveyance, with the panels and wheels tastefully picked out with gilding. A bright white canvas awning protected the bandsmen, in their trim, new uniforms and freshly scrubbed faces, from the sun and rain. Not a speck of dirt defiled this smart turn-out;

'Sing a song of smallpox
Hofmeyr gone askew;
Ashley, Louw and Zoutendyk,
In a pretty stew!
When the scare is over,
These rascals will begin
Their dirty tricks, to stop the bricks
Who would a Clean town win.'
The Lantern,
1 January 1881

The municipal elections of the early 1880s were bitterly contested. The English-language papers threw their full weight behind the reformers. (SAL, *The Lantern*, 15 August 1882)

THE SEARCH FOR ORDER 225

and the pair of well-groomed animals in front pranced proudly along as if they knew that they were chasing away from Cape Town the demons of Slovenliness, Meanness and Dirt.'[32] The result was to put the Clean Party into power.

Despite this temporary triumph in the 1880s, effective victory came only after the franchise had been restructured to exclude the 'mob vote'. When the plural vote was introduced in the municipality in 1893, the town clerk was explicit about the reason behind the move: 'If you were to revert to the system of a single vote ... it would tend to bring about ... a condition of things which actually exists in some districts of England, where there is a great Socialist element – where there is a feeling that working men's dwellings, Municipal workshops, and Municipal soup kitchens should be established ... Assuming that such a condition of things with a thoroughly Socialist Town Council existed in Cape Town, these socialist people would have the power ... of taxing the very people who find the money.'[33]

In the 1890s the reforming clique also acquired a fresh countenance. It included two Afrikaner Bond members, D.P. Graaff and D.C. de Waal, both 'new' urban Afrikaners, politically influential and economically ambitious. Graaff was a director of Combrinck & Co. – soon to become Imperial Cold Storage – which was in the forefront of meat and fruit imports and exports. Another active member of the revamped council was the department-store retailer and property developer John Garlick.

A changing power base and improved prosperity contributed to the emergence of a sense of civic responsibility in the 1890s. This should not be overstated, however, for the notion of a 'civic gospel' as it was understood in Britain was only dimly grasped in Cape Town. Nevertheless, in the 1890s the members of the Clean Party were not only more willing to spend large sums on municipal improvements, but were also in a better position to do so. This is not to say that the lot of the poor improved. On the contrary, what did occur was that the differential between whites and other residents of the city increased as the former began to benefit from the improvements created.

During the 1890s negotiation followed negotiation, hitches abounded, costs expanded, but slowly, haltingly, sewerage and drainage were built. Loans for such improvements were only sanctioned after the new system of plural voting enabled the larger property

Gross mortality rates in Cape Town per 1000 of population, 1892–1910

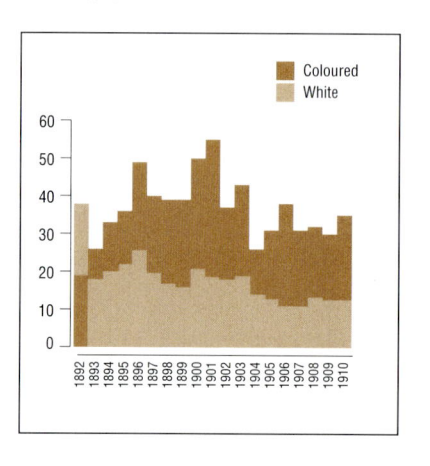

The opening of public works was an opportunity for the display of civic dignity and civic ceremony. The laying of the foundation stone of the Woodhead Reservoir on Table Mountain in 1894, named after the Cape Town mayor Sir John Woodhead, was one such occasion. (SAL INIL 20138)

The construction of the pipe track, to carry water from the dams on Table Mountain, and the building of the dams themselves, provided new employment for the migrant workers entering the town in increasing numbers. (CA AG3525)

Cape Town's Medical Officer of Health

(CA J10527)

*E*dward Barnard Fuller (1868–1946) was a son of the Rev. T. Fuller, who had founded the Free Dispensary. Like many Cape doctors he was educated at the South African College and Edinburgh University. In 1895 he became Cape Town's second medical officer of health and it was he who was responsible for establishing an effective municipal health department. In 1901 he resigned to return to private practice but he retained an interest in public affairs and played a significant role in the creation of a medical school at the University of Cape Town after 1910.

owners to override the vote of the smaller men. An outbreak of typhoid in 1898, which killed the incumbent mayor, Herman Boalch, also encouraged reform. Thus by 1899 Cape Town had many of the amenities of a modern city, including a professional bureaucracy – with a competent town clerk, city engineer and medical officer of health – an adequate water supply, water-borne sanitation and efficient drainage.

One obvious aspect of administrative order in the colonial city was residential segregation. Many colonial towns, whether English, French, Dutch or Spanish, had their white and 'native' sectors. But part of Cape Town's uniqueness was its degree of residential *mixing*, which visitors remarked on repeatedly. At the advent of the mineral revolution segregation in the town was still *de facto* rather than *de jure*. It maintained the equation between whiteness and dominant class status rather than separating all whites from all blacks. One result of the mineral revolution, however, was to force the Cape Town establishment to come to terms with unprecedented economic and demographic changes. Prosperity meant in fact that more black Capetonians could afford entry to the new public and private facilities that sprang up in the course of economic development, thereby challenging the equation between high status and light pigmentation.

With the immigration of white and African workers, miscegenation and residential mingling probably increased towards the end of the century. Perhaps as much as 15 per cent of marriages in Cape Town were mixed at this time. The 1893 Labour Commission was told that 'large numbers' of German and Swedish immigrants had 'lawfully' married coloured women.[34] Immigrant girls were reported to favour Muslim men 'and get thereby husbands who know not billiards and brandy – the two curses of Capetown'. In 1880 the Earl of Stamford married a local 'coloured woman'.[35]

Residentially Cape Town was still a mixed town in the 1870s. The *Cape Argus* reported that 'all shades of colour' inhabited 'the byeways which branch off from Waterkant Street' on the slopes of Signal Hill.[36] Twenty-five years later the 'bulk' of the population in this area was 'Malay' but 'whites and Coloureds also live there',[37] and the different 'races' in inner-city Cape Town were said to be 'closely intermingled in their domestic relations'.[39] Residential mixing also occurred in the suburbs. Norah Henshilwood,

THE SEARCH FOR ORDER 227

Ethnic Mixing in Cape Town

Most mixing in Cape Town was confined to the city's lower ranks, but although the dominant class saw themselves as Europeans or whites, 'many people slightly but still unmistakably off-coloured have made their way into higher ranks of society and are freely admitted to respectable situations and intermarriage with respectable families'.[38] Possession of wealth or education allowed people to 'pass' for white, a feature of Cape Town life that made J.D. Ensor's novel *Sitongo* (1884) more convincing. The eponymous hero, Sitongo, was the product of a marriage between an African chief and a 'white lady' in the eastern Cape. When he arrived in Cape Town, Sitongo had to masquerade as a German music professor, Herr von Lutz, to gain acceptance into 'the higher ranks of society'.

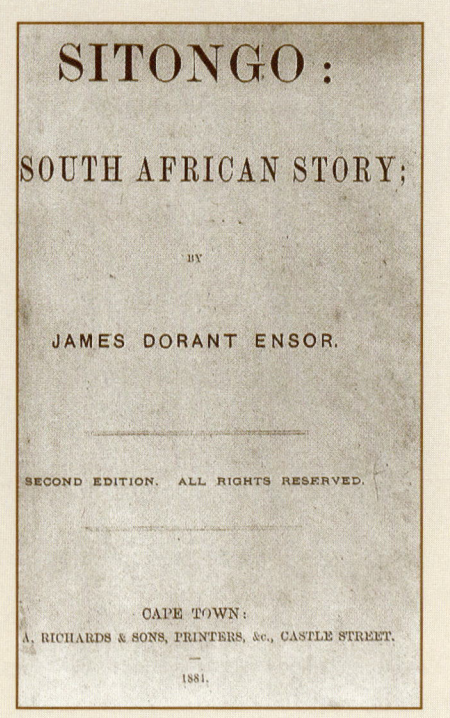

(SAL)

remembering her childhood in Claremont at the beginning of the twentieth century, wrote of an area near the village where 'a mixture of races, shops and income groups blended into an untidy conglomerate'.[40] The squatter settlements which fringed the town were likewise often mixed. In 1883 a 'European' and 'Coloured' family shared a hole in a rock three-quarters of a mile above Roeland Street jail. Dubbed 'Loafer Town' by *The Lantern*, this part of the city was more generally known as the Dry Dock because it sup-

'Anyone who approaches the mountain from the butts, or wanders over Signal Hill, will find at every few steps hollows layered with dried fir branches strewn thickly, the vicinity marked by empty tins and shreds of clothing. There are the ... homeless ... they are of many races' (*SA Licensed Victuallers' Review*, 9 June 1892). (MuseumAfrica 61/1301)

posedly housed dock workers. Here a Mozambican man and an English clergyman's son shared a shelter made of sacking laid across 'two tripods and a cross bar'.[41] Nine years later there were multi-racial squatter settlements above Longmarket Street.

By the end of the century, however, residential segregation, increasingly common in other parts of South Africa, was often being advocated for Cape Town, particularly by the medical authorities. After the 1882 smallpox epidemic the suggestion was made that coloured people be moved out of the town but the notion was rendered abortive partly by the reluctance of Cape Town ratepayers to spend anything on housing for the poor, and partly because of the constitutional implications of segregating an enfranchised population. Apart from docks contractors, few employers wanted their labour inconveniently distant from the places of work, and so there was little pressure from the commercial classes for a separate black location.

While residential segregation remained the pipe dream of a few before the end of the century, racially segregated facilities in official institutions were becoming more common in mission schools, prisons, hospitals and asylums. Not only was segregation seen by the white middle classes as another means of controlling and ordering the town, but some immigrant workers, anxious to stake their claim in the social hierarchy, also supported these moves. Informal segregation in such places as sports clubs and theatres was also becoming more familiar. In 1903 a 'respectable young coloured man' was excluded from the local YMCA; yet this move was not fully accepted, for it occurred 'to the amazement of many and to the disgust of not a few'.[42] Although working-class residential areas were mixed, there is considerable evidence that certain streets or houses had a 'clustering' of whites, coloureds or Africans. Towards the end of the century District Six was expanding rapidly but the majority of the inhabitants were 'the poorest class of the Cape coloured'. Only 'in some parts' of the District was there a growing white population, 'many of these being English mechanics'.[43] African workers often lived together, on wasteland near Salt River railway station or in the hostel of the Cowley Fathers in District Six. The tenements of Horstley Street in the District became notorious as an African slum. For the affluent, on the other hand, it was easier to segregate themselves than to force segregation on others. Racial restrictions in the title-deeds of estate developments in such suburbs as Oranjezicht or Milnerton became more common.

Valkenberg Asylum, situated near the Royal Observatory, represented modern medicine at the Cape both in its segregated facilities and in its philosophy of humane care for the patients. (CA AG15080)

The Robben Island 'lunatic' asylum exemplified the ambivalence of humanist discourse in medical practice at the Cape. After damning reports in the 1860s the asylum was reformed, to become a modern, curatively oriented institution. Patients were categorised primarily according to their gender and mental condition although class distinctions meant that 'better-off' patients, almost invariably white, enjoyed better amenities. By the 1890s new trends in psychiatric treatment combined with growing racism to encourage the argument that white 'lunatics' should be treated separately from blacks. Dr Dodds, inspector of asylums and founder of the all-white Valkenberg Asylum in Observatory, remarked in 1892: 'While colour should not be a dividing line in medicine, and every effort should be made to render happy coloured as well as white, I do not think it right that these two races should mix as they often have to do at present.'[44]

But a number of considerations determined the limits of social segregation in Cape Town. The task of unscrambling Cape Town's inhabitants was not only more daunting but more expensive than in newer South African towns, as the editor of the *Cape Argus*, Edmund Powell, recognised in 1891 when he contrasted Cape Town with 'places that have had a ... modern start ... [which had the possibility] of separating the coloured population in locations'.[45] The permeable colour line, or, as one contemporary put it, the 'infinite gradations of colour in races so mixed as our population', explains too why segregation was informal rather than formal, and why segregation of public institutions was not completely rigid at the turn of the century.[46] As an American visitor remarked, Capetonians were 'a large population of half breeds, so confusing to the ethnologist that it would be an extremely delicate task for a Cape policeman to know whether he was arresting a man more of white than of black blood'.[47] Some schools accepted light-skinned siblings and rejected those with darker skins. These 'gradations of colour' may also explain the continued tolerance of miscegenation.

Attempts to impose order were not confined to a more efficient administration. Late-Victorian reformers tried as well to control the social lives of Cape Town residents. The

Cape Town was certainly 'the Tavern of the Seas'. Police returns for December 1884 showed 314 public houses and canteens in Cape Town compared with a total of 412 for the rest of the colony, including Kimberley. In 1890 (as indicated in the map below) there were 150 licensed drinking places, apart from illegal canteens.

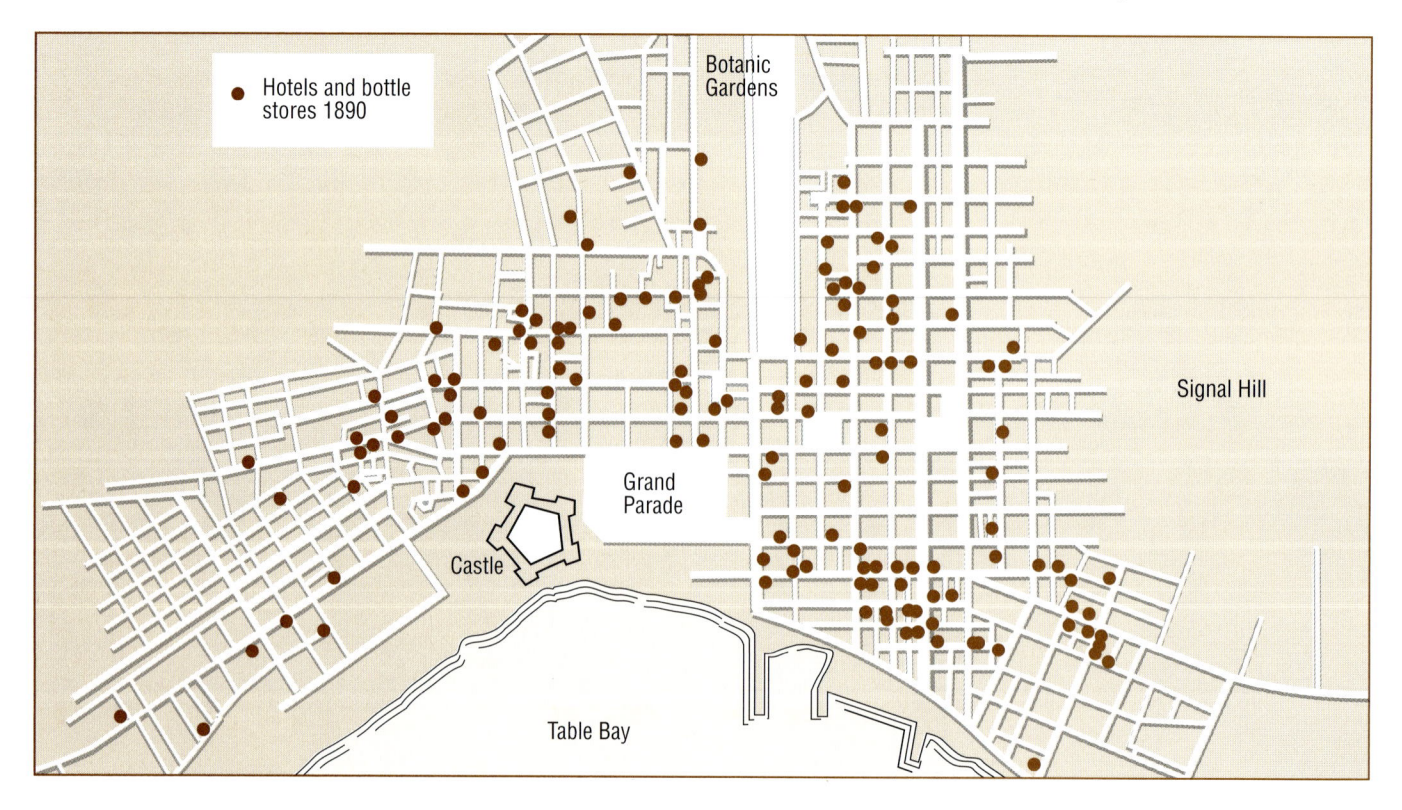

230 CAPE TOWN 1870–1899

daily roll of the magistrates' courts suggested a picture of drunkenness, street violence and petty theft. In December 1884, out of 564 cases before the magistrates' courts, drunkenness and drink-related charges such as abusive language accounted for 243, shouting and screaming 8, vagrancy 40. For the middle classes, controlling the streets was an important part of the daily ordering of the city. Even street games, they felt, blocked thoroughfares, causing too much noise and endangering morals, property and persons. Yet life for Cape Town's middle classes was remarkably secure. Even amongst the poor more serious crimes like murder were uncommon. Indeed, periodic panics about crime tell more about stress in the community than about disorder.

In this low-level civil war over the possession of the streets and open spaces the police, acting as 'domestic missionaries', formed a major agency. Nightly they patrolled the streets and squares, invading the canteens and places of entertainment. But they were ill fitted for this role. The force remained undermanned and underpaid for most of the century. In the 1890s detectives were introduced but little else changed. The result was that only the poorest and most ill-educated whites – coloureds were never employed in the nineteenth century – were recruited into the force. Discipline was a constant problem. Men recruited from Scotland stayed only briefly; 'they complained of the arduous duties and the wretched pay as compared with their duties in Scotland'. Most absconded and the rest left as soon as their contracts expired. The situation reached crisis point when diamonds were discovered: in 1872 half the force decamped for the diamond fields. Composed mainly of British immigrants who could not speak the local *taal*, the language of most of Cape Town's poor, the police were, not surprisingly, bitterly disliked and regularly attacked by the local population, who still called them *dieners*

Drink underlay much of Cape Town's social disorder. To the disgust of employers the productivity of the working class was undermined by the celebration of 'St Monday'. Men were apt to take 'sick leave' on Mondays. If some of these men were indeed the patrons of the Lansdowne Hotel in Claremont, it must have catered for both black and white, though there may have been separate facilities. (UCT Macmillan)

Temperance organisations favoured coffee stalls like this one on Greenmarket Square as an alternative to pubs. (UCT Macmillan)

THE SEARCH FOR ORDER

(officials). The hostility evinced in the cemetery riots was indicative of popular feeling about the forces of law and order.

For the most part social reform in Cape Town was more effectively conducted by voluntary organisations. Moral reform institutions proliferated at the end of the century. These were more than Mother Grundy organisations, for they played an important role in creating a culture of respectability in the town, contributing as well to the formation of a coloured petty bourgeoisie, deeply attached to British values.

The supply and control of liquor proved a constant source of tension in the town. On the one side was the liquor trade, an important part of the Cape Town economy. Beer was the staple of the poor, even Muslims enjoying 'tickey beer' until the 1880s. The brewery industry, dominated by the Swede Anders Ohlsson, had a powerful political voice. On the other side, the 'respectable' classes, living at close quarters with canteens provided the grass-roots membership of the temperance movement in Cape Town. Temperance became a vital source of respectability for the coloured lower middle class, separating them from the stereotypical coloured tippler and justifying their claims to civilised treatment. Leadership of the movement came from the city elite, primarily Nonconformist ministers, but also members of parliament such as the Catholic politician and historian Alexander Wilmot, town councillors and local merchants.

Soldiers and sailors, always a source of disorder in the city, were identified as one focus of reform. A temperance society was started at the Sailors' Home in 1880. When a Soldiers' Home was opened in 1884 'not a few men were reclaimed from drink', it was said.[48] Drunken young male immigrants threatened the moral superiority of whites in the city, as the Rev. L. Nuttall warned the residents of the YMCA in 1889: 'Therefore, not only for the sake of ourselves, but for the sake of those who, as yet uncivilised, and who naturally look up to us for examples, let us seek to glorify God by keeping the Lord's Day holy and avoiding intemperance in its very beginnings.'[49]

By the end of the century the lurid accounts of slummer journalists aroused nightmares of drink-sodden barbarians in the town. African migrant workers, lacking the vote or a firmly established place in the city, proved an easy target for punitive reform. During the South African War the Innes Liquor Act was invoked to prohibit sales of liquor to Africans in Cape Town. But total prohibition raised complex questions of citizens' rights, to which temperance reformers, often people of liberal political views, were particularly sensitive. They felt they had a mandate from African leaders to ban liquor sales to Africans but it was less easy to extend such restrictions to 'Cape boys' who had the vote.[50] Coloured people themselves were ambivalent about liquor restrictions. Although Muslims and churchgoers were prepared to acquiesce in infringements on their rights, emergent politicians were not: at a coloured political conference in 1906 one delegate warned that if the government took away their rights in this area, it could lead to their losing the franchise.[51]

Coercion lay at the heart of the temperance dilemma. How far could men be forced to be sober? 'The European population will never consent to a measure which deprives the temperate man of his right to refreshment because the drink which does him no harm is a cause of stumbling to his weaker brothers,' the *Cape Times* argued.[52] Men had therefore to be seduced into sobriety and showmanship attracted far more adherents than logic. The interdenominational Templar movement, which campaigned for temperance, drew a following from its appeal to the Victorian love of ritual and ceremony. The Independent Order of Grand Templars (IOGT) abounded, for example, in such elaborate titles as the Grand Worthy Chief Templar of the Grand Lodge of Cape Town.

'Therefore, not only for the sake of ourselves, but for the sake of those who, as yet uncivilised, and who naturally look up to us for examples, let us seek to glorify God by keeping the Lord's Day holy and avoiding intemperance in its very beginnings.'
Cape Times,
19 November 1889

This group of members of the Independent Order of True Templars (IOTT) was predominantly white although officially the organisation was the black counterpart of the IOGT. The photograph illustrates both the respectability of the movement and the members' taste for elaborate insignia. (UCT Macmillan)

Meetings were social occasions, providing an alternative to the public houses and canteens. A gathering of the IOGT Long Life Fidelity Lodge was a convivial affair: 'Bro. de Beer gave an address in his customary and vivacious manner, delighting his hearers, and was followed by Bro. Grills, the able WS, & Bro. Steer, WCT. In addition some very amusing readings were given by Bro. Howell, and some songs splendidly rendered, notable among which were those by Sister Alexander, which were tastefully executed and productive of much pleasure ... Finally a vote of thanks was given ... and the meeting duly terminated to the entire satisfaction of all.'[53]

Most renowned of all the temperance organisations in the late nineteenth century was the Salvation Army. In the early 1880s the Salvation Army fanned out into the empire from the industrial slums of Britain, to preach its fiery message of individual salvation. Interested speculation followed its arrival in Cape Town, for the Salvationists' reputation had gone before them. Young men, looking for a lark, turned up in droves to the services, often disrupting them. At first the Salvation Army methods offended conventional churchgoers. *The Lantern*, ever-protective of lower-middle-class values, was downright abusive: 'It would be dishonour, however, to disguise our personal shrinking from the loathsome practices they indulge in ... degrading the dearest sensibilities of the Christian Faith and of the Christian Names to the commonest and vulgarest of vulgar music-hall tunes, the women glib in blasphemy, and mouthing in illiterate dialect the most daring orations to appropriate music-hall gesture and demeanour.'[54] In the months that followed the Army's arrival in Cape Town public reaction continued to be unfavourable. Band members were arrested by the police for creating nuisances, and they were followed down the street after their dismissal from court by a 'jeering mob'. Town councillors suggested that their singing should be ruled a breach of the peace.[55]

THE SEARCH FOR ORDER

In its cartoons *The Lantern* lampooned the Salvation Army. (SAL, *The Lantern*, 3 November 1883)

Regardless of such attacks and despite some police harassment, the Army persisted with its work. Slowly it gained acceptance. Its cheerful red jackets, the lively hymns sung to popular music-hall tunes, and the personal participation of congregants were a far cry from the sober rituals of the mainline churches: they brought colour and interest to the lives of Salvationist adherents. Social acceptance came eventually in 1891 when General Booth himself visited Cape Town to promote his colonisation scheme. The leading inhabitants of the colony were invited to hear him speak. The final accolade was Rhodes's visit to the Army's Social Farm in Rondebosch. From then on the Salvation Army was incorporated into the network of reform in Cape Town. By 1899 the Salvation Army was working in active co-operation with the Colonial Office to provide relief for the destitute. For tickets at 4s 6d a night, subsidised by the government, such men would be housed in the Salvation Army Metropole if they applied to the chief of police for relief.

The Salvation Army would not have attained respectability so rapidly if its values had not fitted smoothly into the dominant culture of middle-class Cape Town. Segregation for instance came easily to the Army. Both coloured and white women were admitted to the Rescue Home but, said the matron, although she had as much regard for black as for white girls, at times there was some difficulty in mixing them.[56] The Social Farm for freed prisoners confined its work entirely to whites. The Night Shelter in Anchor Street, opened in 1896, which provided a refuge for the homeless, excluded coloured men, while the larger Metropole was divided by class as well as race, with different sections for better-off and destitute whites, and separate accommodation for black men.

Closely associated in the public mind with intemperance and disorder was prostitution. Worse still, because domestic servants sometimes practised prostitution, they threatened the sanctity of the Victorian home. But the attitude of middle-class reformers to prostitution was ambiguous. Until the last quarter of the century Cape Town was more concerned with public indecency than with reform. The Victorian 'double standard', which demanded purity and chastity of middle-class women, accepted the sexual needs of young men, as the *Cape Argus* explained in 1868:

> Harlotry, as an institution, ... is of so ancient an origin, that we can hardly now hope to put it down entirely; and perhaps, too, it is not quite desirable, while soci-

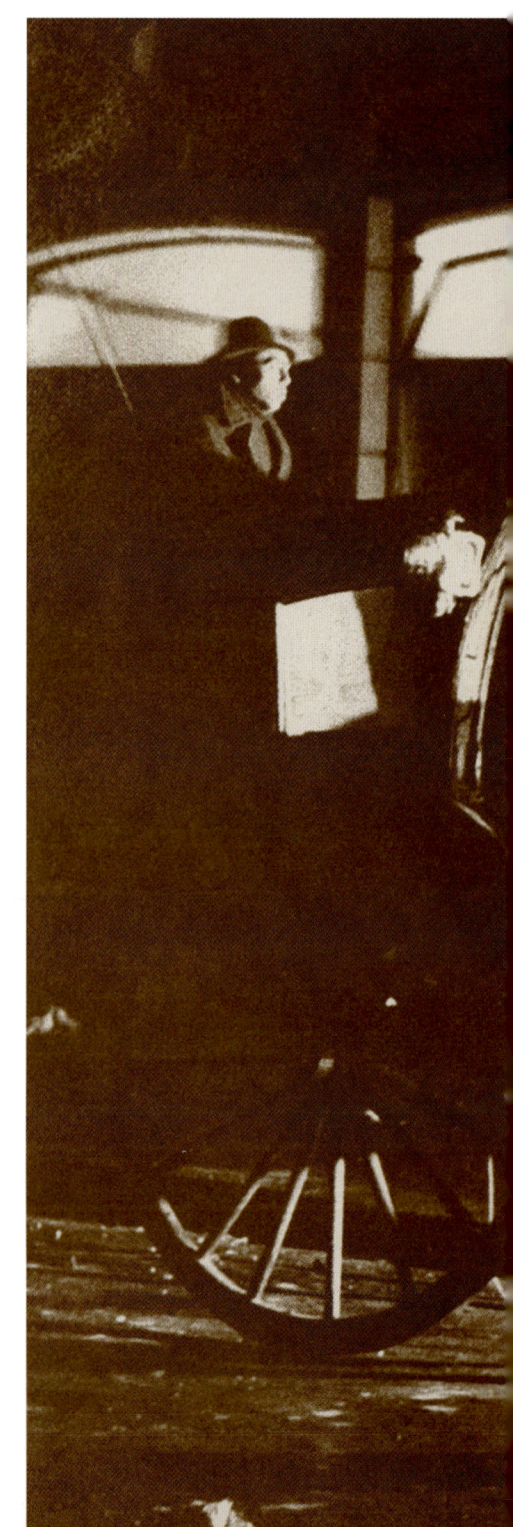

234 CAPE TOWN 1870–1899

ety is constituted as it is, that it should be driven into secret places ... In a measure it must, perhaps, be regarded almost as an institution necessarily attendant on the present state of society; as, in a degree, a safety-valve for public morality, and as some protection to the chastity and purity of our virgins and matrons, guarding them partially from temptations only too seductive![57]

By the end of the century such an attitude was no longer acceptable to evangelical reformers. From pulpit and platform they demanded that men conform to the same moral standards as women. More practically, some people devoted themselves to the rescue of 'fallen women'. Rescue homes proliferated, the Anglicans and the Salvation

Cab drivers were often an invaluable liaison between prostitutes and their customers. Here a cabby waits for clients outside the Queen's Hotel in Dock Road. (SAL BRN 123464)

Prostitution in Cape Town

If these young women hoped that prostitution would bring independence, they rarely found it. Their lives were harsh. The most wretched women lived in holes and bushes on the mountainside, clothed in rags. Others might hire a room for 1s a night. Only the most successful entered brothels though these were insubstantial places, moving location every few months. Violence and brutality formed the daily pattern of their lives. Lizzie Davis, for instance, was beaten up by the pimp and brothel-keeper John Sinclair, a labourer with 15 previous convictions for assault and damage to property. At the same time the women were an integral part of the local community. When Charlotte du Toit was arrested for abusive language to a policeman after she had been ejected, drunken, from a coffee shop, several fellow prostitutes and a number of men came to her rescue. Stephanus Sampson argued, 'All right, I did nothing, the Constable had my girl', while Abdulla Malaliep joined the fray, shouting and trying to pull the girl away.

By the end of the century international criminals were coming to Cape Town. Attracted initially by the pickings of the gold fields, the 'white slave trade' reared its head in the town. The medical authorities implementing the Contagious Diseases Act were inclined to view the European prostitutes with favour. They were a very well-behaved class of women who seemed educated and were careful about disease, Dr Dixon thought. But brothels became larger and more disorderly. William Morris of 48 Barrack Street protested against the inhabitants of no. 52. He objected to the indecent and provocative behaviour of the girls in the street, their drunkenness, quarrelling and bad language, and the constant stream of cabs to the house. It does seem to have been a particularly busy brothel. PC 88 reported seeing 23 white men and 17 coloured men visiting on the night of 26 December 1896. Over 30 cabs arrived and men had to be turned away.

Several of these foreign prostitutes had tragic tales to tell. Julienne Jacqmin was an 18-year-old Belgian, the daughter of farm labourers, who had been brought to South Africa by her sister Antoinette and Antoinette's 'fiancé', Joseph Davis. She had accompanied them, she thought, to Paris but found herself abducted to Cape Town via London. Only when she was placed in a house in Vandeleur Street did she understand her position. Even then she refused to co-operate until Davis raped her and promised to send money home to her mother. Julienne's plight came to the ears of the authorities when Antoinette, annoyed at finding herself displaced by Davis's real partner, Marguerite de Theiss, sought refuge for herself and her sister in the Salvation Army Rescue Home.

The 20-year-old Fanny Kohler was a 'tailoress' from Odessa in Russia. She had been persuaded by Annie Marshall, alias Hannah Alexander, to go with her to Warsaw where prospects of employment were better. From Warsaw she travelled with Hannah and her husband Leon Alexander to London. With each stage of the journey she became more dependent on the couple. 'I had no money in London and could only speak Russian and Yeddish dialects. I asked accused to give me money to pay my passage back to Odessa, and accused said she would be good to me and treat me as a sister.' As in Julienne's case, a combination of kindness and brutality forced her into prostitution, from which she escaped after the Salvation Army rescue workers made contact with her in the Lock Hospital.[58]

Above: Julienne and Antoinette Jacqmin; *below:* Joseph Davis and Marguerite de Theiss. (SAL, *The Owl*, 17 January 1902)

Army being amongst the most active in this respect.

Social purity and temperance provided Cape Town middle-class women with their first public stage. In 1885 the Contagious Diseases Act had been passed in the Cape, ostensibly to protect respectable families from venereal disease passed on by nursemaids and servants. In fact the main effect of the Act was to register prostitutes. But social purity reformers were outraged by legislation which licensed vice and encouraged the double standard. The Women's Christian Temperance Union (WCTU) took the lead in promoting reform for women. Cape Town members resolved at their annual convention in 1891 that 'as a Union, our hearts burn within us at the indignity done to women through the Contagious Diseases Act, and we pledge ourselves to use our influence to bring about its repeal'. Their campaigns led middle-class women to speak out publicly – a novelty in conventional Cape Town. Their embarrassment and determination in doing so were plain to see: women, explained one, had a horror of knowing anything of the sin that was everywhere about them, but they must face the question and do their bit in wresting children from the degradation with which they were threatened. Mrs Walter Searle, wife of a Cape Town merchant, disliked appearing on a public platform, especially on such a topic: it nearly broke her heart, she said, but it was not time to be lackadaisical, sentimental or emotional; it was time to work.[59]

While notions of appropriate behaviour were frequently imposed from without, they were as often assimilated by large sectors of the Cape Town population. Schools and churches were crucial in disseminating such ideas. In 1885 the Anglican Society of St John the Evangelist (the Cowley Fathers) were given charge of mission work amongst Africans in Cape Town. They opened a night school near Zonnebloem and in 1886 a 'Kafir boarding house', St Columba's, which by the mid-1890s accommodated 80 men. A small Christian community emerged in Cape Town as the 'red Kafirs' from the rural Transkei and eastern Cape, or *amagaba*, were converted and acculturated to city life.

The YMCA was a crucial agent for the socialisation of young male immigrants in their new home town. It provided them with accommodation and jobs and attempted to restrain their anti-social energies through prayer, purity and temperance. There was

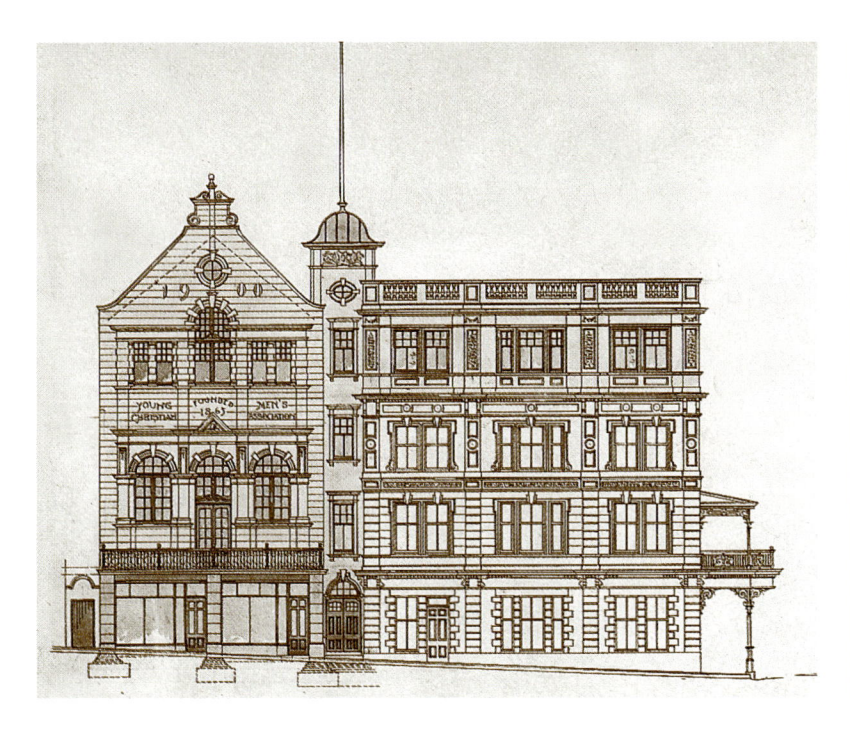

'As a Union, our hearts burn within us at the indignity done to women through the Contagious Diseases Act, and we pledge ourselves to use our influence to bring about its repeal.'
WCTU resolution, 1891

The YMCA and the YWCA (both designed by John Parker) reflected, in their solidity and ornateness, Victorian tastes and values. (UCT BC 729-83, 108)

THE SEARCH FOR ORDER 237

not, however, uniform approval for the YMCA. Despite its virtues it had, the *Cape Times* remarked, an 'Exeter Hall flavour' and the paper suspected that 'the fad of belonging to the YMCA probably requires, on the whole, rather more strength of character than the fad of frequenting bars, and the like resorts of true manliness'.[60]

Self-help organisations were another means of creating a culture of respectability. Friendly societies, a form of personal insurance, were popular amongst the coloured elite and the Dutch. The fact that these 'Weldadigs' and 'Genootschaps' were often actuarially unsound was beside the point: part of their attraction lay in the companionship they provided. To the British, ignoring the likes of the Freemasons and Odd Fellows which had provided the models, they were wonderful specimens of ignorance and ineptitude. 'Most of these are secret societies, with rituals which disclose a strange mixture of paganism and blasphemy.'[61] By the 1890s an increasingly invasive government was anxious to put the friendly societies on a better financial footing. Registration was introduced but was often ignored by people who cherished their independence.

Education, sport and 'rational' leisure all promoted social health, a biddable workforce and an ordered society. Already by mid-century sport had acquired special attrib-

'Most of these [friendly societies] are secret societies, with rituals which disclose a strange mixture of paganism and blasphemy.'

Cape Argus,
3 January 1894

Cricket was enjoyed by poor as well as rich, in the streets of Bo-Kaap or in the pleasant grounds of Newlands. (SAL CW K621; UCT Macmillan)

238 CAPE TOWN 1870–1899

utes in British eyes, reinforcing notions of masculinity and healthiness. In the mission schools, where children were taught 'manners ... habits of diligence ... and order, and also respect and reverence',[62] sport, as much as the three Rs, could instil desirable social behaviour. At most Anglican schools gymnastic drill was part of the curriculum and team sports were encouraged. Father Bull regretted that he had

> missed a famous Cricket Match on Wednesday, when S. Cyprian's Ndabeni eleven played Zonnebloem College second eleven, and wound up the season with a Tea, under Mrs Rousby's auspices, but I have no doubt that the bare feet fielded, and the quick hands caught, and the bright eye flashed upon the ball and bat and wicket, and the ready tongues gave full vent to the feeling of every moment, not less but to the full as much as should any healthy specimens of playing boyhood between eight or sixteen.[63]

Organised sport had a powerful appeal in the late nineteenth century, cutting across lines of class, race and even gender. Women's participation in sports followed the 'me-too' feminist assertion that physical activity could be good for girls as well as boys. In Cape Town a number of games were introduced at such schools as the Good Hope Seminary and Rustenburg Girls' High. Despite male ridicule, middle-class women of the 1880s played cricket, cycled, mountaineered and participated in lawn tennis 'at homes'.

English sports were speedily adopted by other sectors of the Cape Town population. Games ranged from informal football in the street or cricket on the dusty surface of the Docks Location, to formal club matches. In 1887 there was a 'non-European' contest between Cape Town's Albert Cricket Club and Kimberley's Red Crescent Club. The Malay Union Cricket Club was granted permission to play on Green Point Common by 1892. 'Malay' cricketers even formed part of the 1887 Jubilee procession. In the early

CLUB LIFE

City clubs were an important means of asserting and maintaining a masculine culture. The Civil Service Club was started in 1861 'to raise the tone of the Government Service and create a stronger ésprit de corps among the younger members by giving them an opportunity to mix with their elders and, if possible, to keep them out of the public bars'.[64] Confined to the civil service, diplomatic service, army and navy, and learned professions, with merchants only as honorary members, the Civil Service Club expressed implicitly the British aristocratic contempt for trade. By contrast the City Club, formed in 1877, was dominated by merchants. There were few Dutch amongst the founders, apart from a handful of anglicised Dutch such as the Van der Byls and J.G. Steytler. The Owl Club was a purely social club, its purpose encapsulated in the verse:

Of Owls I sing, and of the men whom Fate
Brings every moon to mingle with their kind
In friendly intercourse appropriate
To the Free Arts and Sciences, combined
With eloquence and music ...

Here, in a friendly and relaxed atmosphere, Cape Town's ruling class could meet and strengthen the bonds which were integral to the shaping of a dominant European culture in the town.

Left: Technology introduced other forms of rational recreation although cycling in the rough terrain of the Peninsula was arduous exercise. (CA J2982)

Below: Some activities were designed to cater for both sexes. In the early 1900s J.D. Cartwright, who employed a number of women, took them for a picnic in the grounds of Groote Schuur which had been left to the nation by Cecil Rhodes. (CA J4076)

Bottom: Rational recreation in the form of ballroom dancing was a symbol of respectability for coloured people, the antithesis of the *ghomma* dancing with which they had been associated in the stereotypical view. (CA AG15148)

1890s multi-racial cricket was still possible. In February 1891 there was a 'Test Match' between 'Malays' and 'Europeans', while 18 'Malays' played a team of visiting English professionals in the following year. At least three Peninsula teams – Simon's Town, the Docks and Woodstock – had both coloured and white players.[65]

Within a context of advancing technology and economic change, the pursuit of leisure became more ordered and more commercialised. Railways transformed Cape Town's customary excursions. On 25 March 1862 the first excursion train ran from Cape Town to D'Urban Road (present Bellville). Apart from the considerable excitement of the journey, the attraction was a bazaar presided over by the governor. Return tickets were 1s 6d for first class and 1s 2d for second – beyond the pockets of most – but some trips catered specifically for the less wealthy. An entirely 'fourth class' train was arranged for a trip to Stellenbosch on 1 December 1862 although the 2s 6d return fare was still too much for many poorer people. The opening of the Wynberg line in 1864 made False Bay a genuinely popular leisure destination. In 1883 the line reached the coast at Muizenberg, arriving at Kalk Bay the following year and Simon's Town in 1890. Already at New Year in 1887 large numbers of people camped in tents 'on both sides of the railway' at Muizenberg and Kalk Bay.[66]

The expansion of the railway made new sporting venues in the suburbs accessible. Newlands became the venue for major cricket and rugby matches after land had been acquired near the station by their Western Province organisations in 1887. Horse-racing at Green Point Common, which had been free, declined as the South African Turf Club made Kenilworth the main venue for this activity after 1882 and charged for entry. Professional theatre, established by Sefton Parry in the mid-1850s, suffered a lull in the late 1860s and early 1870s after the middle-class exodus to the suburbs, without evening trains to carry them home. When this omission was rectified, it aided the commercial revival of the late-1870s at the Theatre Royal.

Employers often promoted 'rational' recreation to build morale and loyalty among staff. When Mr Cole took his bakers to Newlands on Tweede Nuwejaar, 1888, he used

In the Tivoli music hall (designed by John Parker) at the corner of Plein and Darling streets, exuberant theatre was contained and ordered. (UCT BC 729-104; CA E7994)

the opportunity to present medals to two apprentices for 'good conduct'. The *Cape Times* commented approvingly that such outings promoted the 'most desirable thing in business – a good feeling between master and men'.[67] The Salt River railway works provided a reading room for its employees, stocked with over 6000 books by 1906. The men were entertained with glee singers, given presents when a manager got married, and taken on summer excursions to places like Nooitgedacht near Stellenbosch where they played cricket. By the 1890s sports teams from individual firms were playing each other, and the docks cricket team was good enough to make the Western Province first league.

Rational recreation was also valued as a safety-valve for anti-social energies. When only a few cases of drunkenness were brought before the courts over the New Year holiday in 1875, the *Cape Argus* took it as proof that 'people here know how to enjoy a short relaxation from work sensibly and rationally'.[68] An Anglican evangelist thought that few 'Malay' men seemed to work in the 1890s, 'but at least they have turned to cricket'.[69]

Alternatives to British Order

As the cemetery riots indicate, attempts to impose British notions of order on the town were constantly contested. Bound up with these notions were definitions of identity whose fixity and racial basis were just as frequently contested. For instance, by no means all Capetonians accepted the correlation of Englishness and whiteness. When a coloured dock labourer was asked by a white visitor in 1897 whether he was a 'native' of the colony, he replied that he was not, that he was English. Pointing to people whom the visitor described as 'coal-carrying Kaffirs', he said that they were the natives.[70]

Census enumerators, on the other hand, made no distinction between English and Dutch, describing both as 'European'. By 1891 'Malays' and 'Mixed or Other' were separately counted, but the term 'coloured' remained fluid, sometimes embracing anyone 'not white'. African tribal groups were carefully distinguished, from 'Kaffir' (Xhosa) to Bechuana and Zulu. 'Hottentots', it was acknowledged, barely existed as an identifiable category in Cape Town although a few people might choose to call themselves by that name. Local people labelled themselves, or others, in many ways. Witnesses in court cases in the 1870s and 1880s used the terms 'coloured', 'white', 'Malay', 'Kaffir', 'Hottentot' and 'Mozambiquer'.

The process was complex, for self-perception also shaped this labelling. 'Malay' had become a white synonym for Cape Muslims by the 1850s. In 1875 almost 7000 Capetonians were described as 'Malays' by the census enumerators. By the 1870s many people also applied this term to themselves, at least in their dealings with whites, though they distinguished themselves too by religion as '*Slam*' (Islam). The observance of Islam, education in Arabic, distinctive dress and culinary and medical practices as well as the use of a version of the Afrikaans language had all become features of 'Malay' ethnicity by the 1870s, underpinned by ties of common work. Muslims still dominated such traditional Cape Town occupations as washing, fishing and artisanal trades. Residentially many were now concentrated around the mosques springing up in District One on the waterfront and on the slopes of Signal Hill. In the 1870s 'Malay' ethnicity was also strengthened by the formation of choral street-bands, such as the Star of Independence Malay Club.

Islam provided the ideology, leadership and a community base for resistance to the imposition of control. White observers commented frequently and disparagingly on the self-confidence of Muslims. 'Formerly the Malays were the trusted servant class. There were bonds of affection between them and their White employers. They were much

These young 'Malay' women in the 1890s dressed fashionably in Western style but retained their ethnic identity in their headdress. (UCT Macmillan)

242 Cape Town 1870–1899

Abdol Burns

(*Cape Argus Weekly*, 27 May 1889)

Abdol Burns (*c.*1838–98) was a cab owner and driver whose surname came from his Scottish father; his mother was 'coloured' and he had been brought up as a Muslim. Unlike most Muslims, who spoke the *taal* and were inclined to be deferential in the face of authority, Burns was articulate in English and confident enough to confront the town council in debate on the issue of smallpox control. He represented the Muslims at a town council meeting on 31 July 1882. The *Cape Times* commented drily of the encounter, that he 'bowled over councillor after councillor like so many ninepins'. One councillor tried to persuade him that he had been wrongly advised by his co-religionists. 'It was no use their saying, however, that religion did not allow this and did not allow that, for the law was superior to religion.' Burns responded, 'No, I beg your pardon.'[74]

---

humbler and more accessible than at present ... Malays were spoken of as specially faithful, though humble citizens ... There is no longer the same intimacy of dependence ... The Malays are now rather exclusive, and independent.'[71] As one of them put it in 1882, 'independence is the aim of everyone who is a little above grovelling in the mud'.[72] Muslim identity became sharpened in conflict with the reforming authorities. When the municipality threatened to ban fish-curing on Roggebaai beach in 1878, Muslim fishermen like Jongie Siers and John Mahomet petitioned the town council. Their protest was couched in the language of English constitutional liberty: 'We always thought that we were emancipated in the reign of our Gracious Majesty Queen Victoria, and freed from tyranny, but it seems that we are mistaken.'[73]

The smallpox epidemic of 1882 brought the issue of control to the fore as Cape Town's medical authorities attempted to impose a severe regime of vaccination and isolation on the town. Although Muslims were marked out as leading the resistance to medical controls, it is almost certain that disaffection went beyond their community. In England, too, there was a long-established tradition of resistance to vaccination, which was imported to Cape Town by working men like James Eayrs, charged in 1894 for failing to have his child immunised. He had lost one child through vaccination, he declared, and another had been permanently injured. Such views may seem obscurantist to modern readers but people had good reason to question the efficacy of current medical practice. A reliable vaccine was only developed after 1891; moreover, arm-to-arm vaccination was an unpleasant procedure which many people understandably rejected.

In Cape Town Dutch resistance to the imposition of British hegemony was by comparison fairly muted but it did emerge over such issues as the closing of the cemeteries, against a background of rising Afrikaner nationalism. Although the Afrikaner Bond dominated parliament, in Cape Town itself the Dutch had lost ground by the late nineteenth century. Fewer of the major commercial institutions were still in their hands and the municipal council was overwhelmingly British. Led by J.C. Hofmeyr, cousin of the better-known 'Onze Jan', the Bond leader, nascent Afrikaners formed the Zuid-Afrikaansche Vereeniging van der Kaapstad in 1884 and fought bitter electoral battles to retain a foothold on the council. By the 1890s they had lost the war, forming part of a silent and resentful minority which came to public notice mainly in times of crisis. In contrast, their successors, men like D.C. de Waal and D.P. Graaff, urbane and partly anglicised, adapted to English values and looked ahead to a more inclusive South Africanism.

If, as we have seen, control of leisure was a means of imposing order on the city, leisure activities could also be a moment for asserting independent identity. In dance, music and song a cross-fertilisation occurred in which different traditions drew on, imitated and even mocked one another. Muslims had long been highly regarded for their musical talents, providing entertainment for white burghers at social events since the seventeenth century. Together with 'Anglo-Afrikaans' forms of square dancing, English country dances – imported in the early eighteenth century – were still performed at 'rainbow balls' in the 1880s. Shortly after arriving from Europe in 1872 Louis Cohen attended one: 'The room was full of men and women of various types. Many owned curly locks, while others had straight hair. It was a mixed breed indeed, and yet the majority of the girls were quite good-looking ... some were white, some nearly black, or tan or snuff-coloured. A few of the European passengers were there ...'[75]

The tradition of song was remarkably eclectic. Street songs were learnt in mission schools, from official parades, concerts, the theatre, circus and music hall. American minstrelsy provides a particularly striking example of the way in which influences were absorbed and adapted in the constant remaking of cultural tradition. American minstrels – white performers, disguised as blacks, who caricatured slave culture – first came to Cape Town with Joe Brown's Band of Brothers in 1848. But the most successful entertainment of this kind was provided by visiting Christy-minstrels in 1862 and 1865. They performed their 'nigger' part-songs, jigs and mocking caricatures of American slaves to all classes of Capetonians in a variety of venues: 'even at the Cape, where the nigger character is so well understood, the caricature created a furore', the *Cape Argus* reported.[76]

The Christy-minstrels spawned innumerable white imitators – the Amateur Darkie Serenaders, Juvenile Christys and Darkie Minstrels. As for Cape Town's slave descendants, they found resonances in the sentiments and ambivalences of minstrel songs like 'I'm leaving thee in sorrow, Annie', 'Poor old Jeff', 'Hard time' and 'Massie's in the cold ground'. Black-face minstrelsy was also to have a direct influence on the New Year carnival, which was pre-eminently the festival of the underclasses. By the 1870s singing and sporting clubs, or *klopse*, were providing troupes of paraders. The disguises they adopted were often influenced by occupation. The Darktown Fire Brigade wore firemen's uniforms and pulled a water pump. The employees of Mr Cole, a leading baker, appeared in the 1887 Jubilee parade as Colonel Baker's Horse, wearing white (the colour of flour) and painting their faces 'black, red and every other conceivable colour'.[77]

In the following year the Cape of Good Hope Sports Club became the first carnival troupe to appear in minstrel garb. By the beginning of the twentieth century some troupes dressed in this way were calling themselves 'Coons'. In 1907 they included both the Jolly Coons Masquerade Troupe and the Jolly Coons. Visits by Orpheus M. McAdoo's Jubilee Singers in the early 1890s were another potent influence.

Places of work could also become sites where the prevailing order was challenged.

The distinction between rational and irrational leisure was not always clearly maintained in late-nineteenth-century Cape Town. (*SA Illustrated News*, 11 April 1885)

Orpheus M. McAdoo's Alabama Cake-Walkers, forerunners of the Jubilee Singers who visited South Africa in the early 1890s. (Hampton Institute Archives, Hampton University)

Opposite, above: Coloured residents of the Cape Peninsula had a tradition of picnicking on public holidays that went back to the days of slavery. (CA E3211)

The ruling class struggled to impose an industrial discipline in an economy in which casual labour predominated and many workers were still partly self-employed. 'Malays' were singled out in the late 1870s and 1880s for their 'idleness' and 'independence', for holidaying at any opportunity. In an attempt to instil work discipline in a putative proletariat the punishment of hard labour was handed out by magistrates for trifling offences in the streets.[78] 'Desertion', 'careless work', 'absence' and virtually any authority-threatening behaviour were defined as misdemeanours.

Perhaps the least free occupation throughout the nineteenth century was domestic service. Liberty was closely monitored by employers and transgressions swiftly punished. Caroline Renaulgh, a monthly servant of Lucy Bernard's on £2 per month, was fined 10s in 1877 for sending a substitute to work after dancing all night herself.[79] Servants faced censure and dismissal from employers for 'immorality', although the experience of 'A slavey' was not uncommon. Unusually, she wrote to the press, complaining of unwelcome sexual advances from her master. Those who fell pregnant usually lost their jobs, with the result that infanticide occurred occasionally. Catherine Windvoge worked in Three Anchor Bay, and gave birth to a baby in her room. She tried to conceal this from her mistress, widow Dinah de Villiers, who testified that because Catherine was unmarried she would have felt the disgrace of an illegitimate child. Hannah Solomon, who worked for Mrs Fitzgerald, was sentenced to death in 1898 after offering Dona Plaatjes 2s 6d to take the body of her baby off the premises in a bucket.[80]

Alternative jobs offered more independence to women yet hours were still long and pay invariably poor. A barmaid could work as much as 18 hours a day, 6 days a week, for £2 per month. Laundering involved fetching and carrying heavy piles of clothes and, for women in town, a journey up the mountain to the stream at Platteklip Gorge. Prostitution may have paid better and allowed greater control over working hours but

THE SEARCH FOR ORDER

involved the danger of disease and assault.

Conditions of employment were altered by the development of small-scale industries in Cape Town, which started with the Salt River railway workshops. For many years hours remained extremely long. Drivers and conductors on the Green Point trams worked from 6 a.m. to 7 p.m., 6 days a week, until the 1900s, with shorter time on Sundays and one day off a month. In the 1890s railway labourers were contracted to work a 6-day week of 12 hours daily in summer and 10 in winter. Their lowest rate of pay was 3s a day. Dock labourers' wages rose from about 2s 6d per day in the 1860s to 4s 6d in the 1890s, for a 10-hour day.

From 1879 employers of dock labour turned increasingly to migrant workers, for they reduced the wage bill and were a more reliable and controllable workforce. On 6- or 12-month contracts, Mozambicans in 1879 were paid 6d a day while Mfengus received 1s in the 1890s. Housed at the docks, migrant workers were subject to extensive restrictions. These included a curfew at night and a prohibition on women visitors and the consumption of alcohol. Accommodation was often appalling. It is not surprising that day labourers in the late nineteenth century called the land they squatted on near Zonnebloem College 'The Orange Free State', perhaps in ironic comparison with the plight of the migrant labourers.

In their free time eastern Cape migrants in the barracks were limited recreationally to group singing. Dances like the *hloma*, which involved stamping on the floor, 'made a great noise, and the good people of Green Point did not like this' and complained to the location superintendent in 1903. He duly banned it. The following year workers still occasionally danced behind barricaded dormitory doors and ignored lights-out regulations. In the 1890s their songs were mainly about rural life, but one sung in 1903 described the 'ringing of the six o'clock bell calling to work at the "docksin" [Docks Location] and ... the hard life of the native in Cape Town, banished from home and comfort, and compelled to eat calves' heads and such poor food'.[81]

Factory production, developing in the 1880s, was confined mainly to service industries like the manufacture of food and clothing. These sectors were traditionally associated with women's work. Female labour with its low rates of pay appealed to employers. In the 1890s some female cigarette workers earned as little as 12s 6d a month. In con-

The dances of migrant labourers in the Docks Location, like the hloma, *which involved stamping on the floor, 'made a great noise, and the good people of Green Point did not like this.'*

Harbour Board, 1903

Dock Labourers

For many years Mozambican dock labourers lived in makeshift accommodation in a coal store and later in a wood store. The Mfengu were housed in the 'Coolie' barracks on the east quay. Here Dr Jane Waterston, formerly a missionary in the eastern Cape who could speak their language, started a night school and gave them medical care.

Dock labourers were particularly susceptible to overseas influences. In 1884, when A.R. McKenzie attempted to reduce their wages they struck work, led by a West Indian, John Titus; his compatriot nicknamed 'Long Dick'; an Englishman, Henry Yateman; and a West African Frenchman named Phillip Susa. Using a nearby pub as their headquarters they organised a picket which became violent when blacklegs were beaten up. An ample reserve of labour and determined action by the police soon ended the episode but it laid the foundations of later worker action in Cape Town.

(UCT Macmillan)

fectionery factories they received between 7s and £1 a week while children were paid 3s a week. Yet women often preferred factory work to the greater restrictions of domestic labour. One indirect result of the mineral revolution was the proliferation of hairdresser salons, cafés, restaurants and shops. Here too, long hours and poor pay encouraged the employment of women. Shop assistants in Plein Street worked from 7.30 a.m. to 6.30 p.m., and until 10 p.m. on Saturdays. Even those in the big Adderley Street stores worked a 10-hour day in the 1890s. Only in 1899 were any shops required to provide seating for assistants.

The situation of domestic servants, migrant workers and shop assistants presents examples of conditions of work before the introduction of labour organisation. British

The Half-Holiday Movement

As early as the 1860s some of the larger Cape Town shops began to close at 2 p.m. on Saturdays. But the 'half-holiday movement', as it became known, had a rocky ride for the next 40 years because of the advantage held by competitors who remained open. The half-holiday disappeared by the 1880s; renewed pressure for its reinstatement only mounted again in the following decade. The immediate cause was a mass meeting of about 500 shop assistants in 1894, which led to a committee that included church representation. The assistants received considerable support from middle-class Capetonians largely because of contemporary considerations of ethnicity and gender: most assistants were English-speaking whites, and a large proportion were women. As 'Pater' commented in a letter to the *Cape Times* setting out the tribulations of shop work, 'what a life for our daughters … can you wonder that they are glad to accept almost any offer to escape this slavery?'

Some shops returned to a half-day, on either Thursday or Saturday, and in 1895 a half-holiday Bill was introduced into parliament in an attempt to make the practice universal. The Bill received support from some members precisely because they were worried that overly long hours prevented female assistants from being 'women', from performing their traditional duties. But they were outvoted by others who thought that legislation of this kind smacked too much of socialism.

Two years later shop assistants tried again. They formed the Cape Town and Suburban Saturday Half-Holiday Association, with subscriptions raised from members. This time the Cape Town Chamber of Commerce also voted in favour of a half-holiday; newspapers published names of shops that participated in the movement; and their owners formed an Early Closing Association. A shop assistant who signed herself 'White slave' advocated a boycott of stores that still held out; this was put into practice by some 'ladies'. A few of the recalcitrant stores were also vandalised. The upshot was that a Half-Holiday Act was passed in 1899, which enforced early closing throughout the colony on a Saturday if two-thirds of the stores in a neighbourhood agreed. But in Cape Town alone shops were allowed to choose between Thursdays and Saturdays, and this option continued to prove a stumbling block. Only after further legislation in 1904 did the vast majority of assistants in all kinds of shops eventually get their half-holiday: Wednesdays in Sea Point, and Thursdays or Saturdays in the rest of the city.[82]

and, later, Australian artisans, imbued with a more militant labour tradition in their own countries, began to influence the climate of employment from the 1890s. The Amalgamated Society of Carpenters and Joiners was reborn in March 1890, and compositors, stonemasons, tailors, plumbers and plasterers followed suit by organising themselves in the next few years. In 1890 a Cape Town and Districts Trades Council began to co-ordinate the push for a 48-hour week. It met with success in 1897, and the subsequent reduction of hours obviously benefited other employees.

In the 1880s there was no precise correlation between divisions of labour and ethnicity in Cape Town. Whites and coloureds regularly worked alongside one another. But a changing economic order opened the way to conflict in the workplace. Fear of displacement or wage undercutting sharpened ethnic division, between coloureds and Africans, between whites and 'others'. Beginning in the 1890s, when African migrant workers from the eastern Cape did the roughest work at the docks at low wages, fights developed with 'Cape boys' who did somewhat lighter work at higher wages – and were sometimes appointed as foremen over African gangs. Conflict increased the mutual sense of distinction. In the depths of a severe depression in 1906 coloured workers and politicians appealed to the government and city council to retrench Africans first and employ only 'local' coloured workers. In response 'Africa' pointed out to the *Cape Times* that 'seventeen years ago Kafirs were brought to Cape Town to do work coloureds wouldn't', and argued that 'Kafirs' were more obedient, trustworthy and hard-working than 'so-called coloured people'.[83]

Predictably, at least some working-class organisations reflected ethnic particularism. In 1880 the constitutions of at least two friendly societies excluded coloured men, or 'any man who is supposed to have coloured blood in his veins'. One of these societies even rejected members whose wives were coloured, 'to keep it as select as possible'. Others had only coloured members. When craft unions were established by immigrant artisans in the 1890s all excluded Africans and women too. Three – the masons, plasterers and carpenters – also excluded coloureds in 1901. While the intention was to prevent the undercutting of wages, the result was that craft pride and ethnic and gender prejudice became closely linked.

Yet if ethnic particularism might divide the working classes, common problems could unite them. Unemployment threatened black and white alike. In the 1870s poverty was still confined to the back streets and margins of the town but the early 1880s saw a new kind of poverty emerge. The dream of diamonds had attracted steamer-loads of young men to the colony; in consequence Cape Town became 'glutted with young gentlemen who have come out to try their fortune here, but who are literally unable to fill any other post than a simple clerkship'.[84] When recession gripped the town in 1883 the presence of indigent whites on the streets began to alter perceptions of poverty. Previously there had been no call for permanent relief institutions. Cape Town's poor were 'naturally malingering and indolent', it was said, and any institution provided for them would merely be a burden on the industrious portion of the community'.[85] Now, as the numbers of unemployed mounted, relief measures were set in place. Early in March 1883 a labour register was established at the *Cape Times* office. A night shelter was also opened for the 200–300 men who, the Rev. Thomas Fuller believed, were sleeping in sheds or on the mountain.

Concern for the unemployed did not alter the grudging and parsimonious charity disbursed by the relief committee. Every applicant

Elaborate moulding like this required new plastering skills, usually provided by immigrant artisans who jealously protected their status. (UCT BC 1074 B5334)

> 'There is scarcely any limit to the horror and repugnance with which we think of England's worst social cancer next to drunkenness – that of organised pauperism. We should fortify ourselves against it here as we would against an epidemic disease.'
>
> *Cape Argus,*
> 30 August 1883

'The crowds marched up, and the crowds marched down, It was the mode in old Cape Town.'

Plein Street on a Saturday morning. (UCT BC 230 M. Leendertz, 'The vanished city', ch. 2; SAL PHA)

was carefully monitored. When work was supplied, men were expected to accept it, however harsh and poorly paid it might be. Clerks struggled to break stones at the Roeland Street quarry for the municipality. For this they earned too little even to pay for board and lodging, and were forced to sleep at the refuge. Behind this lack of generosity lay the prevailing middle-class fear of pauperism: 'There is scarcely any limit to the horror and repugnance with which we think of England's worst social cancer next to drunkenness – that of organised pauperism. We should fortify ourselves against it here as we would against an epidemic disease.'[86]

The new poverty also brought a new militancy on the part of the unemployed, fuelled by social crisis in Britain. Anger flowed over into the colonies. In August 1884 the workless took matters into their own hands and called a public meeting to express their grievances and force public action over their plight. The press was at a loss to report such a phenomenon, for the men on the platform did not wear the air of indigency expected of them. The meeting was substantial, and the committee which was elected represented coloured as well as white artisans. This development, in which the unemployed took charge of their own plight, was unprecedented. The respectable hastened to nip the movement in the bud. At the next public meeting such worthies as the eastern Cape MP Colonel Schermbrucker, Canon Lightfoot, and councillors Stigant, Wiener and O'Reilly took the platform. A register of the unemployed was drawn up which listed 290 men, of whom 140 were married with families to support. The year 1885 brought another wave of protest from the unemployed, with more meetings on the Parade, and the following winter saw a resurgence of unemployment. South Africa, the *Cape Argus* observed sadly, was no longer a land of plenty.[87]

The issue of poverty continued to simmer throughout the 1890s. By 1893 white vagrants were a more common sight in the city than they had ever been before. Night shelters became commonplace. Even before the rinderpest outbreak in 1896 the question of rural white poverty was also beginning to force itself upon the town. This was a matter of national concern, the *Cape Argus* warned. Poor white working men and their families were

> compelled to live in our towns amidst coloured people, and who are sinking, sinking, sinking into the social condition of the snuff-and-butter coloured population. In a Colonial society necessarily based upon class distinction, marked off by Nature herself, it is well worth while to consider the condition of these men ... the poor white working man has had no place for him as yet, and now that our towns are growing so as to make his lot harder than ever, it is time for the sake of the future of the Colony that something be done to give his children at any rate, their fair chance in life.[88]

In this respect too, Cape Town was acquiring the social features of an industrialised society.

SUBURBAN COMMUNITIES

By the end of the century Cape Town's inner-city communities had developed distinct identities. District One, on the waterfront, was perhaps the most impoverished. In Bo-Kaap (District Two) the prevalence of the old mosques meant that there was an unusually high concentration of Muslims. The call of the muezzin, the *madrassah* where the children learnt their Arabic and the verses of the Koran, the Muslim festivals, the exotic dress of the 'Malays', were all prominent features of life in this area. But they should not

THE SEARCH FOR ORDER 249

be overstated: Bo-Kaap was created also by its fairly low-density housing and by its proximity to the docks. Much of the development of the area had occurred after the 1840s, providing housing for artisans who found their first homes here. By no means all were Muslim. In 1865 Rose Street, on the lower boundary of the district, also had a large number of residents with Dutch names. We cannot tell whether Pieter van der Schyff, retail dealer, and Jan Adriaanse, grave-digger, were coloured or white, but it is likely that racial differences between poorer Dutch speakers blurred in these streets. What was striking was the relative absence of British or other European names. The same was true of Chiappini Street, although here the sprinkling of English names was larger. This was an area of small artisans or waterfront workers, from boatmen to fishermen.

In 1867 District Six acquired its familiar name when a new municipal Act divided the town into six districts. Before that it had existed officially as District Twelve or, more colloquially, as Kanaladorp – possibly after the Capel Sluit, or canal, which ran through the area, or else it was derived from the Melayu word *kanala*, meaning 'to help one another'. Early Kanaladorp had been not only ethnically but socially mixed: residents included people like the leading wool merchant, Maximilian Thalwitzer, as well as artisans, tradesmen, labourers and prostitutes. In this, the District was not markedly different from other parts of inner-city Cape Town. By the 1870s, however, the socially mobile were moving out to the suburbs, leaving the District to the poorer classes.

Districts Six and Two in the late nineteenth century.

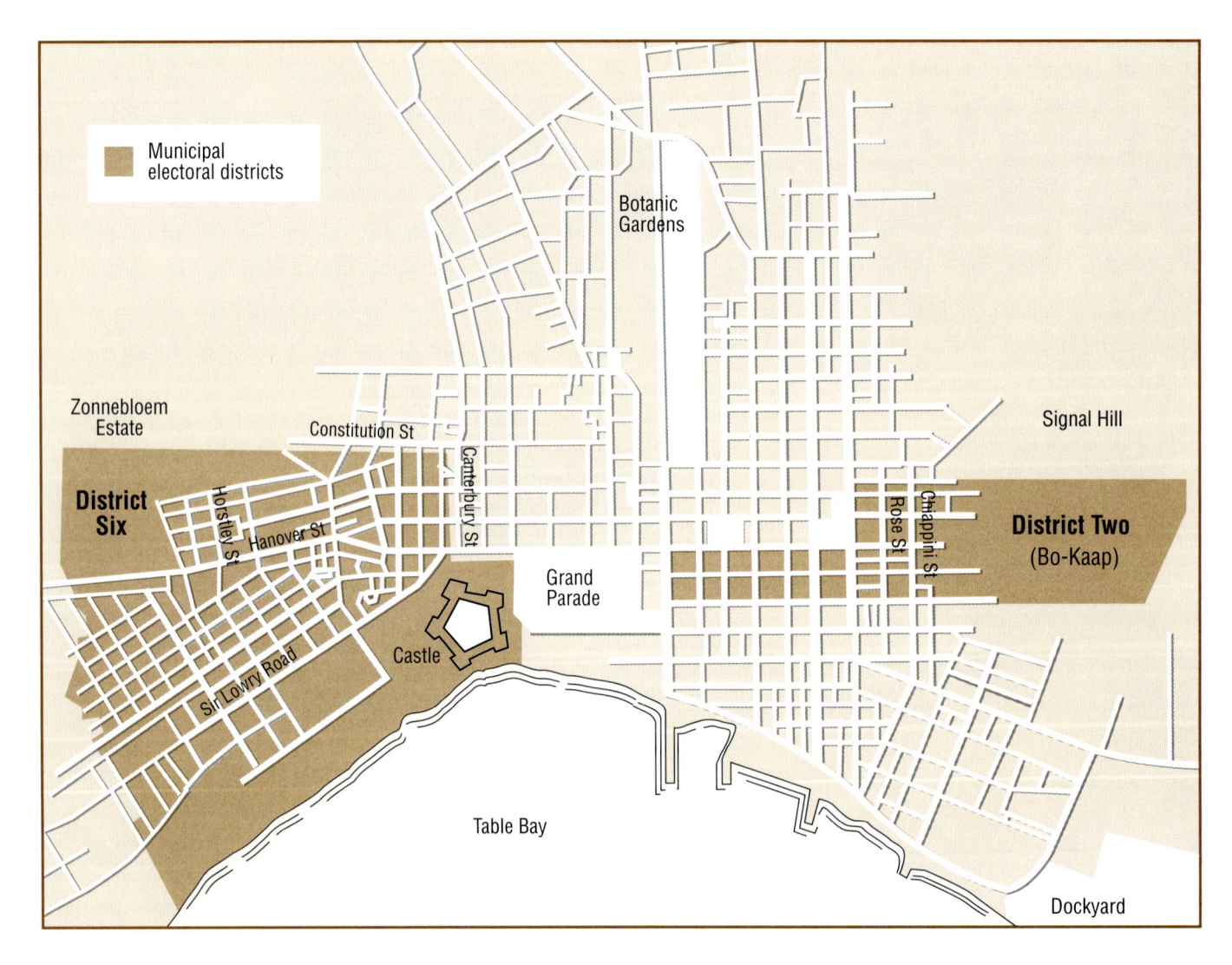

This terrace house in Aspeling Street, District Six, with elaborate late-Victorian moulded parapets and 'broekie lace' iron work typically had residences above and a business below. (SAL PHA)

High-density housing made for affordable rents. What was even more attractive, District Six lay within easy reach of work for the artisans and labourers who lived there. Even the docks on the other side of town could still be reached on foot. District Six became the first place of residence for most immigrants to Cape Town, black and white. By the 1880s it had already acquired many of its well-known features – its varied population, its lively street life. Hanover Street became the local shopping street and Plein Street in town the popular resort on Saturday nights when the shops stayed open until 10 p.m. It also rapidly obtained the reputation for being the most neglected area of Cape Town. 'Another grumbler' complained bitterly in 1881 that District Six was so badly treated by the town council that residents should rebel and make the efforts of the Boers in the Transvaal seem like a 'sideshow'.[89]

Poverty was certainly a hallmark of life in the District but it was moderated by the local community and local institutions. The missions which sprang up – from the Dutch Reformed mission church in Hanover Street, or the Anglican St Mark's Church and St Columba's mission, to the Salvation Army or the City Mission – lent assistance in times of need. But more important, they instilled in their adherents, as did Islam, a sense of self-worth, of 'respectability', which gave people the strength to cope with poverty.

Muizenberg on the False Bay coast provided a sharp contrast to the inner-city communities. In the 1890s the glories of the beach at Muizenberg were described enthusiastically in the *Cape Town Guide* – though it made no mention of the fact that south-easters often raged ferociously, and the guide's oceanic geography was decidedly muddled. The beach was 'alive with gaily dressed ladies and romping children – balmy even when other suburbs are damp and chill. It is situated on the downs of False Bay with its expansive beach safe at all times for bathing, with a unique geographical situation with its balmy breezes laden with the life-giving ozone of the South Pacific.'[90] Separate, screened

The heyday of Muizenberg as a seaside resort began in the 1890s. (SAL PHA)

Sea Point was another fashionable resort. The old Society House became the Queen's Hotel, to provide holiday accommodation for the growing middle classes from the Rand. (CA AG1790)

bathing areas were set aside for men and women visitors, while bathing machines were available for the use of hotel and boarding-house guests as well as some local residents.

This puff about Muizenberg was a sign that Cape Town was being more actively promoted as a holiday destination for people from other parts of southern Africa and overseas. Such a development was aided by faster steamships. The Union, Orient, Currie, Clan and Hamburg lines had all made Cape Town their coaling station by 1882. For most Europeans and Americans Cape Town formed the gateway to southern Africa. Fast trains linked Cape Town to the new centres of population produced by the mineral revolution. Already in 1881, when the railway had reached only Beaufort West, many of the wives and children of wealthier men in Kimberley were coming to Cape Town to escape the intense heat of the summer months.[91]

By the late nineteenth century the suburban villages around Cape Town were blossoming into small, fiercely independent municipalities. Here British immigrants attempted to re-create the idealised communities they had left behind them. Wynberg, no longer the haven of the 'Indians', remained proudly self-sufficient. Further up the

The substantial villa pictured atop, designed by Herbert Baker, was typical of the suburban style which he popularised in Wynberg and Kenilworth. Influenced by the English Arts and Crafts movement, it contrasted sharply with more elaborate and conventional homes (such as that pictured below) produced in the same years by John Parker. (UCT BC 206-265; BC 1074 B5)

In the southern suburbs coloured people also retained a semi-rural lifestyle, as here in Newlands. (CA AG15147)

Rondebosch Primary School was coeducational at first. Sailor suits were a favoured uniform. (UCT Macmillan)

line, Kenilworth was distinguished by its substantial houses. In Claremont the Ardernes, centred on The Hill, still dominated the southern end of the village. Clustering round the mosque on the Main Road, however, was a considerable coloured population. With its breweries on the Liesbeek River, Newlands was semi-industrial in character.

Rondebosch developed as the preserve of the established middle classes. Although it included both the old Dutch farms of Westervoort (Westerford) and Rustenburg and its share of merchant estates – the Ebdens at Belmont and G.P. Moodie at Westbrooke – it was the home of moderately successful business and professional people, setting out to capture a suburban dream of the English village rather than the gentleman's estate.

The ideology of rural England which they evoked had its origins in Britain in the late nineteenth century when the middle classes rejected the sturdy values of industrial northern England, already in decline. The rolling downs of the south, the gentle fields enclosed by hedgerows, the thatched cottages snuggled round village greens, seemed to represent lost values of order, stability and 'naturalness'. A return to country life appeared to offer the only answer to the urban degeneration which was threatening Britain's imperial greatness. In the early twentieth century the Cape's ex-governor Lord Milner was one of many who propagated the idea that a return to the soil was 'the key to the maintenance of a healthy, vigorous and moral race'.[92]

Cape Town's suburban middle classes embraced these notions wholeheartedly, for their identity was bound up with Britain's imperial might. The setting was incongruous: the great buttresses of Table Mountain louring over Rondebosch village were entirely unlike the soft landscape of southern England. But the process of taming the wilderness in which they engaged had been started long before by the Dutch, who had planted the great oaks lining the Main Road. Cecil John Rhodes, the son of a country parsonage, added the perfect touch by introducing squirrels to gambol through their branches.

Rondebosch institutions were central to this rural atmosphere. The two Anglican churches, St Paul's and St Thomas's, in golden stone, reminded parishioners of an older moral order. These English parish churches seemed to express all that was best in the village community. 'These simple, venerable, dear loved village churches, attract to themselves our warmest piety, our deepest reverence.'[93] For their part the local schools epitomised English virtues and the stability of the class hierarchy. The Diocesan College ('Bishops') moved to its Rondebosch site of Woodlands farm in 1850. Its avowed intention was to provide an education for the sons of the English-speaking elite of the Cape and to promote English cultural values. To this end it was modelled on the English pub-

THE SEARCH FOR ORDER 253

Most of the early headmasters at the Diocesan College were clergymen, and school life centred on the chapel as much as the classrooms and the playing fields. The second chapel, built in 1880, was appropriately Gothic in style. (UCT Macmillan)

This group of young women attending Miss Gertrude Hull's finishing school at Rouwkoop in Rondebosch would probably have received a limited education. Schools like this provided one of the few professional employment opportunities for middle-class women. (UCT Macmillan)

lic school system, with a boarding-school which isolated the boys from family life in their most impressionable years. Here British class attitudes and notions of 'imperial responsibility' were inculcated. Located in the midst of a pine forest, the school was designed to resemble the English public school Radley.

Bishops drew its pupils from all over the colony. By contrast, Rustenburg Girls' High School and Rondebosch Boys' High School were community schools, funded by the government and catering to the surrounding villages. Like Bishops they were schools for the middle classes, with similarly spacious grounds and handsome buildings.

Before the establishment of Rustenburg, girls' education was frequently trivial, conducted elegantly in ladies' seminaries, and required no great intellectual exertion. Languages, music, painting and needlework formed the main diet here. Young Emma Rutherfoord's comments on *Uncle Tom's Cabin* sums up the quality of mind that even a conscientious education promoted: 'I think it the most beautiful book of the kind I ever read. I am sure no one could read Eva's death without crying ... Frederic is reading Bleak House but I don't like too many of Dickens they are too long and trifling.'[94] Under the aegis of its first headmistress, Miss Bleby, Rustenburg attempted to provide girls with a more academic education. It instilled in the pupils a 'high seriousness' – 'the sense of belonging to a school with traditions and the high standards that went naturally with it; a sense of discipline and attention to detail, a scorn of anything dishonest or slipshod'.[95] In this, Rustenburg was part of a high-minded feminist tradition which linked Mount Holyoke College in the United States with Huguenot College in Wellington and Bloemhof High School in Stellenbosch. Like the local boys' schools, its education was solidly imperial, from Miss Bleby's own textbook, *South Africa and the British Empire*, to cricket, one of the main sports in the school at the turn of the century.

The mental world of the girls and boys at these schools was remote from Africa. Norah Henshilwood, writing of her girlhood in nearby Claremont in the early years of the twentieth century, remarked that the books they read were entirely British and American, with snowy Christmases and roses in the summer meadows. When Ethel Turner's Australian stories appeared she found them harsh and raw. 'Ours was not a pioneer setting and we felt more at home in the traditional background of the fictitious

Suburban Homes in Rondebosch

*I*ntended to demonstrate the status of their owners, most houses were double-storeyed because height was more imposing. The façades were asymmetrical, gabled and ornamental, achieving the charming irregularity sought by the creators of rural suburbia. These were colonial homes, however, influenced perhaps by Australian models. Verandas, originally built to modify the extremes of climate, proved so appealing that they were often installed pointlessly on the cold south-facing sides of the houses as well. The backs of the houses were strictly utilitarian. Inside there was the same emphasis on display. The public rooms were ornate, with their pressed ceilings and tiled fireplaces. Lothian House had three reception rooms, one ceiling nostalgically decorated with roses, thistles and shamrocks. Bedrooms were usually less ostentatious while the service areas were physically isolated and austere. The names of these houses were reminders of the origins of their owners. In Park Estate, Holmfirth recalled a village near Huddersfield, Mayfield a farm in Berwickshire, Ringmore a Devon village, Restalrig a property in Scotland, Bethel a Cornish village, and Edrom an estate on the Scottish borders.[96]

Liesbeek House in Newlands was more modest than the Silwood houses but embodied the same asymmetry, verandas and love of ornamentation. (Private collection)

THE SEARCH FOR ORDER   255

The white middle class of Rondebosch and Claremont accepted the poor around them as a natural part of their firmament – from the coloured residents of nearby Fraserdale Estate, who provided much of the domestic labour for Park Estate, to the Salvation Army's Social Farm with its invaluable dairy. The Social Farm demonstrated the strength of the rural ideology in Rondebosch, for it was intended to rehabilitate freed criminals in a healthy environment. (CA E7639)

characters whose lives we shared in our reading ... We who lived there [in the Peninsula] were isolated from the rest of our countrymen on the mainland both by geography, situation and by interest. Most of our friends belonged to the Peninsula as we did; they seldom moved out of it and when they did they were more likely to travel overseas than go up-country.'[97]

In Silwood Road and Park Estate the arcadian vision was given tangible form in plaster and cast iron. Located in the silvan neighbourhood of the three schools and Rondebosch Common, the houses built by the middle classes were monuments to the English rural ideology and the cult of domesticity. Although Silwood Road was surveyed already in 1845, development proved slow. In 1889 John Jenkinson, a speculative builder and later mayor of Rondebosch, bought most of the land and began to construct 25 Victorian villas, including Lothian House, which he built for himself. A proviso attached to land acquired from the Diocesan College that no house should be built for under £800 indicates the aspirations of the locality.

The inner-city suburbs of Woodstock, Salt River and Observatory contrasted sharply

256 CAPE TOWN 1870–1899

In the grander houses like Fernwood in Newlands, the billiard room was a male domain, decorated with hunting trophies. (UCT Macmillan)

Salt River, flat, open and windy, was a less desirable suburb than Rondebosch. (UCT Macmillan)

with leafy Rondebosch. Situated in the teeth of the south-easter, they were much less desirable areas to live in. The flat marshes of the Salt River estuary were the least appealing. Here, on the margins of the town, Cape Town's first industrial site – the new railway workshops – was established in 1859. A wool-washing works, Thesen's timber yard and Hare's brickfield, with its 'pungent, sourish smell', added to the industrial atmosphere. After 1900 Lever Brothers soap factory and the Nectar Tea factory in Malta Road also arrived. The lack of trees or open spaces and the terraced housing which was built towards the end of the century all contributed to the industrial character of the district.

So did the residents. The 'navvies' had already brought a rough and vigorous workmen's presence. At first glance Salt River was a typically British colonial working-class suburb. The street names recalled the glories of English literature, as young Barbara Mackenzie learned when she accompanied her general practitioner father on his rounds: 'Addison, Burns, Coleridge, Tennyson, Pope, Goldsmith, Arnold, Lytton, Milton, Kipling and others made up a noble roll call in this humble setting.'[98] The name of the Mackenzie family home, Kandahar (the site of Lord Roberts's victory in Afghanistan), had an appropriately imperial ring.

The culture of the district was also that of the British working classes. Pubs abounded – Goodwin Hotel, Belvedere Hotel, the British Oak and the Junction Hotel – shocking respectable men such as 'A father of a family' who complained of 'the disgraceful scenes, such as those drunken women almost naked on Saturday night'.[99] Although the reality was probably more sober, the efforts of the temperance lobby successfully denied the Salt River Railway Institute a licence for many years. The Institute was typical of that other aspect of British working men's culture, the striving for self-improvement. Founded in 1883 for 'disseminating useful knowledge and encouraging rational amusement amongst all classes of people', the Institute offered training to young apprentices. Its library indicated the tastes of its users: popular literature included *In Darkest Africa*, *Five Years with the Congo Cannibals* and *Bloodtracks in the Bush*, but Gibbon, Macaulay, Conrad, Hardy and Kipling were also stocked. There were only 49 Dutch books out of

THE SEARCH FOR ORDER 257

Salt River market was a community centre as much as a market. (UCT Macmillan)

6088, and the Institute began subscribing to *Die Burger* only in 1925, reflecting the shift in workshop personnel.

Appearances belied the reality. Salt River was an ethnically mixed society, partly an overflow of District Six. A Jewish immigrant compared cosmopolitan Albert Road with London's East End. The Salt River market was a social focus for coloured, Indian and, later, Portuguese residents. A practice remembered by Mrs Wasiela Lagardien in the 1950s probably dated back to the early years of the century: her father's customers, she recalled, 'used to come to the market after their supper when their fathers and husbands had come home from work and everybody would stand around talking and joking and having their after-dinner smokes as the sun went down'.[100]

Salt River life took place on the streets. At lunchtime young men from the railway works in the 1920s 'used to go up to the Main Road and go and pick up the young girls working at OK Bazaars and Oblowitz's and take them down to the beach at Mouille Point and have a royal good time'.[101] Barbara Mackenzie remembered the Salvation Army entertaining her on Saturday nights as well as the errand boys on their bicycles who whistled popular melodies as they passed. She was enchanted by the Coons on 2 January:

> The music and cheering swelled from the direction of Observatory, and I peered expectantly up Albert Road. At last they came, troupe after troupe, all dressed in gorgeous fancy dress, each troupe different from the last. The colours were magnificent, the silks and satins splendid in their richness. But my favourites were the Red Indians with their fringed leather garments, the chief's sweeping down to his very heels, and their tomahawks ... flourished on high as they came leaping wildly and shouting their war cries.[102]

Despite this vitality, Salt River was a community only in a limited sense: labour divided people as much as it united them. Here life was harsher than in the outer suburbs. Work in the railway workshops was long and exhausting. The day began promptly at 7.15 a.m. 'If you were more than two minutes late in clocking in you lost an hour's pay. If you were more than half an hour late you weren't allowed to start work that day for which of course you didn't get paid.' The workshops were choked with smoke. 'If you

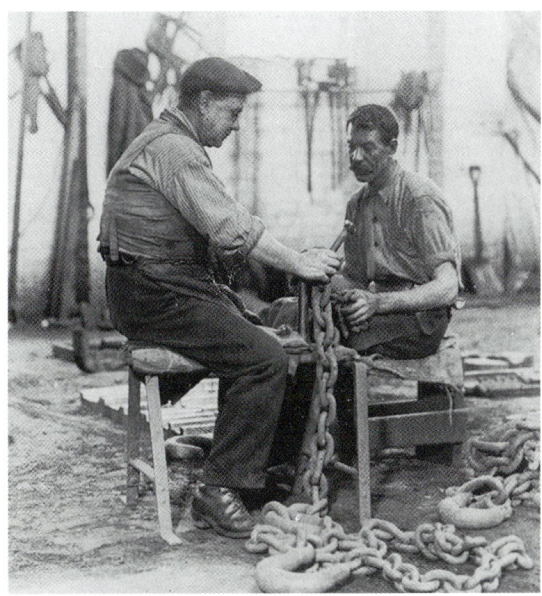

The Salt River railway works, one of Cape Town's first industrial establishments, employed mainly skilled white artisans. (UCT Macmillan)

saw a beam of light in the foundry it was thick solid dust. They used a kind of powder in the castings, plumbago. It's black, it filled the air along with the smoke from the fires.'[103] The railway works were sharply segregated. Unskilled workers were differentiated by colour as well as skill. In the early years they were mainly coloured but by the beginning of the twentieth century most were probably African. Afrikaners entered the works in substantial numbers only after the First World War.

Divided interests and poverty fragmented Salt River society. In addition, the British workers were ambivalent about their status in colonial Cape Town, often rejecting their working-class affiliations. Many of them chose to live in the outer suburbs. Workmen's trains made this possible, as one of them, who lived in Claremont, recalled. 'It was just for the workmen – there were no lights in the compartments. You more or less had your own special seat. In the dark you'd bump into blokes sitting in the wrong places.' They were also embarrassed about their association with Salt River:

'They were very respectable fellows but they undoubtedly had an inferiority complex about being workmen. It was considered very much below the normal thing. The men used to put on white collars and ties to go home to disguise the fact that they were workers ... It was considered quite below any society if you were a Salt River workman. It was a term of opprobrium. "Oh, he's a Salt River workman."'

A workman reminiscing in 1984

They were very respectable fellows but they undoubtedly had an inferiority complex about being workmen. It was considered very much below the normal thing. The men used to put on white collars and ties to go home to disguise the fact that they were workers. They never walked around like mechanics today in blue jeans and slacks. They used to try and give the impression that they were office workers. It was considered quite below any society if you were a Salt River workman. It was a term of opprobrium. 'Oh, he's a Salt River workman.'[104]

Such workers probably felt more at home at the next stop along the line, Observatory. Although it was never a municipality in its own right, then as now its residents nurtured its distinctive character. Here settled the clerks and small tradesmen who flooded into South Africa when the discovery of gold on the Rand made it a land of opportunity for the impoverished British lower middle classes. Avoiding the rougher working-class atmosphere of Salt River, they made their homes in Observatory where speculators were erecting the kind of houses the new settlers wanted and could afford.

A typical development was that of J.C. Wrensch, an immigrant German confectioner. In 1853 he bought the farm Onderneming – 'one of the best in the district' – from

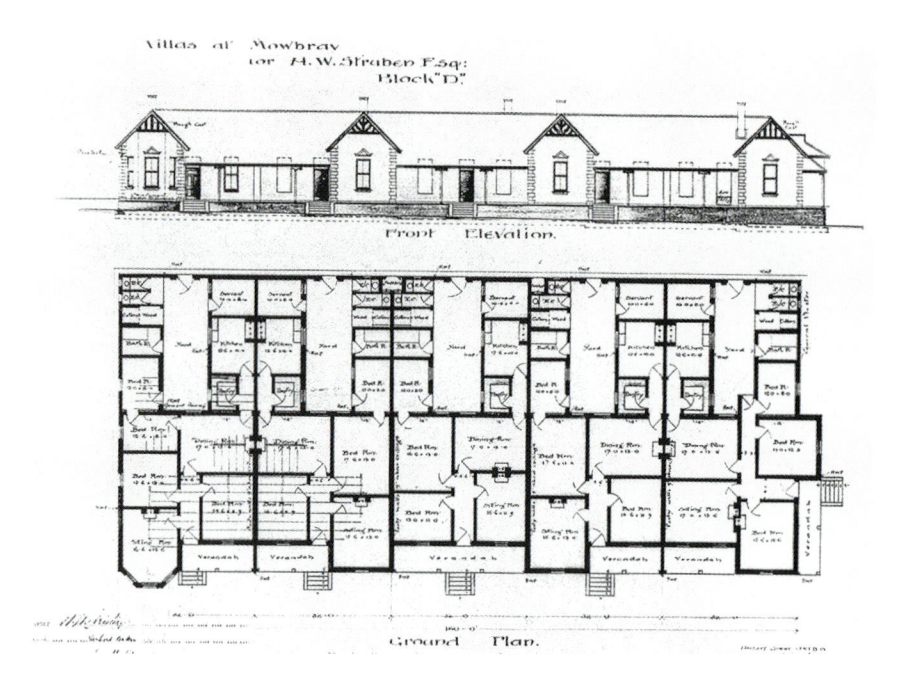

The Rand magnate H.W. Struben was responsible for erecting a number of terrace houses. These 'villas' in Mowbray were designed by Herbert Baker. (UCT BC 206-259)

J.A. Kirsten and grandiloquently changed the name of the homestead to Wrensch House. In 1881, during the economic boom which followed the discovery of diamonds when banks were flush with money, he began to sell the part of the farm that lay west of the railway and east of Lower Main Road. Still determined to leave his name in perpetuity, he called it Wrensch Town. In 1895, in a later boom, he sold the rest of the farm. Much of the land was bought by speculators who could afford to let their investment lie fallow until the demand for housing made building and renting profitable.

The houses, constructed by small builders and contractors flourishing locally, were mainly semidetached or terraced. Single-storeyed (unlike in Britain), they were densely concentrated in narrow streets, ornamented with 'broekie lace', stained-glass panels and brass knockers. These rows of similar houses were deplored by an observer in 1908 who complained of the 'dreadful sameness of architecture'. Relatively few of the new residents owned their own houses. In the early twentieth century 66 per cent were rented but

Lower Main Road, Observatory, was typical of late-Victorian commercial areas in Cape Town with elaborate cast-iron balconies, residences above and shops below. (SAL PHA Observatory)

rentals fluctuated wildly. At the height of the boom before the South African War they rose to £8 10s for a family home, with two months' rent paid in advance. A decade later,, a five-roomed house could be obtained for as little as £2 10s, and many stood empty.

In 1884 the seven listed residents of the area had all been people of status, owning substantial properties. By 1902 the directories listed 630 names, 53 of whom were clerks. Other clerks probably lived in boarding-houses or rented rooms. Many inhabitants were also retailers (in 1903 there were 61), often living above their shops; most could be described as lower middle class, with limited incomes yet careful of their status and respectability. Even in Observatory there was a rough class and race divide: the more genteel, such as the booksellers, music teacher and hairdresser, lived in southern Observatory around Lower Main Road and Station Road, while those with 'dirtier' occupations, like the blacksmith, the four butchers and the coal merchant, lived in the northern area. The six Muslim retailers also operated north of Station Road along with Jewish traders.

Lower-middle-class gentility and a hankering for 'home' stamped the character of Observatory. This was reflected in the house and street names. The rural ideology flourished in the cottage gardens which the owners and tenants lovingly tended.

> The thousand gardens of Observatory are filled with flowers – flowers that fill the narrow, shaded, dusty streets with fragrance; crimson, white, purple, and scarlet flowers. Sometimes the nasturtiums or the roses climb the ornamental iron pillars of the stoep, and reach to the painted galvanized-iron of the roof. Sometimes there are little squares of green on either side of the eighteen inch-wide path in the lit-

A Lower-middle-class Income

A clerk on £10 a month would not have been able to marry on the budget published as a letter in a newspaper in 1904 (see alongside). The writer of this budget lived in the suburbs both because it was healthier and because it was cheaper. His children ate soup rather than meat and his wife baked their bread to avoid 'those disagreeable foreign substances'. Vegetables, 'a good and cheap supply', were delivered to the door.

His wife, and perhaps the daughters, apparently did all the housework, for there was no provision for domestic servants, apart from washing – an impossibly exhausting task in a small, crowded home. Probably church dues fell under 'sundries', for this was also omitted. So was entertainment – 'well, I've got seven children and a small garden, and I candidly confess that I consider that is quite enough recreation and amusement for any one man'.[105]

A Suburban Budget
for three months

	£	s	D
Rent, £4 10s per month	13	10	0
Groceries, 18s per week	11	14	0
Meat, 10s per week	6	10	0
Bread, 10s 6d per week	6	16	6
Lights and fuel, 8s per week	5	4	0
Clothes and boots	4	0	0
Washing	3	0	0
Railway fares	3	0	0
School fees	3	0	0
Vegetables	2	15	0
Milk	2	10	0
Fish	1	15	0
Sanitary fees and rates	1	0	0
Insurance	1	0	0
Sundries	3	5	0
TOTAL	68	19	6

(i.e. £23 per month –
or a lavish income of £276 a year)

THE SEARCH FOR ORDER

Fillis's Circus lent its elephants to St Michael's Church for the occasion of the 1898 bazaar. (SAL G41, *Cape Times Weekly*, 9 February 1898)

tle garden. Sometimes little green bowers have been erected in front of the doors to serve as porches. On every side you see high-sounding suburban names such as 'Clarence Villa' or 'Nottingham Lodge', and stately lawns and gardens.[106]

On limited incomes, carefully budgeted, Observatory residents strove to live honestly, morally, respectably. In 1891 a clerk in the civil service could expect to earn about £10 a month. Rental would be £4–5 a month and his trainfare into town 15s. In 1900 red meat was expensive at 10d per lb; so, as with the inner-city poor, snoek, red roman and stockfish were staple fare.

Church was usually the focal point of family life outside the home. By 1908 Observatory was 'blessed with many churches whose graceful spires and towers rise above the galvanized iron, ornamental roof'[107] – at one stage there were 16, most of which were Protestant. The earliest was the Congregational church in 1893; the Anglican church, St Michael's, a Herbert Baker building, followed soon after. Evangelical Protestantism shaped the minds and actions of the Observatory residents. Nothing demonstrated this more clearly than their determined fight against liquor. Unlike neighbouring Woodstock with its 20 hotels and bottle stores, Observatory remained dry until 1918. The fight for temperance was one aspect of social action. But the churches were also the focus of more relaxing activities such as the 'bazaar of bazaars' held in February 1898 to raise funds for the building of St Michael's. The guest of honour was no less than the governor of the colony, Sir Alfred Milner. The Victorian taste for the exotic was in full display, with a visit from the son of the sultan of Zanzibar, an 'Oriental cigar divan' as one of the stalls, General Gordon's Crimean looking-glass on show, and 'gypsies' telling fortunes. The highlight was the rides provided on elephants.[108]

The Customs House was one of many to display its imperial loyalty in 1887 on the occasion of Queen Victoria's jubilee. (UCT Macmillan)

Queen Victoria's Diamond Jubilee

In 1897 the empire celebrated the Diamond Jubilee of Queen Victoria's long reign. Cape Town participated enthusiastically. The city felt it had good reason to do so. The handsome buildings of Adderley Street, the ordered and pleasant suburbs, the busy harbour, the declining death-rate, all suggested that a city had emerged of which its residents could be proud. If there was poverty and unemployment, it seemed a temporary phenomenon, born of recession on the gold fields. The ethnically mixed population, particularly the 'Malays' with their colourful festivities, added an exotic touch which contributed to Cape Town's charm. The celebrations of 1897 reflected this sense of imperial solidarity and order.

The queen's Diamond Jubilee in 1897 was the last Victorian celebration before Cape Town was plunged into war. *Above*: The corner of Loop and Strand streets; *middle*: Church Square; *below*: outside the railway station. (CA Dr.J. 583, 582[1], 358)

The Search for Order

Into the Twentieth Century

By 1899 Cape Town could describe itself as a city in the fullest sense of the word. It had a well-established municipality, a substantial population and all the amenities that its citizens would expect to find in a colonial capital. Yet the seventeenth-century residents might still have been able to trace the outline of the little town they had known. The shoreline and the Castle at the water's edge were still recognisable, as was the physical layout of the streets. But Cape Town was looking forward, not back; forward, it was hoped, to a new era of prosperity for all its citizens. Yet the road would be harder than anyone could imagine. The city of Cape Town would experience three major wars and much social conflict before it reached maturity.

References

CHAPTER 1

1. Cape Archives (CA), VC 58, 33.
2. R. Raven-Hart, *Before Van Riebeeck* (Cape Town, 1967), 99–100.
3. Camoens, *The Lusiads* (Harmondsworth, 1952), 130–1.
4. Raven-Hart, *Before Van Riebeeck*, 10.
5. Raven-Hart, *Before Van Riebeeck*, 111; H.T. Colenbrander, *Dagh-Register Gehouden in 't Casteel Batavia, 1637–8* (The Hague, 1899), 129.
6. H.B. Thom (ed.), *Journal of Jan van Riebeeck* [*VRJ*] (3 vols., Cape Town, 1952–8), I, 20.
7. H.C.V. Leibbrandt, *Precis of the Archives of the Cape of Good Hope* (Cape Town, 1898–1906), Letters received, I, 12.
8. Ibid.
9. Ibid., 14 and 20.
10. A. Smith, *Pastoralism in Africa* (Johannesburg, 1992), 193–213; A. Smith, 'Adaption strategies of prehistoric pastoralism in the south-western Cape', in M. Hall et al. (eds.), *Frontiers: South African Archaeology Today* (Oxford, 1984), 131–42; A. Smith et al., 'Excavations in the south-western Cape and the archaeological identity of prehistoric hunter-gatherers within the last 2000 years', *South African Archaeological Bulletin*, 46 (1991), 71–91; J. Parkington et al., 'Social impact of pastoralism in the south-western Cape', *Journal of Anthropological Archaeology*, 5 (1986), 313–29.
11. Leibbrandt, *Precis*, Letters received, I, 28–30.
12. S. Abeyasekere, *Jakarta: A History* (Singapore, 1989), 15.
13. Leibbrandt, *Precis*, Letters received, I, 74.
14. *VRJ*, III, 120; I, 317; III, 225, 370.
15. *VRJ*, II, 31, 28–9.
16. *VRJ*, III, 130.
17. *VRJ*, I, 51–2, 128.
18. *VRJ*, I, 142.
19. *VRJ*, I, 243.
20. *VRJ*, I, 79, 143, 147, 151, 245, 275–7; Leibbrandt *Precis*, Letters received, II, 177, 213–14.
21. *VRJ*, I, 35–6.
22. Leibbrandt, *Precis*, Letters received, II, 30–2.
23. *VRJ*, II, 91–3, 131.
24. N. Mostert, *Frontiers* (London, 1992), 129.
25. *VRJ*, II, 227.
26. G.C. de Wet, *Vryliede en Vryswartes in die Kaapse Nedersetting, 1657–1707* (Cape Town, 1981), 196.
27. *VRJ*, I, 115.
28. *VRJ*, I, 116.
29. *VRJ*, I, 292.
30. Ibid.
31. *VRJ*, II, 33.
32. *VRJ*, II, 135.
33. V.C. Malherbe, *Krotoa, Called 'Eva'* (Cape Town, 1990).
34. *VRJ*, III, 196.
35. *VRJ*, III, 146–7, 195–7, 228, 240, 279.
36. *VRJ*, III, 440.
37. Leibbrandt, *Precis*, Letters received, II, 32; *VRJ*, III, 185, 228.
38. Leibbrandt, *Precis*, Letters received I, 20; *VRJ*, III, 185.
39. *VRJ*, III, 185–6, 23–5.
40. K. Jeffreys (ed.), *Kaapse Plakkaatboek* (6 vols., Cape Town, 1944–51), I, 41–2; R. Raven-Hart, *Cape of Good Hope, 1652–1702* (2 vols., Cape Town, 1971), I, 35.
41. *VRJ*, II, 335.
42. *VRJ*, III, 285.
43. CA, VC 39; Leibbrandt, *Precis*, Letters received, II, 205.
44. *VRJ*, III, 172–3.
45. *VRJ*, II, 279.
46. *VRJ*, I, 224.
47. *VRJ*, II, 344–5.
48. *VRJ*, II, 303.
49. *VRJ*, I, 365; III, 209; II, 12; Leibbrandt, *Precis*, Letters received, II, 191–200.
50. Leibbrandt, *Precis*, Letters received, II, 178.
51. Leibbrandt, *Precis*, Letters dispatched, III, 214.
52. CA, C 1, 186.
53. *VRJ*, II, 35; *Resolusies van die Politieke Raad* (9 vols., Cape Town, 1957–81), I, 73.
54. A. Böeseken, *Jan van Riebeeck en sy Gesin* (Cape Town, 1974), 94.
55. *VRJ*, II, 155, 180, 197–8; III, 158.
56. *VRJ*, II, 91–2.
57. Raven-Hart, *Cape of Good Hope*, I, 68.
58. Ibid.; *VRJ*, III, 388.
59. *VRJ*, III, 55.
60. *VRJ*, III, 202.
61. M. Cairns, *Cradle of Commerce: The Story of Block B* (Cape Town, 1974), 15.
62. *VRJ*, III, 422.
63. *VRJ*, I, 106.
64. *VRJ*, II, 346.
65. Leibbrandt, *Precis*, Letters dispatched, III, 376–80.
66. *VRJ*, I, 226; II, 28, 124.
67. *VRJ*, I, 238–43.
68. *VRJ*, I, 61–4, 67–72, 283–4.
69. *VRJ*, I, 155; II, 280–1.
70. *VRJ*, II, 329–30; III, 354.
71. *VRJ*, II, 329–30.
72. François Valentyn, *Description of the Cape of Good Hope* (2 vols., Cape Town, 1973), II, 163.
73. *VRJ*, III, 163–4.
74. Raven-Hart, *Cape of Good Hope*, I, 64–5.
75. *VRJ*, III, 206.
76. Leibbrandt, *Precis*, Letters dispatched, III, 435–7.
77. Ibid.
78. Leibbrandt, *Precis*, Letters received, II, 211.

CHAPTER 2

1. CA, C 1998, 78–9, C 130, 105–7; Otto Mentzel, *A Geographical and Topographical Description of the Cape of Good Hope* (3 vols., Cape Town, 1921–44), I, 60; M. Boucher, *Cape of Good Hope and Foreign Contacts* (Pretoria, 1985), 25 and 88.
2. P. van der Spuy, *Dank-altaar, Gode ter eere opgericht ...* (Utrecht, 1752).
3. A. Böeseken (ed.), *Dagregister en Briewe van Zacharias Wagenaer, 1662–1666* (Pretoria, 1973), 238. Translation by Stephen Gray from M. Hall, 'Small things and the mobile, conflictual fusion of power, fear and desire', in A. Yentsch and M. Beaudry (eds.), *The Art and Mystery of Historical Archaeology* (Florida, 1992), 381.
4. François Valentyn, *Description of the Cape of Good Hope* (2 vols., Cape Town, 1973), I, 79.
5. R. Raven-Hart, 'The Cape in 1759 from the disastrous journey of Jacob Francken', *Quarterly Bulletin of the South African Library*, 22 (1967), 24.
6. D.B. Bosman, *Briewe van Johanna van Riebeeck* (Amsterdam, 1952), 69.
7. Mentzel, *Description*, I, 97.
8. Mentzel, *Description*, III, 27–8.
9. Mentzel, *Description*, I, 61.
10. Otto Mentzel, *Life at the Cape in the Mid-eighteenth Century* (Cape Town, 1919), 97.
11. Valentyn, *Description*, I, 217 and II, 179; Carl Thunberg, *Travels at the Cape of Good Hope* (Cape Town, 1986), 122–3 and 135; C. Woodward, 'The interior of the Cape house, 1670–1714' (M.A. thesis, University of Pretoria, 1982); A. Malan, 'Households of the Cape, 1750–1850' (Ph.D. thesis, University of Cape Town, 1993), 69.
12. Anders Sparrman, *A Voyage to the Cape of Good Hope* (2 vols., Cape Town, 1973–5), I, 57 and n.63.
13. *Resolusies van die Politieke Raad* (9 vols., Cape Town, 1957–81), II, 203.
14. Mentzel, *Description*, I, 133; *Life at the Cape*, 129.
15. L. Duly, *British Land Policy at the Cape, 1795–1844* (Durham, N.C., 1968), 14; L. Hattingh, 'Grondbesit in die Tafelvallei', *Kronos*, 10 (1985), 39 and 44; Mentzel, *Description*, I, 65; Pieter Kolb, *The Present State of the Cape of Good Hope* (2 vols., London, 1731), I, 348.
16. Mentzel, *Description*, I, 101.
17. Ibid., 63–4.
18. Valentyn, *Description*, I, 87.
19. Ibid.
20. Dirk Swart, *Beschrijving van Batavia* (Amsterdam, 1750), 9.
21. Valentyn, *Description*, I, 93.
22. J.D. Buttner, *Accounts of the Cape ...* (Cape Town, 1970), 66.
23. R. Raven-Hart, *Cape of Good Hope, 1652–1702* (2 vols., Cape Town, 1971), II, 409.
24. Mentzel, *Description*, I, 113.
25. A. Grove, *Green Imperialism: Colonial Expansion, Tropical Island Edens and the Origins of Environmentalism* (Cambridge, 1995), 138–9; Raven-Hart, *Cape of Good Hope*, I, 382.
26. H. Pickard, *Gentleman's Walk* (Cape Town, 1968), 93.
27. Sparrman, *Voyage*, I, 130.

28. Algemeen Rijksarchief, The Hague (ARA), Collectie Radermacher 507a.
29. K. Jeffreys (ed.), *Kaapse Plakkaatboek* (6 vols., Cape Town, 1944–51), I, 230, 268, 286.
30. Valentyn, *Description*, II, 221.
31. Raven-Hart, *Cape of Good Hope*, II, 423.
32. Mentzel, *Description*, I, 135–6; Thunberg, *Travels*, 39; Malan, 'Households of the Cape', 20.
33. Malan, 'Households of the Cape', 44; M. Cairns, *Cradle of Commerce: The Story of Block B* (Cape Town, 1974).
34. Leibbrandt, *Precis*, Requesten, 679.
35. Jan de Marre, *Eerkroon voor de Kaap de Goede Hoop* (Amsterdam, 1746), 137.
36. Malan, 'Households of the Cape', 62–73; A. Malan, 'East meets West: freeblack–freeburgher households in early 18th century Cape Town', Society for Historical Archaeology conference, Washington D.C., January 1995.
37. F. Lequin, 'Het personeel van de VOC in Azië in de 18de eeuw, maar in het bijzonder in de vestiging Bengalen' (2 vols., Leiden, 1982), II, 381–2; material on the Company employees is based on analysis of a selection of the VOC muster rolls, ARA VOC 4073 (1714), 5179 (1731), 5214 (1766), 5221 (1773), 5226 (1778), 5230 (1782), 5237 (1789).
38. ARA, Collectie Radermacher 507; ARA, VOC 5179 for Company employees; CA, CJ 3188, 46–57 for *bandieten*; R. Shell, *Children of Bondage* (Johannesburg, 1994), 429 for Company slaves.
39. Mentzel, *Life at the Cape*, 161.
40. ARA, VOC 5221 and *scheepssoldijboeken*.
41. Mentzel, *Life at the Cape*, 128.
42. Thunberg, *Travels*, 271–2.
43. ARA, VOC 5179 and *scheepssoldijboeken*.
44. ARA, VOC 5221 and *scheepssoldijboeken*; C.R. Boxer, 'For love of gain', *Hemisphere*, 23:3 (1979), 136.
45. ARA, VOC 5179 and VOC 5221.
46. CA, CJ 345, 14–26; A.L. Geyer *Das Wirtschaftliche System der Niederländische Ost-Indischen Kompanie am Kap der Guten Hoffnung, 1785–1795* (Munich and Berlin, 1923), 18 n.1.
47. Thunberg, *Travels*, 51 and 152.
48. CA, CJ 787, 288–91.
49. CA, CJ 352, 652–61.
50. Woodward, 'Interior of the Cape house', 289.
51. J.R. Bruijn, F. Gaastra and I. Schiffer, *Dutch–Asiatic Shipping in the 17th and 18th Centuries* (3 vols., The Hague, 1987), I, 69.
52. ARA, Collectie Radermacher 505; Mentzel, *Description*, I, 98; Buttner, *Accounts*, 64.
53. François le Vaillant, *Travels from the Cape of Good Hope Into the Interior Parts of Africa* (2 vols., London, 1790), I, 87.
54. Mentzel, *Life at the Cape*, 125.
55. Thunberg, *Travels*, 22.
56. CA, CJ 14, 9–10.
57. R. Immelman, 'Hollandse matroosliedere op die Kaapvaart in die 17e en 18e eeu – II', *Quarterly Bulletin of the South African Library*, 14 (1960), 126 and 132.
58. CA, CJ 335, 236–38.
59. CA, CJ 360, 1–30.
60. Mentzel, *Description*, I, 53; Valentyn, *Description*, II, 161.
61. Shell, *Children of Bondage*, 301.
62. Mentzel, *Description*, II, 115.
63. Immelman, 'Hollandse matroosliedere – III', *Quarterly Bulletin of the South African Library*, 15 (1960), 14.
64. Valentyn, *Description*, I, 209; D. Moodie, *The Record* (Amsterdam and Cape Town, 1960), 421.
65. CA, CJ 329, 109–25 and CJ 9, 33–4. We are grateful to Robert Ross for alerting us to this case.
66. R. Ross, 'The "white" population of South Africa in the eighteenth century', *Population Studies*, 29:2 (1975), 224–5 and 228–9.
67. ARA, Collectie Radermacher 507. The statistics only include households with children.
68. CA, A 681, letter 13.
69. Raven-Hart, *Cape of Good Hope*, II, 327; Kolb, *Present State*, II, 334–63.
70. Mentzel, *Description*, I, 65–6.
71. Ibid., 117.
72. *Resolusies* II, 27 and 147.
73. ARA, Collectie Radermacher 507.
74. Mentzel, *Description*, II, 88.
75. Raven-Hart, *Cape of Good Hope*, II, 402–3.
76. Valentyn, *Description*, I, 205.
77. Mentzel, *Description*, II, 81.
78. M. Boucher, 'The Cape and foreign shipping, 1714–1723', *South African Historical Journal*, 6 (1974), 23.
79. M. Cairns, 'Genealogical kaleidoscope: Ward 13, Cape Town, 1700–1800', *Familia*, 18 (1982), 38.
80. Mentzel, *Description*, II, 85–7.
81. *Resolusies*, I, 331–2.
82. Mentzel, *Description*, I, 87.
83. Ibid., II, 75.
84. Ibid., II, 79.
85. Thunberg, *Travels*, 141.
86. Malan, 'Households of the Cape', 337 and Table 10.2.
87. Mentzel, *Description*, II, 79.
88. Ibid., 80.
89. Mentzel, *Life at the Cape*, 100, my emphasis.
90. Raven-Hart, *Cape of Good Hope*, II, 249–50.
91. Ibid., 258.
92. Swart, *Beschrijving*, 23–5.
93. Mentzel, *Description*, I, 111–12 and 114.
94. Shell, *Children of Bondage*, 177–89.
95. Ibid., 177.
96. K. Ward, *Bandieten* data base (Cape Town History Project, UCT), and 'The bounds of bondage: forced migration between the Netherlands East Indies and the Cape of Good Hope in the eighteenth century' (Ph.D., Michigan, forthcoming). Thanks to Kerry Ward for this material.
97. R. Ross and S. Koolhof, 'Upas, September and the Bugis at the Cape of Good Hope: the context of a slave's letter', *Sari: Jurnal Institut Bahasa, Kesusasteraan dan Kubudayaan Melayu* (forthcoming, 1997).
98. Thunberg, *Travels*, 103.
99. Mentzel, *Description*, II, 141.
100. Ibid., 89–90.
101. Thunberg, *Travels*, 233.
102. CA, CJ 341, 394–8.
103. J. Franken, ''n Kaapse huishoue in die 18de eeu, uit von Dessin se briefboek en memoriaal', *Archief-jaarboek vir Suid-Afrikaanse Geskiedenis*, 3:1 (1940), 61.
104. CA, CJ 349, 99–120.
105. Mentzel, *Description*, I, 134–5; Mentzel, *Life at the Cape*, 100–2; R. Ross, *Cape of Torments* (London, 1983), 54–72.
106. CA, C 1240, 95–6.
107. Jacob Haafner, *Lotgevallen en vroegere Zeereisen* (Amsterdam, 1820), 74.
108. R. Elphick and R. Shell, 'Intergroup relations' in R. Elphick and H. Giliomee (eds.), *The Shaping of South African Society, 1652–1840*, 2nd edn (Cape Town, 1989), 209.
109. Ibid., 216.
110. Mentzel, *Description*, II, 88.
111. A. Böeseken, *Slaves and Free Blacks at the Cape, 1658–1700* (Cape Town, 1977), 80–1.
112. M. Cairns, 'Appolonia of the Cape, c.1716–1762', *Familia*, 24 (1987), 85–9.
113. Malan, 'Households of the Cape', 44.
114. Thanks to James Armstrong for this information.
115. Malan, 'East meets West', 3.
116. Leibbrandt, *Precis*, Requesten, 252c.
117. Mentzel, *Description*, II, 91.
118. J. Armstrong, 'The Chinese at the Cape of Good Hope in the VOC period, 1652–1795', unpublished paper, 31.
119. V.C. Malherbe, 'Khoikhoi in Cape Town', *Cabo*, 3:2 (1983), 6; William Fehr Collection GH 87/1; see also M. Boucher and N. Penn (eds.), *Britain at the Cape, 1795 to 1803* (Houghton, 1992), 75.
120. Charles Lockyer cited in R. Elphick, *Khoikhoi and the Founding of White South Africa* (Johannesburg, 1985), 181.
121. CA, A 681, letter 17.
122. Gijsbert Hemmy, *Dissertatio juridica inauguralis de testimoniis aethiopum ...* (Leiden, 1770), 60, translated by Margaret Hewitt; R. Viljoen, 'Disease and society: VOC Cape Town, its people and the smallpox epidemics of 1713, 1753 and 1787', *Kleio*, 27 (1995), 22–45.
123. Viljoen, 'Disease and society' and R. Ross, 'Smallpox at the Cape of Good Hope in the 18th century' in C. Fyfe (ed.), *African Historical Demography* (Edinburgh, 1981).
124. Malan, 'Households of the Cape', 52–6 and Table 3.11; A. Malan, 'Beneath the surface – behind the doors: the historical archaeology of households in mid-18th century Cape Town', Centre for African Studies seminar, UCT, 1995, 6.
125. *Kaapse Plakkaatboek*, II, 7–8.
126. J. Hoge, 'Martin Melck', *Tydskrif vir Wetenskap en Kuns*, 12 (1933–4), 203.
127. Mentzel, *Description*, II, 85.
128. A. Th. van Deursen, *Plain Lives in a Golden Age* (Cambridge, 1991), 56 and 59.
129. Mentzel, *Description*, I, 149.
130. *Resolusies*, II, 125, 138, 147
131. M. Marais, 'Armesorg aan die Kaap onder die Kompanjie, 1652–1795', *Archief-jaarboek vir Suid-Afrikaanse Geskiedenis*, 6 (1943), 1–72.
132. Leibbrandt, *Precis*, Journal, 1699–1732, 159. Thanks to Nigel Penn for this reference.
133. John Barrow cited in Boucher and Penn, *Britain at the Cape*, 146.
134. R. Ross, *Beyond the Pale* (Johannesburg, 1993), 72–5.
135. J. Taylor, *The Social World of Batavia* (Madison, 1983).

136. For other early examples, see H.B. Thom (ed.) *Journal of Jan van Riebeeck* [*VRJ*] (3 vols., Cape Town, 1952–8), II, 303, 315, III, 309.
137. R. Raben, 'Bevolking in balans: volkstellingen en segregatiepolitiek in VOC Batavia' (Doctoraalscriptie, Rijksuniversiteit te Leiden, 1988), 71.
138. H. Heese, *Groep sonder Grense* (Bellville, 1984), 20–1.
139. H. Heese, 'Enlightenment, Europeans and slaves in 18th century South Africa', *Kronos*, 14 (1988), 68.
140. M. Cairns, 'Armosyn Claasz of the Cape and her family', *Familia*, 16 (1979), 84–99; H. Heese, *Groep sonder Grense*, 13–14.
141. N. Penn, 'The fatal passion of Brewer Menssink: sex, beer and politics in a Cape family, c.1694–1722', unpublished paper, 1997.
142. H. Heese, 'Challenging certain aspects of intergroup relations in *The Shaping of South African Society*', Kronos, 17 (1990), 75.
143. W. Dooling, 'The Cape Town Castle, 1666–1811', unpublished CSD research report, February 1992, 45.
144. R. Ross, 'A tragedy of manners: status and respectability at the Cape of Good Hope, 1750–1870,' unpublished manuscript, 40–1. We are grateful to Robert Ross for permission to use this material.
145. Mentzel, *Description*, I, 145.
146. *Resolusies*, IV, 365–6; Mentzel, *Description*, I, 66.
147. CA, BRD 35.
148. Ibid., 31 March 1764.
149. CA, BRD 41; *Gleanings in Africa* (London, 1806), 252; D. Warren, 'Merchants, commissioners and wardmasters' (M.A. thesis, University of Cape Town), 3.
150. Leibbrandt, *Precis*, Requesten, 169.
151. CA, A 2276, vol. 321; Thunberg, *Travels*, 124.
152. Ross, 'Tragedy of manners', ch. 2, 29.
153. CA, CJ 39, 30–4; Ross, 'Tragedy of manners', ch. 2, 21–2.
154. Mentzel, *Description*, I, 123.
155. Mentzel, *Life at the Cape*, 73.
156. Leibbrandt, *Precis*, Letters dispatched, III, 479. A 'rasphouse' was a place of correction in the Netherlands where prisoners did hard labour rasping wood.
157. CA, CJ 360, 371–510.
158. Mentzel, *Description*, I, 11.
159. Sparrman, *Voyage*, I, 51–2.
160. De Wet, *Vryliede*, 155.
161. CA, CJ 373; Ross and Koolhof, 'Upas, September and the Bugis'.
162. Woodward, 'Interior of the Cape house', 240–1, 244–5.
163. J.S. Stavorinus, *Voyage par le Cap de Bonne-Espérance à Batavia* (Paris, 1798), 401.
164. D. Varley, 'Joachim von Dessin and his book collection', *Quarterly Bulletin of the South African Library*, 16 (1961), 8–21.
165. K. Jeffreys, *Kaapse Archiefstukke lopende over het Jaar 1778* (Cape Town, 1926), 500.
166. Mentzel, *Description*, I, 132.
167. J. Gerstner, *The Thousand Generation Covenant* (Leiden, 1991), 214–16; Valentyn, *Description*, II, ch. 8.
168. Penn, 'Fatal passion'.
169. L. Herrman, *A History of the Jews in South Africa* (London, 1930), 61–2.
170. E. Schnell, *For Men Must Work: An Account of German Immigration to the Cape* (Cape Town, 1954), 22.
171. CA, CJ 782, 1–18.
172. Thunberg, *Travels*, 49.
173. K. Ward, 'The Sheikh Yusuf tricentenary commemoration in the re-imagining of the Cape Muslim community', unpublished paper, History Department, University of Michigan, 1995, 19–20; S. Dangor, *Shaykh Yusuf* (Durban, 1982), 59.
174. A. Davids, *The Mosques of Bo-Kaap* (Athlone, 1980), 43.
175. Y. da Costa and A. Davids, *Pages from Cape Muslim History* (Pietermaritzburg, 1994), 130–2; M.A. Bradlow, 'Imperialism, state formation and the establishment of a Muslim community at the Cape of Good Hope' (M.A. thesis, University of Cape Town, 1988).
176. Ross, *Cape of Torments*, 20–1.
177. CA, CJ 361, 1.
178. A. Boshoff, 'Slawe orkeste en musiekinstrumente aan die Kaap', *South African Cultural History Museum Bulletin*, 8 (1987), 49–55.
179. Mentzel, *Description*, II, 104.
180. Ibid., II, 104–5.
181. Thunberg, *Travels*, 271.
182. Haafner, *Lotgevallen*, 72.
183. Mentzel, *Description*, II, 93–9; O.H. Spohr, 'Two letters from the promontory of the Cape written in March 1775 by Fr. von Wurmb', *Quarterly Bulletin of the South African Library*, 28:2 (1973), 47.
184. Woodward, 'Interior of the Cape house', 248–53.
185. Ibid., 109–10 and 267–70.
186. Malan, 'East meets West'.
187. Mentzel, *Description*, II, 71.
188. Le Vaillant, *Travels*, I, 91–2.
189. Dooling, 'Cape Town Castle'; W. Dooling, 'The Castle: its place in the history of Cape Town in the VOC period', *Studies in the History of Cape Town*, 7 (1994), 18.
190. Thunberg, *Travels*, 271; Mentzel, *Description*, II, 86.
191. Ross, *Cape of Torments*, 21.
192. Leibbrandt, *Precis*, Requesten, 148.
193. CA, CJ 349, 199–214.
194. Ross, *Beyond the Pale*, 161; CA, CJ 369, 541–4.
195. *Kaapse Plakkaatboek*, I, 227.
196. Leibbrandt, *Precis*, Requesten, 85–6; 679.
197. Thunberg, *Travels*, 157–8.
198. Leibbrandt, *Precis*, Requesten, 1534; R. Shell, 'Rangton van Bali (1673–1720): roots and resurrection', *Kronos*, 1992, 193–4.
199. Mentzel, *Description*, I, 89.
200. Raven-Hart, *Cape of Good Hope*, II, 477.
201. Ibid.; Valentyn, *Description*, I, 59.
202. Raven-Hart, *Cape of Good Hope*, II, 351 and 372; Kolb, *Present State*, II, 13; Valentyn, *Description*, I, 61–2, although Mentzel, *Description*, I, 93 is sceptical of their gullibility.
203. Mentzel, *Description*, I, 90.
204. Le Vaillant, *Travels*, I, 85.
205. Mentzel, *Description*, I, 90.
206. Geyer, *Wirtschaftliche System*, 16–17.
207. J. de Mist, *Memorandum concerning Recommendations for the Form and Administration of Government at the Cape of Good Hope* (Cape Town, 1925), 201.
208. Mentzel, *Description*, II, 111.
209. Cornelius de Jong, *Reizen naar de Kaap de Goede Hoop* (Haarlem, 1802–3), 130; Malan, 'Households of the Cape', 96.
210. L. Wolpowitz, 'The development of the musical life of Cape Town up to the middle of the 19th century', *Quarterly Bulletin of the South African Library*, 48:1 (1993), 21.
211. P. McMagh, *The Three Lieschings* (Cape Town, 1992), 65.
212. T. Baartman, 'Burghers in Cape Town, 1780–1790', Cape Town History Project research paper, History Department, UCT, 1994.
213. A. Bank, 'Liberals and their enemies: racial ideology at the Cape of Good Hope, 1820 to 1850' (Ph.D. thesis, Cambridge University, 1995), 59.
214. R. Ross, 'The last years of the slave trade to the Cape Colony', *Slavery and Abolition*, 9:3 (1988), 209–19; M. Reidy, 'The admission of slaves and "prize negroes" into the Cape Colony, 1797–1818' (M.A. thesis, University of Cape Town, 1997); Shell, *Children of Bondage*, 271.
215. Shell, *Children of Bondage*, 44–5.
216. CA, C 171, 140–2.
217. Malan, 'Households of the Cape', 155.
218. Geyer, *Wirtschaftliche System*, 52–4.
219. De Jong, *Reizen*, 118 and 152.

CHAPTER 3

1. Petrus Borcherds, *An Autobiographical Memoir* (Cape Town, 1963), 26.
2. Ibid., 30.
3. Lady Anne Barnard, *The Cape Journals* (Cape Town, 1994), 155.
4. R. Shell, 'Hudson's Cape Town', *Quarterly Bulletin of the South African Library*, 47:4 (1993), 135.
5. Borcherds, *Memoir*, 279.
6. Ibid., 281.
7. H.G. Nahuys van Burgst, *Adventures at the Cape of Good Hope in 1806* (Cape Town, 1993), 26.
8. G. Theal, *Records of the Cape Colony* (36 vols., Cape Town, 1887–1919), XXVII, 395–6.
9. William Bird, *The State of the Cape of Good Hope in 1822* (Cape Town, 1966), 47.
10. Robert Semple, *Walks and Sketches at the Cape of Good Hope* (London, 1805), 26.
11. Ferdinand Krauss, 'A description of Cape Town and its way of life, 1838–40', *Quarterly Bulletin of the South African Library*, 21 (1966–7), 43.
12. Data from UCT Cape Town History Project, compiled from a variety of sources in the Cape Archives.
13. CA, RDG 121, Wardmaster household returns for 1820. These returns underestimate the total population by about 800, but the shortfall appears to be consistent across all categories of the population and so does not significantly affect the proportions shown.
14. R. Immelman, *Men of Good Hope* (Cape Town, 1955), 25–6.
15. E. Blount, *Notes on the Cape of Good Hope* (London, 1821), 3.
16. Bird, *State*, 151.
17. H. Deacon 'Professionalisation and the state: doctors in the Cape Colony in the early 19th century', Centre for African Studies seminar, UCT, 1995.
18. Robert Percival, *An Account of the Cape of Good Hope* (London, 1804), 324–5.
19. K. McKenzie, *The Making of an English Slaveowner: Samuel Eusebius Hudson at the Cape of Good Hope, 1796–1807* (Cape Town, 1993), 35.
20. CA, RD' 121, Wyk 2.
21. J. Peires, 'The British and the Cape' in R. Elphick and H. Giliomee (eds.), *The Shaping of South African Society*, 2nd edn (Cape Town, 1989), 491.
22. D.S. Evans (ed.), *Herschel at the Cape* (Cape Town, 1969), 69.
23. John Barrow, *Travels into the Interior of Southern Africa* (2 vols., London, 1806), II, 189; Theal, *Records*, assorted figures.
24. Percival, *Account*, 320; Bird, *State*, 158–9.
25. CA, BRD 27; RDG 121.
26. Percival, *Account*, 102; Semple, *Walks and Sketches*, 111.
27. Barrow, *Travels*, II, 50; Barnard, *Journals*, 155; *The Letters of Lady Anne Barnard* (Cape Town, 1973), 41–2.
28. Barnard, *Journals*, 244.
29. Ibid., 271.
30. M. Boucher and N. Penn (eds.), *Britain at the Cape, 1795 to 1803* (Houghton, 1992), 114.
31. Van Burgst, *Adventures*, 75.
32. Barnard, *Journals*, 265; Percival, *Account*, 77–8.
33. Percival, *Account*, 163.
34. Van Burgst, *Adventures*, 25.
35. Barnard, *Letters*, 181, 277.
36. Van Burgst, *Adventures*, 18.
37. Barrow, *Travels*, II, 174.
38. C.M. Elias, 'The African in Simon's Town: a socio-historical study, 1816–1950', paper delivered at the Western Cape: Roots and Realities conference, Cape Town, 1986.
39. CA, RDG 121.
40. Krauss, 'Description', 46.
41. C. Bayly, *Imperial Meridian* (London, 1989), 158.
42. CA, RDG 121.
43. K. Elks, 'Crime, community and police in Cape Town, 1825–1850' (M.A. thesis, University of Cape Town, 1986), 83–4.
44. Barnard, *Journals*, 229.
45. Ibid., 78.
46. Lady Herschel, *Letters from the Cape, 1834–1838* (Cape Town, 1991), 42.
47. Barnard, *Letters*, 101.
48. Bird, *State*, 155.
49. R. Langham-Carter, 'The "Indians" in Cape Town', *Quarterly Bulletin of the South African Library*, 35:4 (1981), 149.
50. *South African Commercial Advertiser* [*SACA*], 20.10.1830, cited in K. McKenzie, 'The South African Commercial Advertiser and the making of middle class identity in early 19th century Cape Town' (M.A. thesis, University of Cape Town, 1993), 192–3.
51. Bird, *State*, 155.
52. Langham-Carter, 'Indians in Cape Town', 148–9.
53. CA, PC 3/1–2; J. Arkin, 'John Company at the Cape', *Archives Yearbook for South African History*, 23:2 (1960), 237–67.
54. J.L. Meltzer, 'The growth of Cape Town commerce and the role of John Fairbairn's *Advertiser* (1835–1859)' (M.A. thesis, University of Cape Town, 1989), ch. 1. The following section is heavily dependent on this thesis.
55. D. Rush, 'Aspects of the growth of trade and the development of ports in the Cape Colony, 1795–1882' (M.A. thesis, University of Cape Town, 1972), 15.
56. Meltzer, 'Growth', 25; D. Warren, 'Merchants, commissioners and wardmasters' (M.A. thesis, University of Cape Town), 53; R. Langham-Carter, 'The Collisons and their achievements', *Quarterly Bulletin of the South African Library*, 24:3 (1970), 234–7.
57. R. Ross, 'The Cape and the world economy, 1652–1795' in Elphick and Giliomee, *Shaping*, 265.
58. P. Philip, 'The vicissitudes of the early British settlers at the Cape', *Quarterly Bulletin of the South African Library*, 41 (1986), 159–70.
59. M. George, 'John Bardwell Ebden: his business and political career at the Cape, 1806–1849', *Archives Yearbook for South African History*, 49:1 (1986), 1–49D.
60. R. Beck, 'Edward Hanbury: Cape Town ship chandler and merchant', *Quarterly Bulletin of the South African Library*, 39:1 (1984), 26–38 and 39:2 (1984), 73–83.
61. Bird, *State*, 147.
62. Evans, *Herschel at the Cape*, 37.
63. Meltzer, 'Growth', 33.
64. CA, PC 3/1–2.
65. Krauss, 'Description', 41.
66. L. Meltzer, 'Emancipation, commerce and the role of John Fairbairn's *Advertiser*' in N. Worden and C. Crais (eds.), *Breaking the Chains: Slavery and its Legacy in the Nineteenth Century Cape Colony* (Johannesburg, 1994), 188.
67. ARA, Collectie Radermacher 507, VOC 4115 (1731); CA, RDG 121 (1820).
68. A. Bank, *The Decline of Urban Slavery at the Cape, 1806 to 1834* (Cape Town, 1991), 22.
69. CA, RDG 121.
70. W.J. Burchell, *Travels in the Interior of Southern Africa* (London, 1822), 29.
71. CA, SO 3/5; Bank, *Decline*, 40.
72. Semple, *Walks*, 17–18, 21.
73. Bank, *Decline*, 174.
74. A. Bank, 'The erosion of urban slavery at the Cape' in Worden and Crais, *Breaking the Chains*, 95.
75. Barrow, *Travels*, II, 94–5.
76. Theal, *Records*, VI, 411.
77. Ibid., 420.
78. R. Ross, *Cape of Torments* (London, 1983), 99; K. Harris, 'The slave "rebellion" of 1808', *Kleio*, 20 (1988), 54–65.
79. Bank, 'Erosion', 96.
80. CA, BRD 27, Wijksrollen 1799, Wyk 13.
81. Bank, *Decline*, 193.
82. C. Iannini, 'Slavery, philanthropy and hegemony: a history of the Cape of Good Hope Philanthropic Society, 1828–1833' (B.A. Honours thesis, History Department, University of Cape Town, 1993).
83. *SACA*, 6.12.1834.
84. Lady Herschel, *Letters*, 125.
85. V. Bickford-Smith, 'Meanings of freedom: social position and identity among ex-slaves and their descendants in Cape Town, 1875–1910' in Worden and Crais, *Breaking the Chains*, 303.
86. CA, 1/WBG Add 1/1/1 52, Jurgens vs. January, 26 February 1835.
87. CA, 1/WBG Add 1/1/1 54, Otto Landsberg vs. Leentje, 27 February 1835.
88. J.G. Steyler, 'Remembrances from 1832–1900', *Quarterly Bulletin of the South African Library*, 25:1 (1970), 25.
89. Krauss, 'Description', 42.
90. CA, CO 441, 48–9.
91. *De Ware Afrikaan*, 4.2.1840.
92. G. Cox, 'Historical background and isotopic analysis of skeletons found near the site of Fort Knokke, Cape Town Foreshore' (B.A. Honours thesis, Archaeology Department, University of Cape Town, 1995).
93. C. Saunders, '"Free, yet slaves": prize negroes at the Cape revisited', in Worden and Crais, *Breaking the Chains*, ch. 4.
94. V.C. Malherbe, 'Diversification and mobility of Khoikhoi labour in the eastern districts of the Cape Colony prior to the labour law of 1 November 1809' (M.A. thesis, University of Cape Town, 1978), 6.
95. CA, RDG 121.
96. Krauss, 'Description', 49; S. Judges and C. Saunders, 'The beginnings of an African community in Cape Town', *South African Outlook*, August 1976, 122–3.

97. J.W. Moodie, *Ten Years in South Africa* (2 vols., London, 1835), I, 51–3.
98. E. Bradlow, 'The Children's Friend Society at the Cape of Good Hope', *Victorian Studies*, 27:2 (1984), 155–77; G. Blackburn, *The Children's Friend Society* (Northbridge, W. Australia, 1993).
99. J. Backhouse, *Extracts from the Journal of James Backhouse* (London, 1840), 7th part, 13.9.1838.
100. S. Judges, 'Poverty, living conditions and social relations: aspects of life in Cape Town in the 1830s' (M.A. thesis, University of Cape Town, 1977), 7.
101. Lady Herschel, *Letters*, 49–50.
102. Ibid., 88.
103. A. Whyte, 'A coloured man and a stranger: the early Cape Town memorials of Antonio Ferreira', paper given at History Department seminar, University of Cape Town, 1993, 27–8.
104. R. Watson, *The Slave Question: Liberty and Property in South Africa* (Johannesburg, 1990), 130–1; A. Bank, 'Liberals and their enemies: racial ideology at the Cape of Good Hope, 1820 to 1850' (Ph.D. thesis, Cambridge University, 1995), 167–70.
105. Blount, *Notes*, 3.
106. S. Hudson, 'The great fire of Cape Town', *Quarterly Bulletin of the South African Library*, 8 (1953–4), 6–11, 138; Boucher and Penn, *Britain at the Cape*, 219.
107. R. Shell, *Children of Bondage* (Johannesburg, 1994), 274–5.
108. Bird, *State*, 162.
109. Percival, *Account*, 116–17.
110. A. Malan, 'Households of the Cape, 1750–1850' (Ph.D. thesis, University of Cape Town, 1993), 179.
111. Krauss, 'Description', 3.
112. Malan, 'Households of the Cape', 190–1.
113. N. Erlank, 'Letters home: the experiences and perceptions of middle class British women at the Cape, 1820–1850' (M.A. thesis, University of Cape Town, 1995).
114. Barnard, *Letters*, 260.
115. H. Robinson, 'Beyond the city limits: people and property at Wynberg, 1795–1827' (Ph.D. thesis, UCT, 1995), chs. 1–2.
116. Meltzer,"Emancipation', 186.
117. K. Wheeler, 'Interior decoration at the Cape, 1815–35', *Bulletin of the South African Cultural History Museum*, 6 (1985), 5–15.
118. K. McKenzie, 'Gender and honour in middle-class Cape Town: the making of colonial identities, 1828–1850' (D.Phil., University of Oxford, 1997), ch. 7.
119. Blount, *Notes*, 9–10.
120. F. Todeschini, *Lion's Head and Signal Hill: historical development and existing cultural landscape* (Cape Town, 1992), 6–8.
121. CA, CO 490-159, Ward 1.
122. Ibid., Ward 2.
123. Ibid., Ward 6.
124. CA, CO 3958-112.
125. *SACA*, 4.7.1829.
126. Judges, 'Poverty', 83.
127. CA, CO 490-159, Ward 6.
128. Judges, 'Poverty', 64.
129. P. Laidler, *A Tavern of the Ocean* (Cape Town, n.d.), 99, 142.
130. Judges, 'Poverty', 4.
131. Ibid., 3.
132. CA, CO 4005-144.
133. *Cape of Good Hope Almanack*, 1841, Statistical index.
134. Judges, 'Poverty', 85.
135. Ibid., 87.
136. J.E. Alexander, *An Expedition of Discovery into the Interior of Africa* (2 vols., London, 1838), II, App. 3, p. 9.
137. P.W. Laidler and M. Gelfand, *South Africa: Its Medical History, 1652–1898* (Cape Town, 1971), 256–7.
138. *Second Annual Report of the Committee of the Ladies' Benevolent Society at the Cape of Good Hope* (Cape Town, 1824), 3.
139. E. Bradlow, '"The Oldest Charitable Society in South Africa": One hundred years and more of the Ladies' Benevolent Society at the Cape of Good Hope', *South African Historical Journal*, 25 (1991), 77–104.
140. CA, CO 481-89, 94.
141. E. Burrows, *History of Medicine in South Africa* (Cape Town, 1958), 107–10; *Dictionary of South African Biography* (Pretoria, 1972), II, 20–1.
142. *Cape of Good Hope Almanack*, 1842, from *Cape Town Mail*, 18.12.1841.
143. Krauss, 'Description', 7.
144. J. Fawcett, *Account of an Eighteen Months Residence at the Cape of Good Hope in 1835–6* (Cape Town, 1836), 8.
145. F. Quinn and G. Cuthbertson, *Presbyterianism in Cape Town* (Cape Town, 1979), 15.
146. A. Namphy, 'Emancipation at the Cape, 1823–53: Christianity and Islam', unpublished paper, 1996.
147. H. Giliomee, *Die Kaap tydens die Eerste Britse Bewind* (Cape Town, 1975), 25–6.
148. H. Ludlow, 'The work of the London Missionary Society in Cape Town, 1812–41' (B.A. Honours thesis, Department of History, University of Cape Town, 1981).
149. R. Shell, 'Rites and rebellion: Islamic conversion at the Cape, 1808 to 1915', *Studies in the History of Cape Town*, 5 (1984), 9.
150. Cited in ibid., 2.
151. J. Mason, 'Social death and resurrection: resistance and the ambiguities of Islam in Bahia and the Cape', unpublished paper, Yale University Contemporary History seminar, 1995, 21.
152. Carl Thunberg, *Travels at the Cape of Good Hope* (Cape Town, 1986), 47–8.
153. Barrow, *Travels*, II, 146.
154. Y. da Costa and A. Davids, *Pages from Cape Muslim History* (Pietermaritzburg, 1994), 52–3.
155. A. Davids, *The Mosques of Bo-Kaap* (Athlone, 1980), 116; Mason, 'Social death', 23–4.
156. A. Davids, 'Words the slaves made: a socio-historical-linguistic study', *South African Journal of Linguistics*, 8:1 (1990), 13.
157. Shell, 'Rites and rebellion', 25–9.
158. For example, CA, 1/WBG Add 1/1/1, cases 17, 25, 27.
159. CA, 1/WBG Add 1/1/1 52, Jurgens vs. January, 26 February 1835.
160. Davids, 'Words the slaves made', 4.
161. Van Burgst, *Adventures*, 37.
162. J.G.Swaving, *Zonderlinge Ontmoetingen en wonderbaarlijke Lotswisselingen* (Dordrecht, 1830), 302–3. We are grateful to Robert Ross for this reference.
163. Davids, 'Words the slaves made', 19–21.
164. W. Mann, *Cape Diary and Letters* (Cape Town, 1989), 21.
165. McKenzie, *Making of an English Slaveowner*, 98–9.
166. Evans, *Herschel at the Cape*, 303.
167. Blount, *Notes*, 97.
168. Ibid.
169. N. Erlank, 'Circulating in Cape Town: material culture and social relations in the life of Lady Margaret Herschel' (B.A. Honours thesis, Archaeology Department, University of Cape Town, 1993).
170. Philip, 'Vicissitudes'.
171. McKenzie, 'Gender and honour', 172–5, 202–4.
172. SAL, MSB 412, Eliza Fairbairn to Mrs Smith, 10.5.1838 and CA, A663 Eliza Fairbairn to Mary Christie, 9.3.1838. We are grateful to Kirsten McKenzie for these references.
173. McKenzie, 'Gender and honour', 131–4; Una Long, *An Index to Authors of Unofficial Privately-Owned Manuscripts Relating to the History of South Africa, 1812–1920* (Cape Town, 1947), 149–50.
174. Krauss, 'Description', 8.
175. Shell, 'Hudson's Cape Town', 139–40.
176. Laidler, *Tavern*, 190; Valentyn, *Description*, I, 109.
177. Fawcett, *Account*, 90.
178. Langham-Carter, 'Indians in Cape Town', 146.
179. Evans, *Herschel*, 42.
180. R. Summers, *A History of the South African Museum* (Cape Town, 1975), 13–16.
181. *SACA* prospectus, 20.12.1823.
182. Krauss, 'Description', 43.
183. Ibid., 46.
184. S.Trapido, 'Van Riebeeck Day and the New Jerusalem', unpublished paper, Institute of Commonwealth Studies, University of London, 1992, 36.
185. H. Botha, *John Fairbairn in South Africa* (Cape Town, 1984), 133.
186. Bank, 'Liberals and their enemies', 163–4.
187. Ibid., 174–8.
188. Fawcett, *Account*, 87.
189. Trapido, 'Van Riebeeck Day', 34.
190. McKenzie, '*South African Commercial Advertiser*'.
191. W.S. Westhuizen, 'Onderwys onder die Algemene Skoolkommissie, 1804–39', *Argief-jaarboek vir Suid-Afrikaanse Geskiedenis*, 16:2 (1953), 114–15.
192. Peires, 'British and the Cape', 477.
193. Krauss, 'Description', 8.
194. Ibid.
195. W. Ritchie, *History of the South African College, 1829–1918* (2 vols., Cape Town, 1918), I, 68 and 96.
196. Westhuizen, 'Onderwys', 94.

197. C. Iannini, 'Contracted chattel: indentured and apprenticed labour in Cape Town, c.1808–1840' (M.A. thesis, University of Cape Town, 1995), 60; George Champion, *Journal of an American Missionary in the Cape Colony* (Cape Town, 1968), 4.
198. Annual Report of Committee of South African Infant Schools, *SACA*, 26.3.1831, cited in McKenzie, '*South African Commercial Advertiser*', 155.
199. Iannini, 'Contracted chattel', 64.
200. N. Erlank, 'Letters home', 53–4.
201. Iannini, 'Contracted chattel', 65.
202. Erlank, 'Letters home', 54–6.
203. Bayly, *Imperial Meridian*, 131.
204. CA, LCA 6, Memorial 33.
205. *SACA*, 4.2.1824.
206. Backhouse, *Extracts from the Journal*, 7th part, 12.8.1838.
207. Elks, 'Crime, community and police', 28.
208. *Moderator*, 7.2.1837; Iannini, 'Contracted chattel', 116–17.
209. *Cape of Good Hope Literary Gazette*, 13.10.1830.
210. Barrow, *Travels*, II, 139.
211. *SACA*, 13.4.1831; McKenzie, '*South African Commercial Advertiser*', 168.
212. M.D. Teenstra, *De Vruchten mijner Werkzaamheden* (Cape Town, 1943), 333–4.
213. Ibid., 334.
214. H. Deacon, *The Island: A History of Robben Island* (Cape Town, 1996), 33–56.
215. Barnard, *Letters*, 216.
216. Ibid., 175.
217. A.M. Lewin-Robinson, 'They came to dinner at Government House: Mrs. Bourke's dinner lists, 1827–8', *Quarterly Bulletin of the South African Library*, 33:4 (1979), 107–11.
218. Blount, *Notes*, 102–3.
219. *Gleanings in Africa* (London, 1806), 37.
220. Bird, *State*, 160.
221. Ibid.
222. *Gleanings*, 258.
223. Percival, *Account*, 51, 101, 161; Barnard, *Journals*, 237; *Gleanings*, 23–4.
224. Teenstra, *Vruchten*, 339.
225. Barnard, *Journals*, 237, 288.
226. Cornelis de Jong, *Reizen naar de Kaap de Goede Hoop* (3 vols., Haarlem, 1802–3), I, 147–8.
227. Barnard, *Journals*, 166.
228. Bird, *State*, 164.
229. Blount, *Notes*, 102.
230. Evans, *Herschel*, 83.
231. Lady Herschel, *Letters*, 26.
232. Borcherds, *Memoir*, 238.
233. Semple, *Walks*, 33.
234. Barrow, *Travels*, II, 98–9.
235. Percival, *Account*, 259.
236. A. Cooper, 'The origins and growth of Freemasonry in South Africa, 1772–1876' (M.A. thesis, University of Cape Town, 1975).
237. A.M. Lewin-Robinson, 'The dangers of a colonial theatre', *Quarterly Bulletin of the South African Library*, 30:2 (1975), 37.
238. Langham-Carter, 'Indians in Cape Town', 146.
239. Evans, *Herschel*, 74.
240. V.M. Golovnin, *Detained in Simon's Bay* (Cape Town, 1964), 59.
241. Trapido, 'Van Riebeeck Day', 31.
242. Lewin-Robinson, 'Dangers of a colonial theatre', 30, 38.
243. Barnard, *Letters*, 12; Blount, *Notes*, 9.
244. Barnard, *Letters*, 42.
245. CA, CO 502–63 & enclosure, 'Report on smuggling houses in Cape Town'.
246. *SACA*, 19.12.1829.
247. Alexander, *Expedition*, II, 286.
248. Judges, 'Poverty', 104.
249. CA, CO 3970–14.
250. *SACA*, 10.7.1833 (letter); CA, CO 3970–14.
251. *SACA*, 17.3.1832.
252. *SACA*, 29.11.1834.
253. *SACA*, 14.12.1831.
254. Fawcett, *Account*, 8.
255. Judges, 'Poverty', 52; Iannini, 'Contracted chattel', 115.
256. Bird, *State*, 166.
257. Percival, *Account*, 294.
258. A. Reid, *Southeast Asia in the Age of Commerce, 1450–1680* (2 vols., New Haven, 1988–93), I, 194.
259. Semple, *Walks*, 86–7.
260. *Gleanings*, 244–6.
261. Bird, *State*, 166.
262. *SACA*, 13.9.1837.
263. *SACA*, 20.9.1837.
264. *SACA*, 8.11.1837.

CHAPTER 4

1. *Cape Argus*, 14, 16, 21.5.1863.
2. R. Damatta, *Carnivals, Rogues and Heroes: An Interpretation of the Brazilian Dilemma* (Notre Dame, 1991), 29.
3. C. Saunders, 'Eliza's Cape Town, 1863', *Quarterly Bulletin of the South African Library* [*QBSAL*] (December 1980), 55.
4. A. du Toit and H. Giliomee, *Afrikaner Political Thought: Analysis and Documents*, vol.1, *1780–1850* (Cape Town, 1983), 24–5.
5. A. Bank, 'Liberals and their enemies: racial ideology at the Cape of Good Hope, 1820-1850' (Ph.D. thesis, Cambridge University, 1994), 282–94.
6. J.L. Meltzer, 'The growth of Cape Town commerce and the role of John Fairbairn's *Advertiser*, 1835–1859' (M.A. thesis, University of Cape Town, 1989), 55, 74. Since published in *Archives Yearbook for South African History*, 57, (1994) this is one of the most significant works for the period.
7. Du Toit and Giliomee, *Afrikaner Political Thought*, 13.
8. Quoted in Meltzer, 'The growth of Cape Town commerce', 209.
9. Ibid., 100.
10. Cited in ibid., 119.
11. Ibid., 118–19.
12. J.M. Smalberger, *Aspects of the History of Copper Mining in Namaqualand 1846–1931* (Cape Town, 1975), 48.
13. Ibid., 41 from *Cape Monitor*, 4.11.1854.
14. Meltzer, 'The growth of Cape Town commerce', 164–7.
15. Ibid., 95.
16. K. McKenzie, 'The *South African Commercial Advertiser* and the making of middle class identity in early nineteenth century Cape Town' (M.A. thesis, University of Cape Town, 1993), 65–6.
17. J. Burman, *Early Railways* (Cape Town, n.d.), 12; P.R. Coates, *Track and Trackless: Omnibuses and Trams in the Western Cape* (Cape Town, 1976), 28.
18. Burman, *Early Railways*, 14; Coates, *Track and Trackless*, 33–4.
19. Coates, *Track and Trackless*, 34.
20. Burman, *Early Railways*, 20.
21. Ibid., 23–6.
22. L. Duff Gordon, *Letters from the Cape* (London, 1931), 140.
23. D.W. Rush, 'Aspects of the growth of trade and the development of ports in the Cape Colony, 1795–1882' (M.A. thesis, University of Cape Town, 1972).
24. SC4-1860, 13, quoted in S. Petersen, 'The development of Table Bay harbour 1860–1870', *Studies in the History of Cape Town*, 3 (1984), 36.
25. Duff Gordon, *Letters*, 28, 32.
26. McKenzie, '*South African Commercial Advertiser*', 60.
27. A. Rabone (ed.), *Records of a Pioneer Family* (Cape Town, 1966), 87–8.
28. *Cape Monitor*, 9.1.1858, cited in A.F. Hattersley, *An Illustrated Social History of South Africa* (Cape Town, 1969), 177.

29. D.J.C. Radford, 'The architecture of the Western Cape, 1838–1901: a study of the impact of Victorian aesthetics and technology on South African architecture' (2 vols., Ph.D. thesis, University of the Witwatersrand, 1979), I, 33; an invaluable source on the topic.
30. P.W. Laidler, *The Growth and Government of Cape Town* (Cape Town, 1939), 345.
31. Radford, 'Architecture of the Western Cape', 73.
32. Ibid., 228.
33. Ibid., 148–9.
34. R.W. Murray, *South African Reminiscences* (Cape Town, 1894), 223–4.
35. Radford, 'Architecture of the Western Cape', 55–6.
36. Cited in D.P. Warren, 'The establishment of Cape Town's first municipality, 1836–1840' (unpublished paper, n.d.), 16.
37. H.W.J. Picard, *Grand Parade: The Birth of Greater Cape Town 1850–1913* (Cape Town, 1969), cited in Warren, 'The establishment', 34.
38. *Cape Town Mail*, 4.2.1842.
39. *Cape Town Mail*, 22.7.1848.
40. D.P. Warren, 'Merchants, commissioners and wardmasters; municipal politics in Cape Town, 1840–54' (M.A. thesis, University of Cape Town, 1986), 13; much of my argument is drawn from this source.
41. Quoted in Meltzer, 'The growth of Cape Town commerce', 133 n.2.
42. Quoted in ibid., 133 n.4.
43. Warren, 'Merchants, commissioners and wardmasters', 196.
44. H.C. Botha, *John Fairbairn in South Africa* (Cape Town, 1984), 203.
45. *South African Commercial Advertiser*, 7.7.1849; *Cape Town Mail*, 7.7.1849.
46. Warren, 'Merchants, commissioners and wardmasters', 224; *Cape Town Mail*, 26.4.1853.
47. Meltzer, 'The growth of Cape Town commerce', 137.
48. Quoted in ibid., 147.
49. A 20-1866, *Census of 1865*.
50. C. Saunders, 'Between slavery and freedom: the importation of prize negroes to the Cape in the aftermath of emancipation', *Kronos*, 9 (1984), 36–43; C. Saunders, 'Liberated Africans in Cape Colony in the first half of the nineteenth century', *International Journal of African Historical Studies*, 18 (1985), 223–39.
51. J.C. Chase, *The Cape of Good Hope*, (Cape Town, 1843), 237, cited in L. Rushby, 'The Cape and immigration, 1839–1854' (B.A. Honours thesis, University of Cape Town, 1983), 64.
52. CA, CO 4068-241, Memorials, 16 August 1853.
53. L. Duff Gordon, quoted in C. Swaisland, *Servants and Gentlewomen to the Golden Land: The Emigration of Single Women from Britain to Southern Africa, 1820–1939* (Oxford, 1993), 78.
54. *Standard Encyclopaedia of Southern Africa*, III, 27; E. Rosenthal, *Today's News Today: The Story of the Argus Company* (Johannesburg, 1956), 3.
55. CA, MC 29, 370; M. Naudé, 'The role of the Free Dispensary in public health care in Cape Town, 1860–1910' (B.A. Honours thesis, University of Cape Town, 1987), 45.
56. *Cape Argus*, 24.8.1867.
57. *Cape Argus*, 24.10.1865.
58. *Cape Argus*, 26.10.1865.
59. SAL, MSB 323, Mary Maclear's diary, 29.4.1862.
60. *Cape Argus*, 27.3.1860.
61. *DSAB*, I; A. Brooke, *Robert Gray, First Bishop of Cape Town* (Cape Town, 1947), 37.
62. H.C. Hopkins, *Die Moeder van ons Almal: Geskiedenis van die Gemeente Kaapstad, 1665–1965* (Cape Town, 1965), 235.
63. R.D.T. Cameron, 'The Anglican Church in Cape Town during the episcopacy of Bishop Gray, 1848–1872' (B.A. Honours thesis, University of Cape Town, 1974), 76.
64. A. Davids, *The Mosques of Bo-Kaap: A Social History of Islam at the Cape* (Cape Town, 1980), 50.
65. Duff Gordon, *Letters*, 34–6.
66. Ibid., 37.
67. D.P. Faure, *My Life and Times* (Cape Town, 1907), 11–12.
68. *Cape Argus*, 6.8.1863.
69. *Cape Argus*, 8.8.1863.
70. P.W. Laidler, *A Tavern of the Ocean* (Cape Town, n.d.), 148.
71. Ibid., 12–13.
72. *Cape Argus*, 17.3.1863.
73. *Cape Argus*, 29.3.1862.
74. J. Fletcher, *The Story of Theatre in South Africa: A Guide to its History from 1780–1930* (Cape Town, 1994), 86, 90; P.W. Laidler, *The Annals of the Cape Stage* (Edinburgh, 1926), 60; O. Racster, *Curtain Up!* (Cape Town, 1951), 48–50.
75. Picard, *Grand Parade*, 55.
76. L.G. Green, *I Heard the Old Men Say* (Cape Town, 1964), 149.
77. *Cape Times*, 1.8.1877, 3.8.1877, 3.9.1877.
78. *Cape Argus*, 4.1.1868.
79. *Cape Argus*, 2.1.1866.
80. C. Winberg, '"The Goemaliedjies" of the Cape Muslims: remnants of a slave culture' (unpublished paper, University of Cape Town English Department seminar, 1991), 17.
81. J. Mackinnon, *South African Traits* (Edinburgh, 1887), 114–15.
82. Faure, *My Life and Times*, 12.
83. *Cape Argus*, 3.1.1871, 2.1.1873, 3.1.1874.
84. *Cape Times*, 4.1.1886.
85. *Cape Argus*, 24.12.1859.
86. *Cape Argus*, 26.12.1857.
87. *Cape Argus*, 29.12.1859.
88. J. Murray (ed.), *Mrs Dale's Diary, 1857–1872* (Cape Town, 1966), 60.
89. *Cape Argus*, 2.12.1862.
90. *Cape Times*, 26.6.1876.
91. *Cape Argus*, 17.1.1857, 28.10.1885; *Cape Times*, 23.3.1865.
92. *Lantern*, 3.5.1884.
93. *Lantern*, 28.6.1884.
94. Faure, *My Life and Times*, 12; D. Kennedy, *Kennedy at the Cape* (Edinburgh, 1879), 15.
95. Kennedy, *Kennedy at the Cape*, 13–15.
96. *Cape Argus*, 12.4.1860.
97. S.M. Feast, 'The policeman as thief-taker, streetcleaner and domestic missionary: police and policing in Cape Town in the 1860s and 1870s' (B.A. Honours thesis, University of Cape Town, 1988), 79.
98. R. Holt, *Sport and the British* (Oxford, 1990), 86–134.
99. *Cape Argus*, 26.8.1862, 11.9.1862, 13.9.1862.
100. M. Kuttel, *Quadrilles and Konfyt: The Life and Journal of Hildagonda Duckitt* (Cape Town, 1954), 17.
101. G. Lister, *Reminiscences of Georgina Lister* (Johannesburg, 1960), 50–2.
102. A Lady, *Life at the Cape a Hundred Years Ago* (Cape Town, 1963), 53.
103. J. Murray (ed.), *In Mid-Victorian Cape Town: Letters from Miss Rutherfoord* (Cape Town, 1968), 80.
104. *Evening Express*, 4.5.1880; *Cape Times*, 27.9.1884, 26.7.1887; CA, 1/CT, 20.6.1885, 5.6.1886, 21.6.1886, 28.6.1886.
105. Lister, *Reminiscences*, 11.
106. P. Morgenrood, 'Philip Dominicus Morgenrood: the squire of "Wijnberg's Hoogte,"' *QBSAL*, 37: 3 (March 1983), 288.
107. H. Robinson, 'Beyond the city limits: people and property at Wynberg, 1895–1927' (Ph.D. thesis, University of Cape Town, 1995), 86, 138–41.
108. Murray, *In Mid-Victorian Cape Town*, 47–8.
109. Lady Herschel, *Letters from the Cape, 1834–1838*, ed. B. Warner (Cape Town, 1991), 78.
110. A Lady, *Life at the Cape*, 64.
111. Cited in E. Green, '"Helpmeet and counsellor": the letters of Agnes and John X. Merriman', *QBSAL*, 44: 4 (June 1990), 134.
112. Ibid., 133, 135.
113. Maclear, *Diary*, 12.4.1862.
114. Murray, *Mid-Victorian Cape Town*, 98.
115. E. Bradlow, 'Women at the Cape in the mid-nineteenth century', *South African Historical Journal* [*SAHJ*], 19 (Nov. 1987), 58; a seminal article. See also N. Erlank, 'Letters home: the experience and perceptions of middle class British women at the Cape 1820–1850' (M.A. thesis, University of Cape Town, 1995).
116. Bradlow, 'Women at the Cape', 58.
117. J. Murray (ed.), *Young Mrs Murray*, 10, cited in Bradlow, 'Women at the Cape', 62.
118. Bradlow, 'Women at the Cape', 61.
119. *Cape Times*, 3.8.1900.
120. Duff Gordon, *Letters*, 116, 61.
121. Bradlow, 'Women at the Cape', 62.
122. Lady Herschel, *Letters*, 158.
123. Duff Gordon, *Letters*, 38.
124. A Lady, *Life at the Cape*, 12.
125. J.V. Bickford-Smith, 'The impact of European and Asian immigration on Cape Town: 1880–1910' (unpublished paper, University of Cape Town, 1978), 12–13; CA, PWD 2/8/20.
126. CA, A 515, Maclear–Mann Papers, cited in Bradlow, 'Women at the Cape', 72.
127. Murray, *Mid-Victorian Cape Town*, 19.

CHAPTER 5

1. *Cape Argus*, 18.1.1886.
2. *Cape Times*, 2.2.1886.
3. E. Bradlow, 'The Cape community during the period of responsible government' in B. Pachai (ed.), *South Africa's Indians: The Evolution of a Minority* (Washington D.C., 1979), 135.
4. V. Bickford-Smith, *Ethnic Pride and Racial Prejudice in Victorian Cape Town: Group Identity and Social Practice, 1875-1902* (Cambridge, 1991), 39. Much of my argument on the subject in this chapter is drawn from Bickford-Smith's work.
5. A. Mabin, 'The rise and decline of Port Elizabeth 1850–1900', *International Journal of African Historical Studies*, 19, 2, (1986), 298–9.
6. *Cape Monthly Magazine*, in VRS, NS2, IX, 266–7.
7. D.J.C. Radford, 'The architecture of the Western Cape, 1838–1901: a study of the impact of Victorian aesthetics and technology on South African architecture' (2 vols., Ph.D. thesis, University of the Witwatersrand, 1979), I, 255–6.
8. P. Buirski, 'An analysis of the changing composition of Adderley Street, Cape Town, between 1867 and 1885', *Studies in the History of Cape Town*, 3 (1984), 18–29.
9. L. Bean and E.B. van Heyningen, *The Letters of Jane Elizabeth Waterston 1866–1905* (Cape Town, 1903), 187.
10. R.S. Soloway, *Demography and Degeneration. Eugenics and the Declining Birthrate in Twentieth-Century Britain* (Chapel Hill, 1990), 13.
11. G. Stedman Jones, *Outcast London* (Harmondsworth, 1976), 309.
12. J. Mackinnon, *South African Traits* (Edinburgh, 1887), 107.
13. P. Lewsen (ed.), *Selections from the Correspondence of John X. Merriman 1890–1898* (Cape Town, 1963), II, 54.
14. Ibid., 49.
15. *Ons Land*, 4.6.1903.
16. A. Mayne, *Representing the Slum: Popular Journalism in a Late Nineteenth Century City* (Melbourne, 1990), 6.
17. *Cape Argus*, 8.1.1876.
18. *Cape Times*, 11.3.1881.
19. *Cape Times*, 16.5.1878, 22.5.1878, 12.6.1878.
20. *Lantern*, 3.9.1881.
21. *Cape Times*, 20.7.1881.
22. *Cape Times*, 7.12.1889.
23. *Cape Argus*, cited in C. Knox, *Victorian Life at the Cape 1870–1900* (Cape Town, 1992), 86.
24. *Lantern*, 16.2.1884.
25. *Spectator*, 22.11.1902.
26. *Lantern*, 13.9.1879.
27. E.B. van Heyningen, 'Public health and society in Cape Town, 1880–1910' (Ph.D. thesis, University of Cape Town, 1989), 239.
28. Ibid., 108.
29. Ibid., 111; *Lantern*, 31.7.1880, 2.
30. *Cape Argus*, 5.5.1880.
31. V. Bickford-Smith, 'Commerce, class and ethnicity in Cape Town, 1875–1902', (Ph.D. thesis, University of Cambridge, 1989), 120; A13-1881, 68.
32. A 8-1897, 4–5; Bickford-Smith, 'Commerce', 285.
33. *Cape Argus*, 15.8.1882.
34. G39-1893, 24.
35. *Lantern*, 14.4.1883.
36. G.M. Fredrickson, *White Supremacy* (New York, 1981), 133.
37. *Cape Argus*, 8.1.1876.
38. *Cape Times*, 26.3.1901.
39. CA, GH 35/40.
40. N.G. Henshilwood, *A Cape Childhood* (Cape Town, 1972), 31.
41. *Lantern*, 14.4.1883, 8.9.1883.
42. *SA News*, 9.9.1903.
43. *Cowley Evangelist* (1893), 107.
44. H. Deacon, 'Madness, race and moral treatment: Robben Island Lunatic Asylum, Cape Colony, 1846–1890', *History of Psychiatry*, 7 (1996), 295.
45. *Cape Argus*, 21.2.1891.
46. *Cape Times*, 9.9.1882.
47. P. Bigelow, *White Man's Africa* (from *Harper's Magazine*, c. 1897).
48. *Cape Times*, 9.1.1884.
49. *Cape Times*, 19.11.1889.
50. *Cape Times*, 10.3.1904.
51. *SA News*, 5.1.1906.
52. *Cape Times*, 24.5.1904.
53. *Cape Times*, 9.5.1881.
54. *Lantern*, 10.3.1883.
55. *Cape Times*, 29.10.1883, 24.5.1883.
56. *Cape Times*, 16.8.1892.
57. *Cape Argus*, 11.6.1868.
58. E.B. van Heyningen, 'Prostitution and the Contagious Diseases Acts: the social evil in the Cape Colony, 1868–1902', *Studies*, 5 (1984), 79–123.
59. Ibid., 108.
60. *Cape Times*, 4.7.1895.
61. *Cape Argus*, 3.1.1894.
62. *South African Native Affairs Commission*, II, 191.
63. *Cowley Evangelist* (1907), 135–8.
64. *Cape Argus*, 24.2.1891; *Cape Times*, 6.11.1897.
65. *Cape Argus*, 3.1.1885; *Cape Times*, 3.1.1887.
66. C.G. Botha, *History of the Civil Servce Club 1858–1938* (Cape Town, 1939), 27.
67. *Cape Times*, 3.1.1888.
68. *Cape Argus*, 5.1.1875.
69. G39-1893, *Select Committee Report on Labour*, 120.
70. *Cape Argus*, 3.4.1897.
71. *Cowley Evangelist*, (August 1899), 'The Malays of Cape Town'.
72. *Lantern*, 23.9.1882.
73. Bickford-Smith, *Ethnic Pride*, 223 n.44.
74. *Cape Times*, 1.8.1882.
75. Louis Cohen, *Reminiscences of Kimberley* (London, 1911), 13–14.
76. *Cape Argus*, 20.11.1862, 23.11.1865.
77. *Cape Times*, 3.1.1888; *Cape Argus*, 22.6.1887.
78. H. Deacon, 'A history of the Breakwater Prison from 1859 to 1905' (B.A. Honours thesis, University of Cape Town, 1989); L. Chisholm, 'The pedagogy of Porter: the origins of the reformatory in the Cape Colony, 1882–1910', *Journal of African History*, 27: 3 (1986), 481–95.
79. P. van der Spuy, 'Women and crime: the involvement of women in violent crime as processed by the institutions of justice in Cape Town 1860–1879' (B.A. Honours thesis, University of Cape Town, 1988); *Cape Times*, 8.12.1876, 25.1.1877; *Excalibur*, 28.2.1890; *Cape Argus*, 26.9.1892.
80. *Cape Argus*, 4.3.1893; CA, 1/CT 6/177, 28.11.1884; *Cape Times*, 23.7.1898.
81. *Cowley Evangelist* (Nov. 1893), 90; *South African Native Affairs Commission* [SANAC], II, 110; CA, CHB 266, Chief Inspector to General Manager TBHB, 25.7.1904.
82. A32-1899; A27-1904; *SA News*, 12.9.1901, 28.9.1904, 26.12.1904; *Cape Argus*, 3.1.1863, 14.12.1894, 8.5.1895; 27.6.1895, 14.6.1897; *Cape Times*, 3.11.1896, 3.3.1897, 8.3.1897, 23.9.1897, 27.9.1897, 13.1.1898, 29.1.1898, 4.10.1897, 6.10.1897, 2.12.1897, 29.1.1898, 7.9.1897, 6.1.1898, 23.4.1898, 29.10.1897, 2.6.1908.
83. *Cape Times*, 28.12.1896, 24.11.1897, 10.9.1906.
84. *Lantern*, 10.1.1880.
85. *Cape Times*, 18.10.1882; see also *Cape Times*, 10.10.1879.
86. *Cape Argus*, 30.8.1883.
87. *Cape Argus*, 11.7.1887.
88. *Cape Argus*, 21.12.1892.
89. *Cape Times*, 27.1.1881.
90. *Cape Town Guide for 1897* (Cape Town, 1897).
91. *The Cape Argus Centenary Supplement*, (Cape Town, 1957), 21.
92. Cited in Howkins, 'The discovery of rural England', 67–8.
93. *South African Church Magazine and Ecclesiastical Review*, cited in Radford, 'The architecture of the Western Cape', 40.
94. J. Murray, *In Mid-Victorian Cape Town: Letters from Miss Rutherfoord* (Cape Town, 1968), 18.
95. J. McIntyre, *White Stoep on the Highway. Rustenburg School for Girls: A History 1894–1994* (Cape Town 1994), 27.
96. Henshilwood, *Cape Childhood*, 68–9.
97. M. Cairns, *Park Road Estate: Rondebosch. Looking Back* (Rondebosch, 1992).
98. B. Mackenzie, *Salt River Doctor* (Cape Town, 1981), 35.
99. S. O'Sullivan, 'Workers with a difference: life and labour in the Salt River workshops, 1900–1935' (B.A. Honours thesis, University of Cape Town, 1984), 15.
100. *Cape Argus*, 10.6.1982.
101. O'Sullivan, 'Workers with a difference', 55.
102. Mackenzie, *Salt River Doctor*, 54.
103. O'Sullivan, 'Workers with a difference', 55–6.
104. Ibid., 55, 46.
105. J. Young, 'A town in the suburbs: a history of Observatory: 1881–1913' (B.A. Honours thesis, University of Cape Town, 1994), 4–15.
106. *Argus Christmas Annual*, 1904, cited in Young, 'A town in the suburbs', 5–7.
107. Young, 'A town in the suburbs', 6–12.
108. Ibid., 6–15; *Cape Times Weekly*, 9.2.1898.

Index

A

Abdul Jemaalee 187, 189
Adamastor 12
Africa Club 143
African people *see* ethnic identities: African
Afrikaner nationalism 157, 243
Afrikaner people *see* ethnic identities: Afrikaner
agriculture 16, 38, 39, 45–8, 90, 200, 213; early struggles 19–20, 29; links between town and country 67–8; Khoi 21; wool 159–60
Alexander, Hannah *see* Marshall, Annie
Alexander, Leon 236
Allemann, Rudolf 59
Almeida, Francisco de 13–14
Amiens, Treaty of 86
Amsterdam 19, 27, 36
Amsterdam Battery *see* Table Bay: batteries
Andrews, Thomas 166
Angela of Bengal 64–5
Angola 27, 32
Anti-Convict Association *see* politics
Appolonia van der Caab 65
apprenticeship 107–8
Arabic *see* language
architecture and building 48–9, 112–13, 116–17, 168–70, 184, 186, 187, 214–16, 251, 260; Arts and Crafts movement 253; Macfarlane iron foundry 214–15; plastering 248
architects: Baker, Herbert 253, 260, 262; Freeman, Charles 214–15, 217; Greaves, Harry 217; Inglesby, T.J.C. 169, 214; Lewcock, Ronald 184; Penketh, P. 170; Ransome, G. 216; Thomson, Alexander 'Greek' 116; *see also* Parker, John
Arderne family 201, 253
Arderne, Henry Mathew 201
Arderne, Ralph Henry 129, 201, 225
army *see* military
art 30, 36, 156, 167, 175; panoramas of Cape Town 42, 46–7, 87, 114–15
artists: Angas, George French 77, 136; Anreith, Anton 87; Baines, Thomas 125, 165, 172; Bell, Charles Davidson 65, 130, 149, 156, 163, 188–9, 192, 204; Bowler, Thomas 96, 116, 152, 156, 171, 175, 184–5, 189, 197; Cloete, Catherine 117; Comfield, John 75; Davis, Samuel 44, 48; De Meillon, H.C. 53, 63, 103, 116, 131, 138; Duff, George 108, 147; Egersdorfer, H.H. 217; F.B. 114–15; Frederici, J.C. 86; Gordon, Robert Jacob 46; Herbert, Thomas 22; Huntley, W. 128; I'Ons, F.T. 106; Kolb, P. 45; Langschmidt, W.H.F. 116, 167; Leeuwenberg, Jürgen 53; Malan, Solomon Caesar 101; Michell, Charles Cornwallis 91, 135; Mundy, Peter 15; Poortermans, J.C. 116, 163, 173; Rach, Johannes 42, 43, 45, 49, 54, 61, 66, 67, 73, 78; Regnault, Pieter 60; Ritter, W. 189; Sabatier, Leon 113; Schonegevel, Johan 90; Schouten, Wouter 30; Schumacher, Johannes 46; Sellar, John 12, 17, 25; Stade, E.V. 38; Trench, P.C. 163; Van Ryne, Johannes 36; W.R.H. 97; *see also* Barnard, Lady Anne; D'Oyly, Sir Charles; Thompson, George
Arthur, Mary 186
Atlantic Ocean 92, 98

Australia 215, 218
Autshumato 14, 21, 23

B

Bailey, Dr Samuel 122, 148, 181
balls *see* dancing
bandieten 50, 61, 64, 65, 77, 109–10
banks and banking *see* financial institutions
Banks, Joseph 158
Bantam (Indonesia) 12, 14, 15
Banten, Sultanate of 76
Barbara, Johanna 202
Barbier, Estienne 65–6
Barkat van Timor 63
Barker, Mrs S. (retailer) 90
Barkly, Sir Henry 213
Barnard, Lady Anne: as an artist 48, 62, 76, 81, 87, 92, 112, 145; comments on Cape society 93, 96, 117, 139, 143–4, 144, 146
Barracks (Great) 81, 92
Barrow, John 69, 105, 143
Barry, Dr James 122
Barry, Joseph 160
bars, canteens, 'hotels', public houses, shebeens, smuggling houses, taphouses and taverns 28, 54, 58, 78–9, 195, 257; economics of 146–7; Belvedere Hotel 257; Het Blaauwe Anker 58; De Blaauwe Haan 54; British Oak 257; Goodwin Hotel 257; De Goude Leeuw 58; Junction Hotel 257; 't Laatste Stuivertje 58; London Tap 195; Schotse Tempel 58, 68; Thatched Tavern 86, 171; West of England pub 180; Het Witte Hart 58; *see also* brewing; drink and drugs
Basson family 69
Batavia 19, 27, 29, 36, 61, 64, 65, 98; comparisons with 18, 26, 39, 48, 49, 56, 70, 75
Batavian government 87–8, 144
batteries *see* Table Bay: batteries
Beard, Henry 201
Beard, Joanna (*née* Arderne) 201
Beaufort West 213, 252
Beaulieu, Augustin de 12
Beaumarchais, P.A.C. de 81
Bell, Colonel John 130
Bellville 212
Belmont (Rondebosch) 253
Bengal 97
Bergh Valley 24
Bernard, Lucy 245
Bible and Tract Society 130
Bird, Christopher 123
Bird, William Wilberforce 97, 143, 145, 148
Bishop's Court 186, 195
Blake, Colonel 128
Bleby, Miss 254–5
Bleek, Dr Wilhelm 156
Blouberg 46, 212; Battle of 87
Blount, Edward 90, 112, 118, 128
Bo-Kaap 187, 238, 249–50; origins of 118–19, 127
Boerij, Jacob 52
Bogaert, Abraham 80
Boland 38, 99
Boniface, Charles Etienne 133, 144, 157, 158
Boom, Annetje 28

Boom, Hendrik 18
Boomplaats, Battle of 191
Booth, General William 217–18, 234
Borradailes, Thompson & Pillans 102
Botanic Gardens *see* Gardens
Bourbon *see* Réunion
Bourke, Elizabeth, Lady 140
Brand family 173
Brand, Christoffel Joseph 133, 158–9, 186–7, 192, 206
Brand, President J.H. 192
Brazil 27
Breede River 160
brewing industry 57; South African Breweries 210, 253
Brill, Francina 200
Brink, Melt 192
Brink, P.M. 158
British people *see* ethnic identities: British
Brits family 70
Bugis people *see* ethnic identities: Bugis
Bull, Father 239
Burdett-Coutts, Angela 178
Burgher Council and Senate *see* Cape Town municipality
Burgher House *see* Town House
Burns, Abdol 196, 210, 243

C

Cabo *see* Cape Town
caffers 61, 63, 77, 137
Calcutta 97
Caledon, Earl of 124
Cameron, James 129
Camoens, Luis de 12
Camps Bay 162, 222
Canigou (Rondebosch) 204
canteens *see* bars etc.
Cape Almanac 179, 202
Cape Flats 16, 25, 138, 162, 212; hunting on 140–1
Cape Hanglip 63
Cape of Good Hope 13, 15, 17, 200; Colony 87
Cape of Good Hope Gas Light Company 172
Cape of Good Hope Philanthropic Society 107
Cape of Good Hope Telegraph Company 162
Cape of Good Hope Trade Society 101, 106
Cape of Storms *see* Cape of Good Hope
Cape Town: administration 70–1; as a port 38; as gateway to South Africa 252; as a health resort 96–7; British annexation 87–8; civic gospel 226; as a commercial centre 45, 113, 168; coexistence of old and new 113; Dutch claims to 24, 36; depictions of 36, 38, 39, 42–3, 46–7, 66, 97, 112–13; emergence of urban community 27–9, 36, 39, 56, 71, 82; Great Fire 112; as a frontier, 43; growth 36–9, 112–22, 212–13, 215; images 12–13, 15, 19, 25, 30, 36, 142–3, 156, 158, 167, 168; nomenclature 36; origins of settlement 12–24; physical structure 38–43; precolonial settlement 16; public buildings 40–2, 45; Riebeeckstad 88; reform of 44–5, 134, 211, 218, 220–1, 223–6, 233–5; settlement 17–19, 29; social order 72–3, 152–3, 220–1, 238, 242; vulnerability of early settlement 17–20, 32–3; water supply 40, 45, 49, 54, 62, 120, 224, 226

276 INDEX

Cape Town municipality; Burgher Council and Senate 70–1, 87–8, 90, 99, 101, 122, 133; commissioners 129, 172, 173, 174; corruption 91, 172, 174; depictions of 224, 225; elections 221, 225; franchise 172, 221, 226; mayors 169; municipal government 171–7, 222; Ordinance of 1840 171–2, 173; Act of 1867 172; municipal public works and services 172, 173, 214, 226; public meetings 172, 175, 176; Raad der Gemeente 88; rates 174; reform 179–80, 225–6; suspension of government 88; wardmasters 71, 94, 171, 172, 173–4, 176

Cape Town and Suburban Saturday Half-Holiday Association 247

Cape Town Railway and Dock Co. 160, 162

Capel Sluit 250

carnivals and festivals 77, 78, 152, 190; 1 December (Emancipation Day) 106, 108, 195; Christmas 195; Coon Carnival 194, 258; Eid 126; Guy Fawkes 194; laying of foundation stone of Houses of Parliament 217; New Year's Eve/Day 77, 106, 193, 194, 210, 241; Prophet's birthday 124, 126, 127; Queen's Birthday 193; Ramadan 124, 126; Tweede Nuwejaar 193, 194, 241; Whitsun 195; *see also* music and song

Cartwright, J.D. 240

Castle 39–43, 70, 72, 77, 86, 87, 88, 93, 108, 113, 119, 152, 184, 195, 224; building of 37–8, 66; depictions of 18, 36, 38, 41, 114; life in 78; social events at 139; Van Riebeeck's fort 17, 29

Catharina of Bengal 69

Celebes 15, 61

cemeteries 41, 181, 210, 211; Chinese 46, 76–7; Muslim (including Tana Baru) 126, 210, 211; riots 210–11, 242

census and population 112, 213, 222; Dutch period 26, 38, 49–51, 55, 56; 1731 census 50; British period 89, 93, 212; 1865 census 153, 177–8; 1875 census 153; 1891 census 222

Ceylon 39, 49, 87, 98, 100

Chamber of Commerce 247

Changuion, Dr Antoine 154, 157–8, 175

charity *see* poverty: relief of; women: philanthropy

Chavonnes Battery *see* Table Bay: batteries

Children's Friend Society 110

Chinese 18, 26, 54, 56, 65–6; hostility to 218; *see also* ethnic identities: Chinese

Christie, John 201

Christie, Lydia (*née* Arderne) 201

churches 123–4, 262; church bazaars 262; *Anglican* 180, 184–5; St George's Cathedral 116, 123, 125, 180, 184–5, 217; St Mark's mission 186, 251; St Michael's (Observatory) 262; St Paul's (Bree St) 178, 180; St Paul's (Rondebosch) 253; St Saviour's (Claremont) 185; St Thomas's (Rondebosch) 253; *Catholic* 75, 115, 120, 123, 178; Harrington St chapel 123; St Mary's Cathedral 123; St Michael's (Rondebosch) 169; *Congregational* 122, 124, 201, 262; Union Chapel 124, 129, 130, 201; *Dutch Reformed* 74, 75–6, 123, 153, 159, 167, 184, 186–7, 206; Groote Kerk 36, 43–4, 75, 133, 186, 217; Nieuwe Kerk (Bree St) 186; Ou Kerk (Hanover St) 186, 251; St Stephen's 121, 145, 184; *Lutheran* 43, 46, 68, 75, 76, 115, 123, 200; *Methodist*; Central Methodist Church 214, 215; *Moravian* 212; *Presbyterian* 123; St Andrew's 116, 123; *Salvation Army* 217, 233–4, 236, 251, 258; *see also* missions and mission work; religion

City Tramways Company *see* Tramways Company

Claremont 187, 201, 213, 253, 255, 256, 259; municipality 222

Claasz, Armosyn 70

class 69, 161, 173–4, 184, 190, 195, 221, 239; class distinctions 43, 48, 72–3, 96, 112, 139–40, 145, 191, 205, 234; class prejudice 218; elite 67–8, 128, 139–40, 152; inculcation of class attitudes 254; lower middle class 173, 213, 218, 259–62; middle classes 121, 122, 128–35, 152, 173–4, 201, 256; middle class fear of working classes 217–18; working classes 93, 109, 152, 213; education 135; rejection of working-class status 259; social mobility 56, 69, 153, 173; *see also* respectability

climate 19; earthquakes 76; floods 224; southeaster 18, 96–7, 223

Cloete, Bonnie 199

Cloete, Hendrik 62

Cloete, Hon. Henry 158

Cloete, Josias 157

Cloppenburg, Abraham 63

Clos, Christian 52

clubs (social) 77–8, 130, 143, 239; City Club 239; Civil Service Club 239; Concordia Club 143; Harmony Club 143; Owl Club 239

Cochoqua *see* Khoi people

Colenso, Bishop J.W. 185

Cole, Mr (baker) 241–2, 244

Cole, Sir Lowry 140

Collison, Francis 99

Collison, John 99

Collison, Starkey & Co. 99

Colombo 56, 61

Colonial Medical Committee 122, 223

Colonial Office (British) 165

Colonial Office (Cape) 155, 173, 234; reorganisation 223

Combrink, W.G. 193

Combrinck & Co. *see* Imperial Cold Storage

commemorative events 30, 88; centenary of settlement 36, 38; Queen's Diamond Jubilee (1897) 152, 263; Queen's Golden Jubilee (1887) 152, 191, 239, 244, 262; death of William IV 149; marriage of Prince Albert (15 May 1863) 152–3, 190; Queen Victoria's accession to the throne 149; visit of Prince Alfred (1860) 152, 155, 166, 189

Commercial Exchange 99, 100–1, 113, 129, 130, 131, 132, 144, 149, 154, 184, 193

Committee for the Encouragement of Juvenile Emigration 122

Committee of the High Court 71

communications 161–8, 213, 214; omnibus 154, 162, 163; post 161, 163, 164; railways 162–3, 166, 197, 213, 241, 252; roads 39, 161–2; telegraph 162; trams 214; wagon 45; *see also* ships and shipping

Constantia 77, 157, 200

convicts *see* prisons and prisoners

Coode, John 166

Coons *see* Carnival troupes

Cornelissen, Leendert 30

Council of Justice 29, 52, 70, 72, 91, 92

Council of Policy 29, 30, 32, 56, 58, 71, 72, 75

Cowie, Mary 178, 183

Craig, Major-General James 86

crime and punishment 30, 32–3, 52, 62, 137, 178, 183–4; moral panic 136; reform 136–7; bigamy 55; gambling 79, 147; infanticide 245; pub brawls 36, 54–5, 79, 81; murder 63, 80; punishment 72–3, 137–9, 183; theft 76, 137

Cruywagen, Adriaan 91

culture 71–80; British 117, 129, 143, 153–6, 159, 190, 197, 201, 255–6, 257–8; colonial 129; Dutch 30, 71–3, 141–2, 156–9; French 81; 'Malay' 189, 192, 193–4, 207, 249–50; 'Malay magic' 128; material 78, 83, 113, 117, 118, 200; middle-class 129, 128–36; popular 30, 36, 75, 78–9, 146–9, 190–5; working-class 190, 195, 198, 257–8

Customs House 112, 138, 262

Cutting, William 162, 163

D

Dale, Mrs Langham 195, 205

dancing 135, 139, 148–9, 195, 199, 243; depictions of 149, 240, 244; *hloma* 246; rainbow balls 148, 195–6, 243

Danielssen, Jan 32

Darnell, Bryan H. 179

Darwin, Charles 155, 217

Davis, Joseph 236

Davis, Lizzie 236

De Jager, J.C. 221

De Jong (naval officer) 83, 141

De Kock, Servaas 158

De la Fontaine, Jan 50

De Lima, J.S. 133, 144, 145, 157, 158, 159; almanacs 159

De Lorentz, Baron Charles 137, 173

De Meuron, Captain 82

De Mist, Commissioner J.A. 81, 88, 144

De Roubaix, P.E. 188

De Smidt family 200

De Smidt, Abraham 180

De Smidt, Henry 222

De Theiss, Marguerite 236

De Villet, Charles 119

De Villiers, Dinah 245

De Vyf, Abraham 65

De Waal, D.C. 226, 243

demography *see* census and population

Denyssen, Daniël 133

Descartes, René 82

Devil's Peak 12, 39, 62, 199

Diderot, Denis 74

Die-si-en (Chinese exile) 65

Diep River 117, 200

Dinah (cook) 205

District One (waterfront) 219, 242, 249

District Six 129, 158, 184, 186, 212, 250–1; elections in 221; residents of 107; origins of 119, 170, 172; living conditions 224, 225

Divisional Council 222

Dixon, Dr 236

Dollie, Hadji Mohamet 193

D'Oyly, Sir Charles 86, 90, 93, 94, 95, 97, 99, 103, 109, 110, 111, 113, 118, 119, 120, 123, 140, 141, 146, 148; *Tom Raw, the Griffin* 142
Drakenstein 67
dress 253; as a mark of social status 146, 202; Muslim 127, 128, 187, 189, 193, 242
Driekoppen *see* Mowbray
drink and drugs 146–8; culture of drink 93, 147–8, 181, 195
drosters see slaves and slavery
drugs *see* drink and drugs
Du Toit, Charlotte 236
Duminy, François 82
Dundas, Admiral Sir John 156
Dundas, Major-General F. (governor) 112, 140
Durban Rd 212, 241; *see also* Bellville; Durbanville
Dutch East India Company *see* VOC
Dutch people *see* ethnic identities: Dutch
Dutch West India Company 20, 27

E

Early Closing Association 247
earthquakes *see* climate
East Africa 82
East London 165
East India Company 12, 14, 96, 97, 102, 112
East Indies 36, 59, 61, 63; importations from 60, 148; links with 26
Eastern Province 99, 165, 166, 171, 177
Eayrs, James 243
Ebden family 253
Ebden, Dr H.A. 223
Ebden, John Bardwell 99, 100, 102
economy 39, 67–9, 98–102, 158, 159–69, 213–14; auctions 78, 100, 113; book trade 131, 154; boom 83, 102; coastal trade 98, 160; commerce and trade 20, 36, 54, 159–70; depression 99–100, 182; disparities of wealth and poverty 67–8, 120, 173; emergence of wage labour 104, 107, 108–9; export trade 100; fruit industry 214; inflation 83, 93; informal trading 171; markets 113, 115, 121, 163; mercantile community 83, 99–102, 128–9, 216, 243; military costs 81–21, 61, 161; mineral revolution 211; money 71; monopolies, removal of 133; pre-industrial economy 96, 179; slave compensation money 102, 107, 117, 158, 174; prices 59; retail trade 58–9, 60, 90, 100, 169, 212; standards of living 115, 121, 181, 261–2; wages and salaries 122, 179, 205, 246–7, 261–2; wine trade 99, 101, 146–7; wool trade 102, 160; *see also* brewing industry; industrialisation; industries
education 74–5, 134–6, 153, 154, 185–6, 238, 253–6; literacy 74, 126, 131, 153–4, 190–1, 195, 203, 257–8; Muslim 119, 125, 126, 135, 136, 189; mission schools 135–6, 189, 195, 239; private tutors 58, 135; Bloemhof High School (Stellenbosch) 255; Catholic Academy 123; Classical and Commercial Academy 134; Diocesan College 185, 197, 253–4, 256; Gertrude Hull's finishing school 254; Good Hope Seminary 239; Huguenot College (Wellington) 255; Mrs Swaving's French Academy 135; Mount Holyoke (USA) 255; Rondebosch Boys' High School 254; Rondebosch Primary School 253; Rustenburg Girls' High School 239, 254–5; St Cyprian's 185; St Cyprian's (Ndabeni) 239; School of Industry 136; South African College 129, 131, 132, 134–5, 154, 169; Tot Nut van 't Algemeen Society School 133, 134; Zonnebloem College 185–6, 198, 237, 239, 246
Eerste River 162
Effendi, Abu Bakr 187, 188–9
Effendi, Achmat 221
Eliza (Transkei visitor) 152
Elgin 106
Elphinstone, Admiral Keith 86
Elsenburg (Stellenbosch) 67
English, Mr 193
English East India Company *see* East India Company
English Fund for Promoting Female Emigration 178
English people *see* ethnic identities: English
The Enlightenment 82, 129, 132, 144
environment: changes to 25, 39
ethnicity and identity 184–9, 190, 191, 195, 242–4, 248; Dutch–English intermarriage 93, 99, 122, 133; Dutch–English tension 87, 133, 144, 177; ethnic diversity 61, 86, 89–96, 177, 202, 212–13, 258; middle class 128–36, 149, 169, 217, 225; stereotypes 67, 128, 137, 142, 147–8, 156, 217–18, 220, 243, 245, 248
ethnic identities: African 61, 195, 213; Afrikaner 158, 187, 225; British 132, 149, 178, 213, 217–18, 225, 253; Bugis 61; Chinese 76, 159; Dutch 88, 89–91, 128, 132–3, 156–9, 177, 186–7, 192, 211, 243; English 96, 213, 218; French 195; German 51, 76, 89, 213; Indian 61, 93, 212; Indonesian 61; Irish 93/96, 111, 112, 123, 137, 178, 191, 205; Jews 212, 258; Khoi 23; Malagasy 61; 'Malay' 63, 127–8, 137, 158, 191, 242; Mosbiekers 178, 192; Muslim 186, 189, 211, 242–3; St Helenans 178; San 137; Scots 96, 99, 123, 153, 179; slave and free black 61, 107, 137; South African 174–5, 243; West African 93
eugenic beliefs 217, 253
Europe, Northern, immigrants from 26
Eva *see* Krotoa

F

Fairbairn, Eliza (*née* Philip) 130
Fairbairn, John 97, 101, 106, 110, 129, 130, 137, 138, 154, 158, 159, 171, 174–7, 190; unpopularity 133; values 132, 134, 148
False Bay 25, 46, 53, 63, 81, 86, 92; as a holiday destination 241, 251–2
family life 50
Faure (village) 77
Faure, Abraham 133
Faure, D.P. 190, 194
Fawcett, John 133
Feldhausen (Claremont) 202
Fernwood (Newlands) 257
festivals *see* carnivals and festivals; *see also* commemorative events
financial institutions 83, 99, 102, 159, 160, 213, 216; legislation 160; Board of Executors 102, 158; Cape of Good Hope Bank 100, 102, 159; Cape of Good Hope Savings Bank 129; Colonial Bank 216; Equitable Fire Assurance Company 129, 160; General Estate and Orphan Chamber 169; Good Hope Fire and Life Assurance Society 122; London and South African Bank 160; Old Mutual 154, 160, 169, 181; De Protecteur Fire and Life Assurance Company 158, 160; South African Bank 158; South African Fire Insurance 169; Standard Bank 169, 213, 214, 215, 216; *see also* Commercial Exchange
The Firs (Claremont) 201
Fish Hoek 16
Fitzherbert, Humphrey 12
floods *see* climate
Foreshore 16
Fort *see* Castle
Fort Knokke 46, 109, 198
Francken, Jacob 39
Frans van Bengal 127
Fraserdale Estate (Rondebosch) 256
free blacks 50–1, 64–5, 69, 89, 105, 107, 118, 202; occupations 54, 94–5, 106–7, 111; slave ownership 107
free burghers 20–1, 23, 24, 26, 28, 29, 41, 50–1, 55–8, 68
Free Dispensary 180–1, 223
Freemasons 144, 168, 217, 238; De Goede Hoop Lodge 144, 177, 206; Hope Lodge 144
French people *see* ethnic identities: French
Frijkenius, Commissioner S.H. 83
Friday (domestic servant) 199
friendly societies 181, 206, 238, 248; St Andrew's Friendly Society 121; St Patrick's Society 121
frontier war (1846), 187, 188–9
Fuller, Rev. Thomas 179, 181, 248
funerals 72, 206–7

G

Gadney, W.G. 129
gardening 261–2
Gardens 116, 129, 131, 134, 146, 152, 170; VOC garden 17–19, 20, 40, 44, 45, 103; attempt to close 145
Gardens (suburb) 214
Garlick, John 221, 226
Garrick, David 144
Gcaleka 139
Geens, Barbetjie 57
Genadendal 212
gender 50, 53, 55, 129–30, 156, 184, 190, 220, 239; education 135, 254; attitudes to women 161, 234–5; demography 55, 93, 213; education 135, 254; leisure 77–8, 195, 198–200; masculinity 130, 196–8, 237–8, 239, 257; in the theatre 144; position of women in society 96; stereotypes of women 220; women's occupations 28, 59, 90, 94–5, 96, 100, 130, 178, 186, 199–200, 202, 245–6, 254; women disguised as men 26, 55
Genootschap van Kunsten en Wetenschappen 133
Die Genootskap van Regte Afrikaners 193
German people *see* ethnic identities: German
Gerrit (slave) 104
Glynn, J.W. 170, 180, 195
Gonnema 28

278 INDEX

Gorachoqua *see* Khoi people
Gordon, John 57
Gordon, General Charles 217, 262
Gordon, Lucie, Lady Duff 164, 168, 178, 187, 189, 205
Gorinhaiqua *see* Khoi people
Government House 106, 131, 140, 152
Graaff, D.P. 226, 243
Graham, Mrs (shopkeeper) 169
Grahamstown 92, 139, 162
Gray, Bishop Robert 176, 180, 184–5
Gray, Sophia 185
Green Point 92, 115, 118, 122, 162, 199, 246; as a military encampment 210; depictions of 119; race-course 141, 241; and Sea Point municipality 222
Green Point Common 191, 196, 239
Greig, George 131, 132
Gregory, Dr Alfred John 223
Grey, Sir George 166, 169, 181, 183, 186
Griffith, Bishop Patrick Raymund 123
Groot Constantia 62
Groote Schuur 200, 240
Guinea (Africa) 27

H

Haafner, Jacob 63
Hadji Mattarm 77
Hadji Sulaiman Shah Mohammed 77
Hanbury, Edward 100
harbour *see* Table Bay
Harfield Cottage 201
Harington, Captain 97, 99
Harington House 97
Harry *see* Autshumato
Hartog, Abraham 55
Haupt, Mr (slave owner) 104
health and sanitation 19, 113, 119–20, 179–81, 211, 223–6; 1867 disease 44, 121, 139; epidemics 181; 'lunacy' and 'lunatics' 60–1; medical culture 211, 223; mortality rates 26, 51, 56, 121, 181, 226; Muslim medicine 189; smallpox 56, 66, 121, 139, 211, 243; Vaccine Institution 122
Hendricks, Omaar 106
Henshilwood, Norah 255–6
Heren XVII *see* VOC directors
Herman, Dr C.L. 223
Herschel, Sir John 132, 143
Herschel, Margaret Lady 96, 111, 205
Herschel (Claremont) 201, 202
Hesse, Elias 59
Hiddingh family 158
Higgs, Mr 180
Hill, Colonel 152
The Hill (Claremont) 201, 253
Hodgson, Janet 186
Hofmeyr family 158
Hofmeyr, J.C. 243
Hofmeyr, J.H. 158
Hofmeyr, J.H. ('Onze Jan') 243
holidays *see* carnivals and festivals; commemorative events
Hondeklip 165
Hooper, James 105
hospitals 60–1; Company hospital 29, 44, 50, 81, 92; Lock Hospital 236; Merchant Seamen's Hospital 122; New Somerset Hospital 181, 224; (Old) Somerset Hospital 92, 122, 139, 148; *see also* Robben Island
hotels and boarding houses 57–8, 90, 96, 129, 178; George Hotel (Wynberg) 191; St George's Hotel 106; Queen's Hotel (Dock Rd) 106, 234–5; Queen's Hotel (Sea Point) 169, 252; Rathfelder's Inn 191, 200, 205
Hottentots *see* Khoi people
Hottentots Holland mountains 25, 38, 138, 161
houses and housing 260 ; domestic interiors 60, 113, 118, 255, 260; slums 120, 219; names of 255, 257, 262; representation of slums 179–80; spatial organisation of 48–9, 83, 117, 255
Hout Bay 16, 24, 36, 81
Hudson, Samuel 96, 112, 113, 128, 141

I

identity *see* ethnicity and identity
Île de France *see* Mauritius
Imhoff Battery *see* Table Bay: batteries
immigration and migration 36, 93/96, 111, 165, 177–8, 212–13; colonial emigration as a means of relieving metropolitan poverty 218; Emigrant Depot 178; hostility to 217, 218; rural to urban migration 108; places of residence 251; sources of 51–2, 93; women 178, 218
imperialism 217–18, 254, 263
indentured servants 110
Indian Mutiny (1857) 161
Indian Ocean 52, 61, 92, 98
Indian people *see* ethnic identities: Indian
'Indians' 96–7/9, 117, 131, 140–1, 163, 185, 252
Indonesian people *see* ethnic identities: Indonesian
industrialisation 164, 210, 246, 257–9; Afrikaners 259; factory production 246–7
industries: Hare's brickfield 257; Imperial Cold Storage 226; Nectar Tea factory 257; Thesen's timber yard 257
insurance companies *see* financial institutions
Irish people *see* ethnic identities: Irish
Irish Town 96, 111, 123

J

Jacobs, Katie 107
Jacqmin, Antionette 236
Jacqmin, Julienne 236
Jakarta *see* Batavia
James I (king) 12
Jameson Raid 221
Jan van Bougies 107, 127, 202
January (slave) 126
January van Tutocorijn 62
Jansz, Lucas of Groningen 33
Jarvis, H.C. 174, 176
Java 12, 15, 61, 79
Jenkinson, John 256
Jewish people *see* ethnic identities: Jews
jingoism 217, 218
John Collison & Co. 99
Jones of Bloemhof 112
journals and newspapers 154, 159, 179–80, 218; freedom of the press 132; slummer journalism 218–20; values 223; *A.P.O.* 107; *Die Burger* 258; *Cape Argus* 179, 182, 184, 190, 194, 195, 242, 244; values 234–5, 249; *Cape Monthly Magazine* 154–5; *Cape of Good Hope Literary Gazette* 137; *Cape Times* 217, 220, 221, 238, 242, 243, 247, 248; values 218; *Cape Town Mail* 172, 177; *Folk-lore Journal* 156; *Graaff-Reinet Herald* 168; *Journal of the Asiatic Society of Bengal* 132; *Kaapse Cyclopedie* 133; *The Lantern* 210, 220, 221, 234; values 218, 233; *Het Nederduitsch Zuid-Afrikaansch Tijdschrift* 133; *The Owl* 218; *South African Advertiser and Mail see South African Commercial Advertiser*; *South African Commercial Advertiser* 97, 101, 121, 131, 132, 174, 179; and abolition 106, 107; values 129, 132, 133, 134, 149; *South African Quarterly Journal* 132; *South African Spectator* 221; *De Verzamelaar* 133; *Ware Afrikaan* 108; *De Zuid-Afrikaan* 132, 133, 144, 158
jubilee *see* commemorative events

K

Kaapsche Vlek *see* Cape Town
Kaapstad *see* Cape Town
Kalk Bay 200/202, 222, 241
Kanaladorp *see* District Six
Kelly, Michael 105
Kenilworth 213, 241, 253
Keurboom River 201
Khoi people 12, 16–17, 32, 50, 66–7, 89, 109, 139, 156; apprenticeship 137; conflict with 13–14, 18, 20–5, 26, 29, 32–3, 36–7; depictions of 14, 16, 22, 30, 43, 66–7, 133; 'purchase' of land from 36–7; responses to settlement 28; social mobility 67; trade with 14, 15, 16–17, 21, 22, 36; transhumance 16, 20–3; *see also* military: Khoi regiment
Kimberley 213, 252
Kindersley, Mrs 66–7
King, Inspector John 173
Kinniburgh, Mrs 144
kinship 201
Kirsten, J.A. 260
Klein Oude (Wynberg) 202
Kloof Nek 162
knegts 68
Knysna 165
Kohler, Fanny 236
Krauss, Ferdinand 117, 132
Krieger, Jan 73
Krotoa 23, 67
Krynauw, R. 180

L

labour and work 244–8; Australian militancy 248; conditions of 30–2, 246, 258–9; discipline 245; disputes 163, 180, 246, 248; hours of 246–7; labour relations 242; rhythms of 190; shortages 19, 26
labour unions 247–8; Amalgamated Society of Carpenters and Joiners 248; Cape Town and Districts Trades Council 248
Ladies' Benevolent Society 121–2, 130, 136
'A Lady' 199, 203, 205
Lagardien, Mrs Wasiela 258
Lancaster, Mrs 205
Landsberg, Dr J.P. 223
Landsberg, Otto 107

INDEX 279

landscape 80; control of 17, 18–19, 39–40, 253; mapping and naming of 20, 24, 25; romantic 30, 199
Langa 183
Langalibalele 183
languages 71, 127; linguistic divide 144; Afrikaans 127, 158, 193, 194; Afrikaans in Arabic, 127, 158, 188; Arabic, 125, 154, 158, 221, Bugis 74; Chinese 71, 74; creole 71, 127; Dutch 71, 91, 127; English 91, 127, 133, 153; French 81; Khoesan 71, 156; Malagasy 71, 124; Melayu 127–8, 250; Yiddish 218
law 158–9; anti-immigration legislation 218; Batavian codes 30; Chinese Exclusion Act 218; Contagious Diseases Act 236, 237; discriminatory laws 70, 111–12; English law 91–2; financial legislation 160; General Dealers Act 218; Half-Holiday Act 247; inheritance laws 59; Masters and Servants Act (1855) 204; Ordinance 50 109; Roman-Dutch law 59, 90, 138, 158; slave codes 63, 105, 106, 107; sumptuary laws 73; vagrancy legislation 137
Layard, E.L. 155
Le Vaillant, F. 78
Leeb, Philip 200
Leentje (slave) 107
leisure 77–80, 139–49, 190–200, 238, 243–4; baboon-baiting 79; changes in 196, 241–2; cockfighting 79, 148; gambling 79; games 196, 212; picnics 240, 241–2, 244–5; rational leisure 240, 242, 244; social life 81, 97, 140; social visits 77, 141; *see also* clubs; sport
Lesar, J.H. 121
Lever Brothers soap factory 257
liberalism 129, 132
libraries *see* South African Library
Liesbeek House (Newlands) 255
Liesbeek River 25, 57, 117, 210, 253
Liesbeek Valley 20, 23, 24, 25, 27, 28, 29, 38, 39
Liesching, Friedrich 76
Liesching, Louis 91
Lightfoot, Rev. Thomas Fothergill 178, 180, 182, 184, 249
Lion's Head 12, 19, 23, 30, 42, 78, 152
Lion's Rump *see* Signal Hill
Lister, Georgina 199, 200
Literary and Scientific Institution 122, 131–2, 155
Literary Society *see* Literary and Scientific Institution
Lloyd, Lucy 156
London Metropolitan Police 173
'Long Dick' 246
Lothian House (Rondebosch) 255, 256
Louis (slave) 105
Louw, Mr 177
Lovedale College 193

M

Maatschappij ter Uitbreiding van Beschaving en Letterkunde 133
Macartney, George, Earl 87, 96, 105, 117
McCombie, Thomas 218
McElroy, Rev. Mr 178
McKenzie, Andrew R. 166, 170, 221, 246
Mackenzie, Barbara 257, 258
Mackinnon, Rev. James 218

Maclear family 206
Maclear, Mrs Mary 203
Maclear, Mary 184, 203, 205
Maclear, Thomas 96, 155, 156, 157
Madagascar 19, 83, 92; slaves from 23, 60, 109, 148
Madras 98
Mahe, Louis 195
Mahomet, John 243
Maitland 16, 222
Makhanda (Xhosa prophet) 139
Maker, Rukea 188
Malacca 33, 36
Malagasy people *see* ethnic identities: Malagasy
'Malay' people *see* ethnic identities: 'Malay'
mandoors see slaves and slavery
Maqoma (Xhosa chief) 139
Maria of Bengal 27
Marquard, Leopold 167, 186
Marshall, Annie 236
Mascarenes 53, 82, 100
Mathew, Thomas James 129, 201
Mauritius 14, 16, 27, 32, 81, 92, 165; trade with 83, 98, 100
Maynard, James 200, 202
Mecca 76, 187
Mechanics' Institute 155
Melck, Martin, 67–8, 76
menagerie 119
Menssink, Willem 70
Mentzel, Otto 44, 45, 53, 56, 60, 62, 64, 68, 71, 78, 80; life 58
Menzies, William 119
merchants *see* economy: mercantile community
Merriman, Agnes 203
Merriman, John X. 196, 203, 218
Metropolitan and Suburban Railway Company 214
Mfengu 110, 246
Mhala, N.C. 198
military 81, 89, 92–3, 161, 197–8; fortifications 42, 81; impact on town 92–3; naval mutiny 93; free black militia 70; German mercenary regiments 87; Khoi militia 86; Luxembourg regiment 81; Swiss regiment 81, 82; Württemberg regiment 76, 81, 91; British Army 92, 196–8; 75th Regiment 162; 73rd Regiment 178; Scotch Brigade 99; Royal Navy 92; Khoi regiment 92; Malay Corps 126, 187, 188–9; town militia 29, 112; volunteer forces 197, 210, 211; Cape Royal Rifles 197; Cape Town Cavalry ('Sparklers') 197; Cape Town Highlanders 210; the Dukes 210
Mills, Sir Charles 218
Milner, Sir Alfred (later Lord) 253, 262
Milnerton 92, 222
missions and mission work 123–4, 130, 181, 180, 184, 186, 251; City Mission 251; Cowley Fathers 237; London Missionary Society 124, 130, 135, 186; Society of St John the Evangelist *see* Cowley Fathers; St Columba's 237, 251; Zuid-Africaans Genoodschap 123–4, 135; *see also* churches
Mitchel, John 176
Molteno, Sir John 213
Monomotapa 13, 25

Montagu, John 161–2, 165, 175, 183
Moodie, Benjamin 110–11
Moodie, G.P. 253
Moor, Paay 69
Moore, W.E. 158
Morgenrood, Philip 200, 202
Morris, William 236
Mosenthal Bros 189
mosques 118, 127, 187; Auwal Mosque 125–6; Jami'a (Queen Victoria) Mosque 187, 188; Palm Tree Mosque 107, 127, 187, 202
Mouille Point 53, 258
Mount Nelson 174
Mowbray 86, 212, 213, 260; municipality 222
Mozambican people *see* ethnic identities: Mosbiekers
Mozambique 14, 27; slaves from 60, 82, 106, 109, 124, 148; labourers from 246
Mozambique Channel 99
Muizenberg 200, 241, 251–2; Battle of 86, 92
Murray, Andrew jun. 157, 187, 204
Murray, R.W. 170, 177, 179–80
museums *see* South African Museum
music and song 77, 108, 148, 178, 191–2, 194, 196, 243–4; Amateur Darkie Serenaders 244; American minstrels 243–4; Christy-minstrels 152, 190, 244; Colonel Baker's Horse 244; Darkie Minstrels 244; Darktown Fire Brigade 244; depictions of 118, 149; Joe Brown's Band of Brothers 244; Juvenile Christys 244; *Carnival (Coon) troupes* 244; Cape of Good Hope Sports Club 244; Jolly Coons 244; Jolly Coons Masquerade Troupe 244; Orpheus M. McAdoo's Jubilee Singers 244, 245; *ghommaliedjies* 189, 190, 192, 193–4; *klopse* 244; Star of Independence Malay Club 242; sailors' songs 54, 55
Muslim people *see* ethnic identities: Muslim
Mutual Life Assurance Society (Old Mutual) *see* financial institutions

N

Nahuys, Baron 93
Namaqualand 160–1
Napier, Sir George 172, 173
Napoleon 92, 98, 99
navy *see* military: Royal Navy
Ndlambe (Xhosa tribe) 139
Nederburgh, Commissioner S.C. 83
Netherlands 55, 68, 133; comparisons with 75; immigrants from 26
New South Wales 100, 102, 139
Newlands 118, 200, 210, 213; coloured residents 253; cricket grounds 238, 241; Paradijs 25, 50
Newlands House 199
Newlands Forest 50
Noble, Roderick 154
Nooitgedacht (Stellenbosch) 242
Norden, Benjamin 189
Norden, Joseph 176

O

Observatory (suburb) 132, 200, 213, 256, 259–62; Lower Main Rd 260, 261; Station Rd 261

occupations 28, 43, 49–52, 56–59, 86, 90–2, 94–5, 179; architects 169–70; artisans 56, 62, 96, 111, 179, 259; bakers 28, 94; barmaids 245; boatmen 166, 179; carpenters 28, 179; civil servants 91–2, 179; clerks 213, 248, 249, 259, 261; dock labourers 110, 166, 178, 179, 246, 248; domestic servants 108, 111, 178, 179, 195, 199, 204–6, 218, 245; fishermen 62, 64, 65, 95, 121, 124, 179; hawkers 63, 86, 103, 109; labourers 179; lamplighters 179; legal profession 90; medical profession 28, 56, 76, 90, 91, 179, 223; navvies 182; professions 50, 179; sailors 54–5, 93; seamstresses 95; shop assistants 247; soldiers 50–2, 93; tailors 28; tram-drivers 246; washerwomen 62, 95, 167, 179, 190, 195, 245; water carrier 167
Odd Fellows 238
Ohlsson, Anders 221
Ohlsson's Breweries see brewing industry
Old Moses 154
Onderneming (Observatory) 259–60
Orange Free State 192
'Orange Free State'(Cape Town) 246
O'Reilly, T.J. 249
O'Rourke, Terry 193
Orphan Chamber 91
Orphan House 134
orphanages 121, 186; Granite Lodge 186; St Michael's Home 186
Osingkhimma (Khoi captain) 36
Ottoman Empire 188, 189
Overberg 99, 160

P

Palmyra House (Claremont) 201
Papenboom 57
Papendorp see Woodstock
parades see carnivals and festivals
Park Estate (Rondebosch) 255, 256
Parker, John 237, 241, 253
parliament 158, 177; building of 214, 216–17; House of Assembly 221; Legislative Council 100, 171, 174, 176; Legislative Assembly 171, 177, 211; parliamentary representation 158, 165–6, 171–7, 213, 221
Parry, Sefton 193, 241
Patriot movement see politics
Pauper Establishment 122
Peers Cave (Fish Hoek) 16
Penstone, Charles 218
Percival, Robert 113
Persent, Jan 106
Philip, Mrs Jane 122, 130
Philip, Dr John 122, 129, 133, 201
Philip, John jun. 201
Philip, Marianne (née Arderne) 201
Philippi 213
photography 158, 187, 202
Pickering, E. 163
Pieterscon, Joost of Leiden 33
Pillans, C.S. 97, 99
Platteklip Gorge 46, 62, 80, 106, 190, 245
plays see theatre and plays
Plettenberg Bay 165
Plumstead 117, 202, 213
Pocock family 205

police 61, 137, 172–3, 210–11
politics: Afrikaner Bond 221, 226, 243; anti-convict agitation 166, 173, 175–7, 190; Patriot movement 82, 83, 144, 176; influence of French revolutionary ideas 105; Orangist forces, 82, 83; see also parliament
Politieke Raad see Council of Policy
population see census and population
Port Elizabeth 159, 165, 213
Port Jackson 98
Port Louis 83
Port Natal 98
Port Nolloth 165
Port Office 119
Porter, William 171
Portuguese 12–14
Post Office 103, 169, 214, 215
poverty 108, 120–2, 179, 248–9, 251, 259; aged 122; attitudes to 68, 182, 184, 218–19, 248–9; free blacks 65; poor whites 248, 249; poor relief 68–9, 121–2, 181, 182–3, 195, 234, 248–9, 251; unemployment 108, 182, 248–9
power relations 17, 22, 211
press see journals and newspapers
Prince of Ternate 61
Pringle, Thomas 134
prize negroes 89, 106, 108–9, 177
prisons and prisoners 61, 110, 122; convicts 162, 166, 183–4; Breakwater Prison 166, 182, 183; House of Correction 122, 178; Lock Hospital 169; Roeland Street jail 169, 183; Strand St jail 138; see also Amsterdam Battery; Robben Island
property ownership and speculation 48, 67–8, 117, 119, 129, 170, 173, 200–1, 222, 259–60; coloured 202; free black 64–5; tenants 119–20, 259–61
prostitutes and prostitution 57, 158, 178, 190, 195, 234–7, 245–6; brothels 58, 79; rescue homes 235, 236, 237
Protea see Bishop's Court
Prussian civil service 58
Public Gardens see Gardens
pubs see bars
punishments see crime and punishment

Q

Queen Rebecca 161
Quinn, Mrs 178

R

Raad der Gemeente see Cape Town municipality
Rabinowitz, Rev. Joel 189
Rabone, W.H. 168
race 69–70, 239; miscegenation 27, 69–70, 188; racism 70, 111–12, 184, 205, 218, 220; racial categorising 112, 222, 242
Rachel van die Kaap 202
railway station 263
railways see communications
Rangton van Bali 79
Ras, Hans of Angel 33
Ravensworth (Claremont) 201
Raw, Tom see D'Oyly, Sir Charles
Registry of Deeds 169

religion 30, 75, 123–8, 184–9; Chinese 76; Christianity 16, 30; Africans 237; evangelicalism 123–4, 129, 130–1, 235, 262; pietism 123; Islam 76–7, 124–8, 184, 187–9; khalifa 126, 127; rampi-sny 127; ratiep see khalifa; Hinduism 76, 127; Judaism 157, 159, 189
Renaulgh, Caroline 245
respectability 73, 149, 176, 184, 186, 205–6, 234, 237–8, 240, 261–2
Rets, Lodewijk 61
Réunion 81, 83; trade with 98, 100
Rhodes, Cecil John 221, 234, 240, 253
Riebeeckstad see Cape Town
Rietvlei (Milnerton) 92
Rio de Janeiro 165
The Rise (Claremont) 201
ritual 72–3, 152, 168, 206, 226
Robben Island 23, 53, 183; animal life 19, 25; as a hospital 139, 181, 182; as a prison 15, 50, 61, 77, 124, 139
Robertson, A.S. 154
Robertson, Ds. William 187
Roebuck, Disney 193
Rogers, G.J. 106
Roggebaai 120, 124, 186, 224, 243
Rondebosch 39, 42, 62, 118, 169, 184, 199, 200, 213, 223, 253–6, 257; Common 256; military encampment 92; municipality 222; Salvation Army Social Farm 234, 256
Ross, Hamilton 99, 100, 106, 158, 174, 177
Ross, Dr W.H. 223
Rotterdam 55
Rousby, Mrs 239
Rousseau, J.-J. 82
Rouwkoop (Rondebosch) 254
Rowan, Colonel 173
Royal Observatory 132, 155, 157, 158, 203
Rust en Werk (Wynberg) 202
Rustenburg (Rondebosch) 118, 253
Rutherfoord, Emma 157, 199, 202–3, 204, 206, 254
Rutherfoord, H.E. 214
Ryklief, Philip 202

S

Saar, Johan 32
Sacharias, Jan 27
Sailors' Home 168
St Helena 14, 16, 27, 83, 92; trade with 98, 99; see also ethnic identities: St Helenans
St Helena Bay 99
St James 200
St Leger, Frederick York 218
St Martin-in-the-Fields (London) 116
St Matthew's mission (Keiskammahoek) 152
St Pancras (London) 116
Saldanha, Antonio de 12
Saldanha Bay 16, 21, 27, 32, 36; hunting at 141
Salt River 13, 25, 37, 39, 42, 105, 162, 163, 212, 256–9; as a community 258–9; Albert Rd 258; Malta Rd 257; market 258; Railway Institute 257–8; railway works 242, 246, 258–9; street names 257
Salvador (Brazil) 109
Sampson, Stephanus 236
San people 16; see also ethnic identities: San

INDEX 281

Sandile 166
sanitation *see* health and sanitation
Sans Souci (Claremont) 174
Schagger *see* Osingkhimma
Schermbrucker, Colonel 249
schools and schooling *see* education
Scotland Yard *see* London Metropolitan Police
Scots people *see* ethnic identities: Scots
Sea Point 16, 78, 129, 169, 214, 247; depictions of 119; as a holiday destination 252
Searle, Mrs Walter 237
Secretariat 91
Sedgwick, James 97, 99
segregation and lack of segregation 48, 234; labour 69, 248; marriage 56; residential 48, 111, 167, 250, 261; occupations 259; sport 153, 239/241; theatre 145, 193
Semple, Robert 89, 104, 148
Serrurier (*predikant*) 44
Sheikh Yusuf 76, 77
Shillinge, Andrew 12
ships and shipping 28, 52–3, 81–2, 83, 98, 102, 163–5, 168; shipping lines 252; shipwrecks 15, 53, 109, 165; trade routes 14, 15–16, 28, 32, 36; *Alabama* 189, 190; *Bosphorus* 164; *Drake* 36; *Enterprise* 163, 164; *Erasmus* 32, 33; *Gentoo* 178; *Haerlem* 15–16, 21; *Neptune* 46, 176, 190; *Pacquet Real* 109; *Roode Vos* 32; *Sea Bride* 190; *Tulp* 19; *De Vis* 53
shops and shopping 216; half-holiday movement 247; Garlicks 216; Juta's bookshop 215, 216; Oblowitz 258; OK Bazaars 258; Stuttafords 169, 214, 216
Shortt & Berry 98
Siers, Jongie 193, 243
Signal Hill 12, 36, 66, 78, 106, 115, 152, 181, 191; cemeteries on 41, 46, 77, 126; farming on 39; fortifications 81; development of 118, 119, 224, 242; quarry 124, 148; signalling 52, 53; views from 114–15
Silwood (Rondebosch) 255, 256
Simeon (black sportsman) 153
Simon's Town 53, 128, 162, 176, 200, 202, 241; municipality 222; naval station 92
Sinclair, John 236
Sintler, Jan 202
Sir Lowry's Pass 161
Sivewright, Sir James 218
Slabbert family 70
Slave Lodge 44, 60–1, 70, 74, 75, 103, 109; *see also* Supreme Court
slaves and slavery 26–7, 50, 60–4, 69, 75, 102–12; auctions 104; Company slaves *see* government slaves; conversion to Christianity 123–4; demography 27, 50, 60–1, 89, 102; desertion 32–3, 80, 108; emancipation and manumission 64, 74, 75, 102, 104, 105–8, 133, 137; government slaves 103; hire of 103–5; legal status of children 70; leisure activities 148–9; *mandoors* 60; origins and supply 27, 60, 82; occupations 61–2, 103–6, 141; punishment 32, 62–3, 105; religion 124, 126; resistance 63, 105, 107; trade 82–3, 99, 102, 108–9; urban slavery 103–5; women 105–6; *see also* apprenticeship; *bandieten*; ethnic identities: slave; prize negroes
slums *see* housing
Sly, Sam 169–70

Smith, Sir Harry 176
Smuts, Anna 59
Smuts, J.J.L. 158, 180
Smuts, Michiel 63
Smyth, Charles Piazzi 157, 158
Snow, William Barclay 170
social control 136–9
social purity movements 237–8
Society House (Sea Point) 78, 119, 252
Society of the Jewish Community of Cape Town 189
Soga, Tiyo 166
Solomon, Hannah 245
Solomon, Saul 129, 154, 177, 178, 179, 213
Somerset, Lord Charles 97, 128, 131–2, 134, 141
South African Cultural History Museum 103
South African Folklore Society 156
South African Literary and Philosophical Society *see* Literary and Scientific Institution
South African Medical Society 122
South African Museum 109, 131, 155
South African people *see* ethnic identities: South African
South African Public Library 154, 155; Dessin collection 74, 131; Grey collection 156
South African War (1899–1902) 168, 261, 263
south-easter *see* climate
Southey, Richard 211
Sparmann, Carel 158
Sparrman, Anders 71
sport 196–8, 238–41: archery 199; cricket 196, 197–8, 238, 239, 241; croquet 199; cycling 240; football 196–7, 239, 241; horse-racing 97, 141, 191, 241; hunting 140–1, 191; mountaineering 196; pub games 195; rowing 198; rustic 152, 195; swimming 199; tennis 199, 239; women 198–9, 239
sports clubs: Albert Cricket Club 239; Alfred Rowing Club 198; Cape Civil Service Rowing Club 198; Hamilton Sea Point Rugby Football Club 198; Malay Union Cricket Club 239; Red Crescent Club (Kimberley) 239; Reformed Club 198; South African Turf Club 241; Union Rowing Club 198
Stavorinus, J.S. 74
Stein, John 177
Stegmann, Ds. G.W. 187
Stellenbosch 67, 86, 241
Stellenbosch Dutch Reformed seminary 218
stereotypes *see* ethnicity and identity
Stewart, Dr P.G. 223
Steytler, J.G. 157
Stigant, P.J. 249
Strandlopers *see* Khoi people
streets and squares: naming of 39; street signs 44; *Adderley St* 153, 168, 169, 174, 216, 224, 247, 263; development 170, 214, 216–17; Alfred St 170; Anchor St 234; Aspeling St 251; Barrack St 225, 236; Berg St 92, 100, *see also* St George's St; Bloem St 167; Boom St 225; Bree St 55, 101, 113, 136, 153, 170; Buiten St 170; Buitenkant St 40, 152, 192, 193, 196; Buitengracht St 39, 46, 153, 170, 186, 195; Buitensingel 40; Burg St 48, 90, 153; Caledon Square 81; Caledon St 193; Canterbury St 250; Castle St 29, 64, 90, 117, 119; Chiappini St 187, 195, 250; Church Square 75, 124, 263;

Coffee Lane 219; Constitution Hill 96, 119, 120, 123, 192; Constitution St 195, 250; Darling St 169, 210, 241; Dock Rd 147, 235; Dorp St 125, 126; Elbow Lane 159; Glynn's Square 170, 195; Glynnville Terrace 170; Government Avenue 174; *Grand Parade* 40, 45, 92, 97, 100, 112, 113, 115, 133, 146, 152, 157, 176, 194, 195, 197, 249; Great Rd *see* Sir Lowry Rd; *Greenmarket Square* 49, 86, 87, 104, 113, 137, 152, 153, 171, 214; buildings 215; Hanover Square 195; Hanover St 186, 250, 251; Harrington St 97, 123, 170, 186, 193; Heerengracht 40, 43, 44, 45, 48, 72, 90, 100, 111, 113, 119, 120, 143, 154, 170; Heerestraat *see* Castle St; Helliger Lane 224; Herman Lane 196; Hope St 118; Horstley St 250; Hottentot Square *see* Riebeek Square; Hout St 29, 64, 100, 119, 124; Keerom St 136, 178, 196; Kerk St 41; Klipfontein Rd 212; Lansdowne Rd 201, 212; Long St 119, 121, 124, 127, 134, 167, 187, 202; Longmarket St 119, 180, 210; Loop St 263; Looyer's Plein 131; Napier St 170; New St *see* Queen Victoria St; New Church St 170; Oliphants St *see* Hout St; Palmyra Rd 201; Pepper St 121; Plein St 92, 96, 123, 144, 193, 241, 247, 249, 251; Prestwich St 170; Queen Victoria St 134; Reijger St 29; Riebeek Square 144; Roeland St 119, 152, 170, 186, 249; Rose St 224, 250; St George's St 44, 100, 113, 174, 214; Shortmarket St 107, 210; Sir Lowry Rd 113, 163, 193, 210, 250; Somerset Rd 170, 181, 200, 206, 210, 211; Stal Plein 40, 131; Stanley Rd 201; Steen St 41; Strand St 43, 46, 48, 58, 67, 115, 119, 138, 153, 194, 200, 263; Sydney St 111; Vandeleur St 170, 236; Venus St *see* St George's St; Wale St 116, 119, 153, 173; Wandel St 180; Waterkant St 220; Wesley St 170; Zee St 48, 64
Struben, H.W. 260
Stuurman, David 139
suburbs 19, 20, 117–18, 200–6, 212, 241, 249–62; boundaries 25; municipalities 221–3, 252; rural dream 210, 252–4, 256, 261–2
Sulawesi *see* Celebes
Supreme Court 87, 103, 217
surveys and surveying 115, 157, 170, 180
Susa, Phillip 246
Swartland 16, 21, 105
Swellendam 99, 163
Swellengrebel, Hendrik 52

T

taal *see* languages: Afrikaans
Table Bay 12–14, 16, 19, 20, 21, 25, 36, 72, 81, 86, 93, 100, 109, 163, 176, 190, 192, 200; as a coaling station 164, 252; batteries 36, 41, 42, 53, 54, 72, 120, 166, 167, 186; breakwater 62, 102; building of harbour 53, 166, 168, 175, 181, 213; depiction of 30, 46–7, 54, 65, 189; Docks Location 239; Harbour Board 222; jetties 29, 101–2; lack of safety 27, 53; settlement 17, 18, 38; shipping in 15, 92, 98, 102, 164–5; shipyard 54; waterfront 24; Alfred Basin 168; Robinson Dry Dock 168; South Arm 168; Victoria Basin 168

Table Mountain 12, 19, 25, 30, 62, 63, 106, 199, 253; climbing 58, 180; depictions of 15, 46, 80; farming on 39, 46, 115; fortifications 81; squatters 110, 120; Woodhead Reservoir 226
Table Valley 24, 29, 39, 67, 90
Tamtanko (Chinese) 76
Tana Baru *see* cemeteries
taphuisen see bars
taverns *see* bars
Teengs, H.W. 192
Teenstra, M.D. 138
telegraph *see* communications
temperance 232–3, 237, 257, 262; Independent Order of Grand Templars 233; Independent Order of True Templars 233; Temperance Society 122, 133, 148
Tennant, Alexander 99, 202
Thalwitzer, Maximilian 160, 250
theatre and plays 143–5, 190–1, 192–3, 241; African Theatre 144–5, Aurora group 192, 193; Bijou Theatre 193; Drawing Room Theatre 193; Drury Lane Theatre 192; Good Hope Theatre 193; New Music Hall 193; Theatre Royal 193, 241; Tivoli Music Hall 241; Tot Oefening en Smaak 145; Africander Amateurs 144; Cabinet of Froglands 192; Fillis's Circus 262; Garrison Players 143; Mr McCollum's Circus 193; Severo's Italian Circus 192; *The Barber of Seville* 81; *Bombastes Furioso* 144; *Brown and the Brahmins* 193; *The Irish Tutor* 193; *The Haunted Inn* 144; *Katherine and Petruchio* 144; *The Lady of Lyons* 193; *De Moord van Dingaan aan Pieter Retief* 192; *The Snake in the Grass* 190–1; *De Temperantisten* 133
Theepesio (Chinese) 76
Three Anchor Bay 245
Thom, Rev. George 124
Thompson, George 92, 101, 115, 116
Thomson, J.D. (Thomson, Watson & Co.) 177; 'flat iron' building 215, 216
Thompson & Pillans 97
Thoole, Lumke 55
Thunberg, C.P. 61, 62
Tijger Valley *see* Tyger Valley
Timor van Bali 63
Titus, John 246
Tokai 213
Tot Nut van 't Algemeen 133, 134
Town House 45, 71, 86, 87, 88, 104, 133, 152, 156, 171, 176, 181
Tramways Company 129, 214
transport *see* communications
Tredgold, Clarkson Sturge 201
Tredgold, Elizabeth (*née* Arderne) 201
Tredgold, John Harfield 129
Tredgold, Henry Knight 201
Tredgold, Susanna (*née* Arderne) 201
Tristan da Cunha 27
Trompetter, Hans 139
Truter, Sir John 91, 92, 158
Tuan Guru (Imam Abdullah ibn Qadi Abd al-Salam) 124–5, 127, 211
Tuan Said 77
Tulbagh, Rijk 36, 38
Tyger Valley 39
Tygerberg 212

U

Uitvlugt 212
Union Steam Ship Navigation Company 164
United States of America 89, 218
University of Cape Town 109
Upas (slave) 74

V

Valentyn, François 38, 45
Van Burgst (Dutch visitor) 127
Van de Graaff, C.J. 81
Van den Berg, widow 58
Van den Berg, Catherina 99
Van der Henghel, Mr (fiscal) 68
Van der Spuy, Petrus 36
Van der Stael, Pieter 27
Van Diemen's Land 162, 176
Van Meerhoff, Pieter 23
Van Oudtshoorn, Baron Pieter van Reede 72
Van Reenen family 99
Van Reenen, Johanna 160
Van Riebeeck, Jan 12, 15–19, 23–30, 36, 64, 156; attitude to Khoi 16, 21; coat of arms 88; departure 33,
Van Riebeeck, Johanna 39, 65
Van Sittert (surgeon) 59
Vermeulen family 69
Voltaire, J.F.M.A. de 82
Von Dessin, Joachim 63, 74, 77
Virginia Company 12
VOC 12, 25, 27, 29–30, 33, 159; administration 70–1; desertion from 32–3, 51; employees 18, 19, 26, 28, 29–33, 43, 49–52, 55, 61, 90–1; directors 17, 29; governors 52; hierarchy 29–30, 49–50, 72–3, 128; in East Indies 32; occupation of the Cape 14–15; permanent settlement 37–8; trading policy 36, 81

W

Wagenaer, Zacharias 38
warfare 83; alliance with French 81–3; between Dutch and English 17, 36, 80; between Dutch and French 17, 36, 38, 52–3; between English and French 87; British conquest of the Cape 38, 86–7; Napoleonic Wars 87, 93, 98, 108
Wasie, Abdul 64
Water Kasteel *see* Table Bay: batteries
'Watermen' *see* Khoi people
Watermeyer, F.S. 158, 176
Waterston, Dr Jane 217, 246
Wellington 162, 163
Weltevreden (Claremont) 201
Wernich, Joachim 60
West Africa 99; *see also* ethnic identities: West African
Westerford (Rondebosch) 200, 253
White, Arnold 217
Wicht, A. 170
Wicht, C. 170
Wicht, J.A.H. 158, 170, 174, 180
Wicht, J.C. 170
Wicht, J.H. 158
Wicht, J.U. 170
Wiener, Ludwig 249
Wilberforce, W. 106
The Wilderness (Claremont) 201
Wilkers, Johanna 73
Windvoge, Catherine 245
women 50; domesticity 130, 202–6, 256; feminism 255; marriage 204; philanthropy 121–2, 130, 237; in public affairs 237; sexuality 203–4; in trade 59; *see also* gender
Women's Christian Temperance Union 237
Woodhead, Sir John 226
Woodlands (Rondebosch) 253
Woodstock 178, 186, 198, 212, 213, 241, 256, 262; Africans in 220; municipality 222
World War I 259
Woutersz, Jan 69
Wrensch, J.C. 259
Wrensch House (Observatory) 260
Wrensch Town (Observatory) 260
Wylde, Sir John 118
Wynberg 25, 117, 118, 162, 163, 191, 200–2, 213, 252; military encampment 92, 93; municipality 222
Wynberg Railway Act (1861) 162

X

Xhosa nation and people 92, 139, 183, 186

Y

Yateman, Henry 246
Young Men's Christian Association (YMCA) 237–8
Young Women's Christian Association (YWCA) 237
Yonge, Lady 117, 144
Yonge, Sir George 117, 144, 145

Z

Zandvliet *see* Faure
Zanzibar 187
Zasman, Abraham 202
Zeekoe Vlei 212
Zonnebloem 184, 250; *see also* education
Zuid-Afrikaansche Vereeniging van der Kaapstad 243